Short Ride in a Fast Machine   Sandra Kranich

Wilhelm-Hack-Museum
Verlag für moderne Kunst

In seiner Außenstelle, der Rudolf-Scharpf-Galerie, einem ehemaligen Künstleratelier, das der Stadt Ludwigshafen überantwortet wurde, zeigt das Wilhelm-Hack-Museum neue Positionen der zeitgenössischen Kunst. Die Rudolf-Scharpf-Galerie bildet damit das experimentelle Spielbein des Wilhelm-Hack-Museums, dessen Standbein eine umfangreiche Sammlung der Kunst des 20. und 21. Jahrhunderts ist.

Tatsächlich ist Sandra Kranichs künstlerische Arbeit, die Skulptur, Performance und Pyrotechnik kombiniert, äußerst experimentell.

Spätestens seit dem 15. Jahrhundert gibt es in Europa Feuerwerke. Auch heute erfreuen wir uns an Neujahr oder anlässlich unterschiedlichster Festivitäten an diesen Spektakeln, die über die Jahrhunderte hinweg nicht an Reiz verloren haben. Die Verwendung von Pyrotechnik im Bereich der Bildenden Kunst war bisher nur vereinzelt im fernöstlichen Kulturkreis, wie bei dem chinesischen Künstler Cai Guo-Qiang, bekannt. Der Schweizer Künstler Roman Signer verwendet zwar Explosionen jeglicher Art, allerdings nicht im Sinne von Pyrotechnik.

Den Reiz der kontrollierten Explosion, des Feuers und Lichtspiels nützt auch Sandra Kranich für ihre performativen Installationen und Ereignisse. Dabei kombiniert sie auf ganz bestimmte Weise jene der verschiedenen Aspekte, die in den genannten künstlerischen Ansätzen stecken: Zum einen die poetische Seite des Feuer- und Farbenspiels, zum anderen der Aspekt der Kraft, der

Zerstörung und des Zufalls. Bei Sandra Kranich zielt der Einsatz von Pyrotechnik zumeist nicht allein auf das kurzfristige Spektakel. Das Feuerwerk ist über den Moment hinaus Bild definierend und bestimmend. Die abstrakt-konstruktiven Kompositionen ihrer Wandarbeiten werden durch die Explosionen einem zerstörerischen Kalkül ausgesetzt. Der kalkulierten Konstruktion, wie beispielsweise bei *Dark Triangle, Firework 05/04/2013* wird eine unberechenbare destruktive Kraft entgegen gesetzt. Auch bei der jüngsten Werkserie, *Echo Return*, erhält die Skulptur erst nach der Zündung des Feuerwerks ihre entscheidende Form.

Ich danke Sandra Kranich für ihr Engagement für die Ausstellung in der Rudolf-Scharpf-Galerie des Wilhelm-Hack-Museums und diese begleitende Publikation. Ein großer Dank gilt Astrid Ihle für die Kuratierung der Ausstellung sowie dem gesamten Team des Wilhelm-Hack-Museums. Ebenso danke ich Harald Pridgar für die Gestaltung des Kataloges sowie dem Verlag für moderne Kunst in Nürnberg. Für die gute Zusammenarbeit danke ich PPC Philipp Pflug Contemporary. Darüber hinaus möchte ich dem Oldenburger Kunstverein und der Union Investment Stiftung für die grosszügige Unterstützung der Publikation danken.

René Zechlin

Wilhelm-Hack-Museum is showing new positions in contemporary art at its satellite space, the Rudolf-Scharpf-Galerie, a former artist's studio bequeathed to the City of Ludwigshafen. As such, Rudolf-Scharpf-Galerie constitutes the experimental venture of Wilhelm-Hack-Museum, whose primary focus is its extensive collection of 20th- and 21st-century art.

And indeed, Sandra Kranich's artistic work, which combines sculpture, performance and pyrotechnics, is extremely experimental.

Fireworks have been around in Europe since the 15th century at the latest. Even today we still marvel at the spectacular displays at New Year or on various festive occasions; centuries later they have lost none of their appeal. The use of pyrotechnics in the realm of visual art had hitherto been seen only sporadically in Far Eastern cultures, for instance in Chinese artist Cai Guo-Qiang's work. Swiss artist Roman Signer makes use of all kinds of explosions in his art, but not in the sense of pyrotechnics.

Sandra Kranich also makes use of the appeal of controlled explosions, fire and the play of light for her performance-based installations and events, in so doing combining various aspects of the named artistic approaches in a very particular way: on the one hand the poetic nature of the play of fire and color, on the other the aspect of force, destruction and chance.

In using pyrotechnics Sandra Kranich does not generally seek to create a short-term spectacle alone. The fireworks define and determine the image even after the moment of explosion has passed. The abstract-constructive compositions of her wall pieces are exposed to calculated destruction by means of the explosions. The calculated construction, as in *Dark Triangle, Firework 05/04/2013* for example, is set against an unpredictable, destructive force. In her latest series too, *Echo Return,* the sculpture takes on its definitive form only after the fireworks have been ignited.

I wish to thank Sandra Kranich for her commitment to the exhibition at Wilhelm-Hack-Museum's Rudolf-Scharpf-Galerie and this accompanying publication. Many thanks go to Astrid Ihle for curating the exhibition and the entire team at Wilhelm-Hack-Museum. I would also like to thank Harald Pridgar for designing the catalog and Verlag für moderne Kunst in Nuremberg. For the very positive cooperation I wish to thank PPC Philipp Pflug Contemporary. I am moreover grateful to Oldenburger Kunstverein and Union Investment Foundation for their generous support for the publication.

René Zechlin

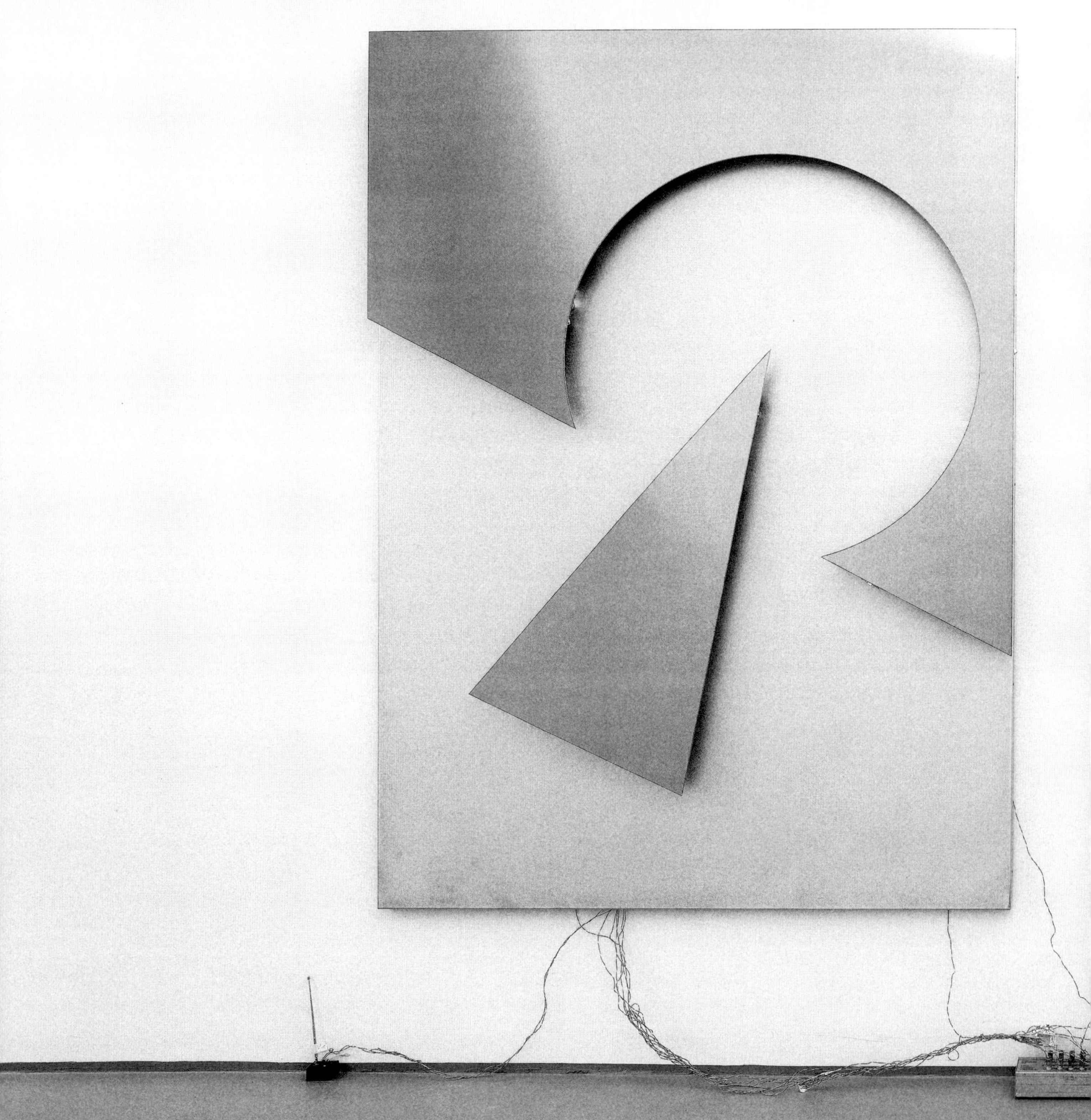

Echo Return, 2014, PPC Philipp Pflug Contemporary, Frankfurt/M.

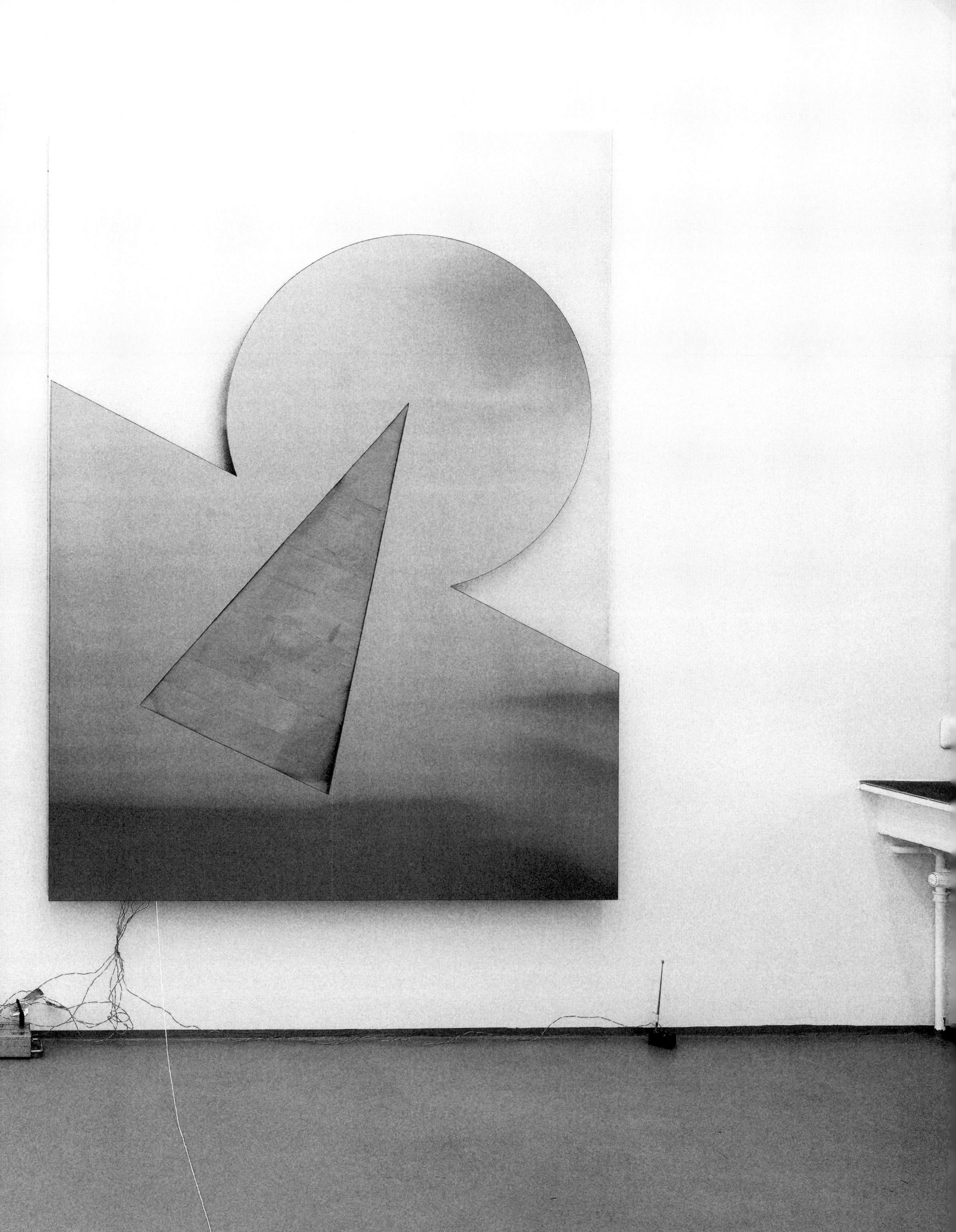

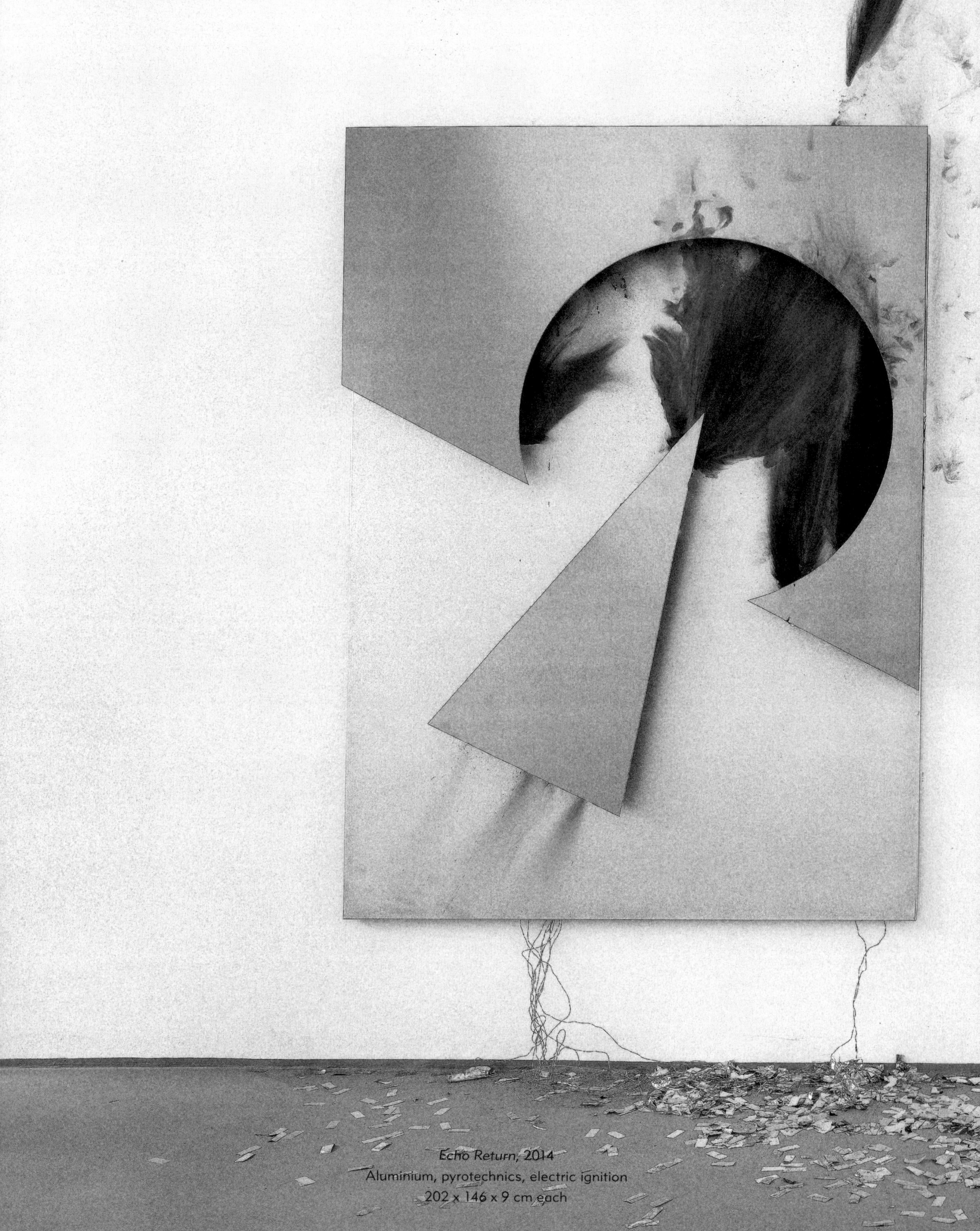

Echo Return, 2014
Aluminium, pyrotechnics, electric ignition
202 x 146 x 9 cm each

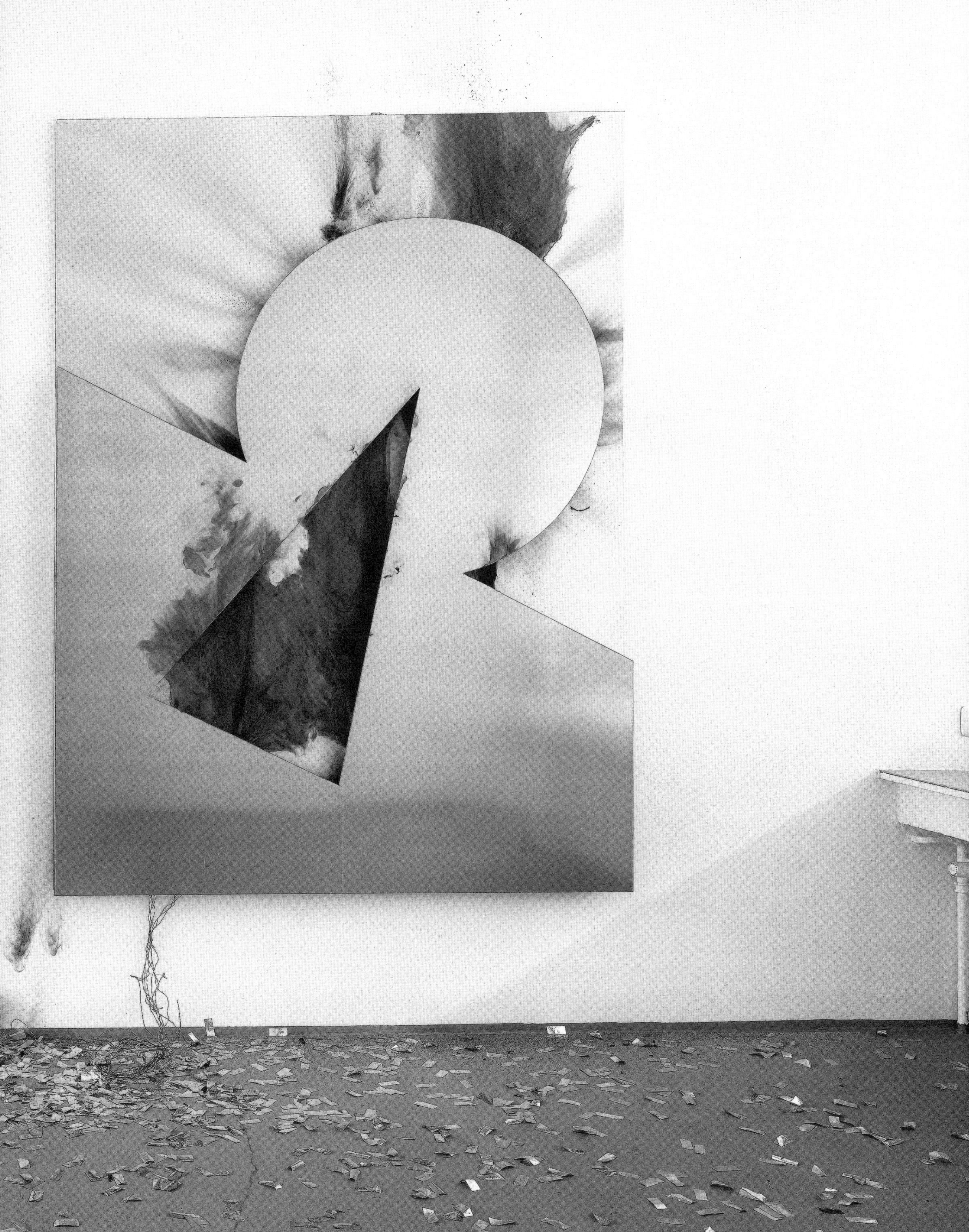

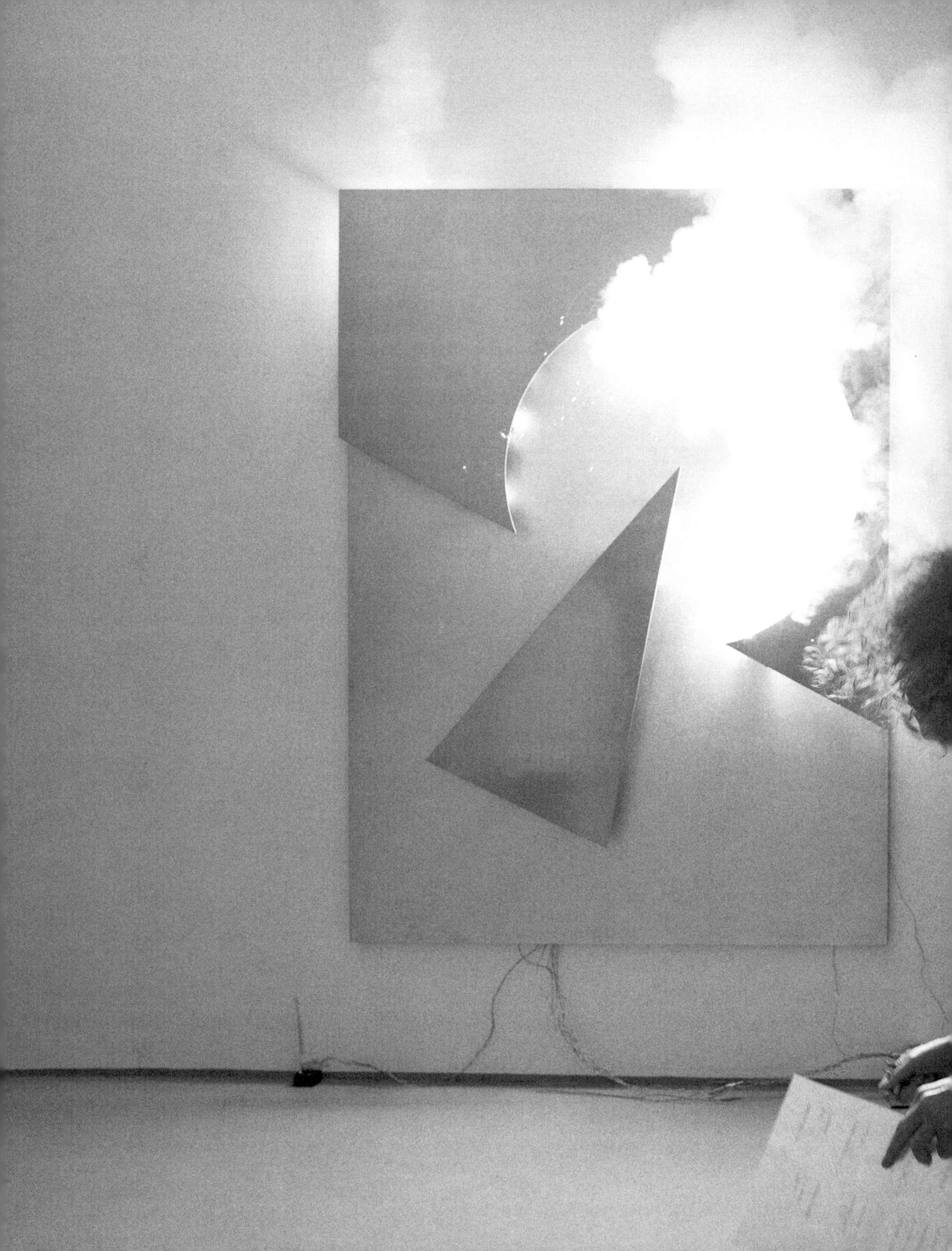

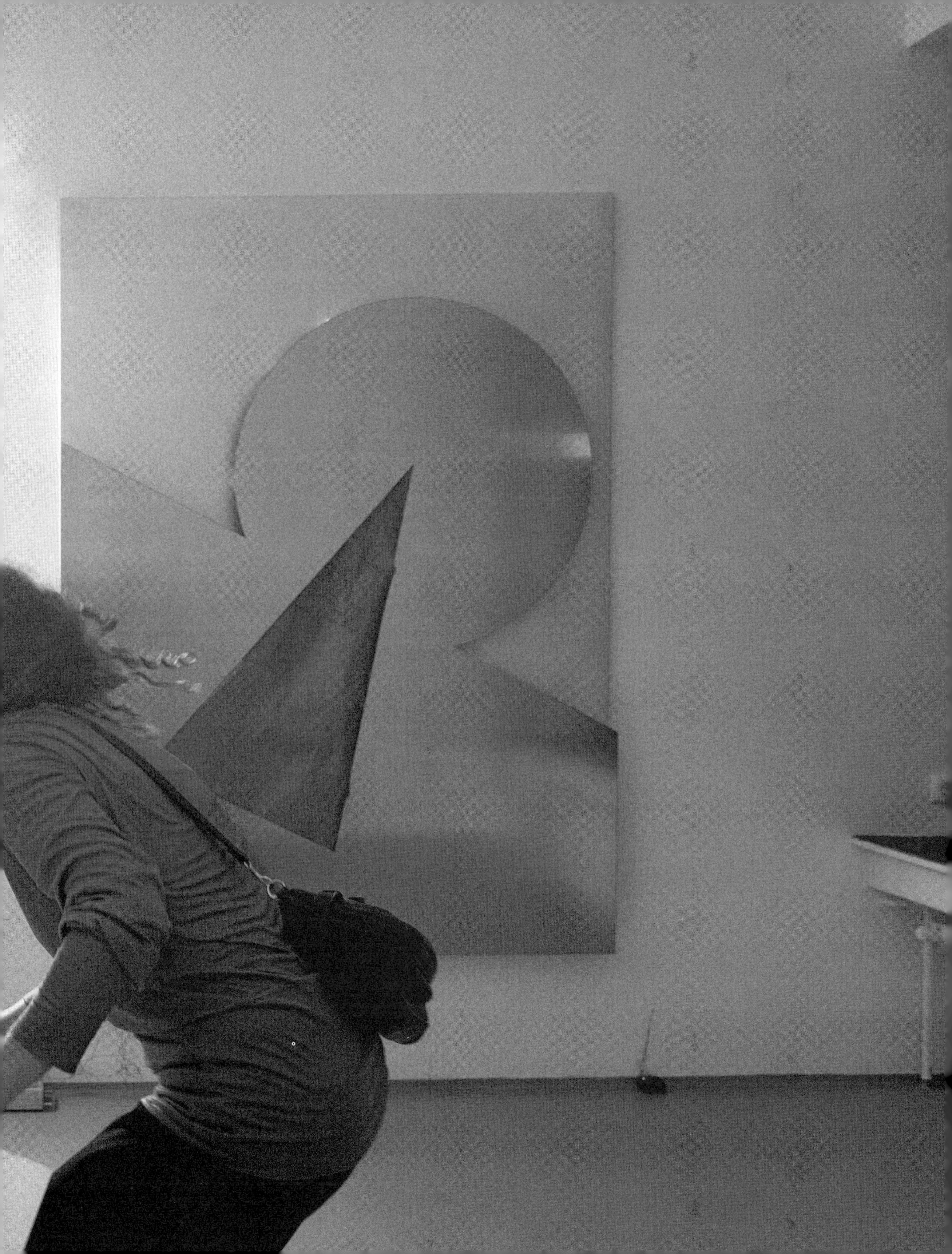

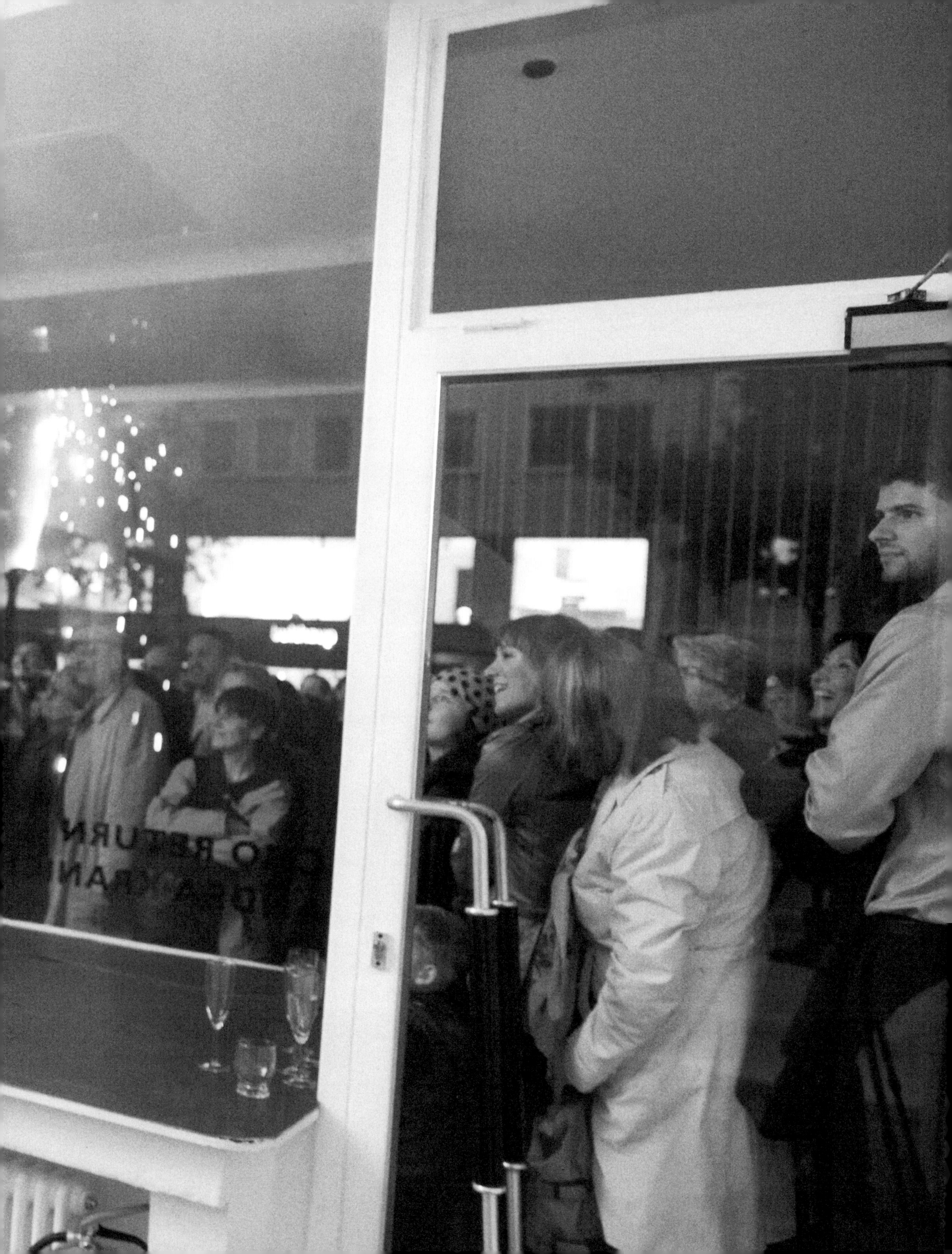

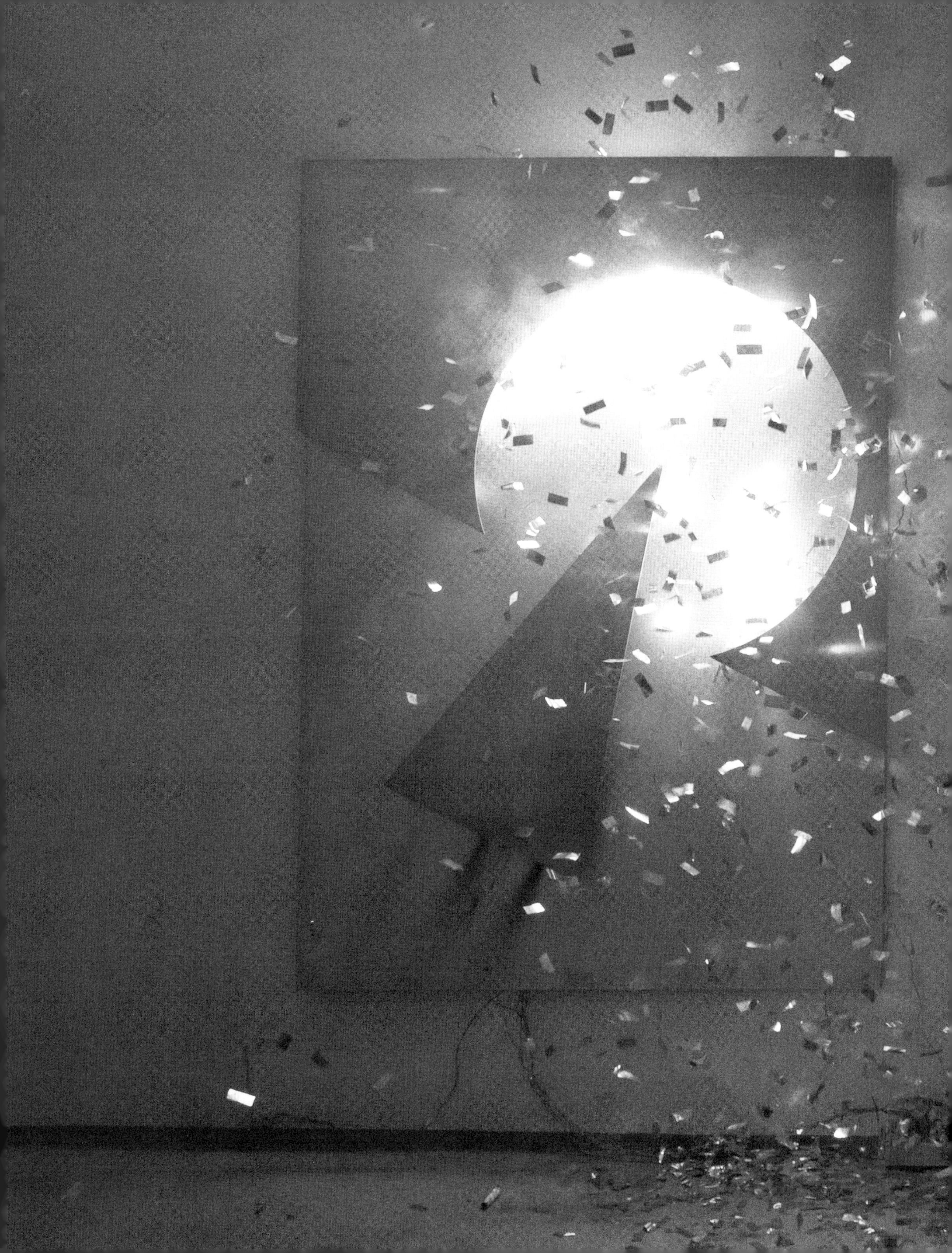

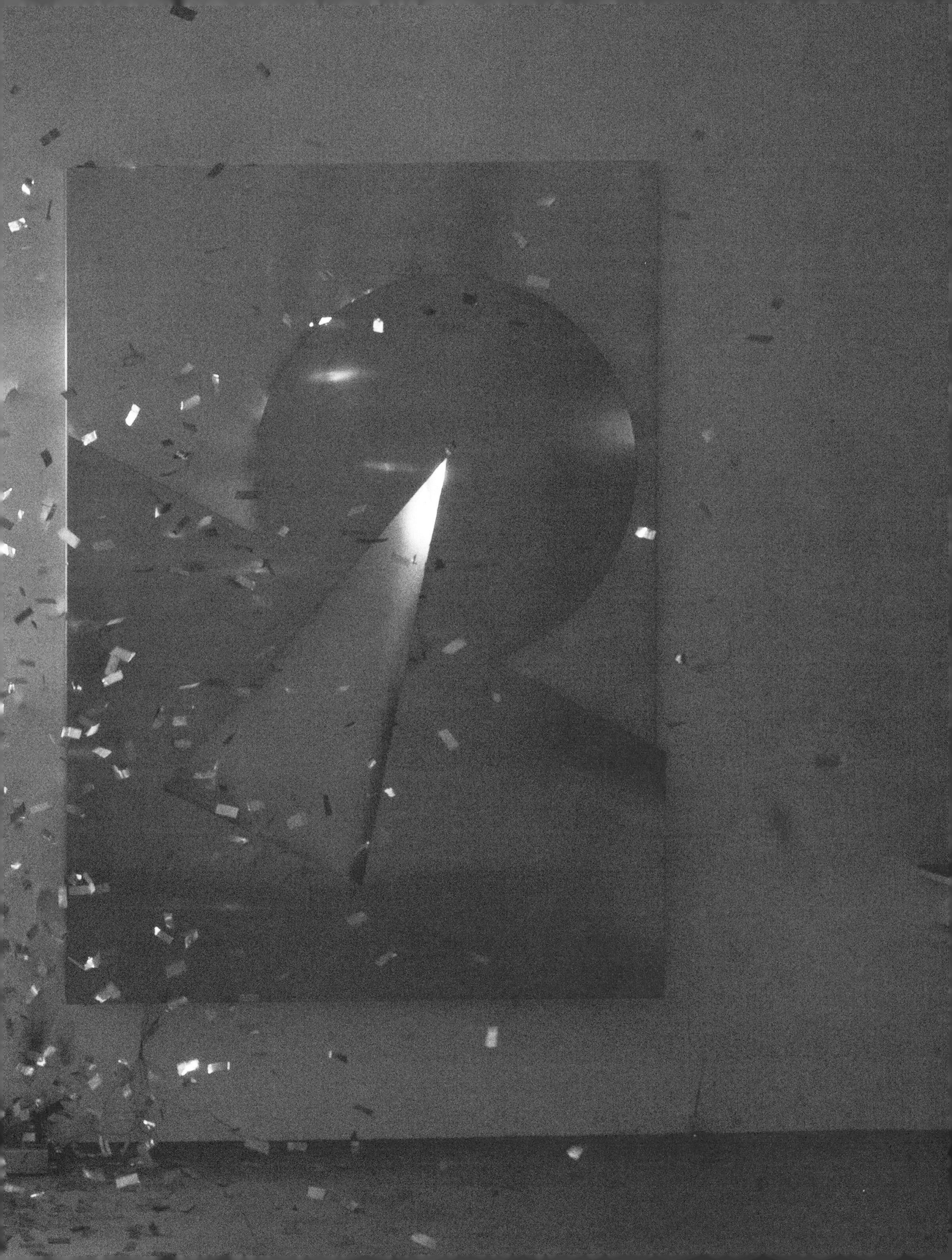

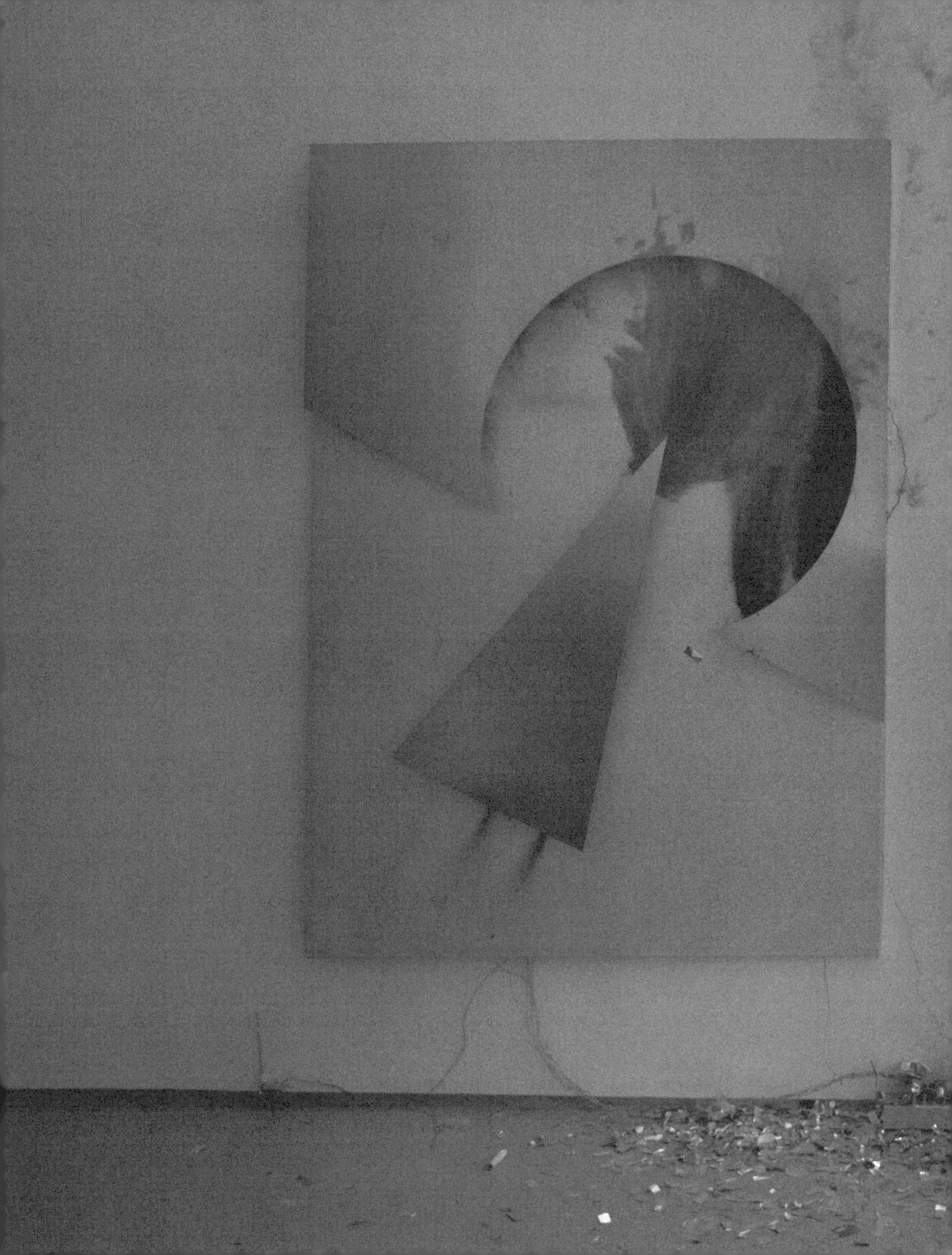

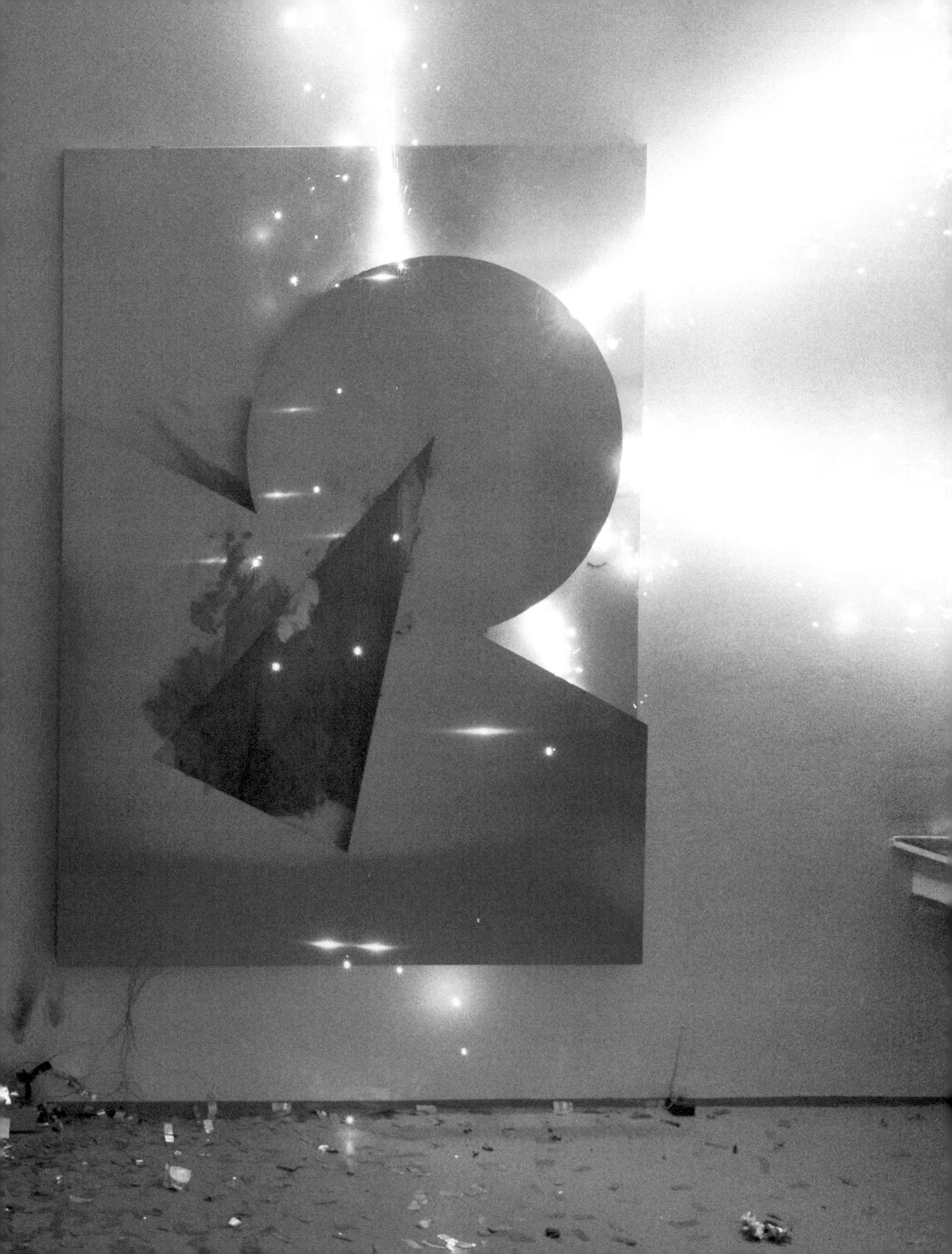

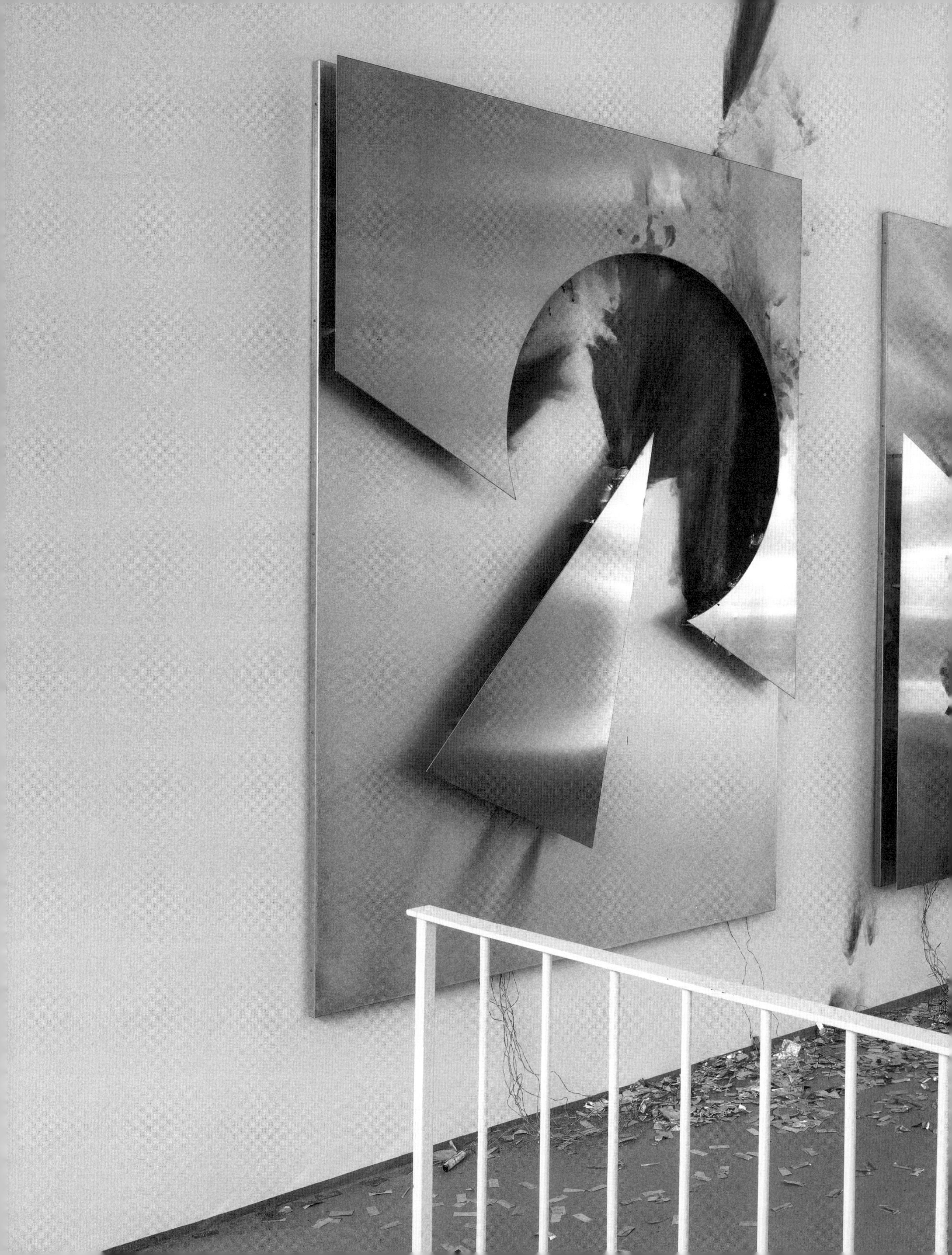

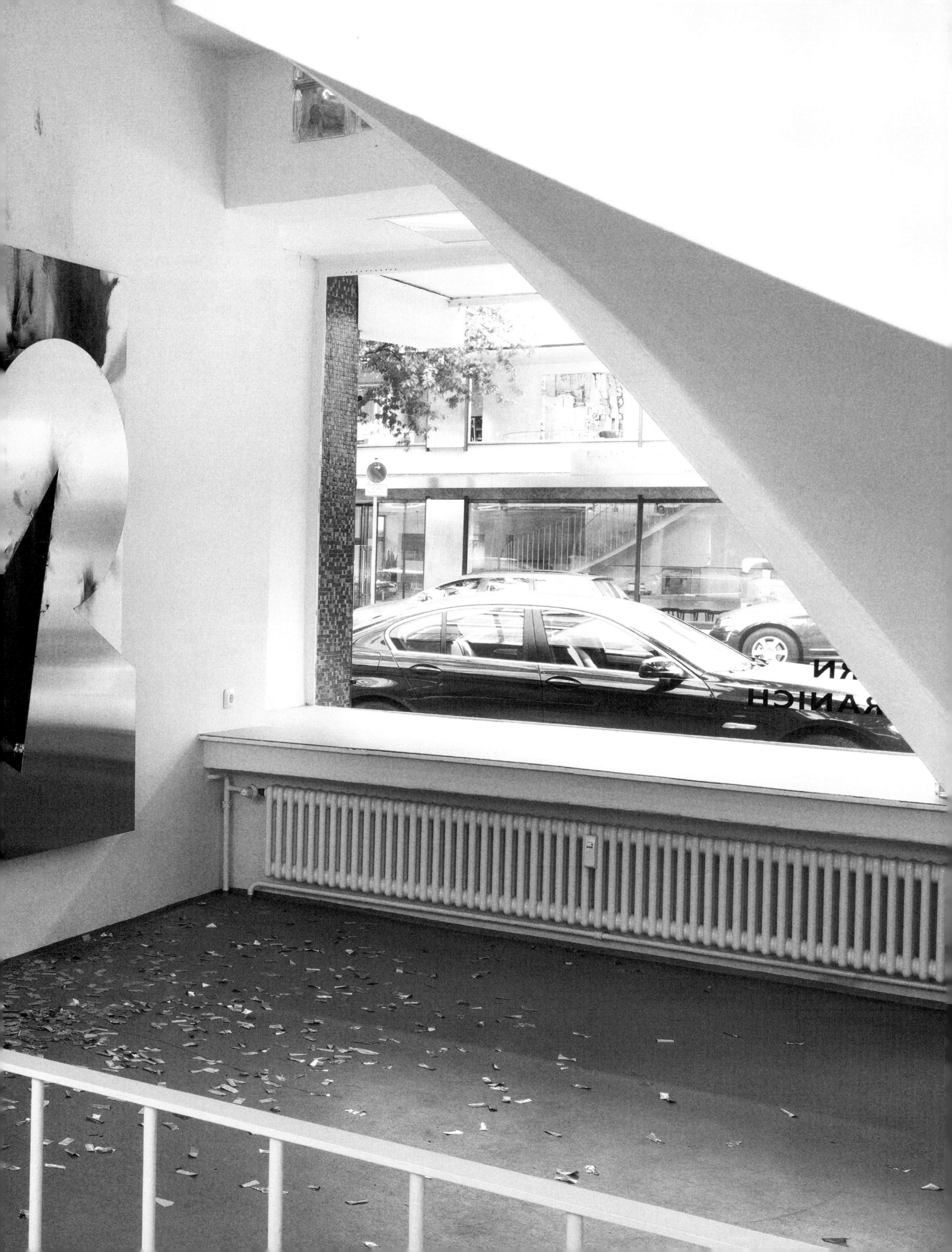

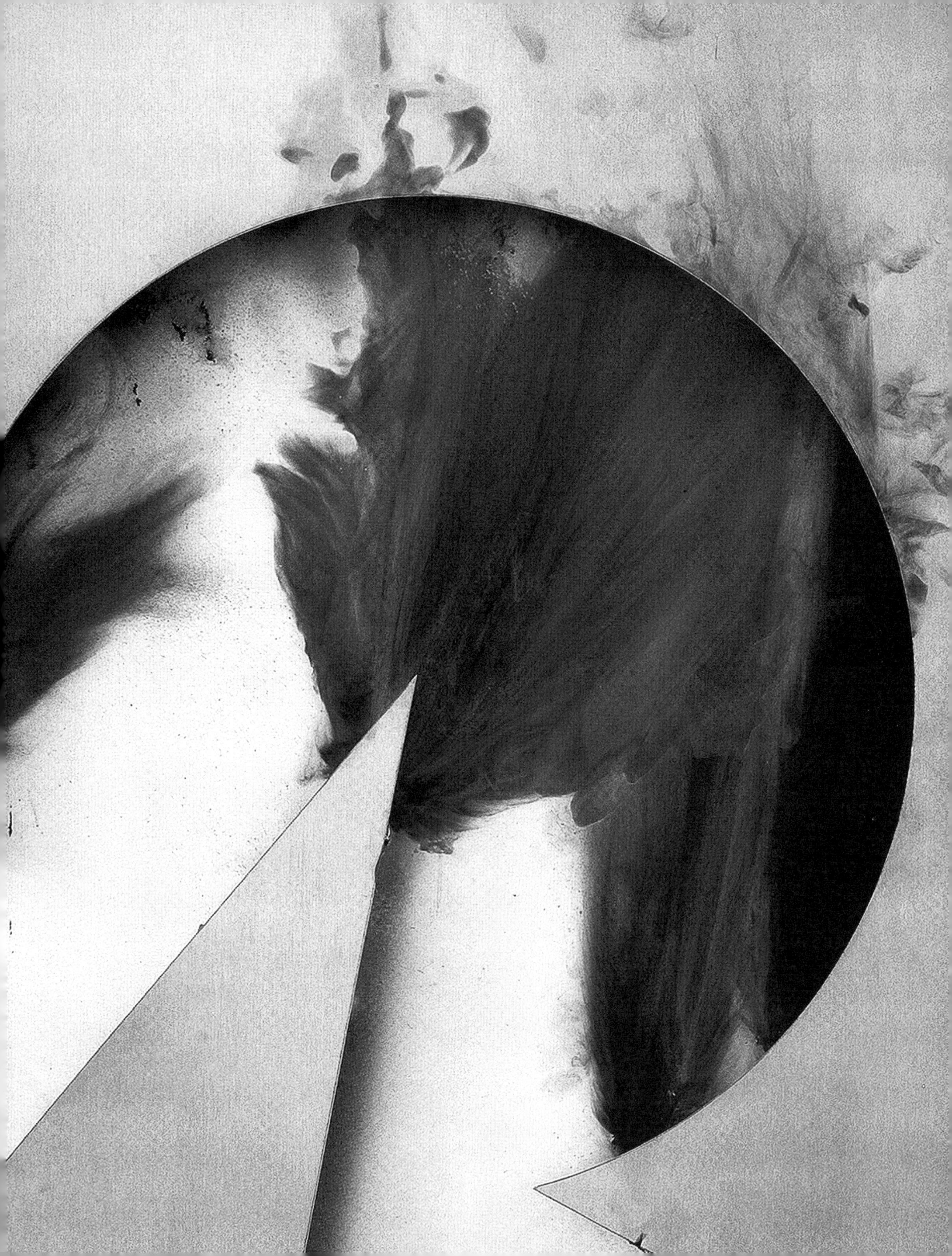

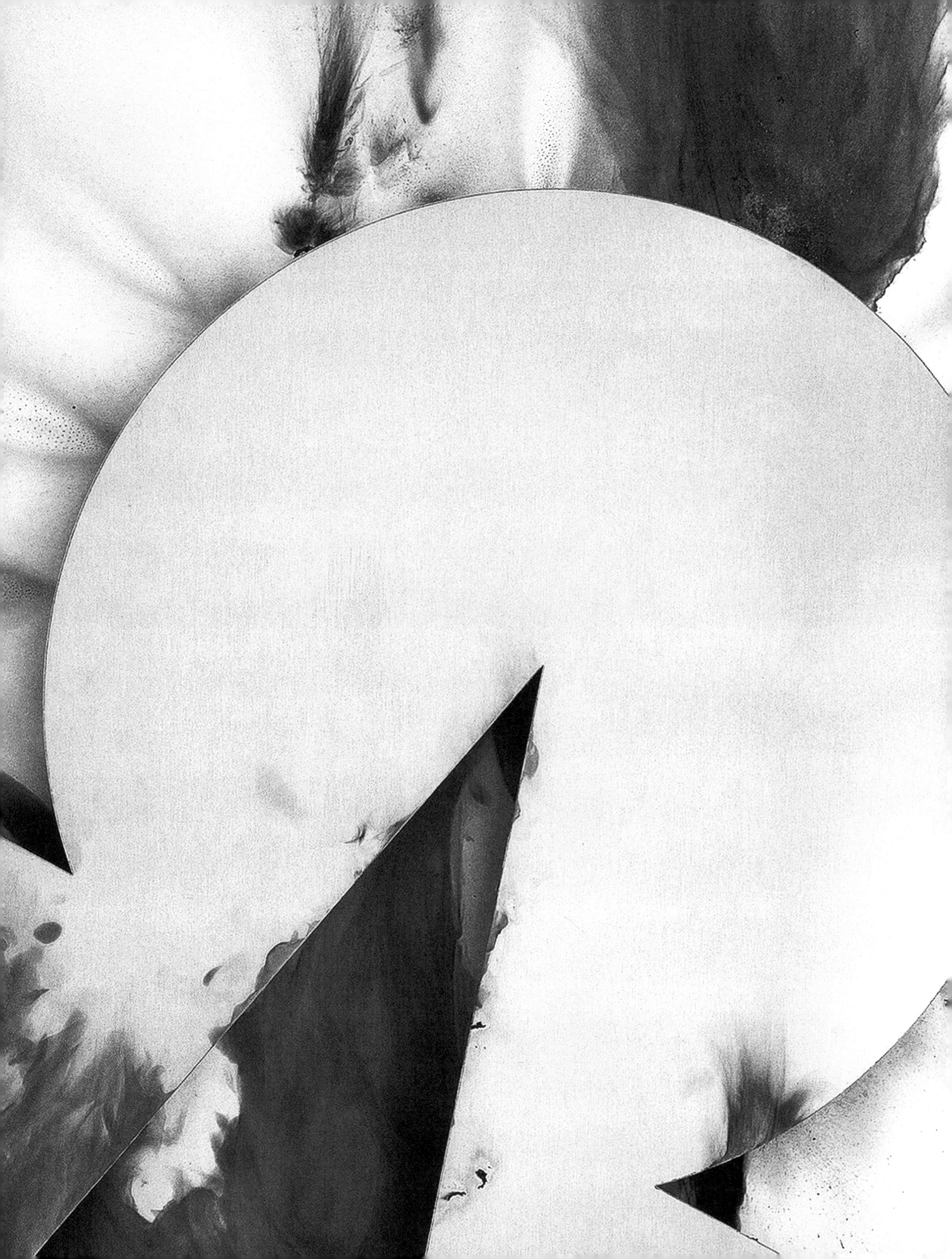

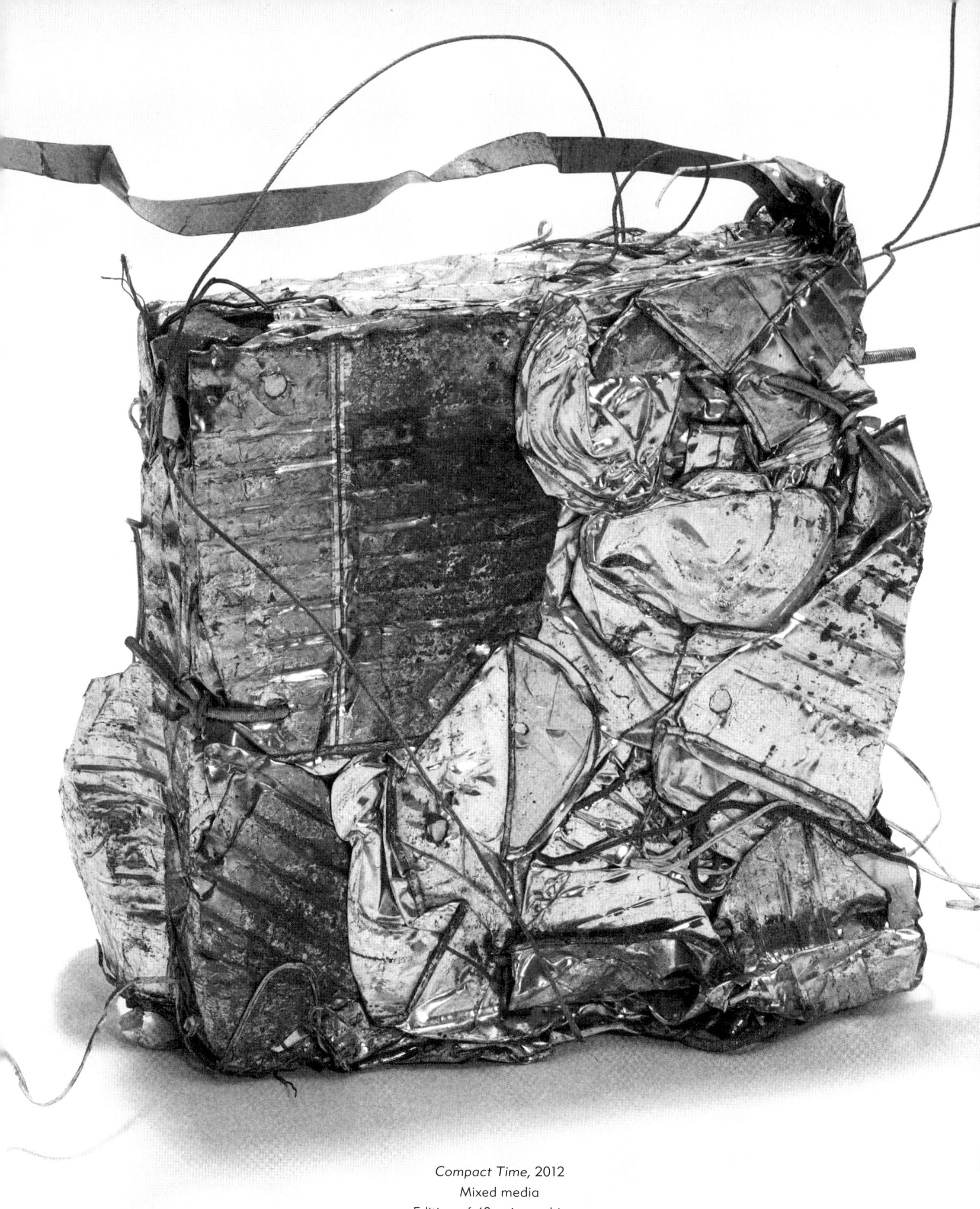

Compact Time, 2012
Mixed media
Edition of 40 unique objects

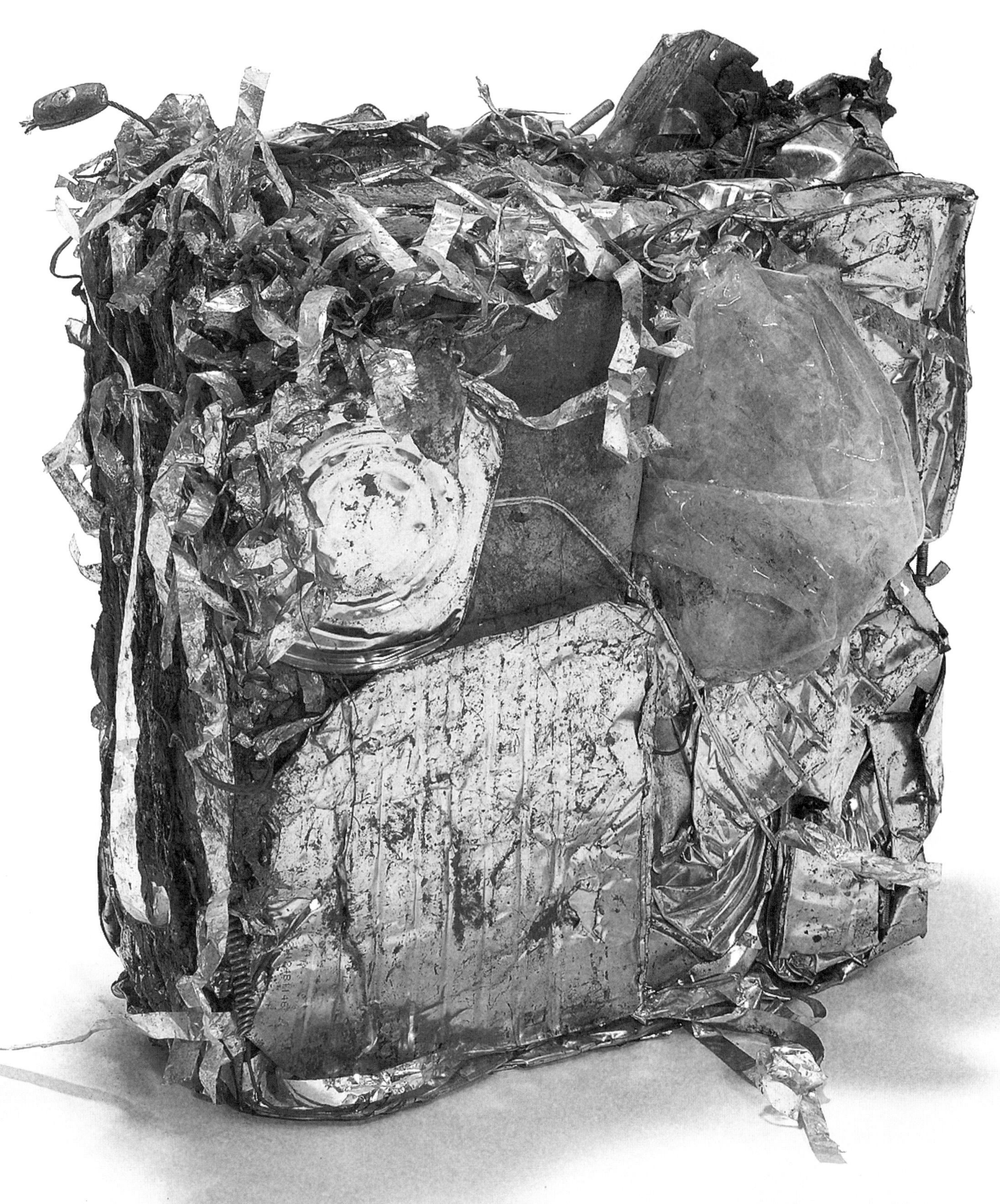

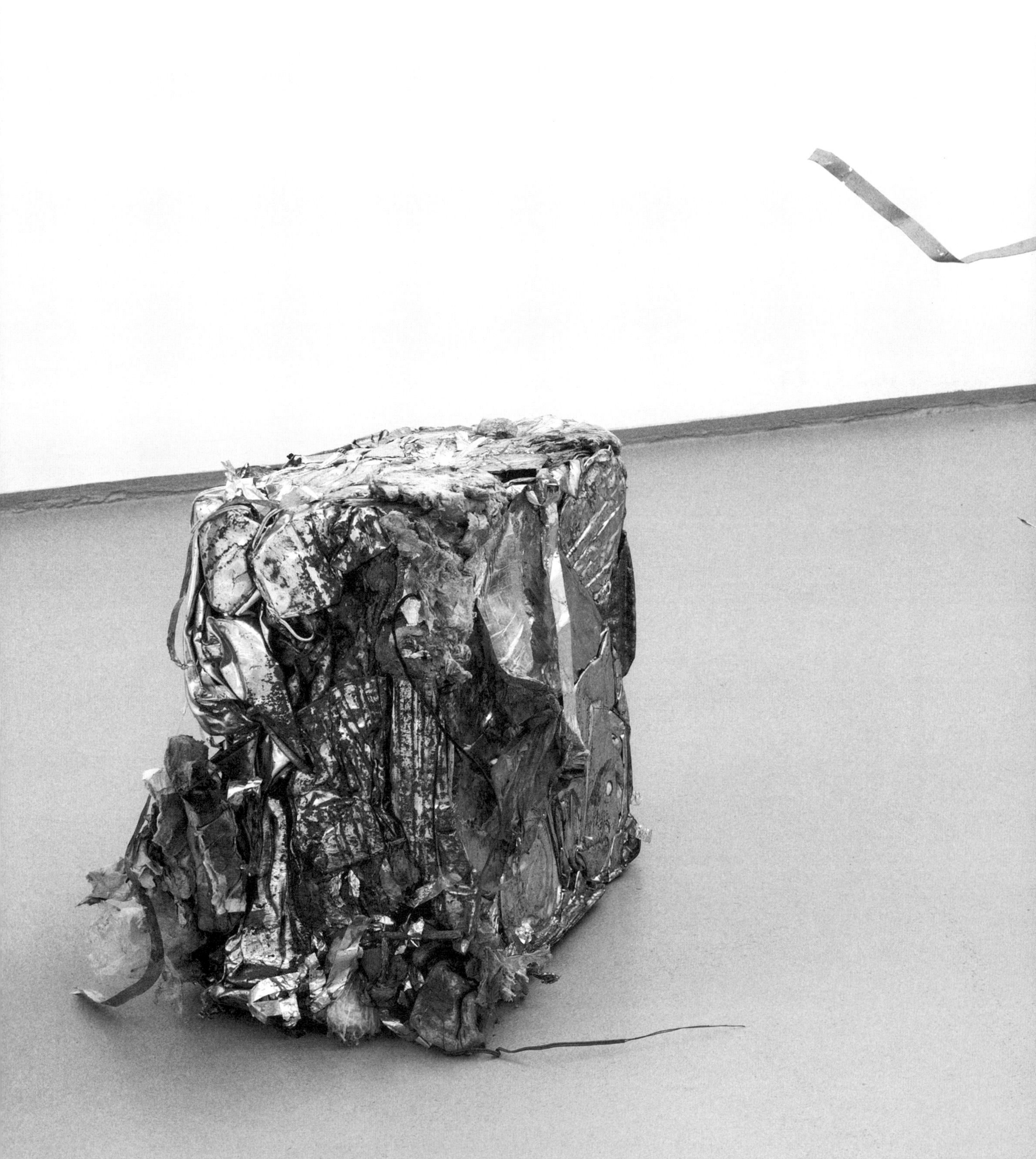

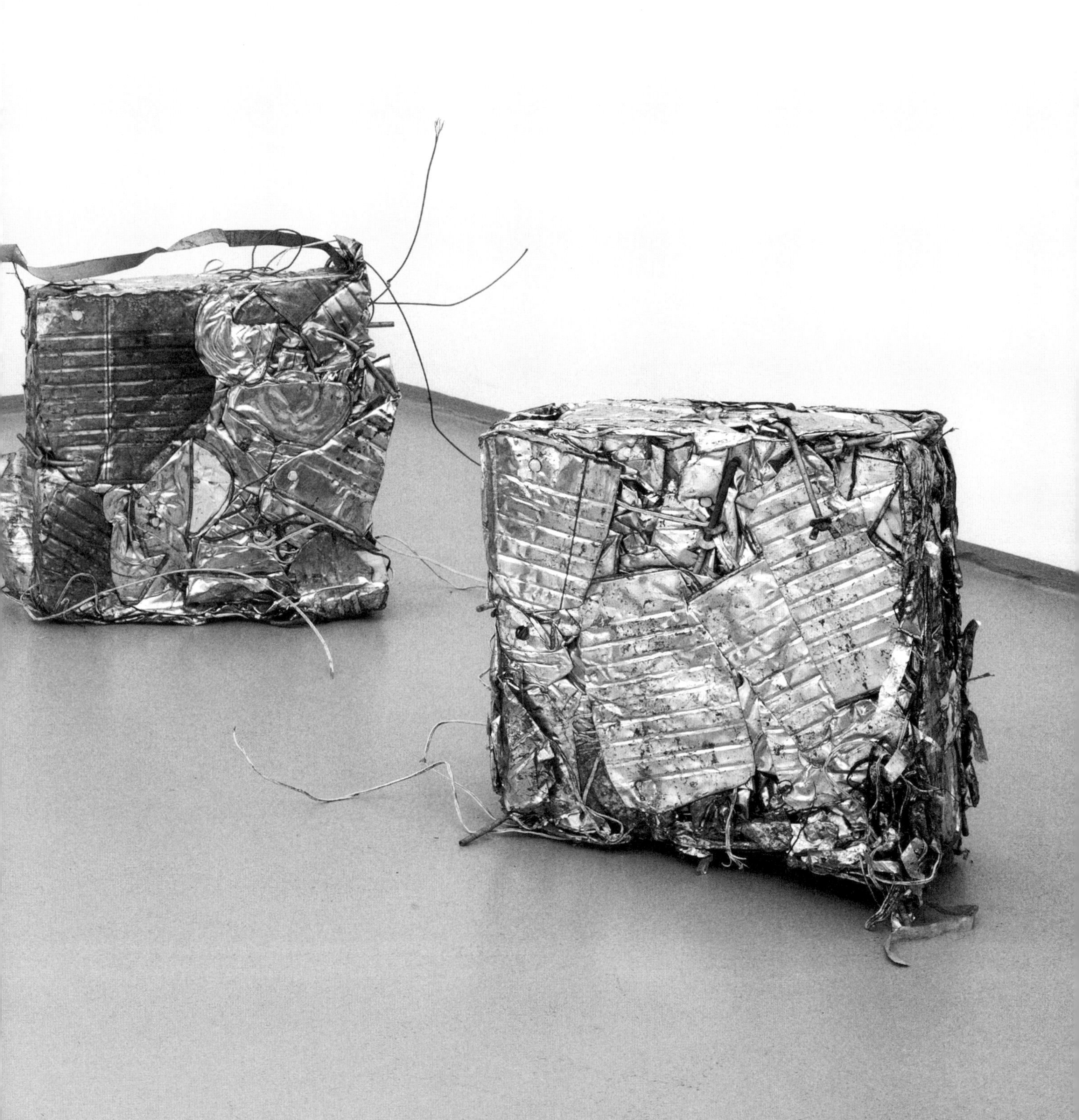

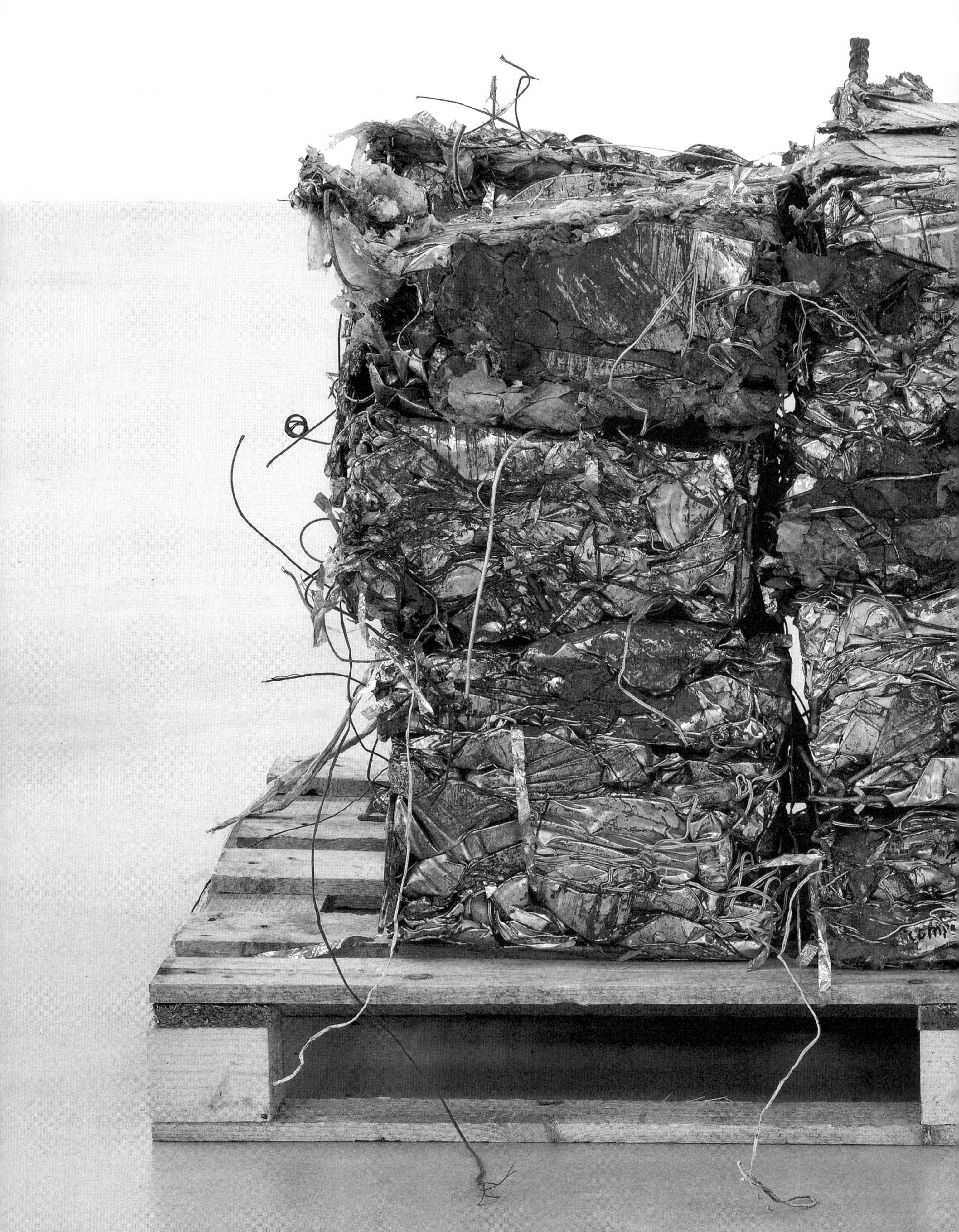

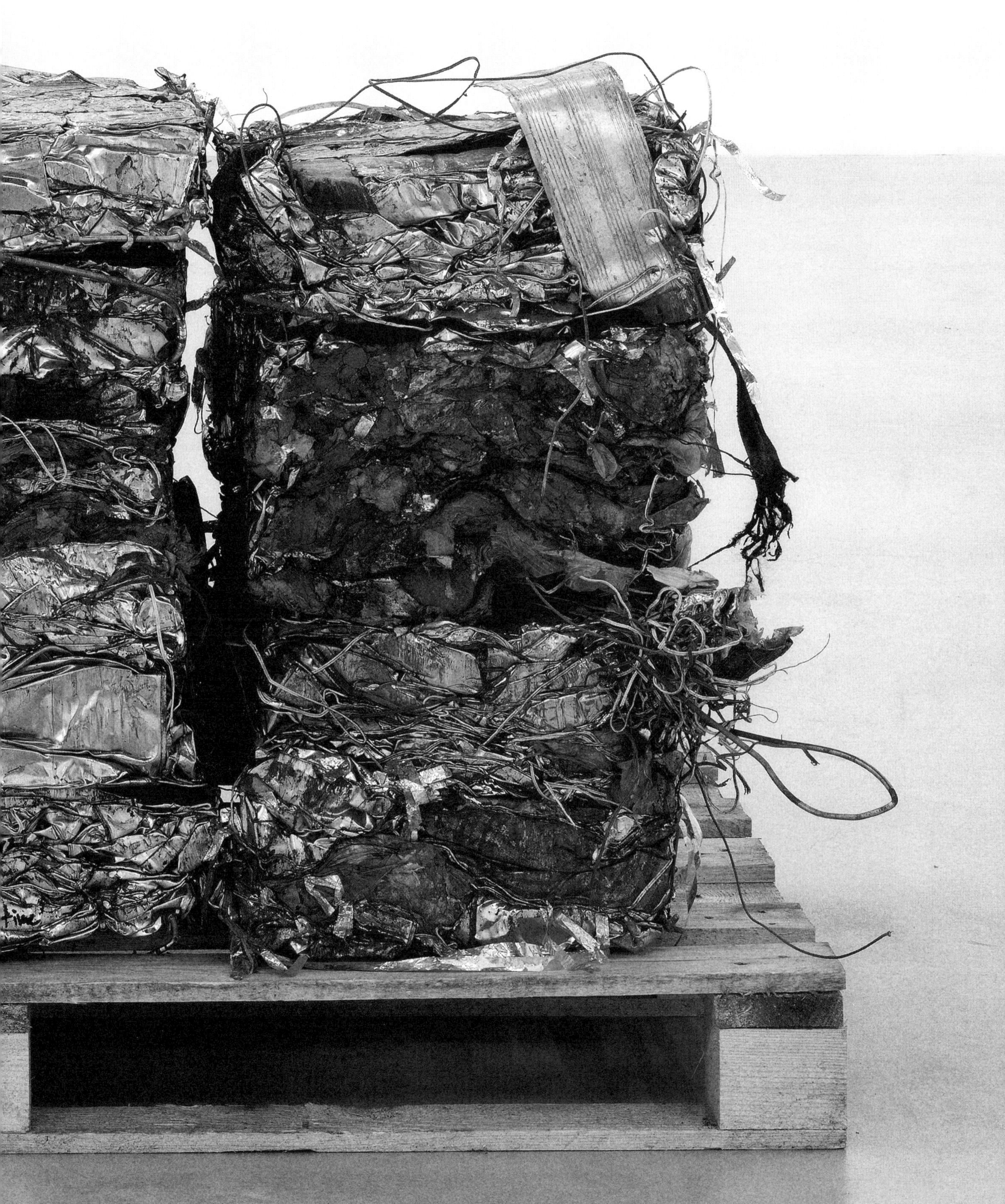

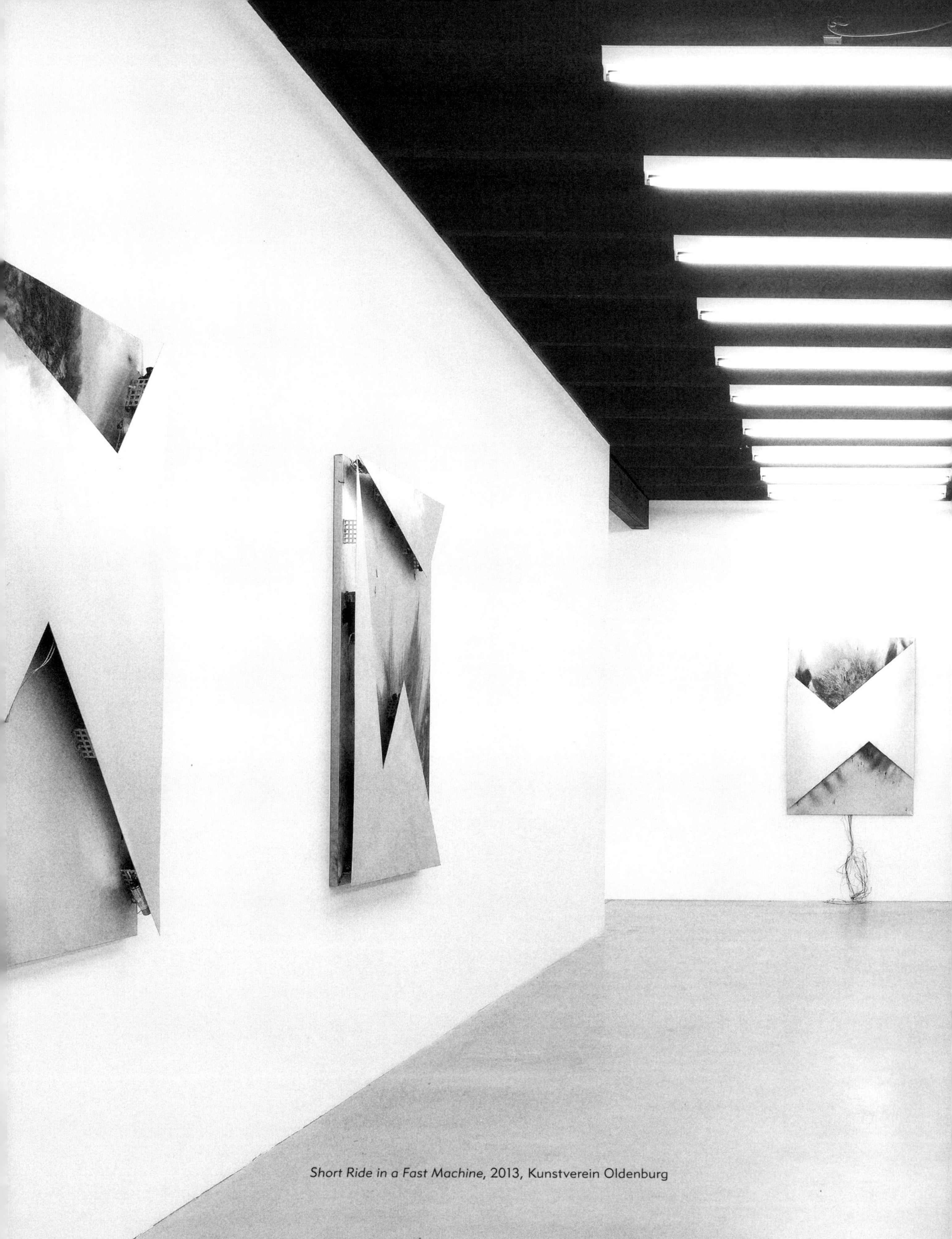

Short Ride in a Fast Machine, 2013, Kunstverein Oldenburg

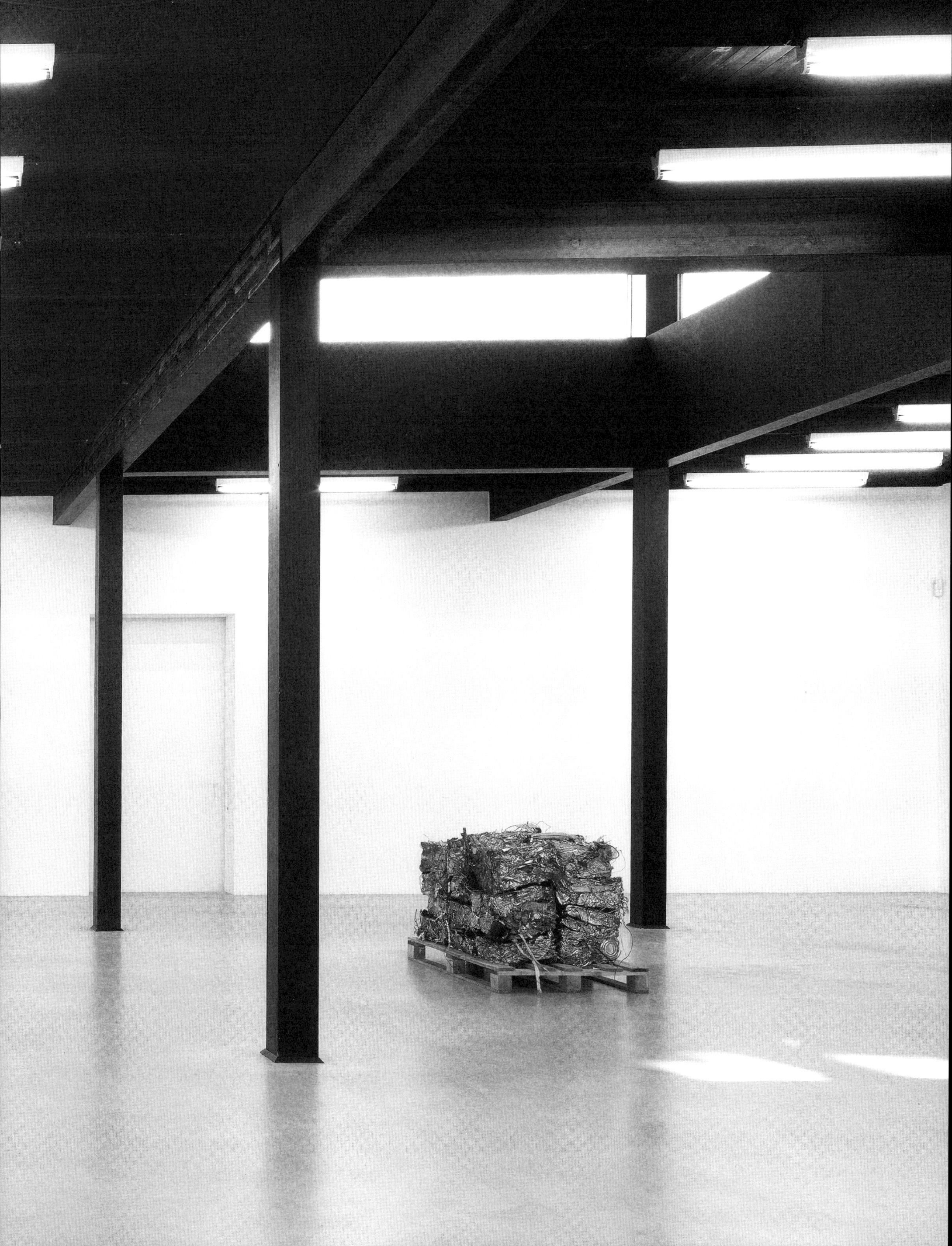

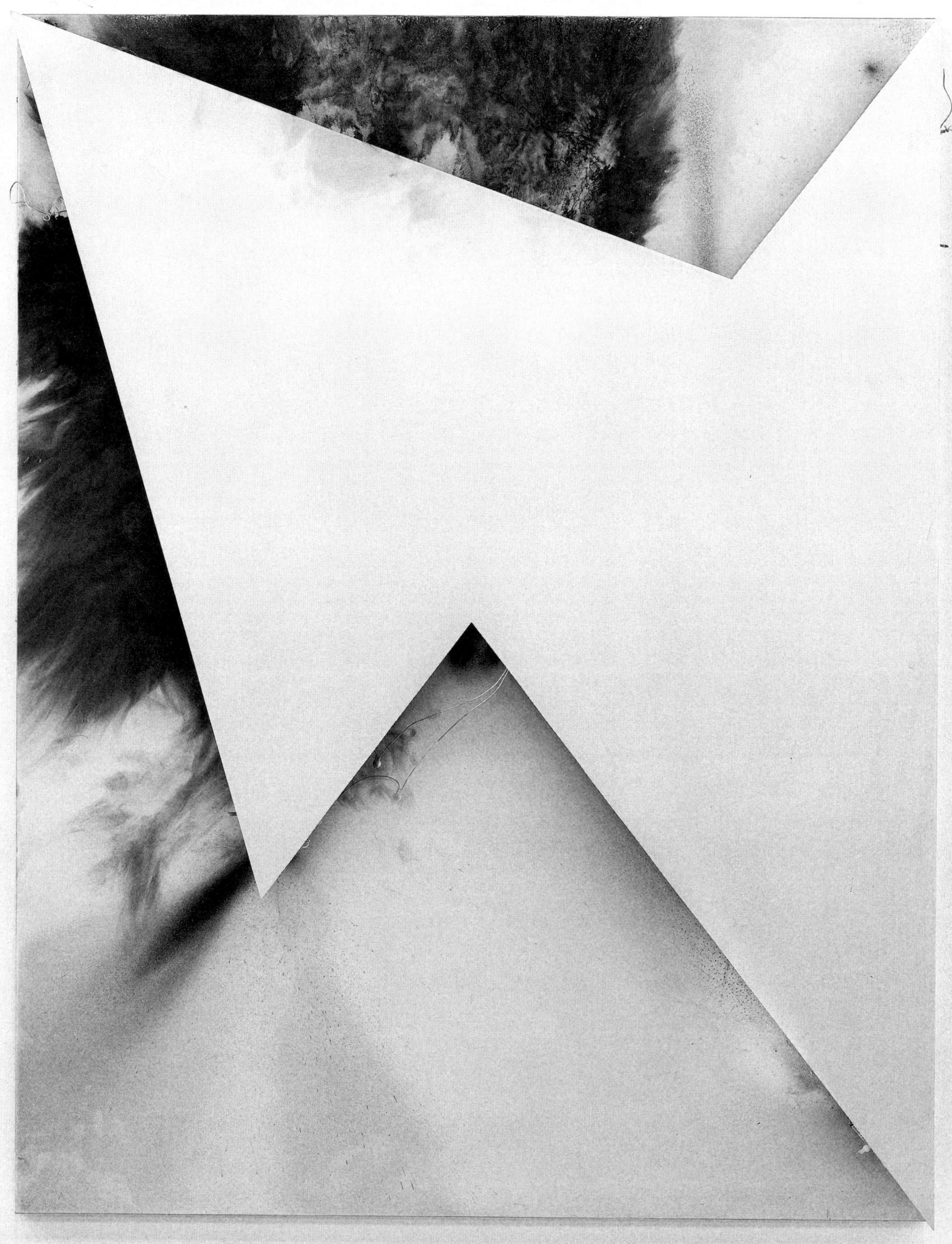

Flashforward 1 & 2, 2012
Aluminium, pyrotechnics, smoke residue, electric ignition
144.5 x 109 x 6 cm each

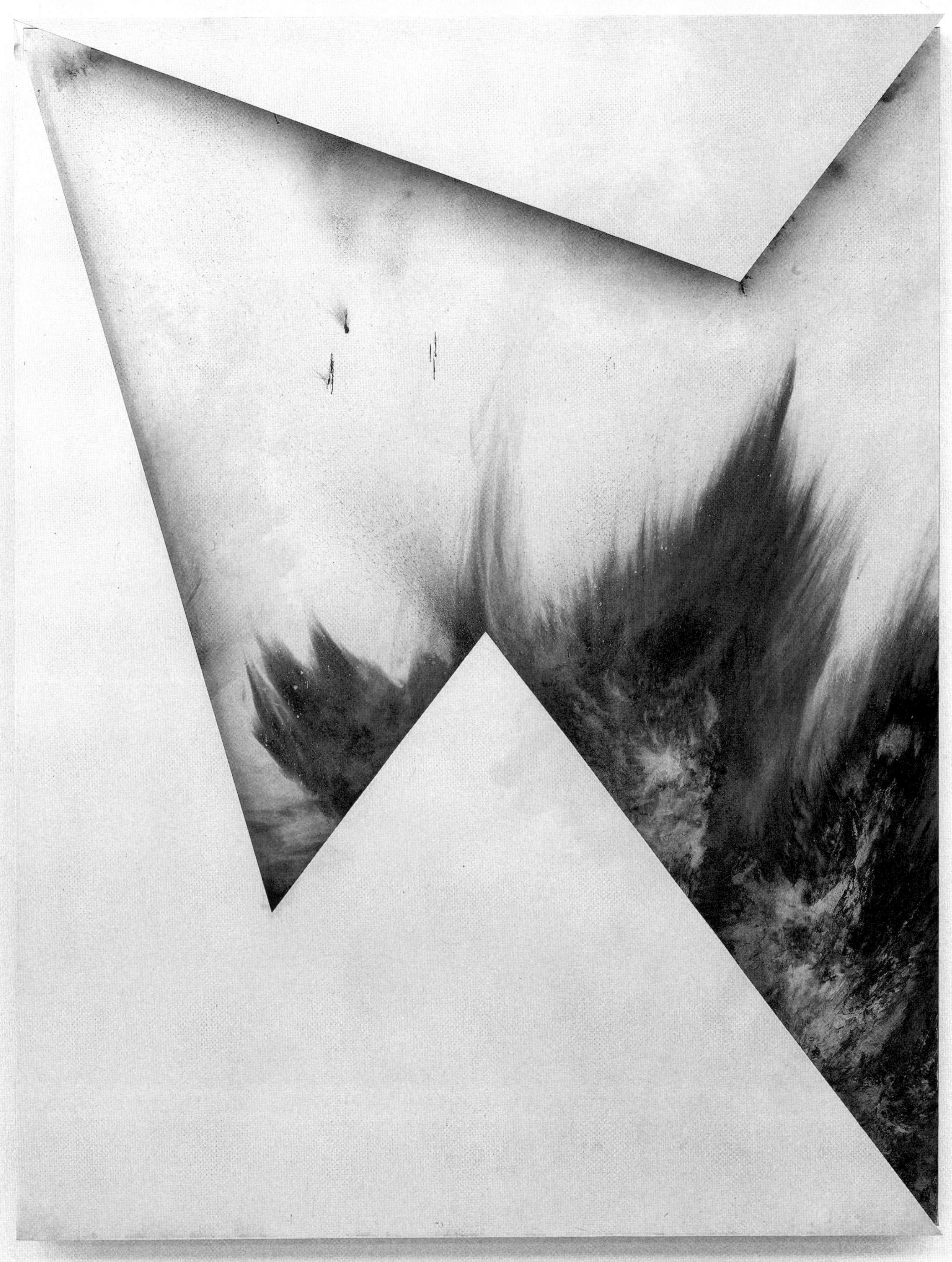

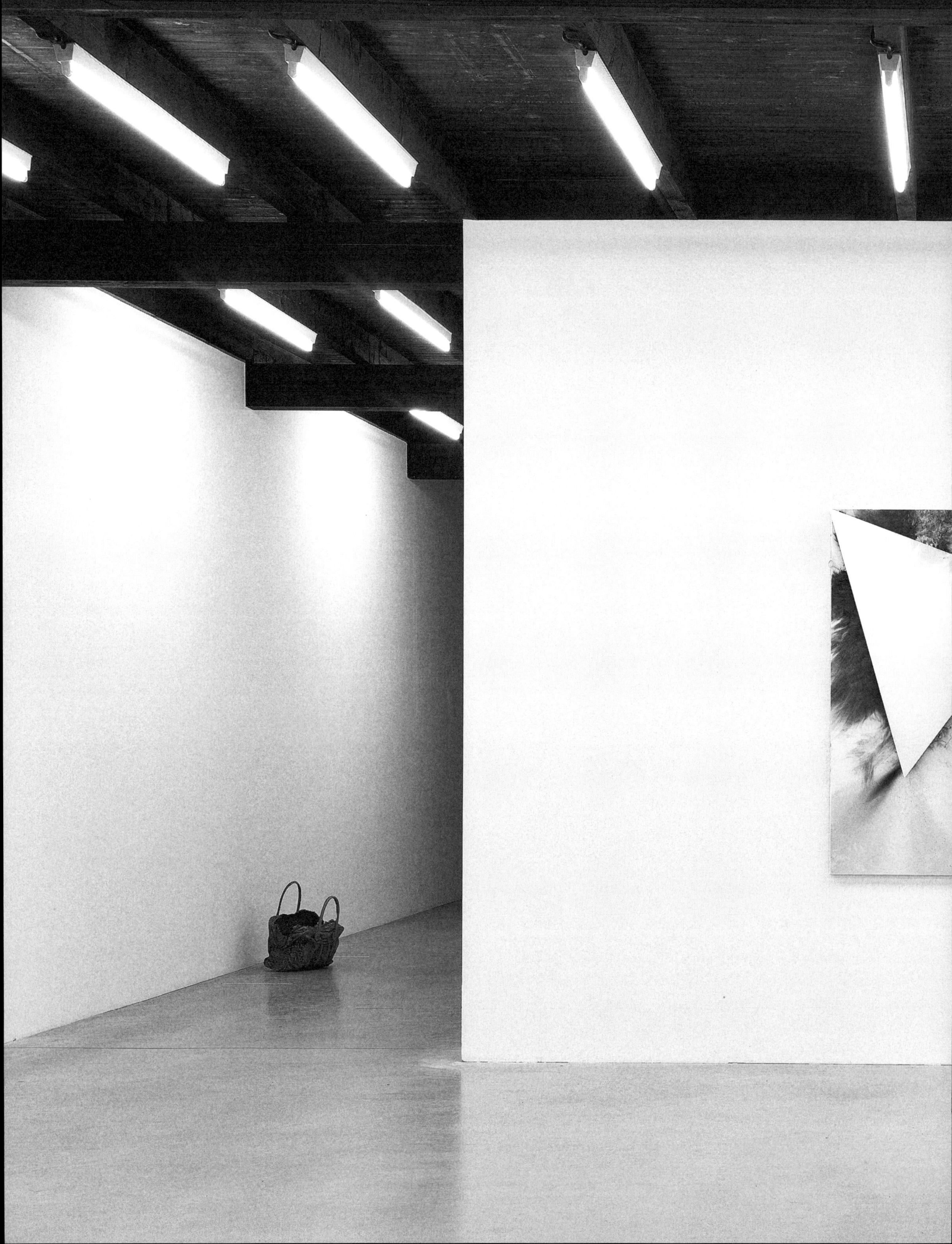

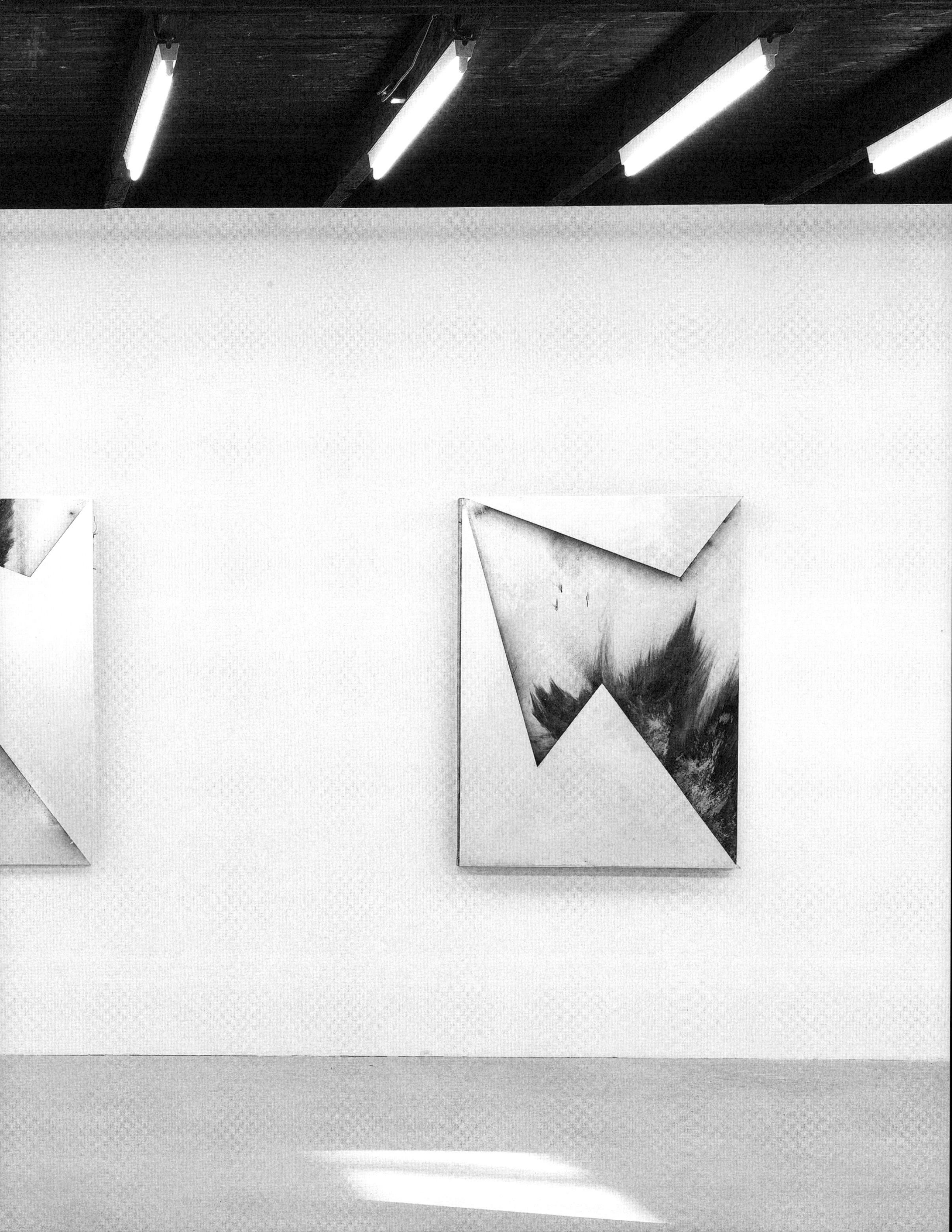

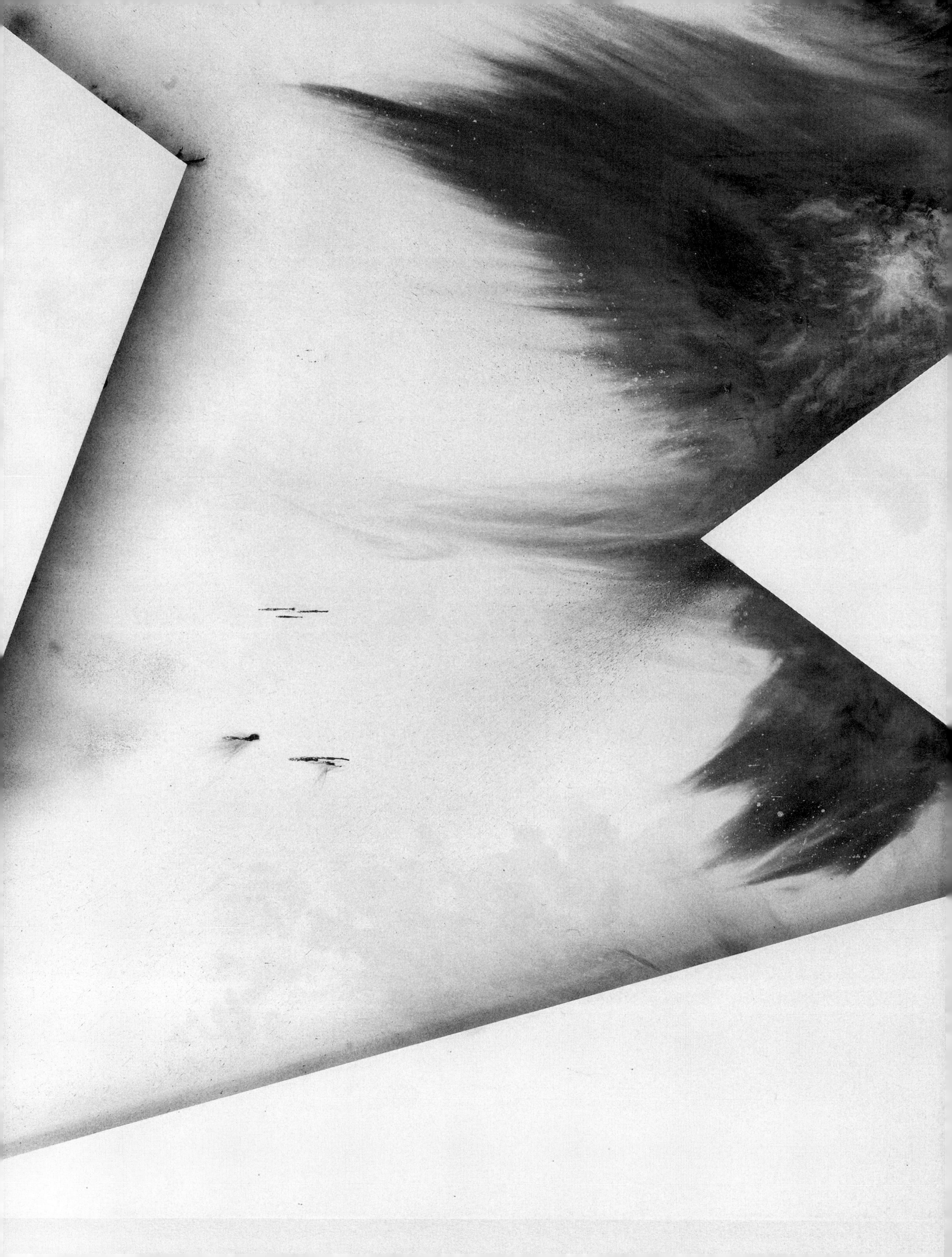

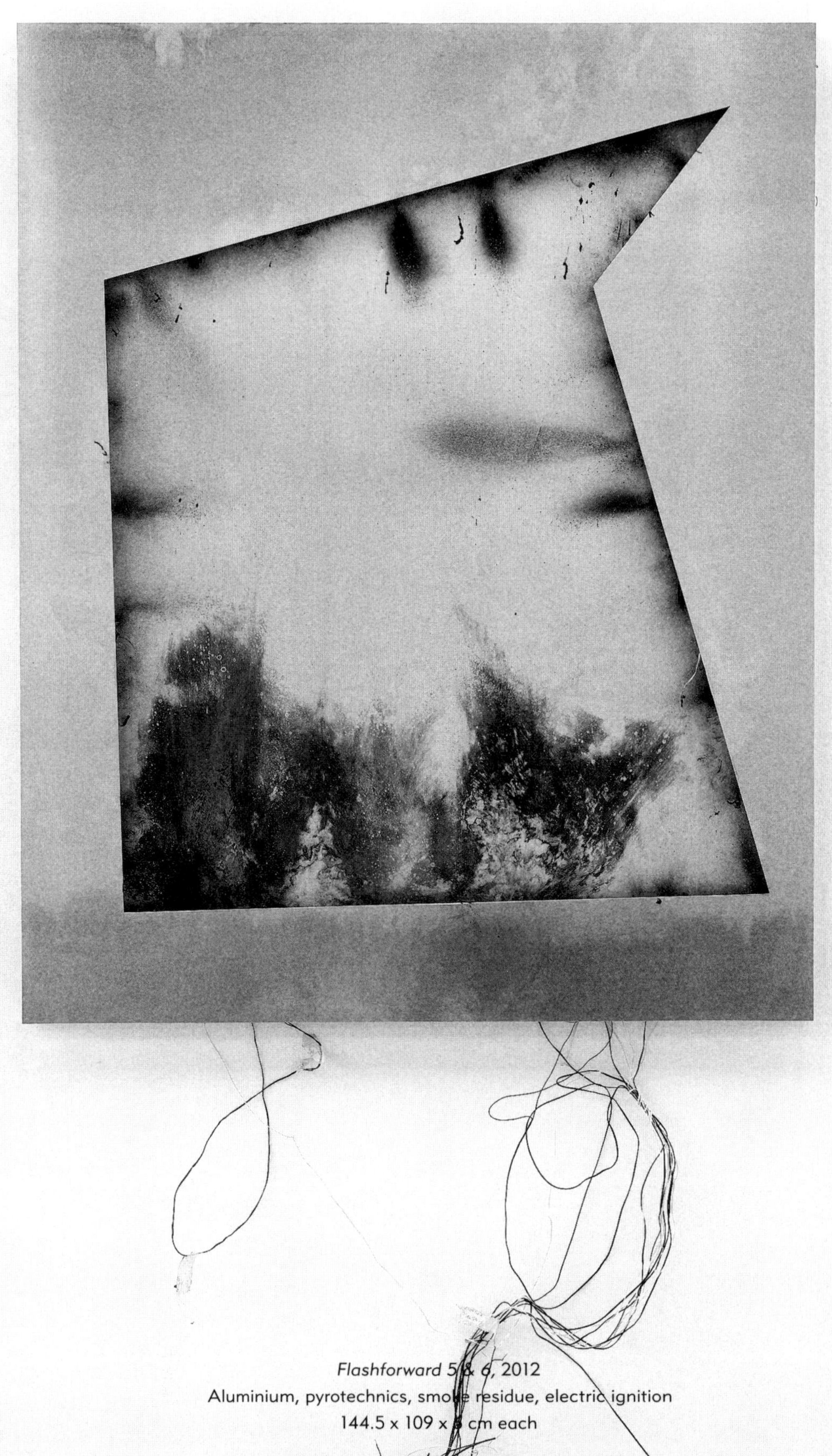

Flashforward 5 & 6, 2012
Aluminium, pyrotechnics, smoke residue, electric ignition
144.5 x 109 x 8 cm each

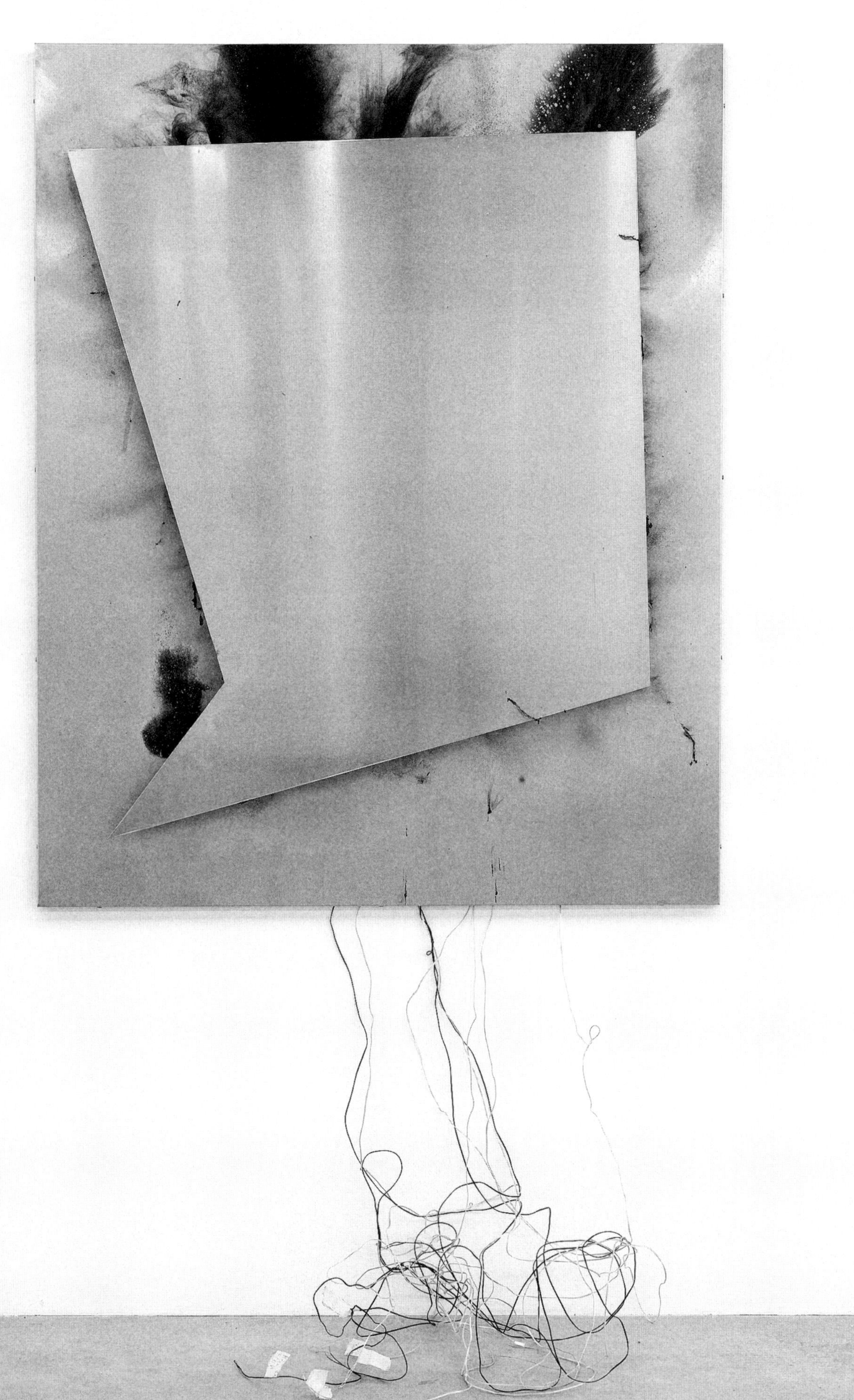

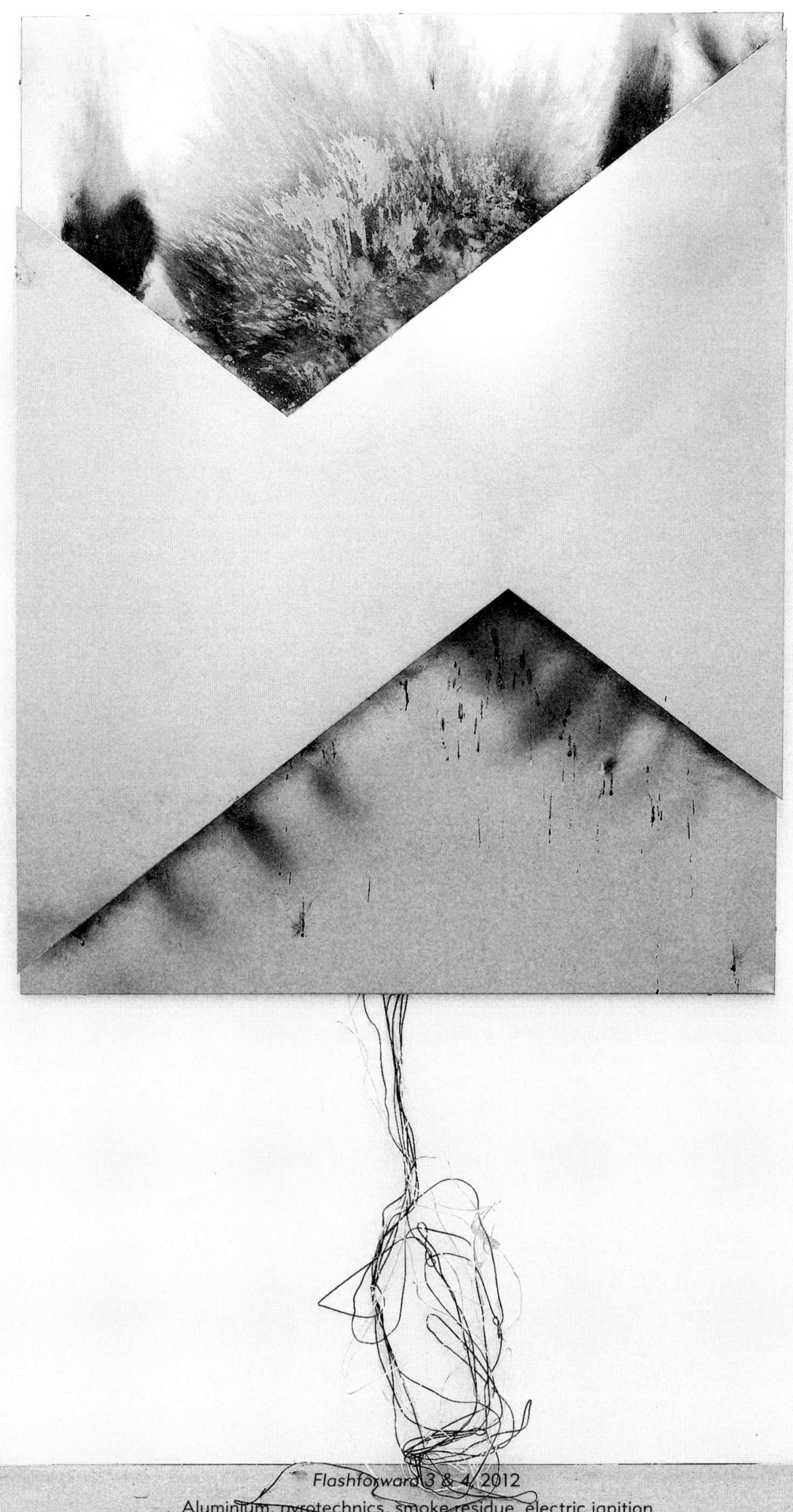

Flashforward 3 & 4, 2012
Aluminium, pyrotechnics, smoke residue, electric ignition
144.5 x 109 x 6 cm each

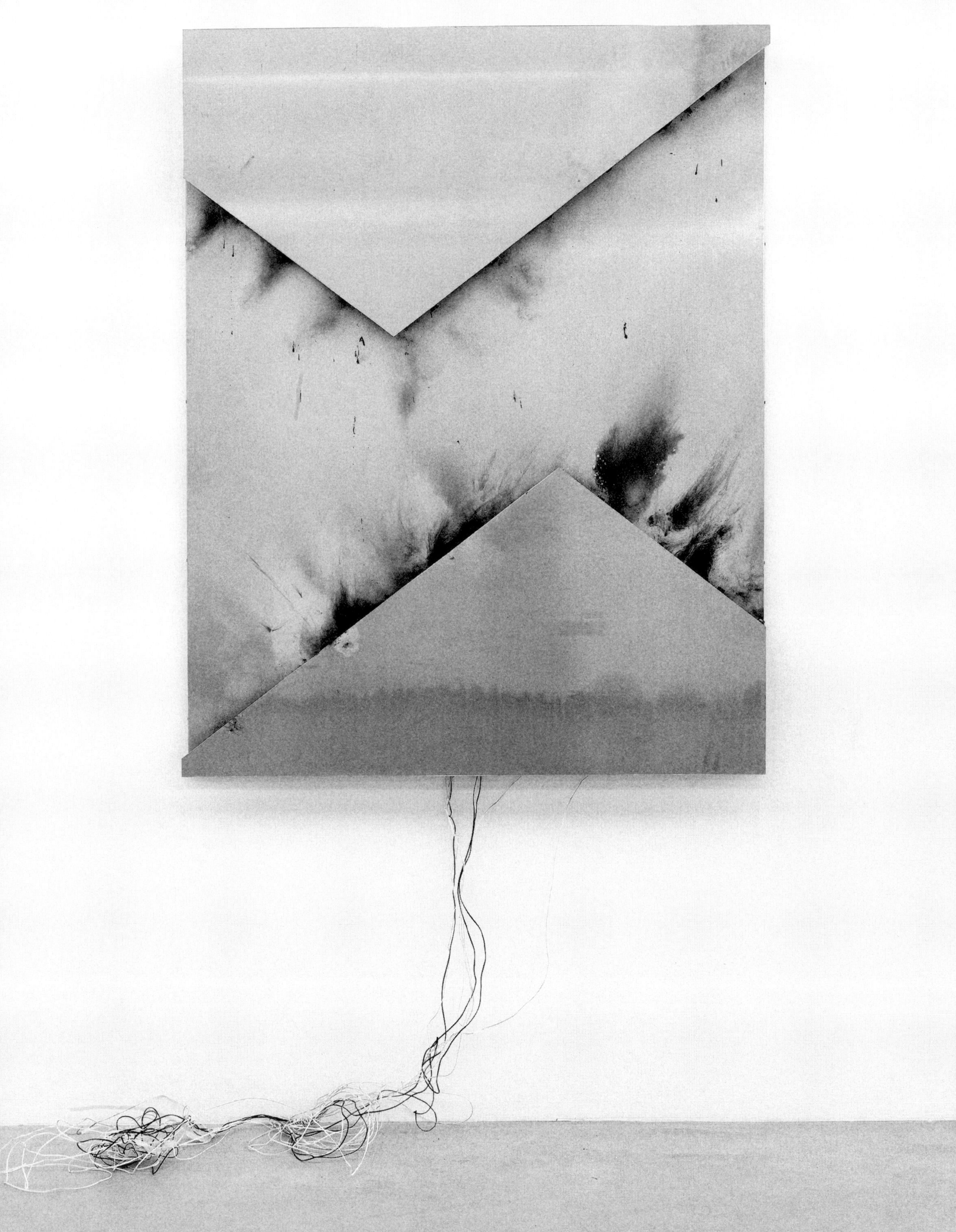

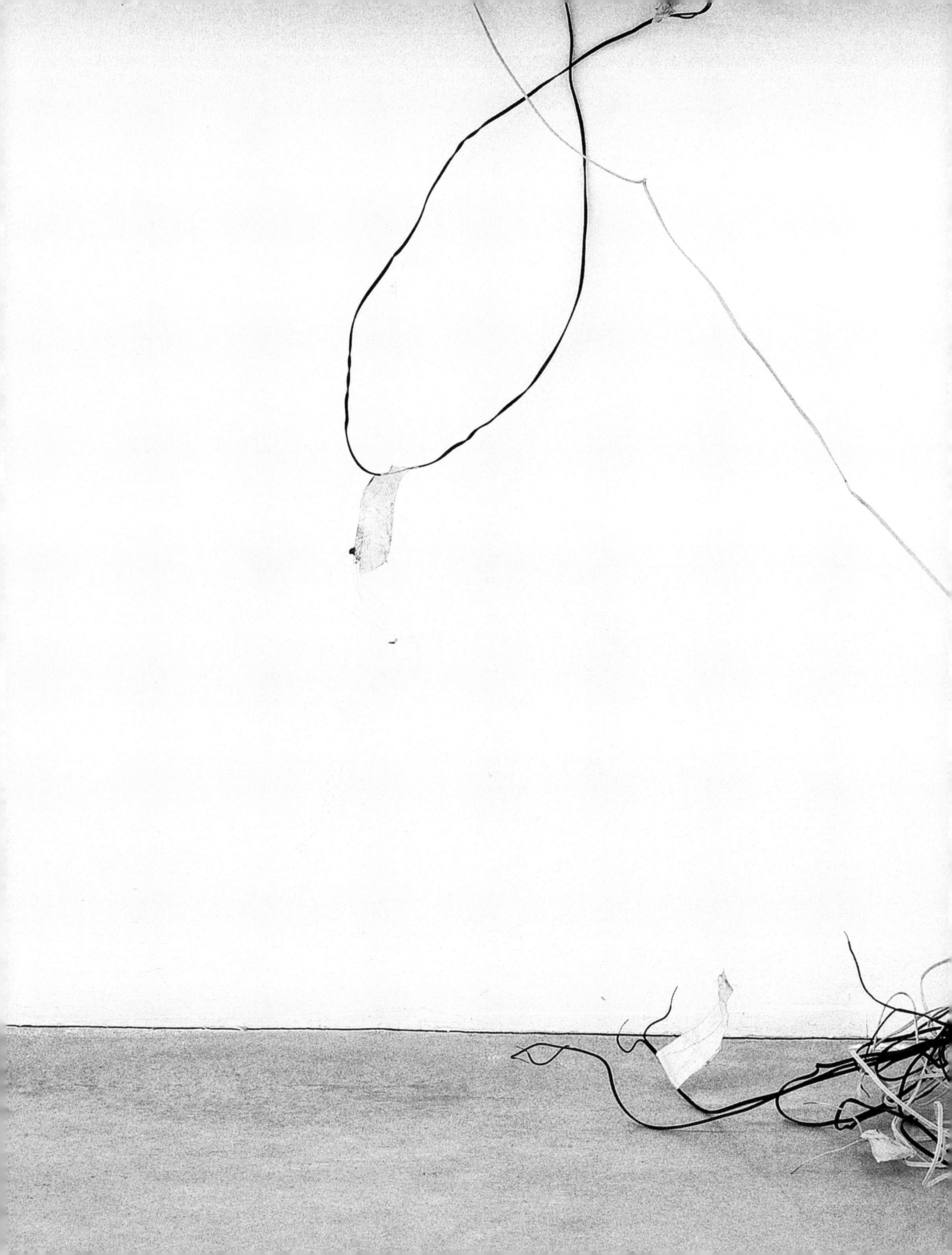

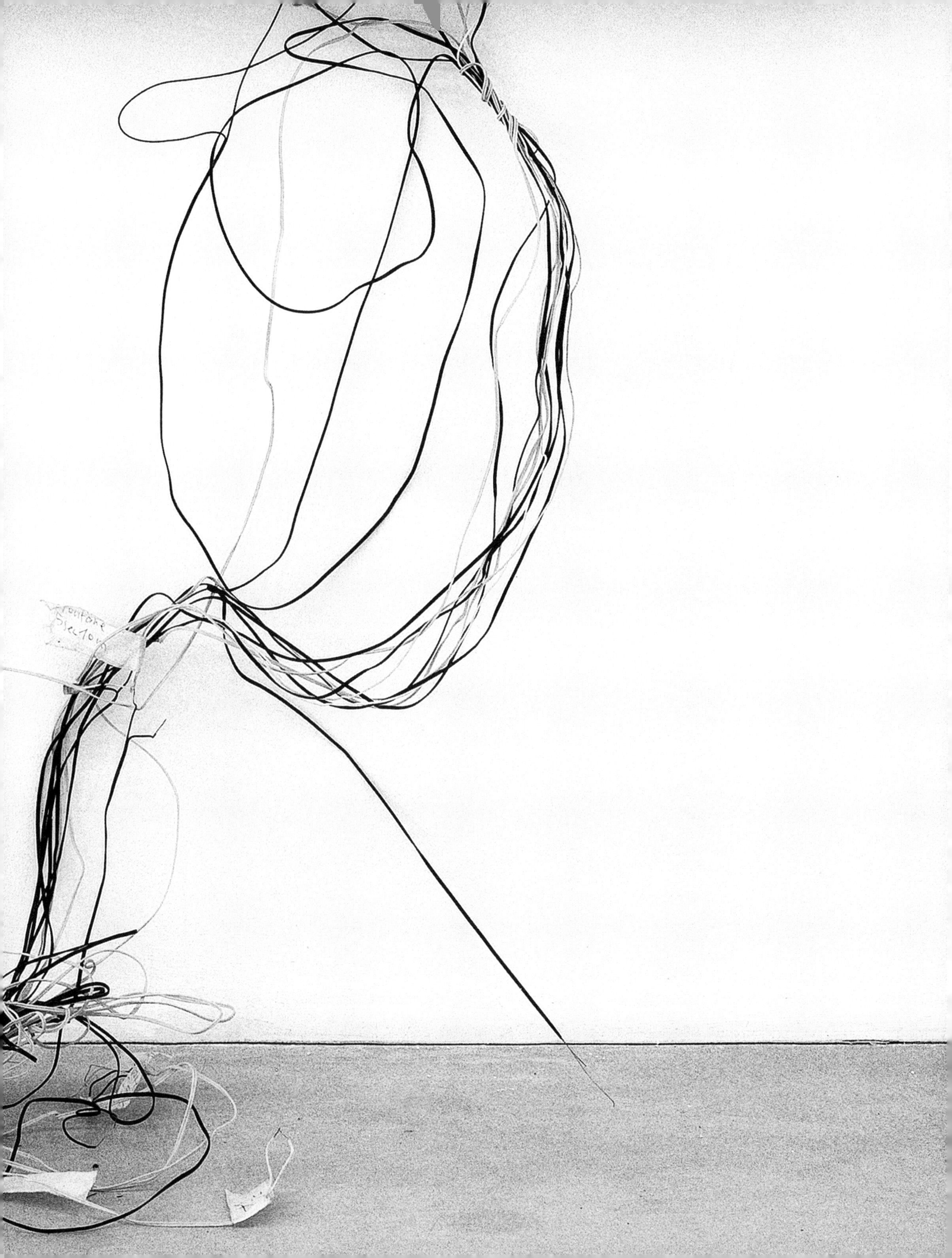

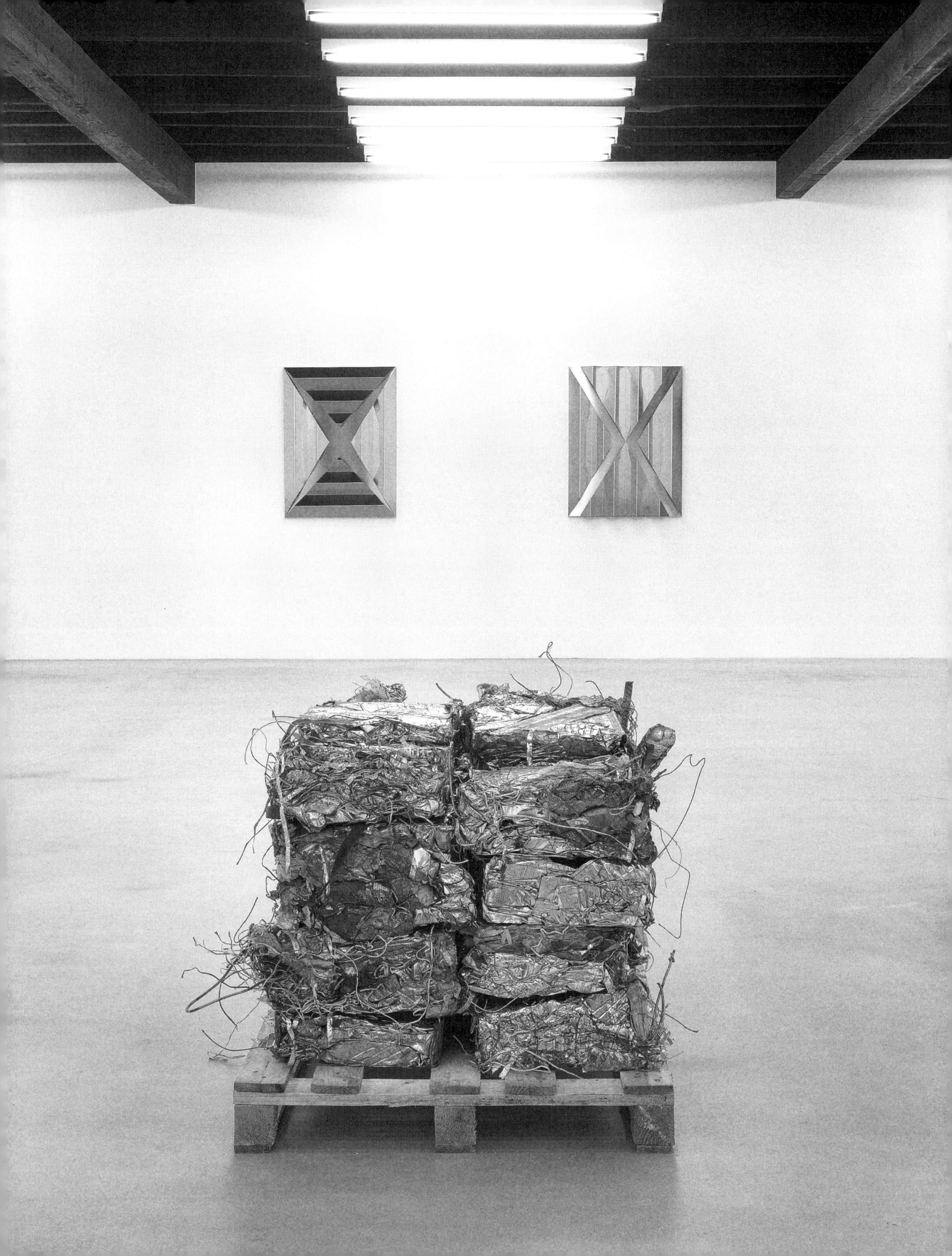

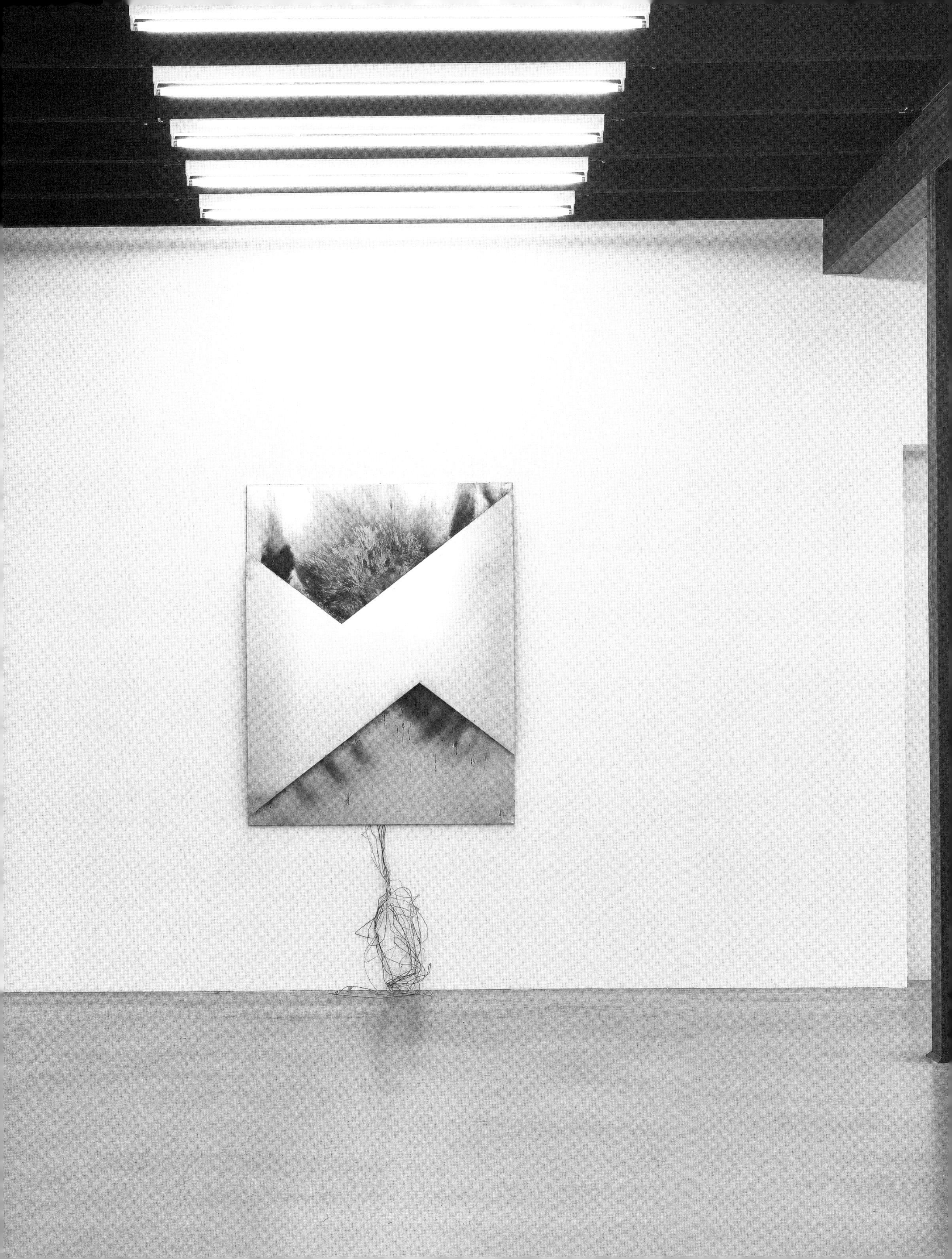

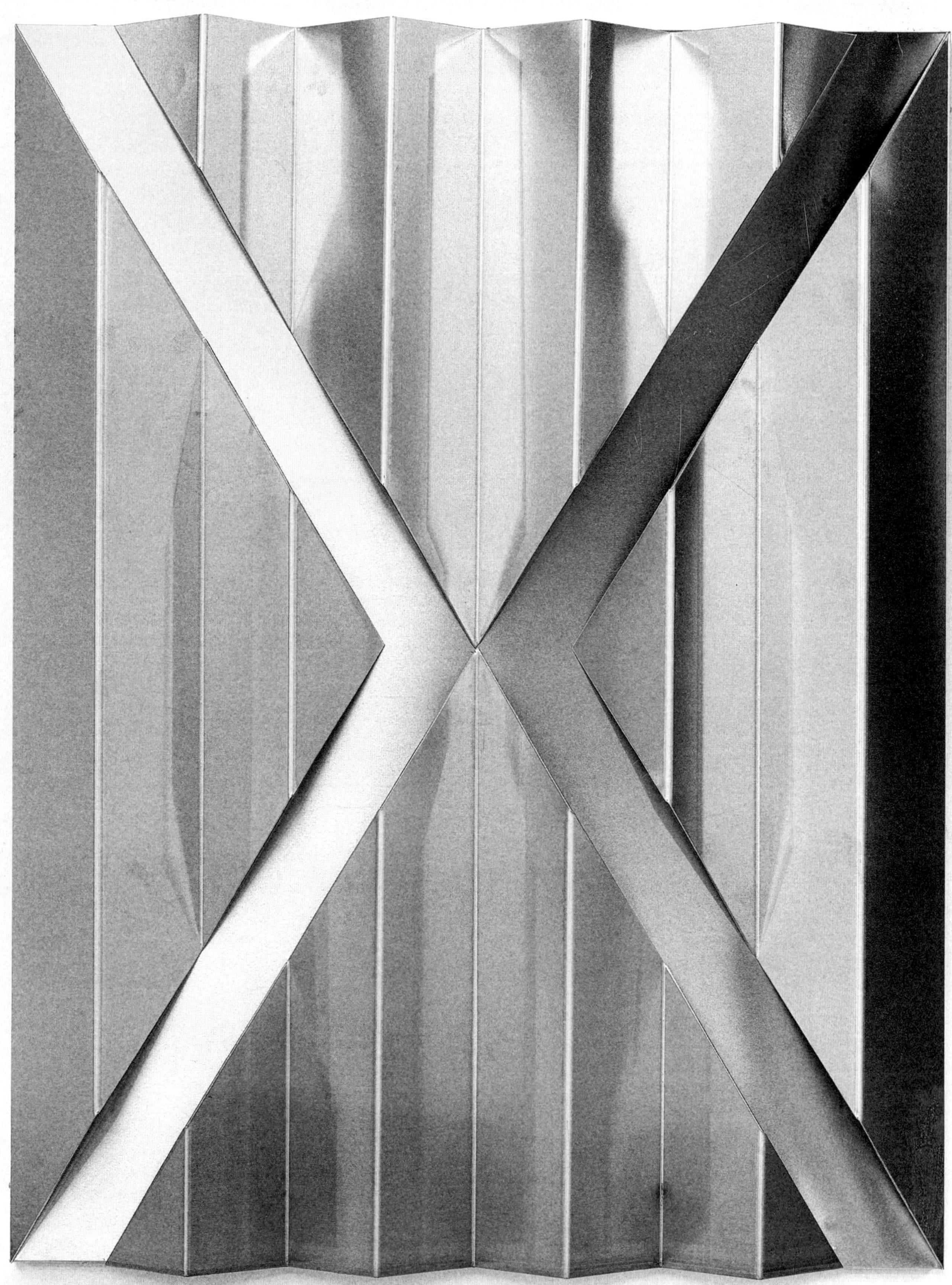

Untitled, 2012
Aluminium
100 x 75 x 9 cm each

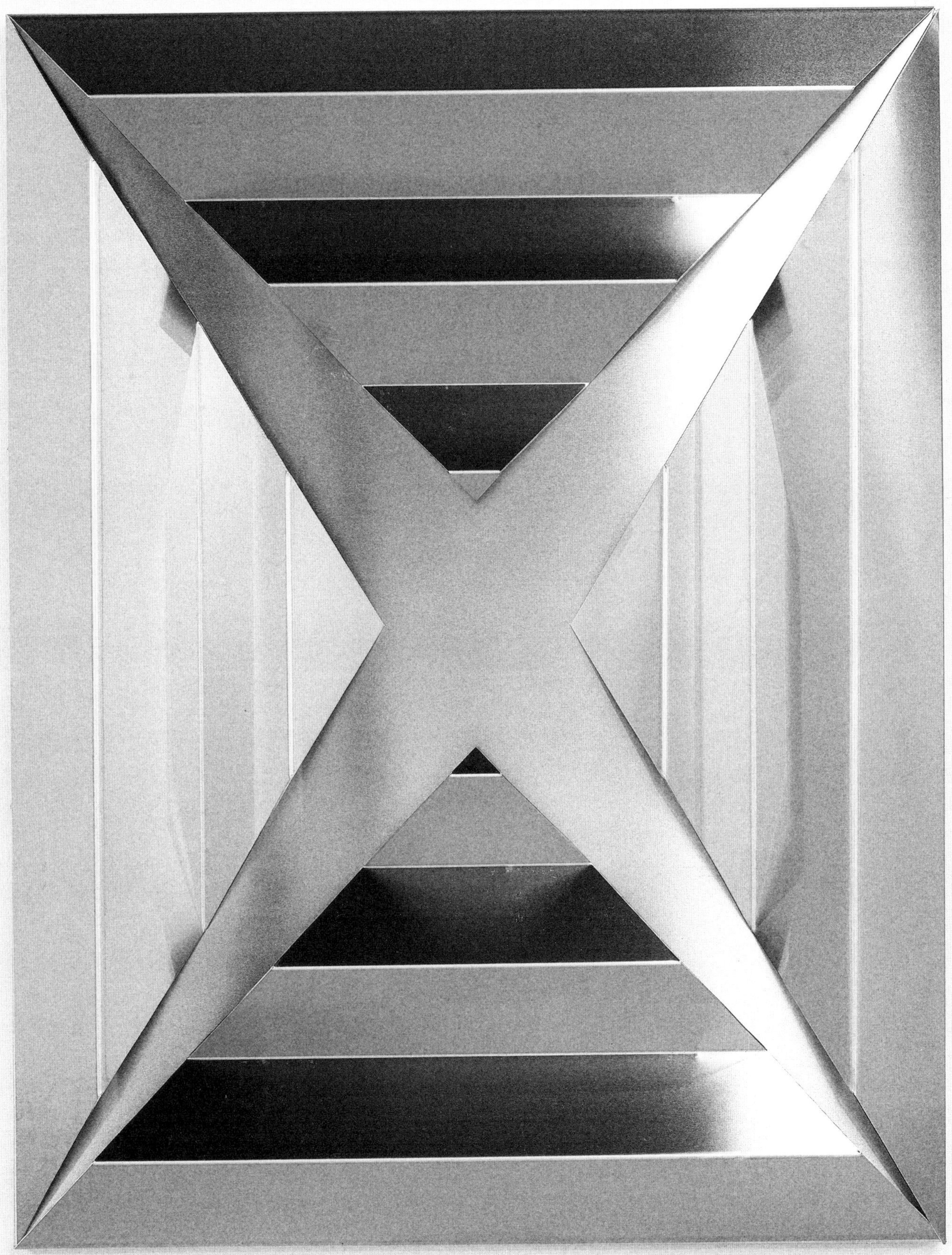

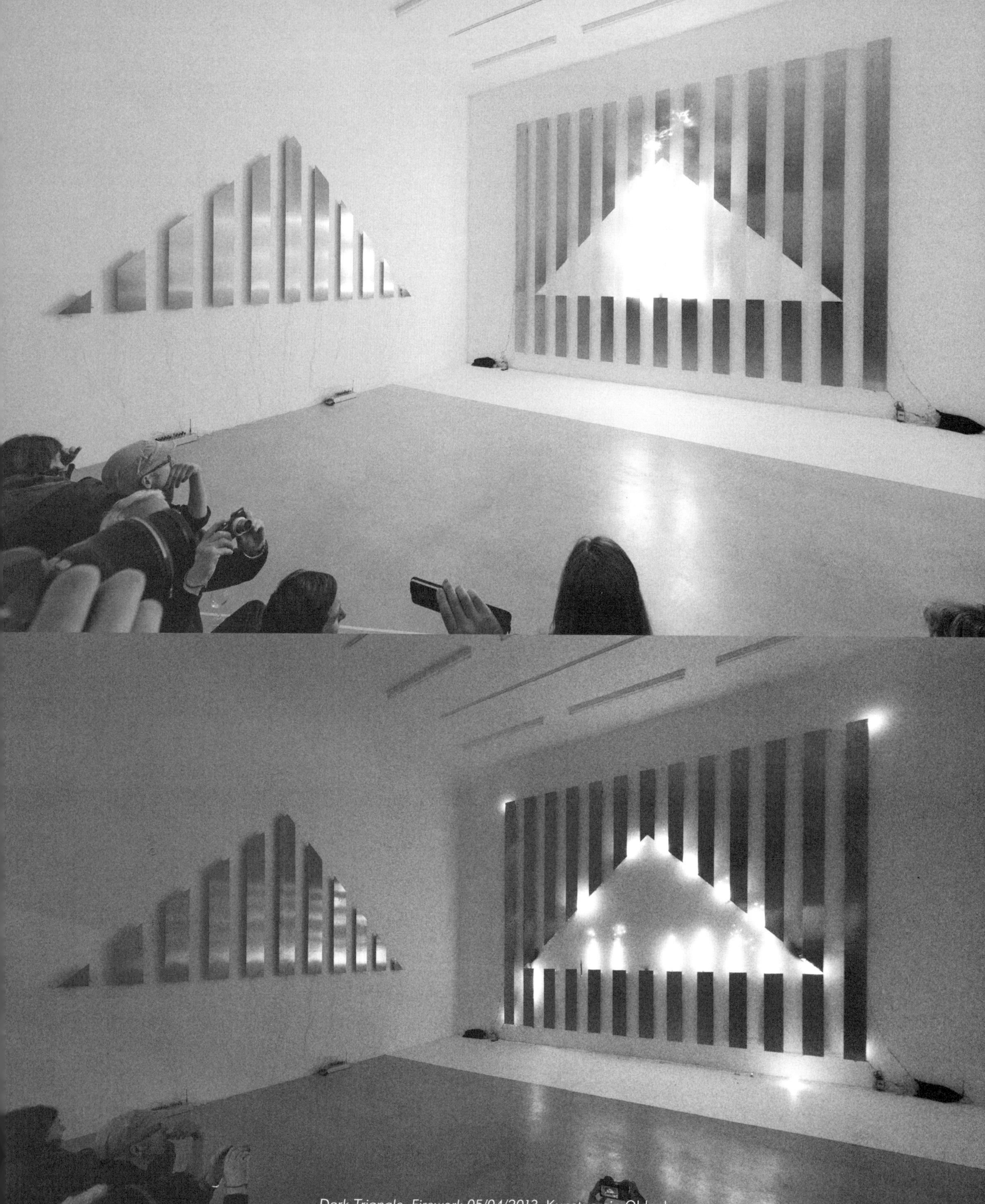

Dark Triangle, Firework 05/04/2013, Kunstverein Oldenburg

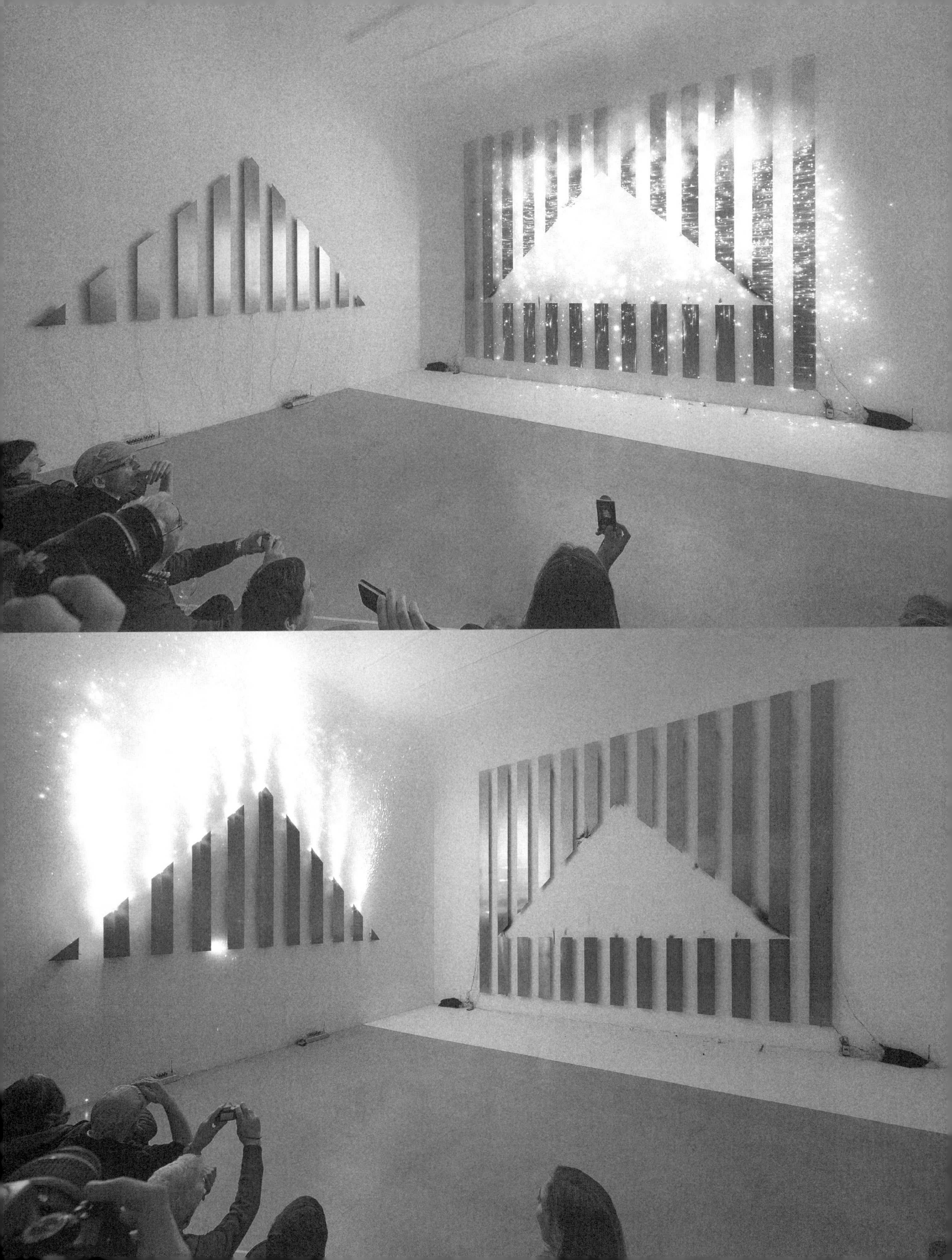

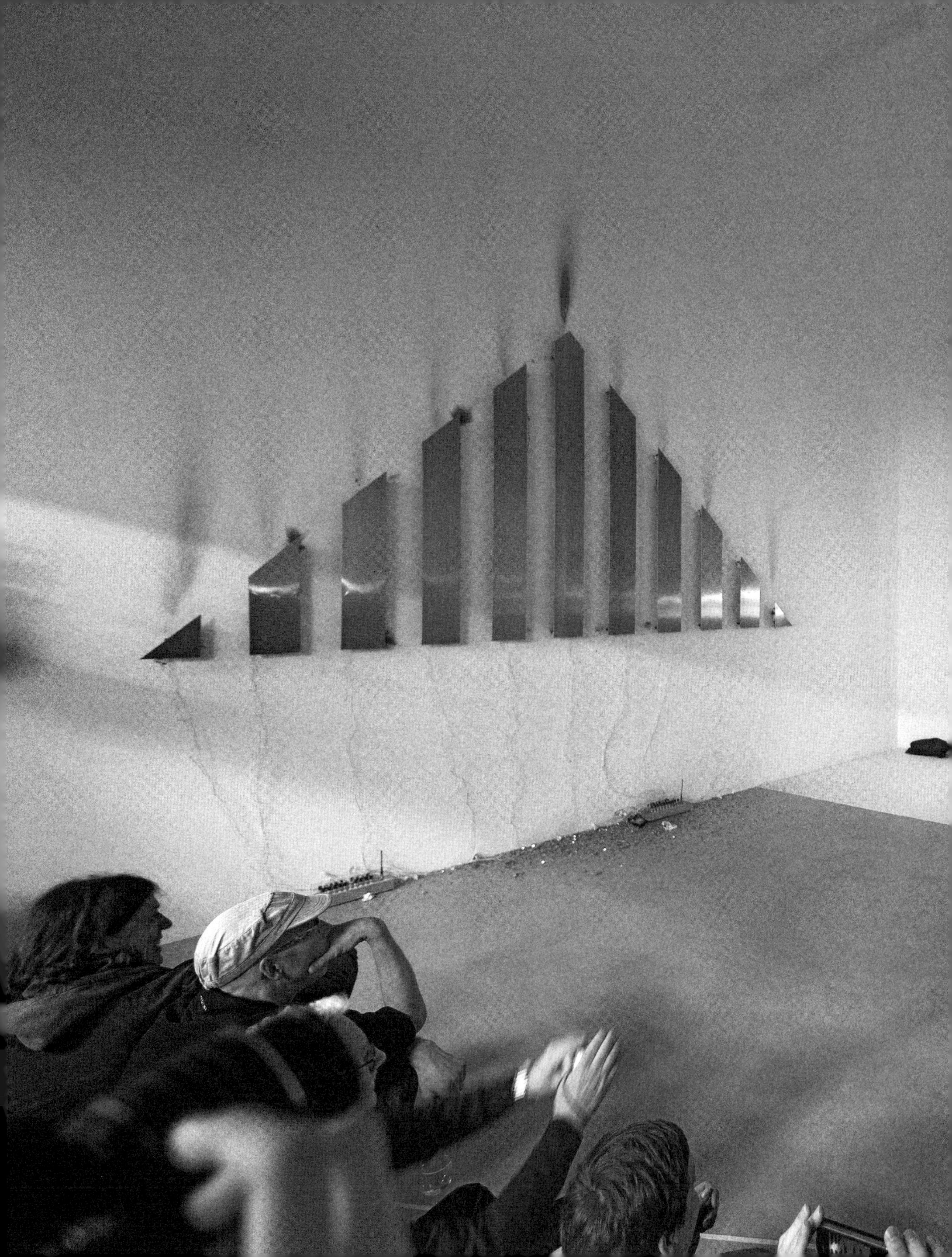

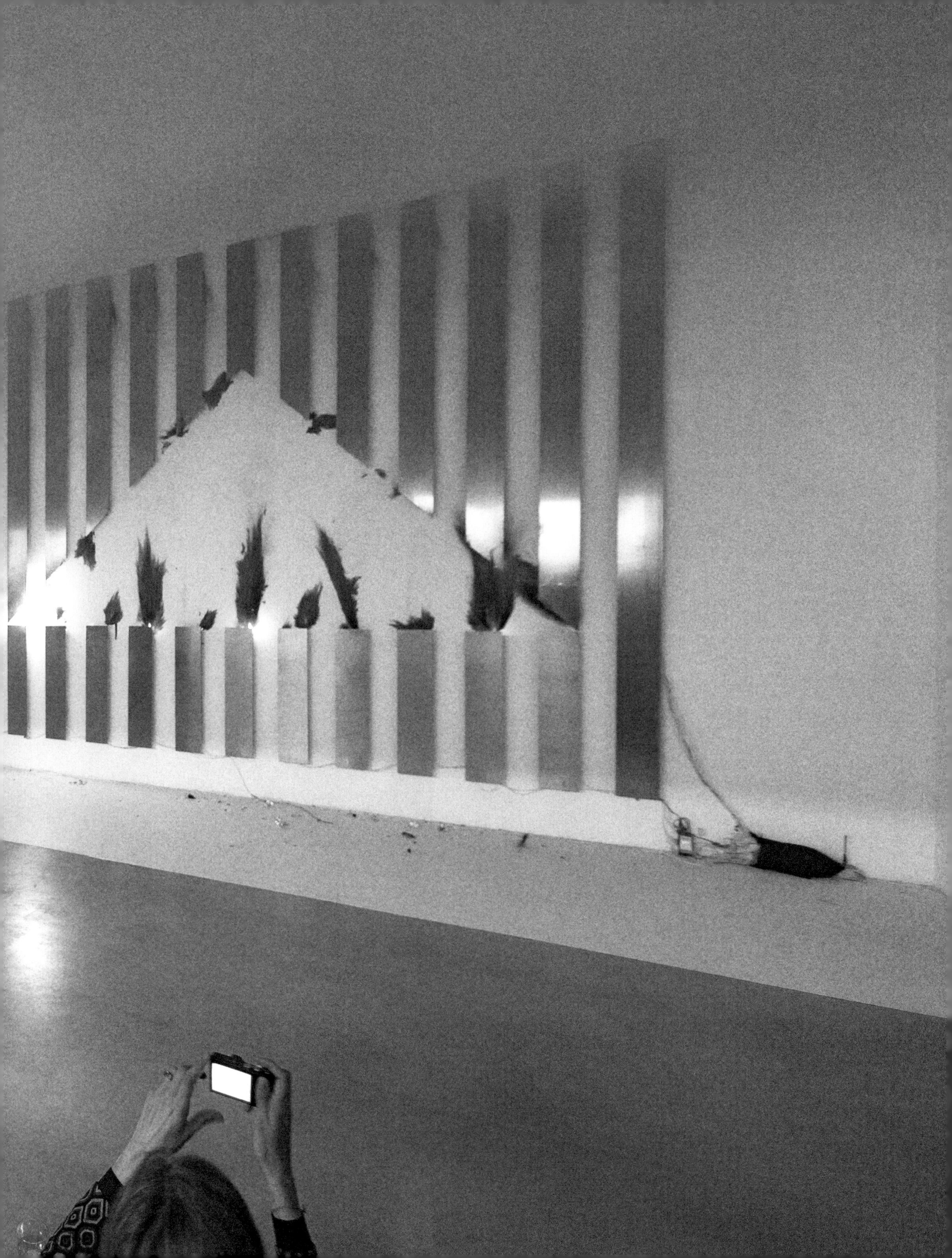

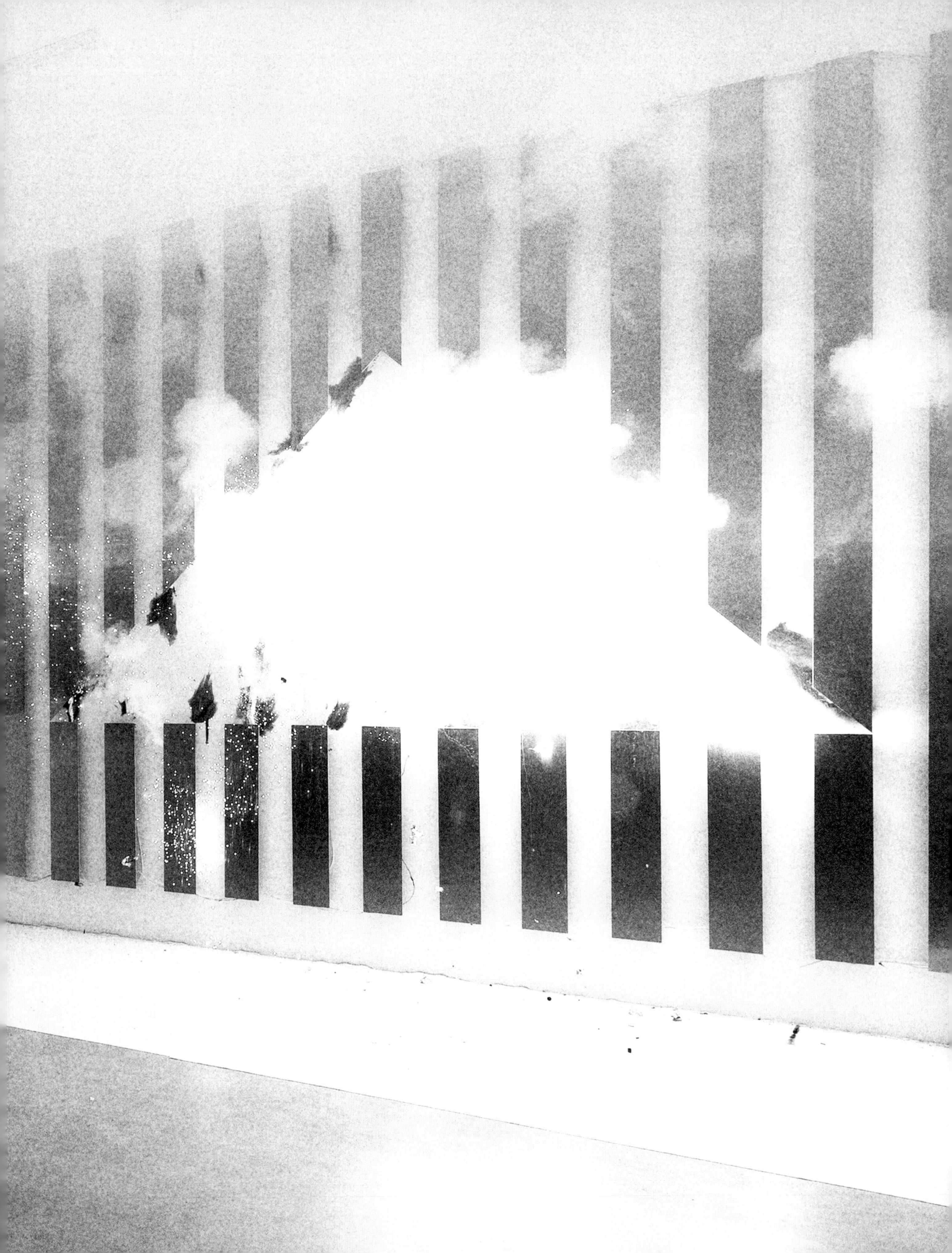

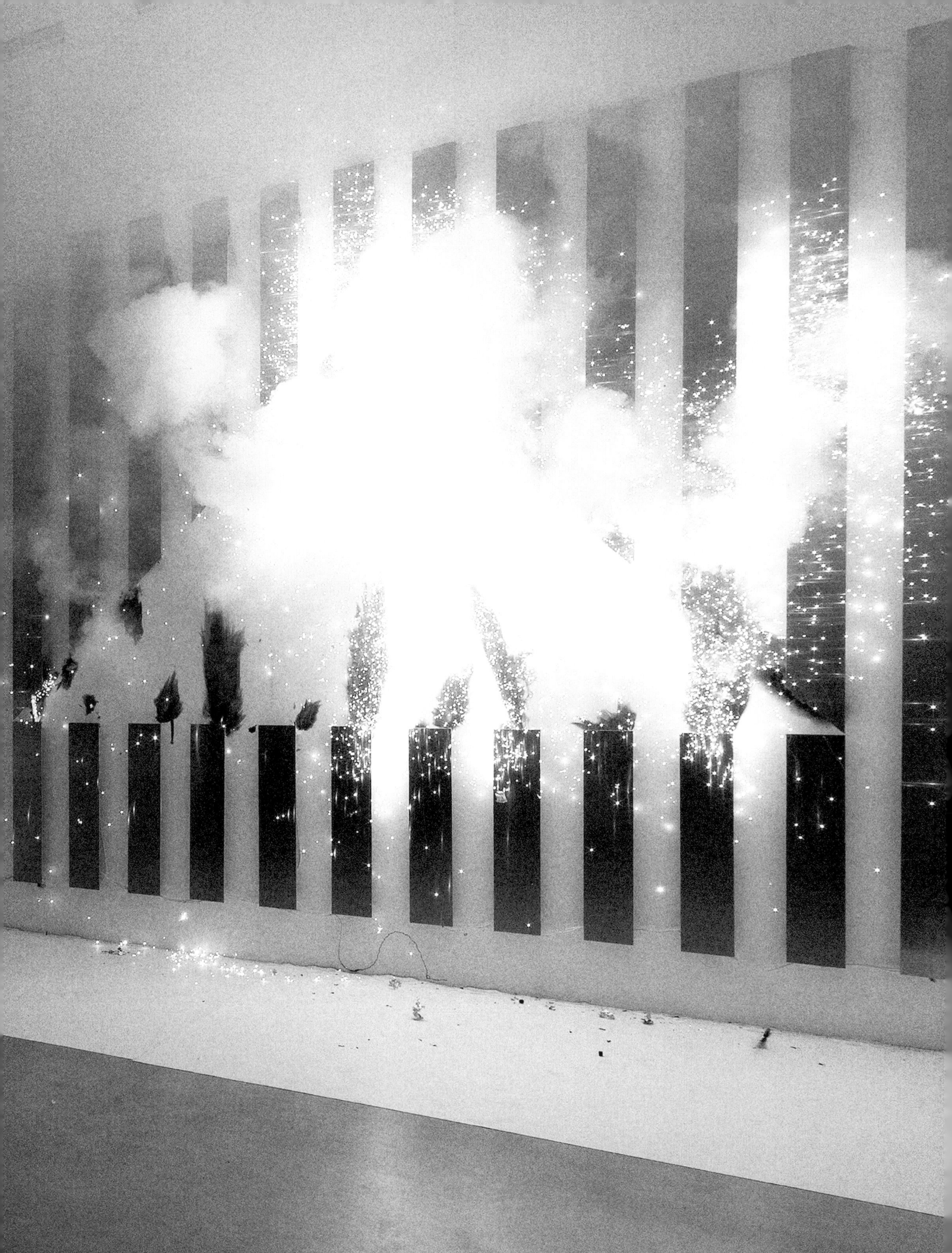

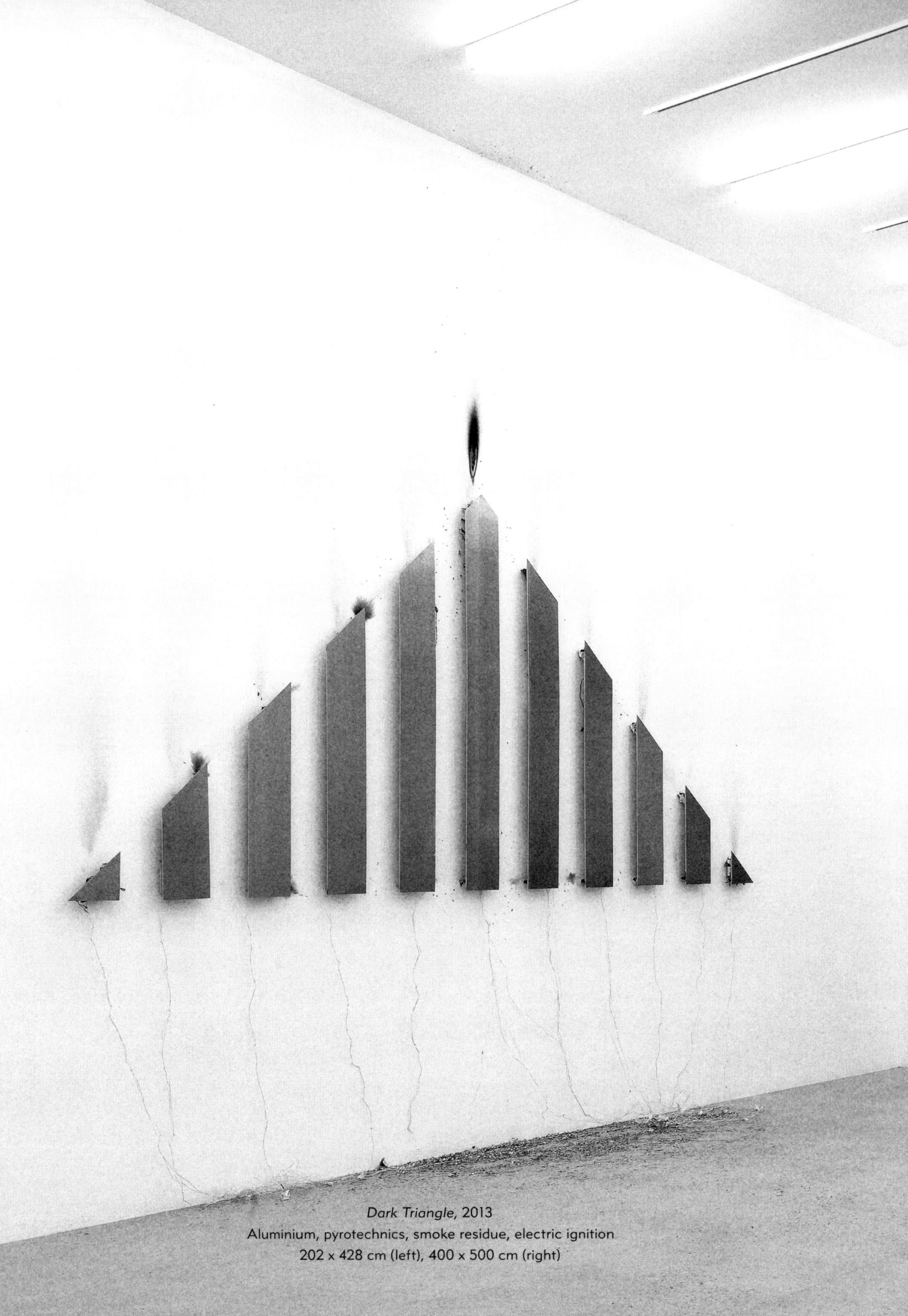

Dark Triangle, 2013
Aluminium, pyrotechnics, smoke residue, electric ignition
202 x 428 cm (left), 400 x 500 cm (right)

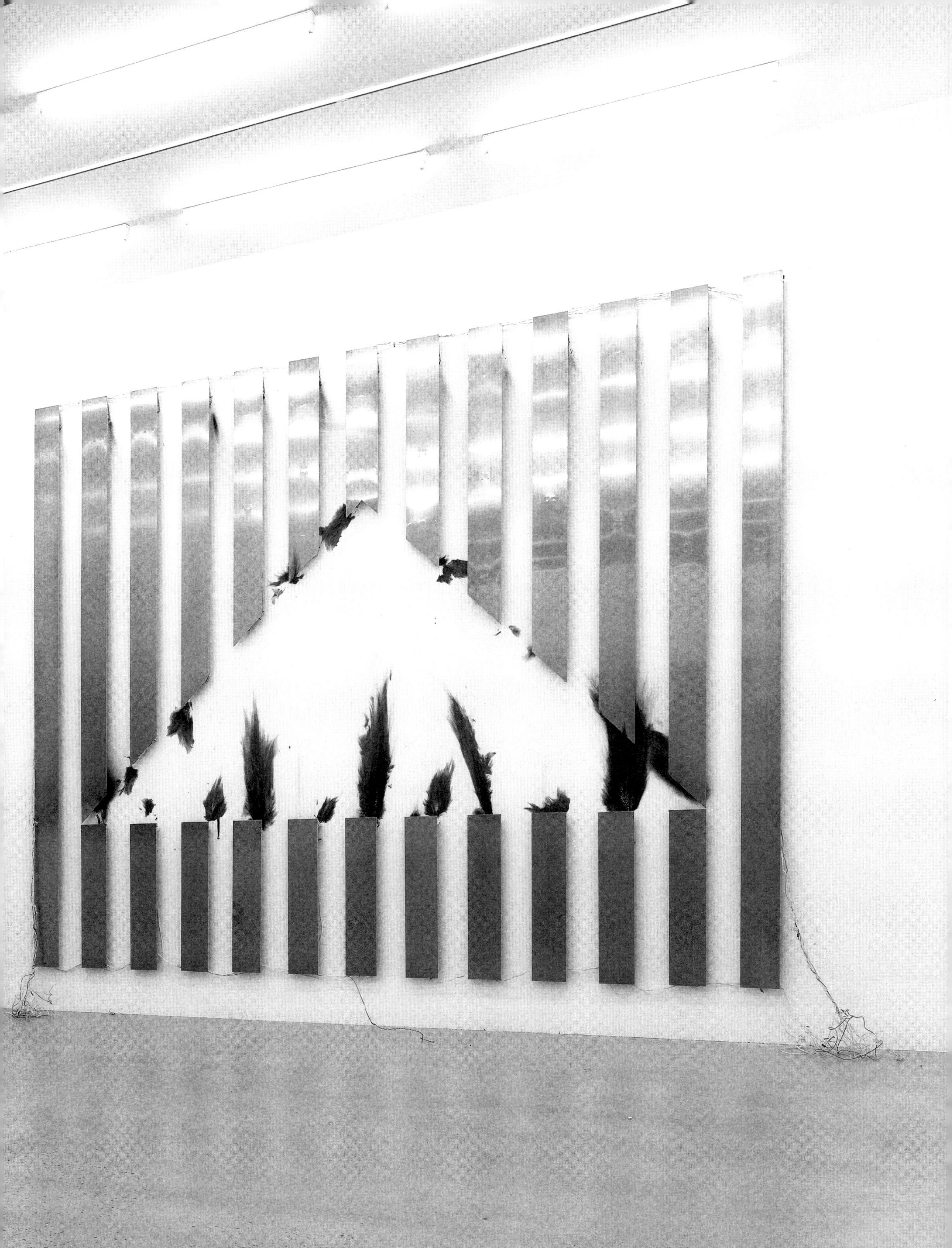

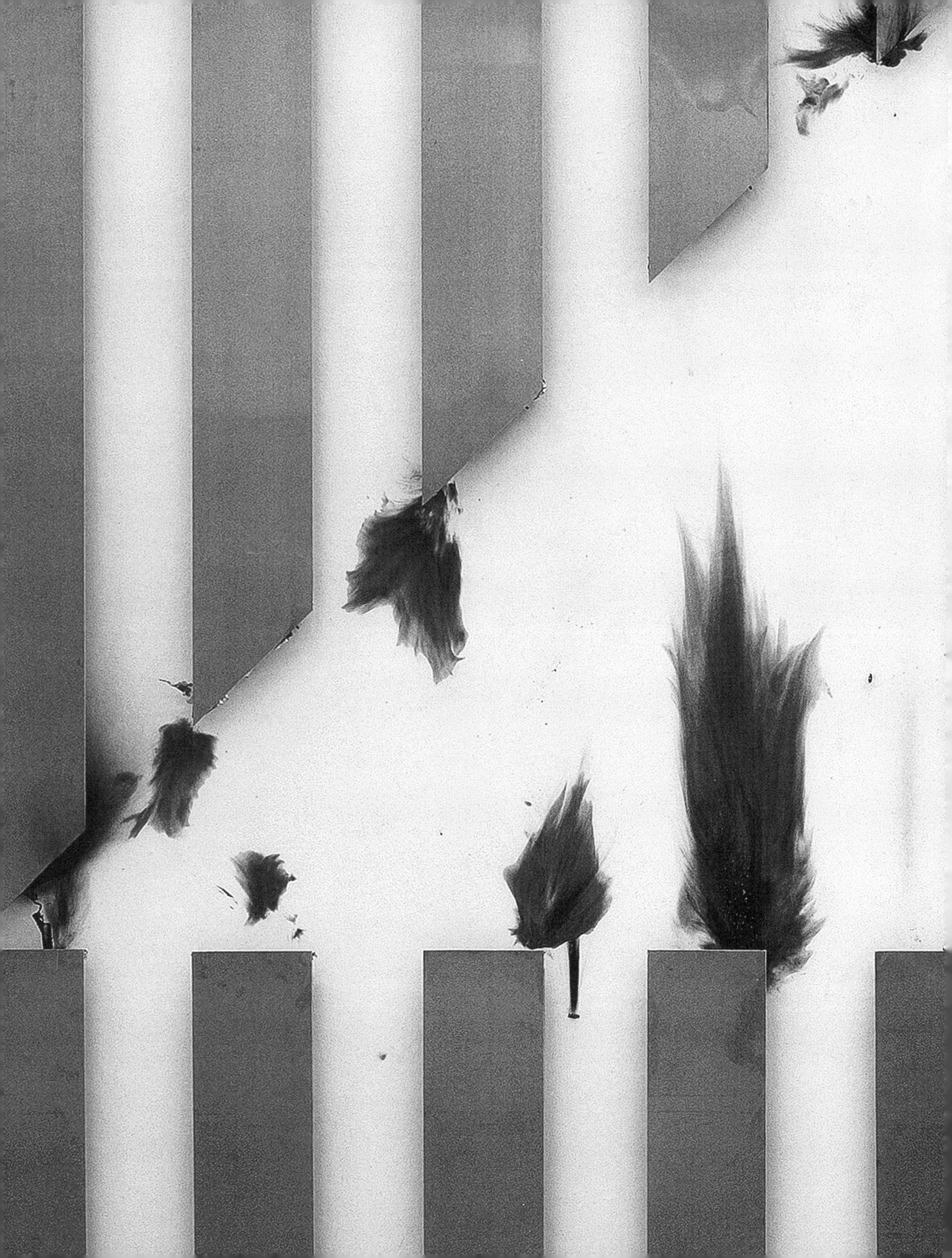

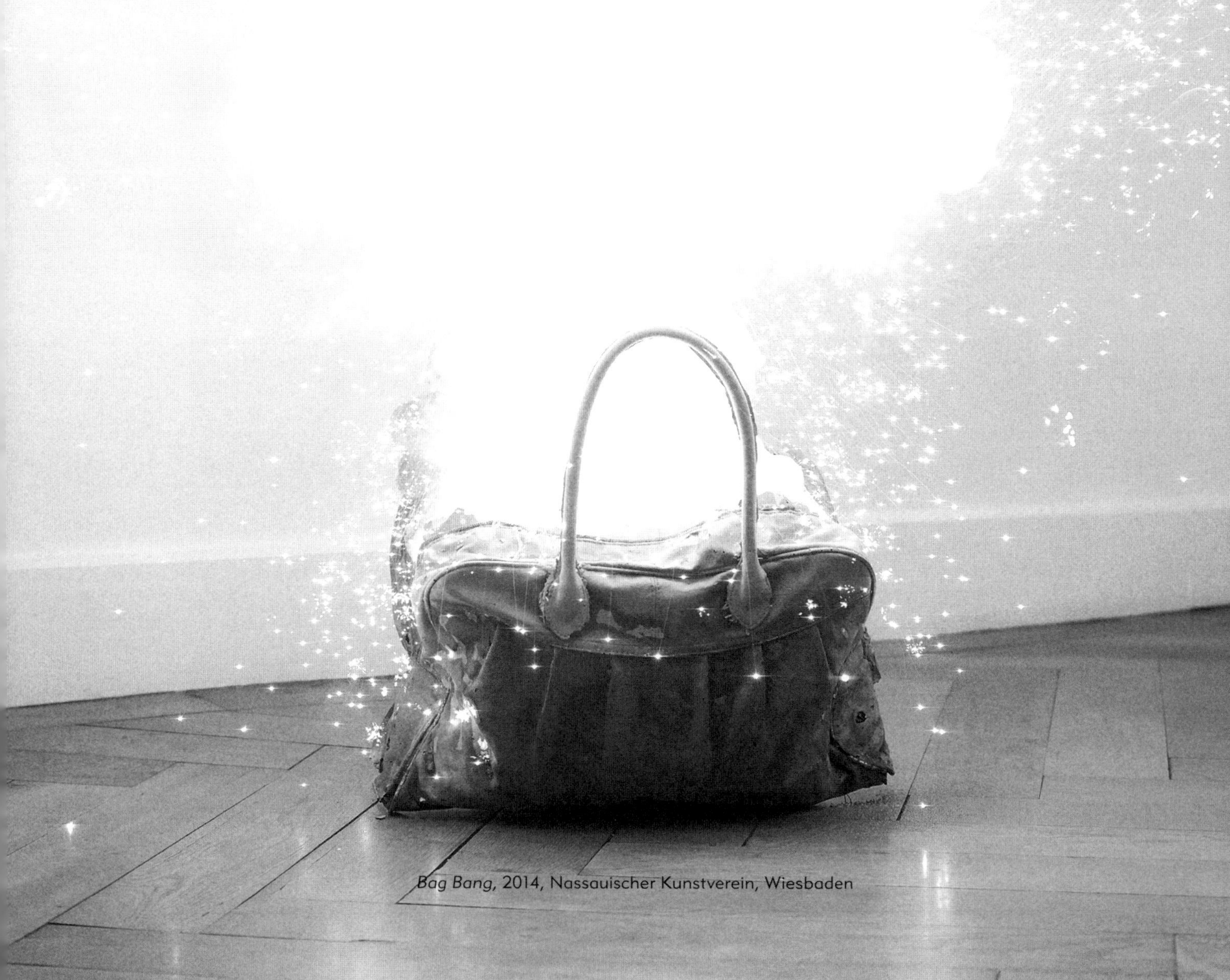

Bag Bang, 2014, Nassauischer Kunstverein, Wiesbaden

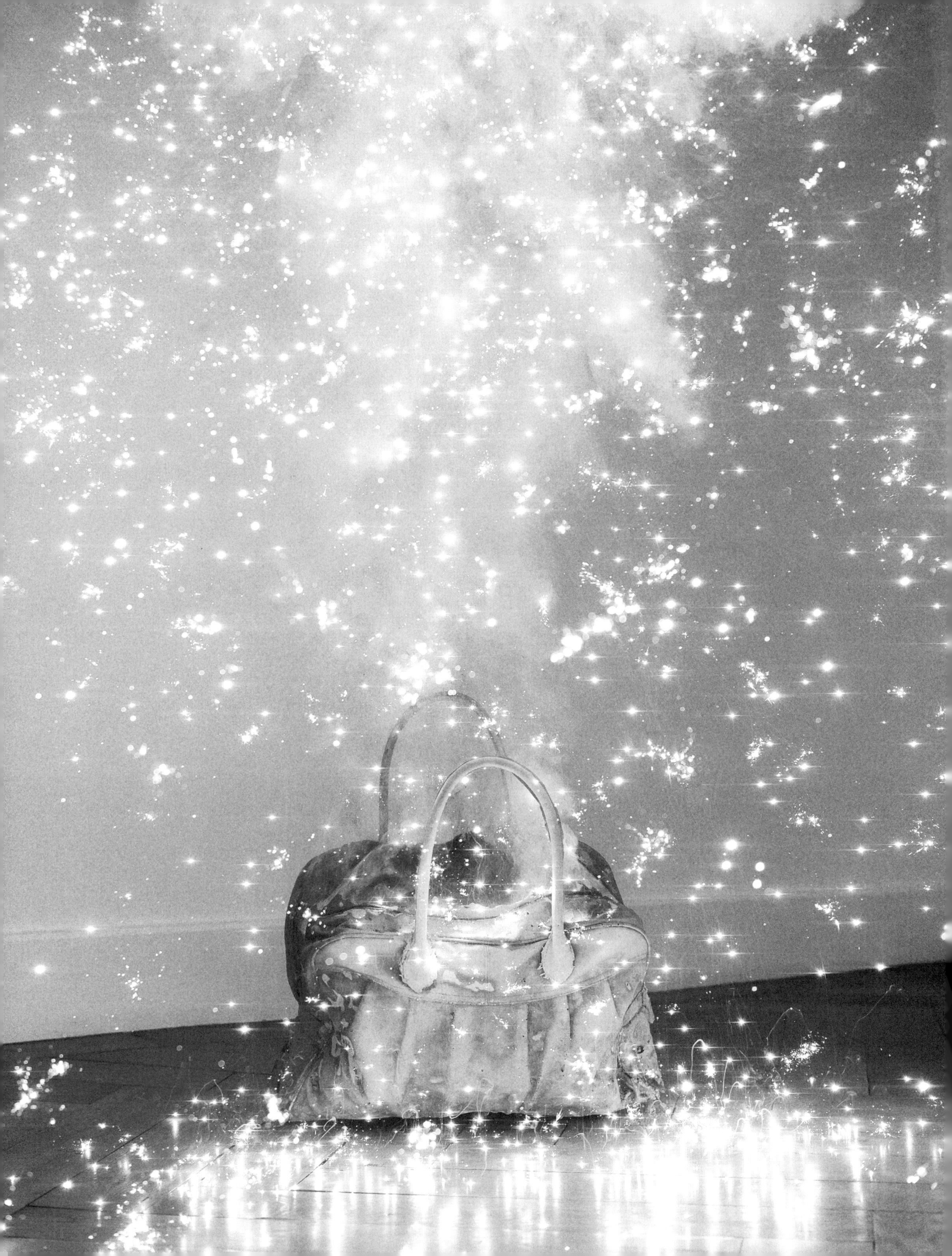

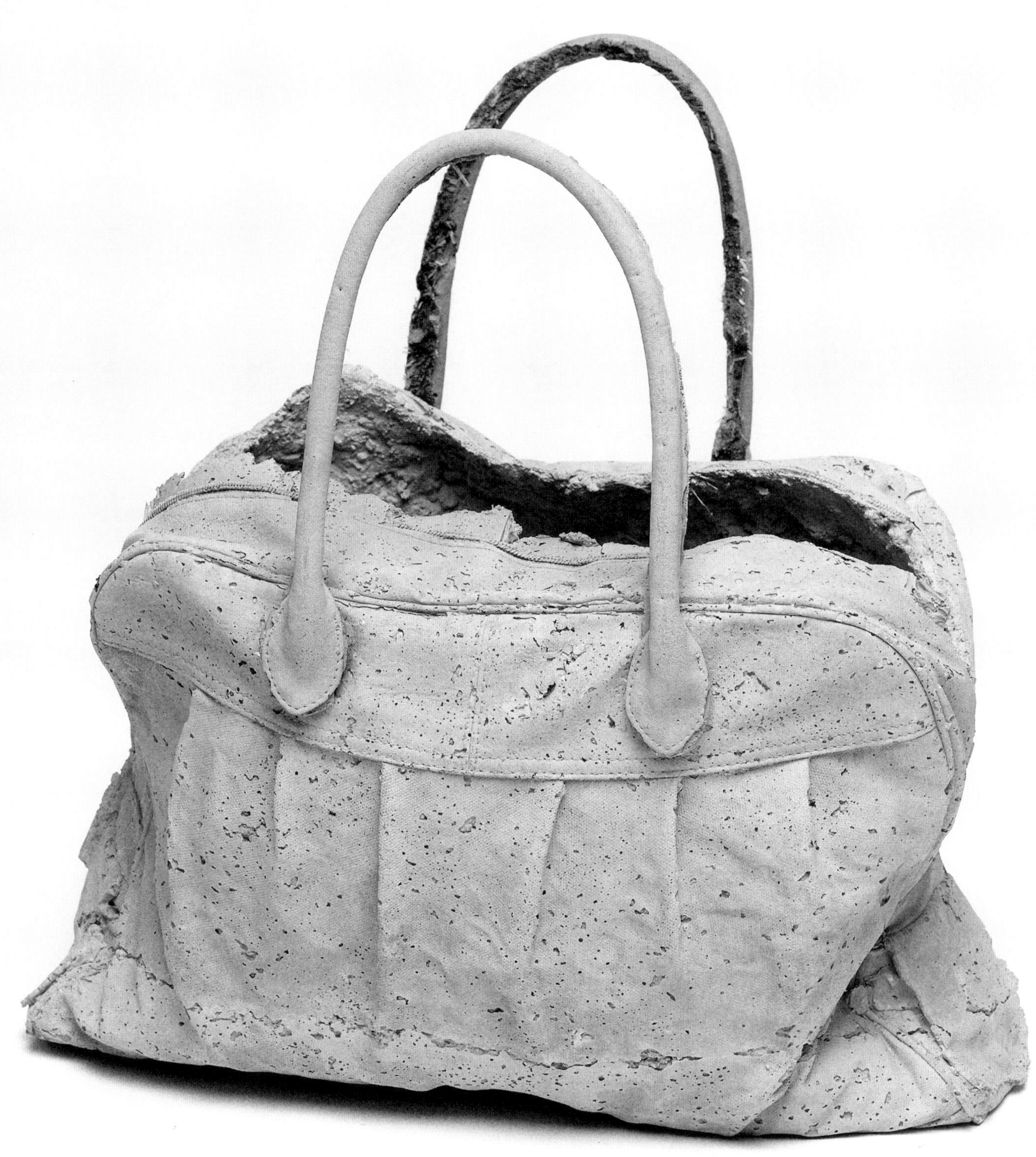

Bag Bang, 2013
Concrete, electric ignition
50 x 43 x 27 cm each

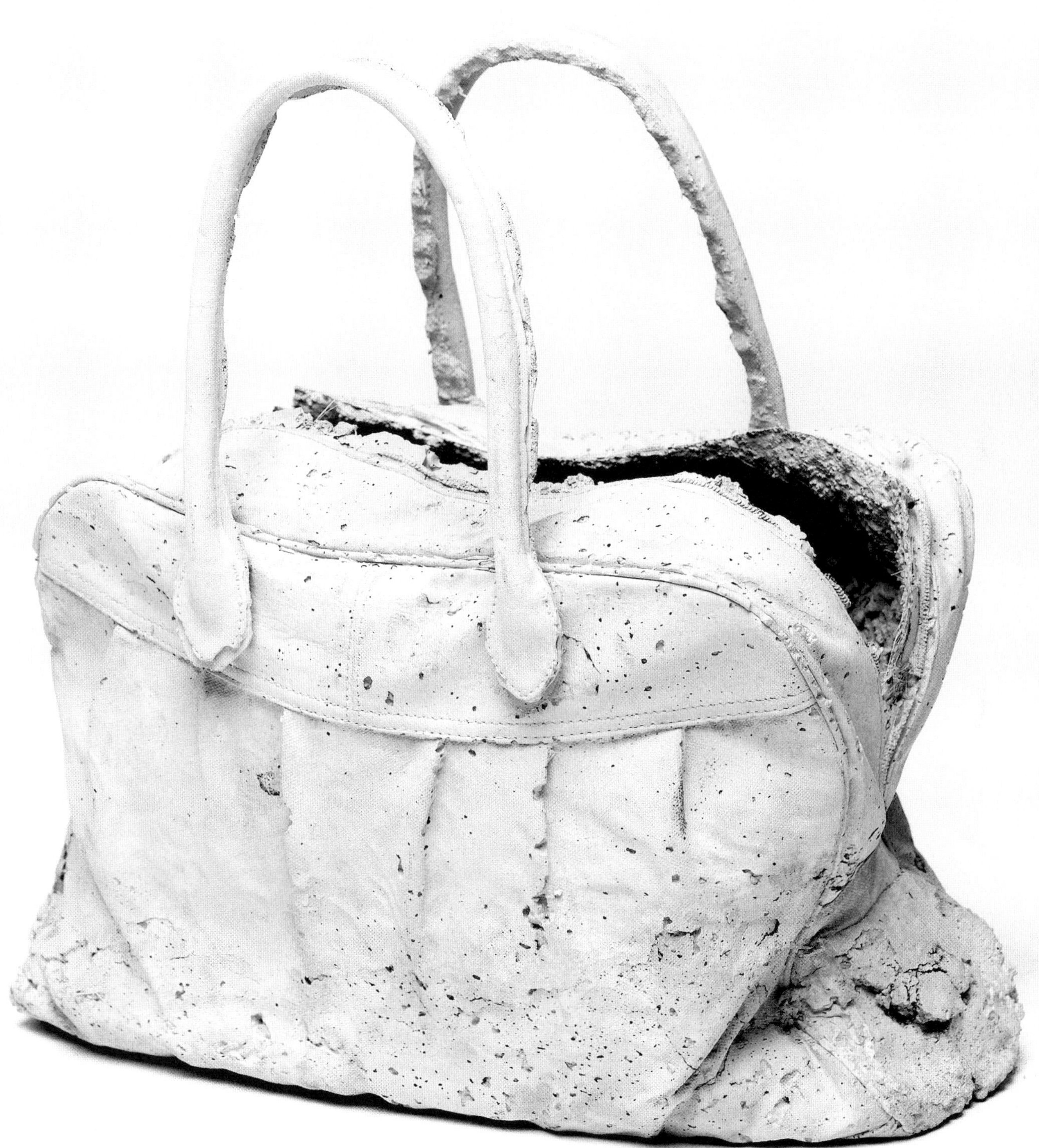

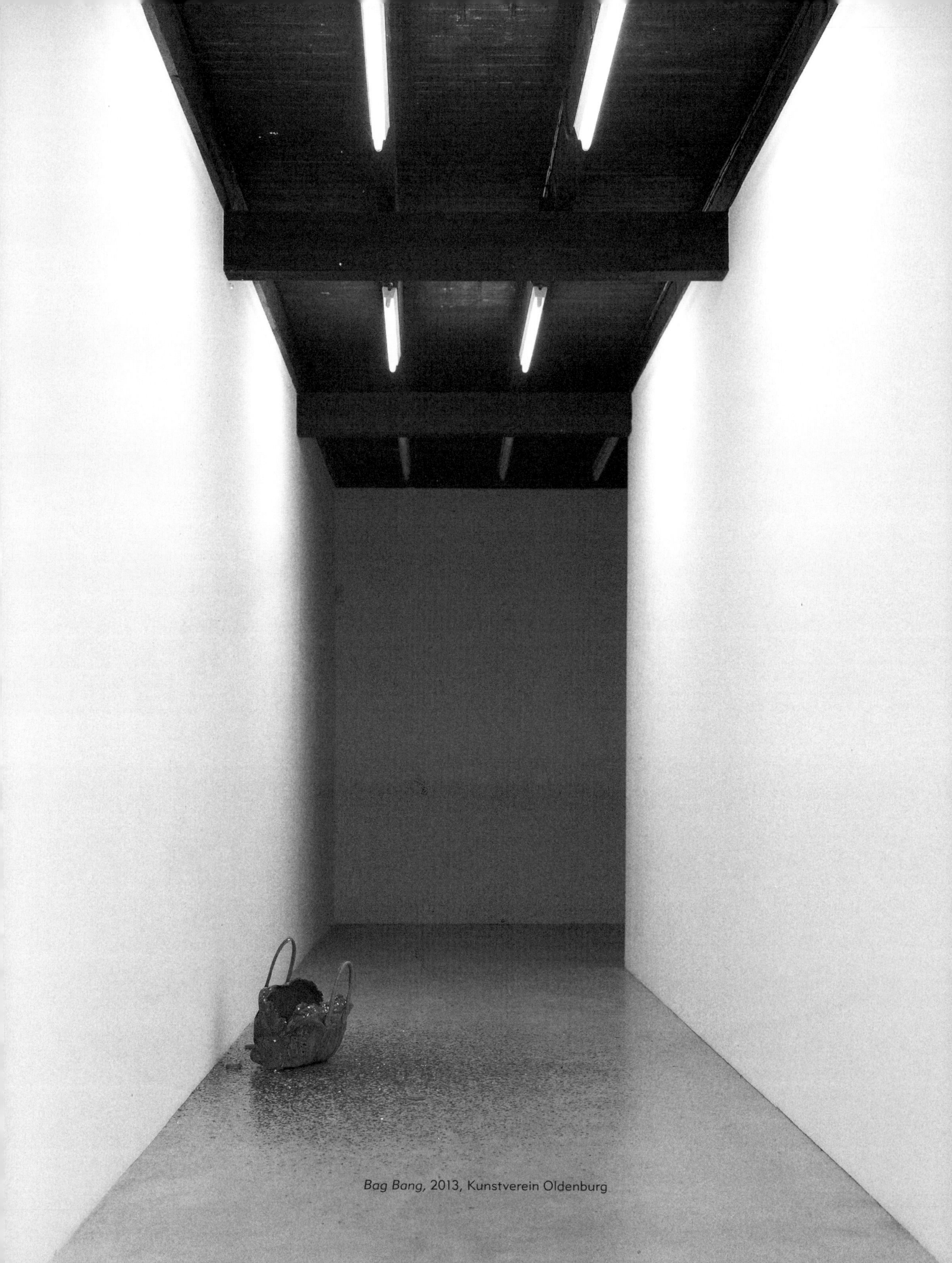

Bag Bang, 2013, Kunstverein Oldenburg

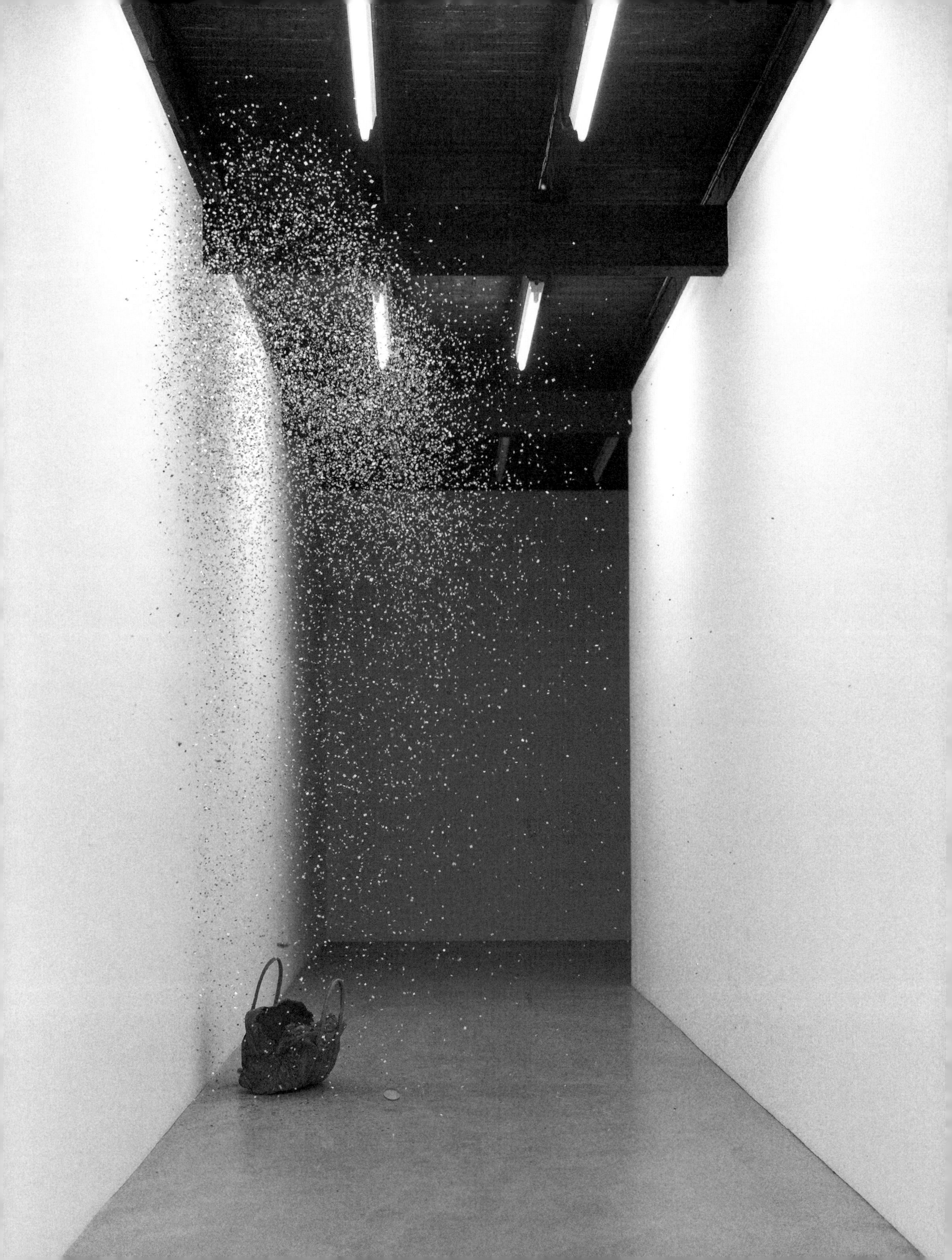

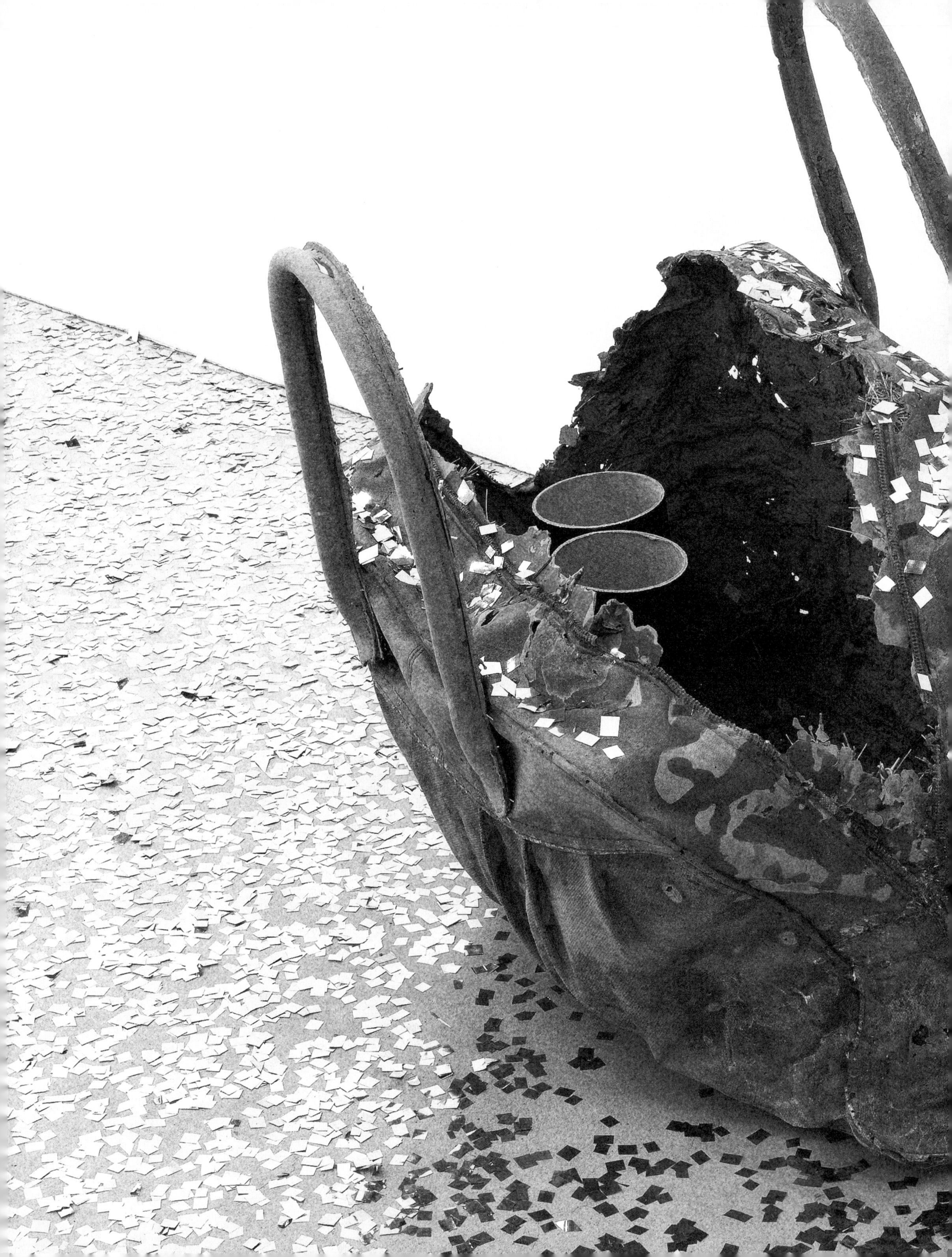

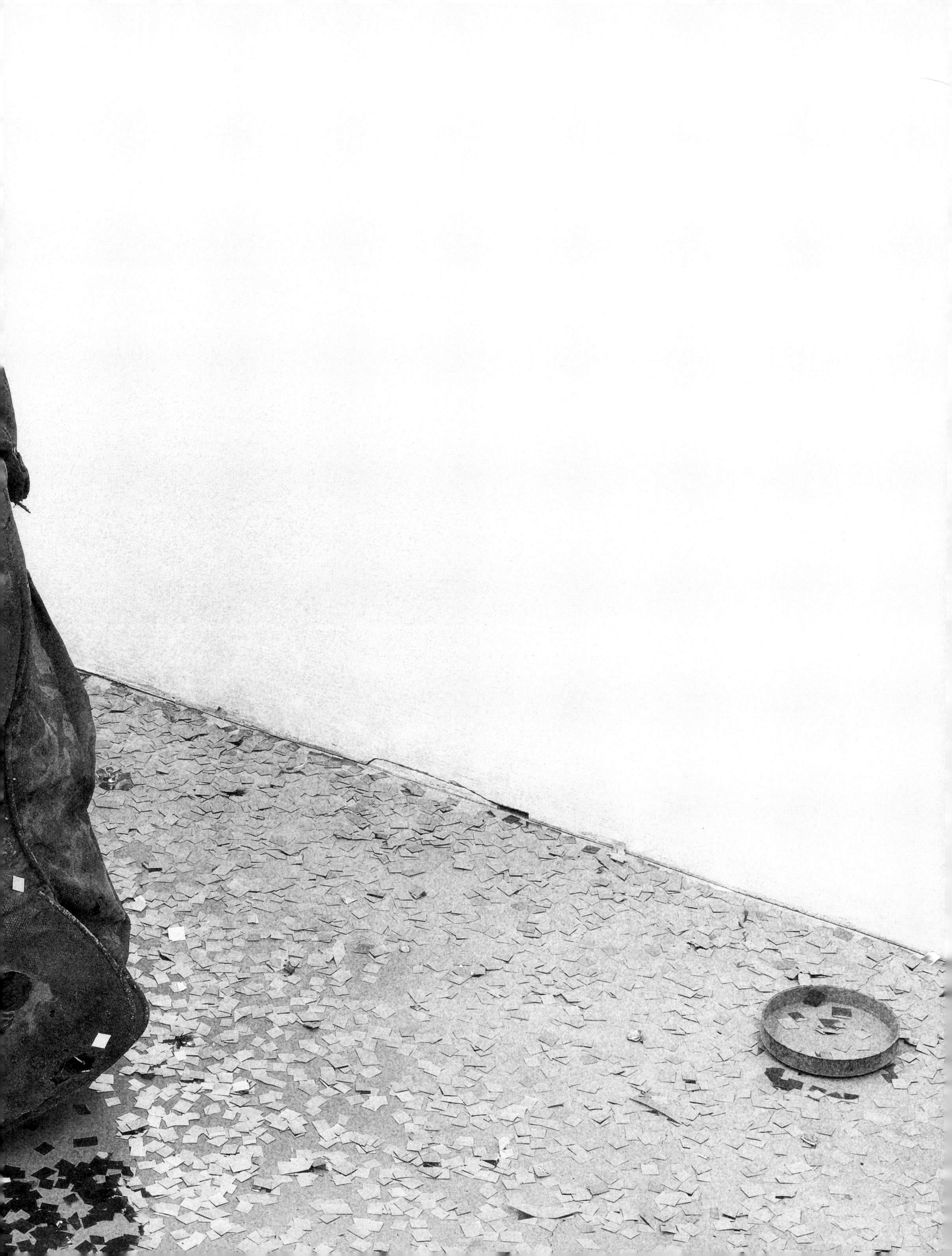

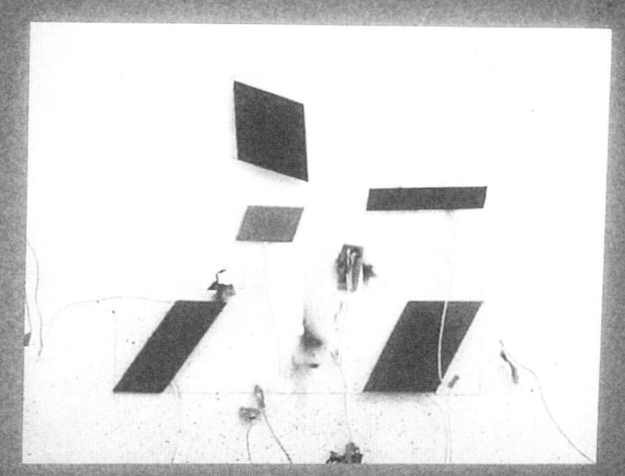

Back 1-3, 2010, video installation, Kunstverein Oldenburg

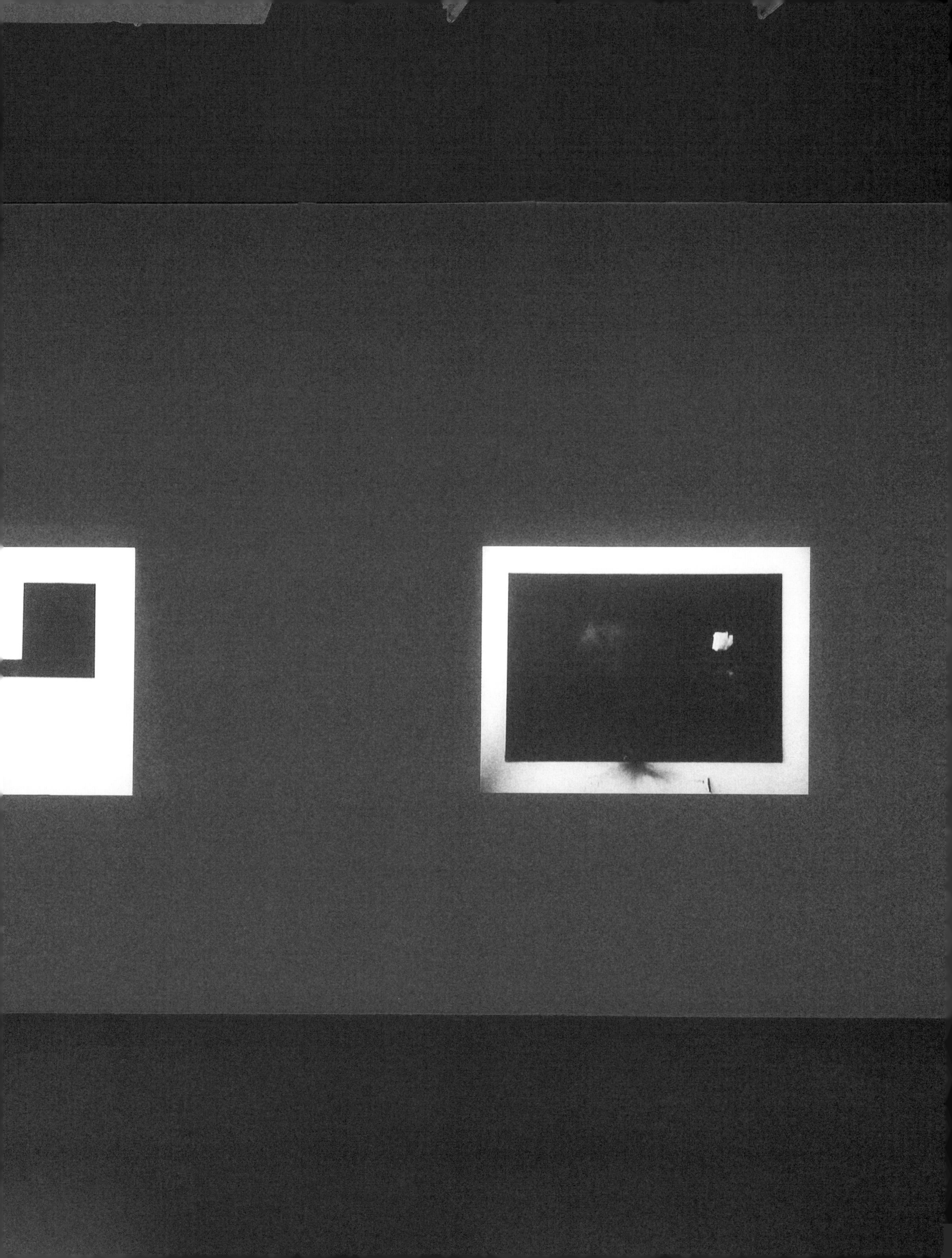

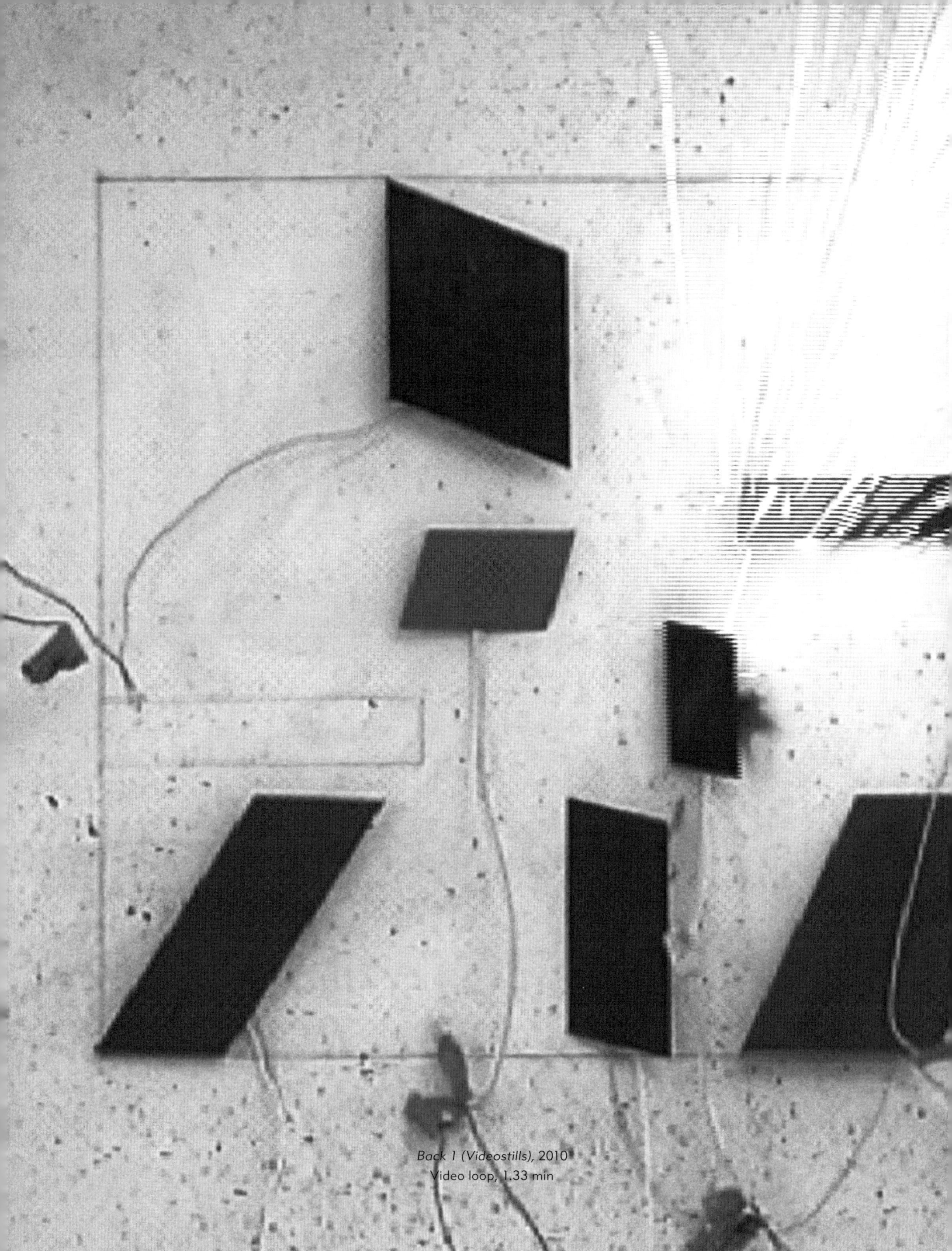

Back 1 (Videostills), 2010
Video loop, 1.33 min

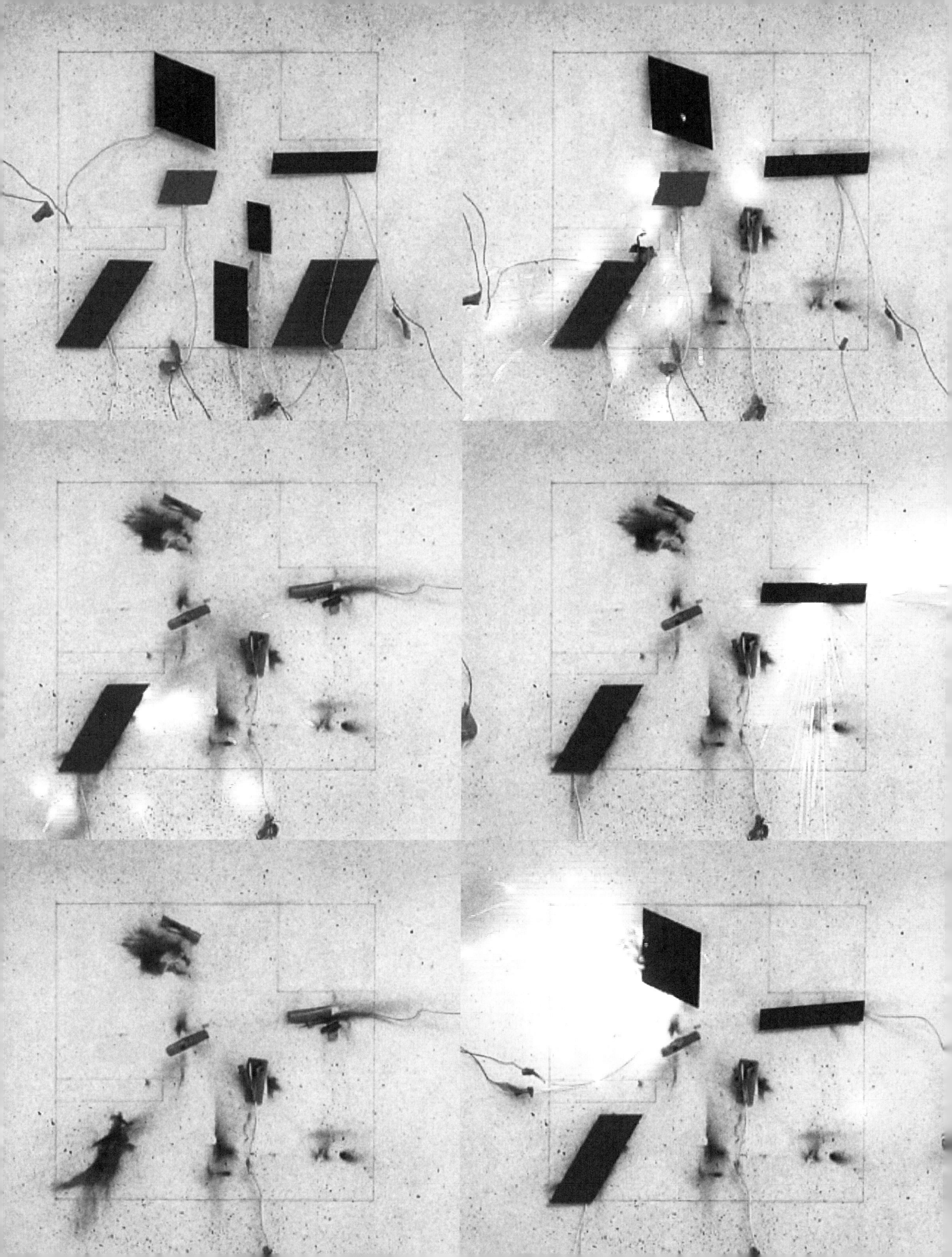

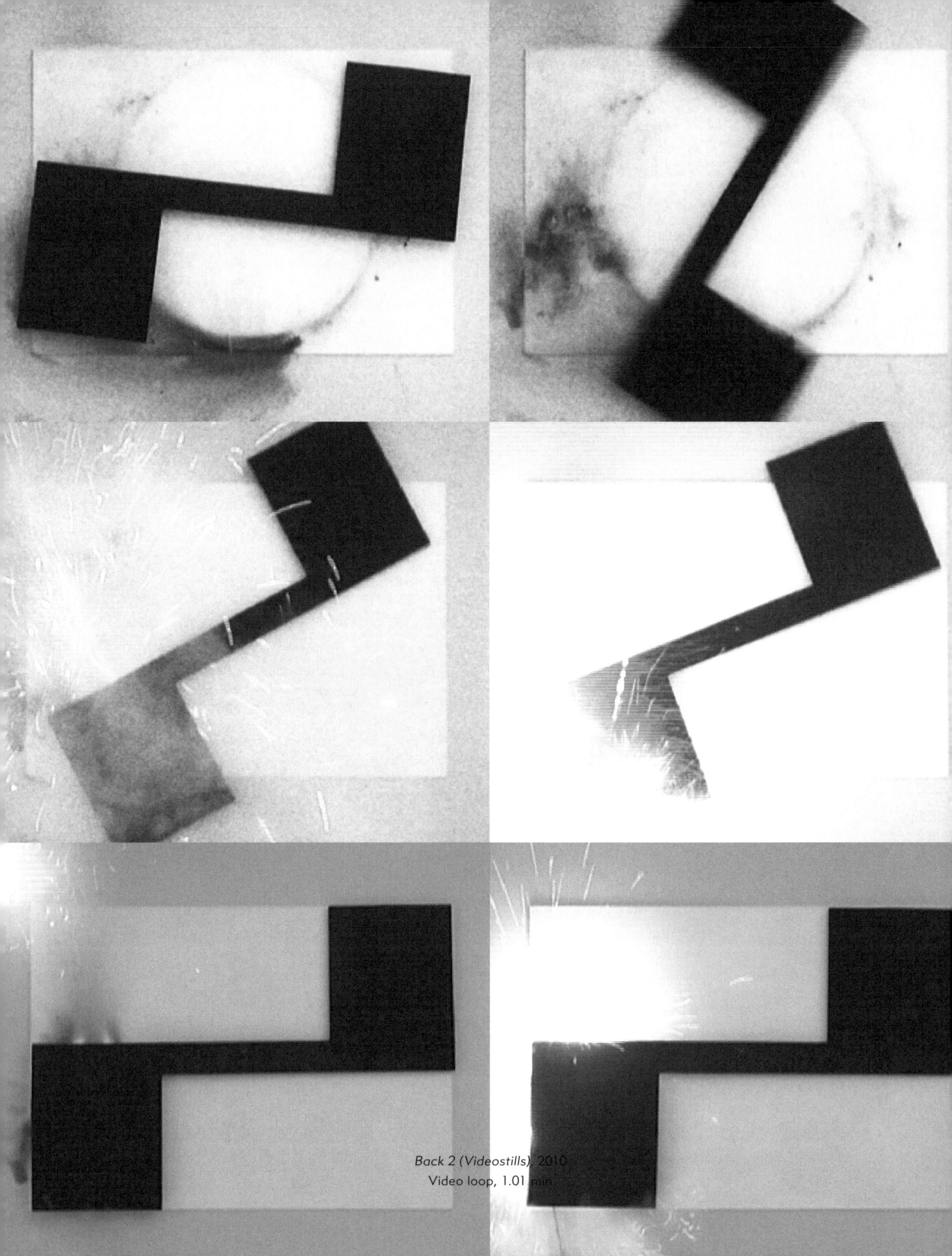

Back 2 (Videostills), 2010
Video loop, 1.01 min

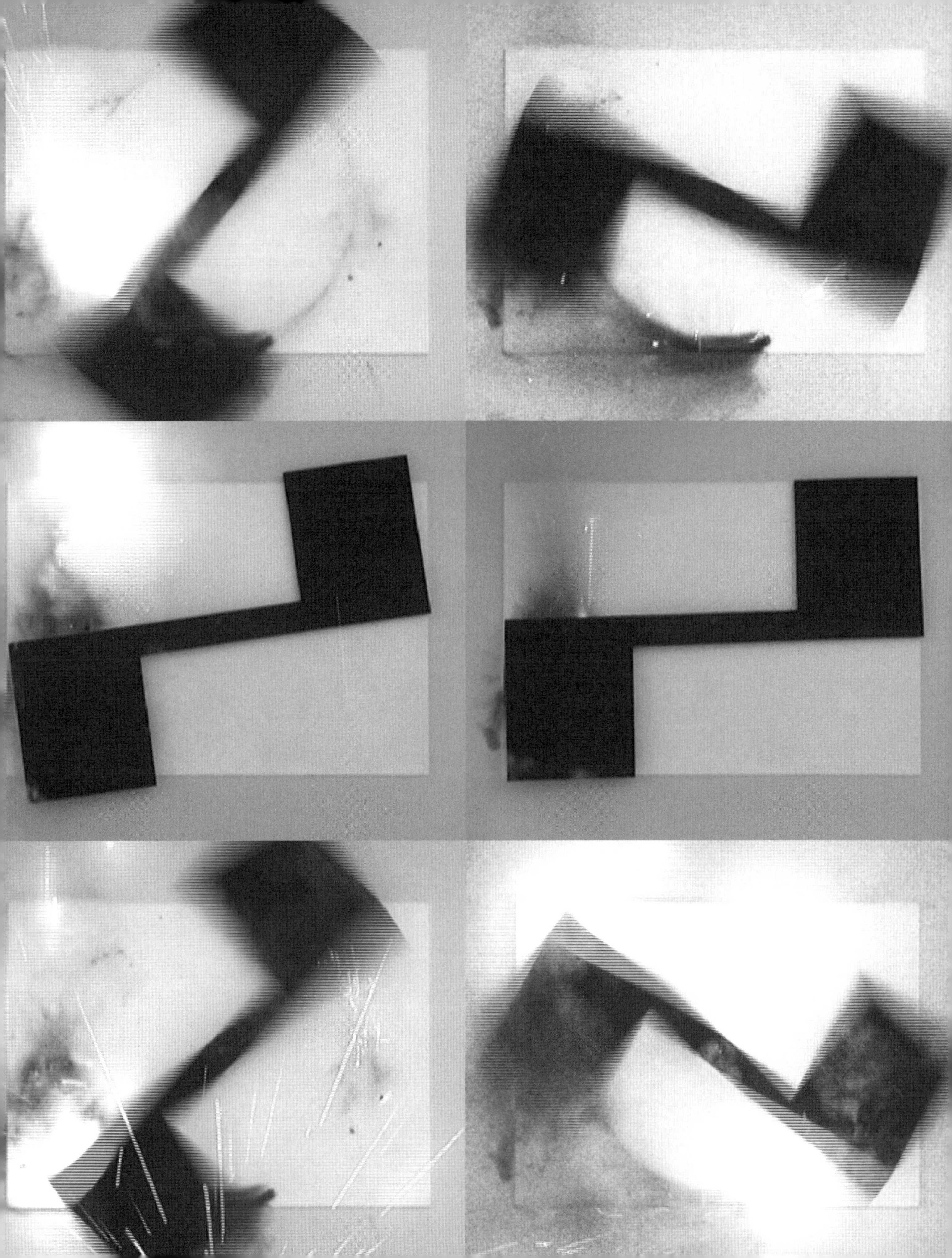

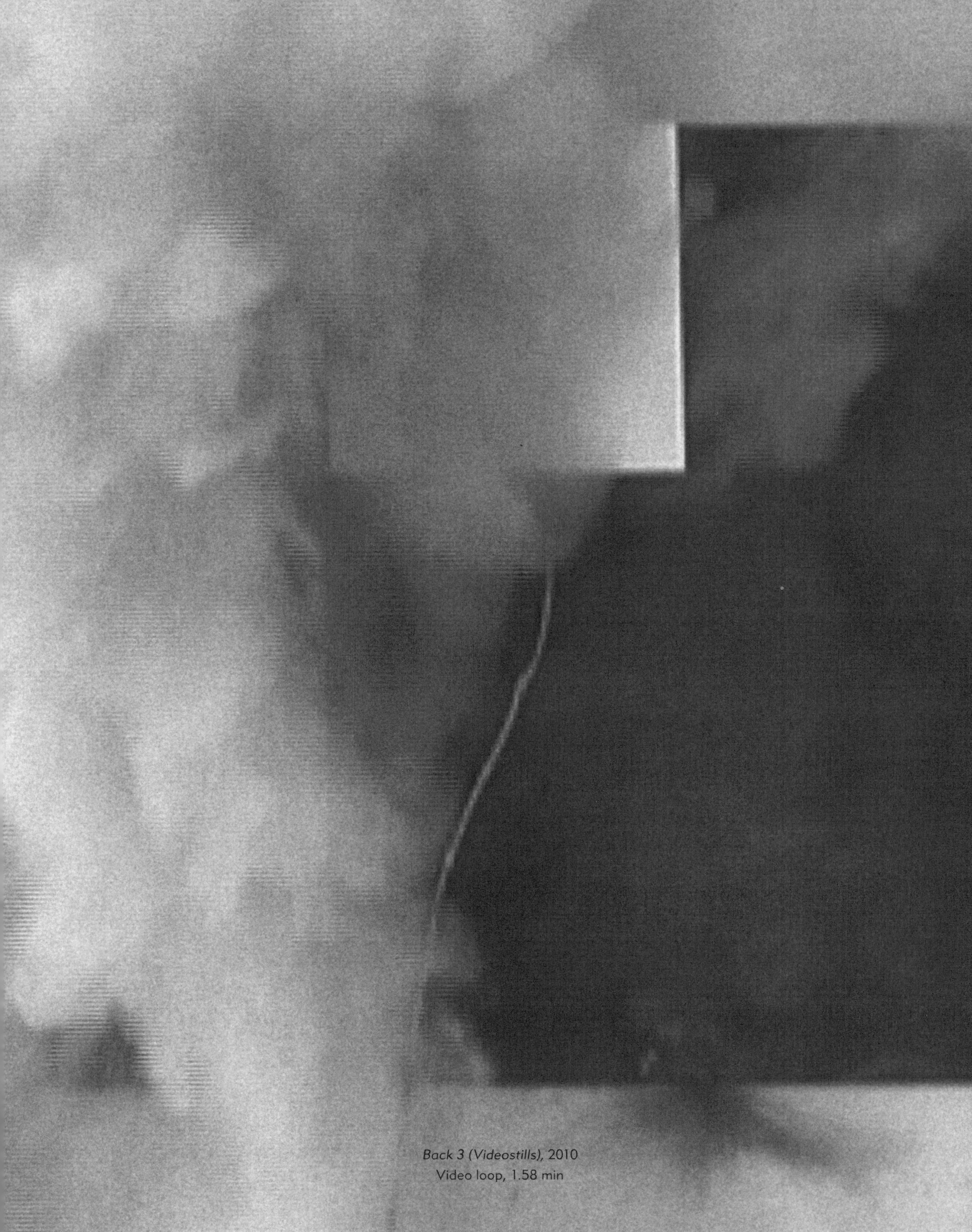

Back 3 (Videostills), 2010
Video loop, 1.58 min

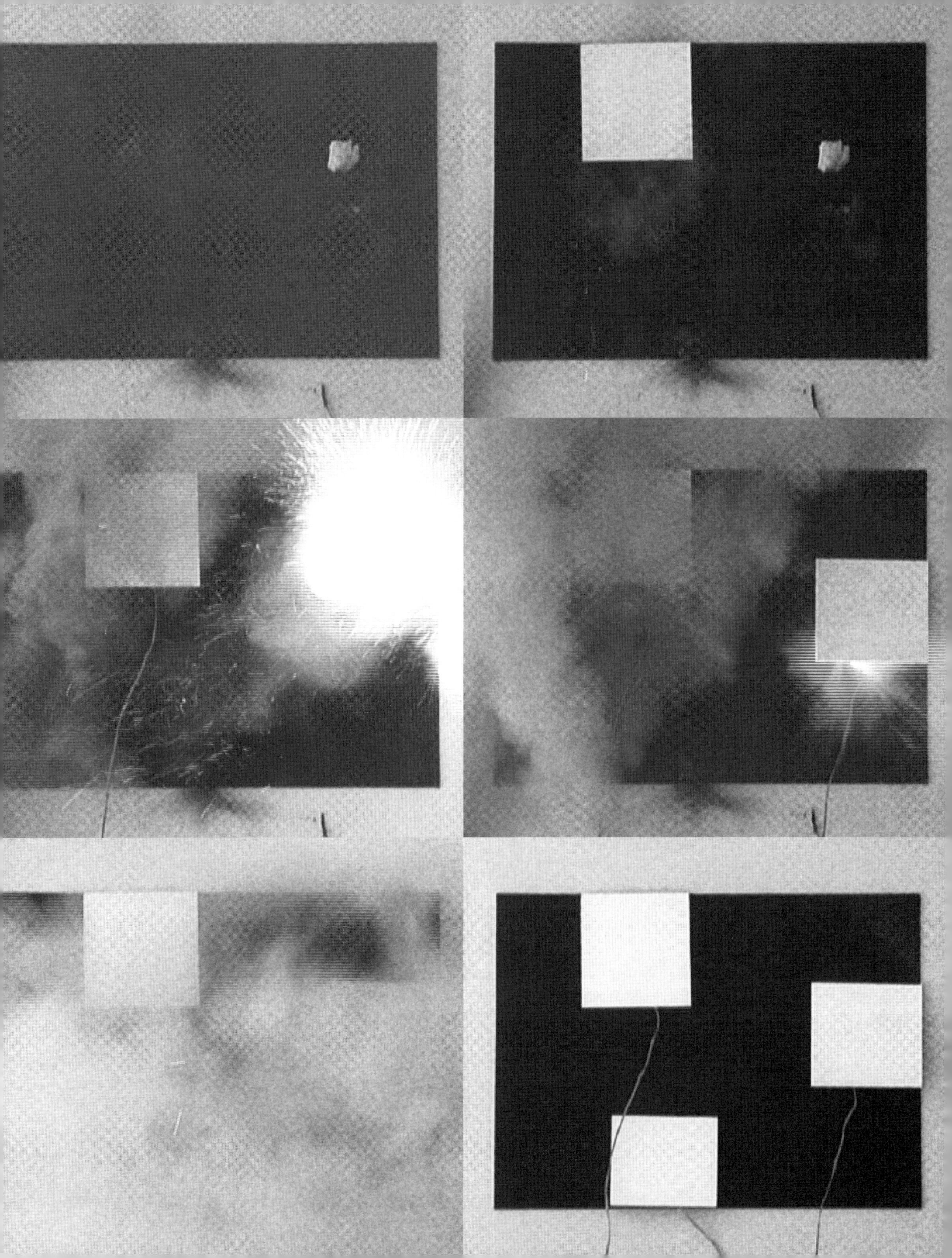

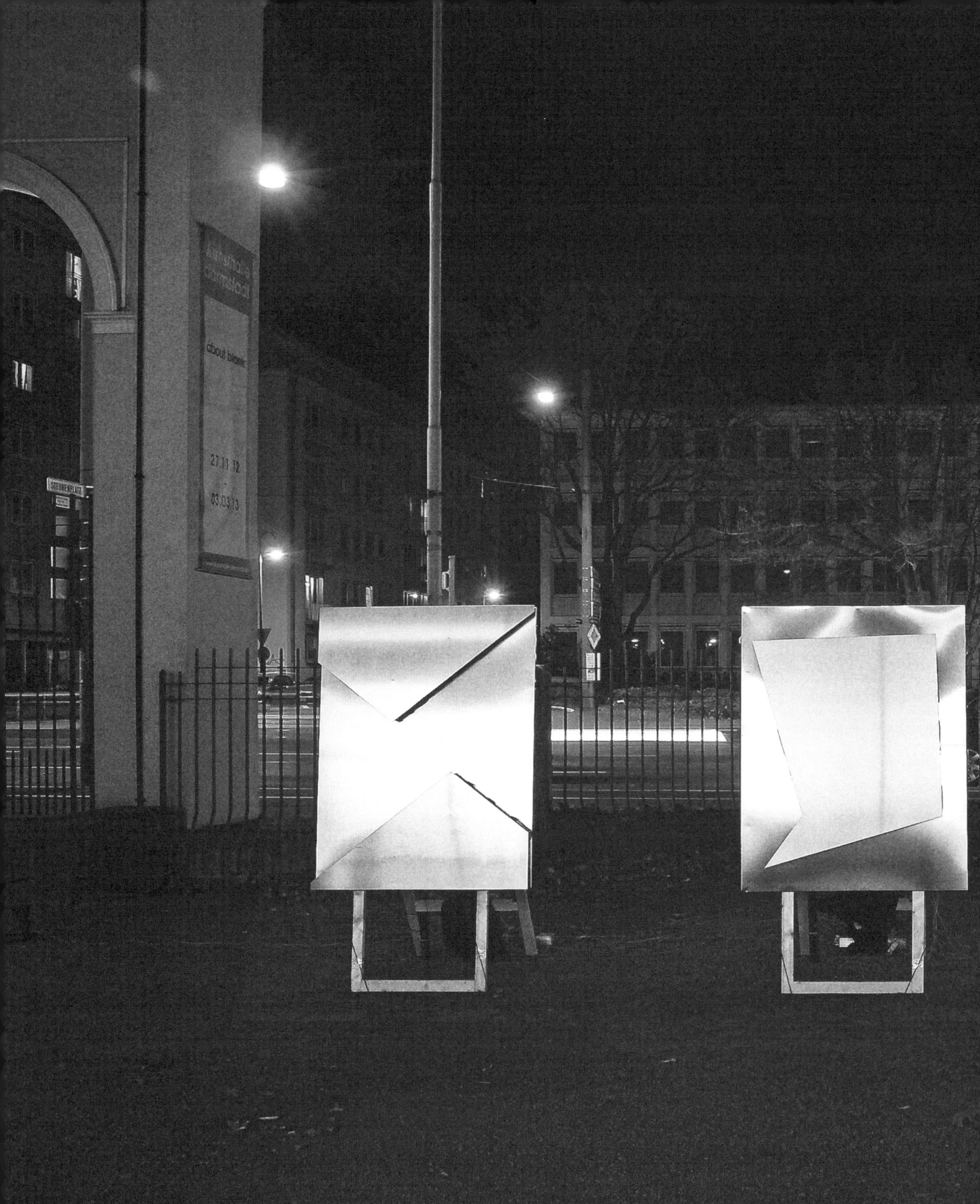

Flashforward 3-6, Firework 11/26/2012, Kunsthalle Darmstadt

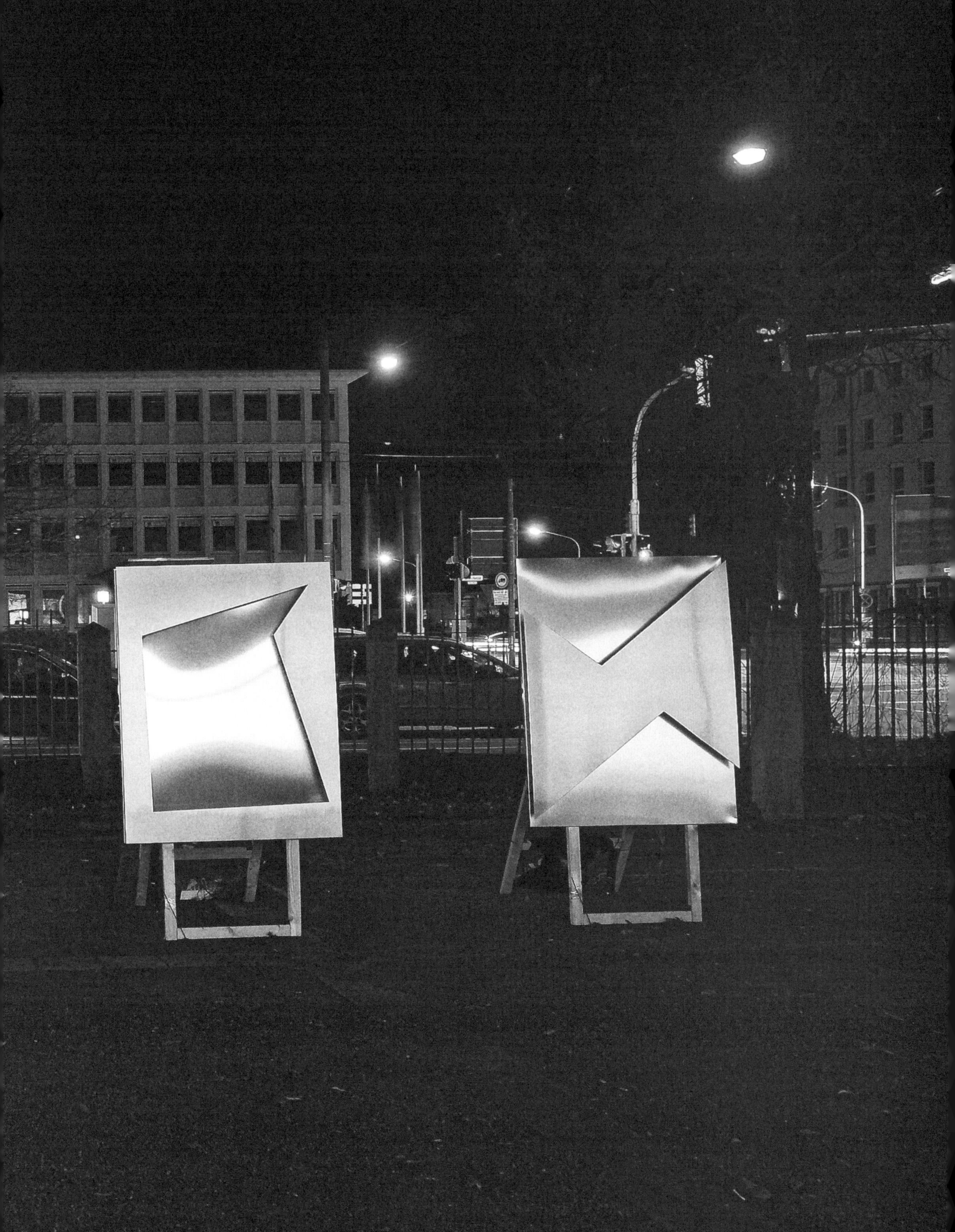

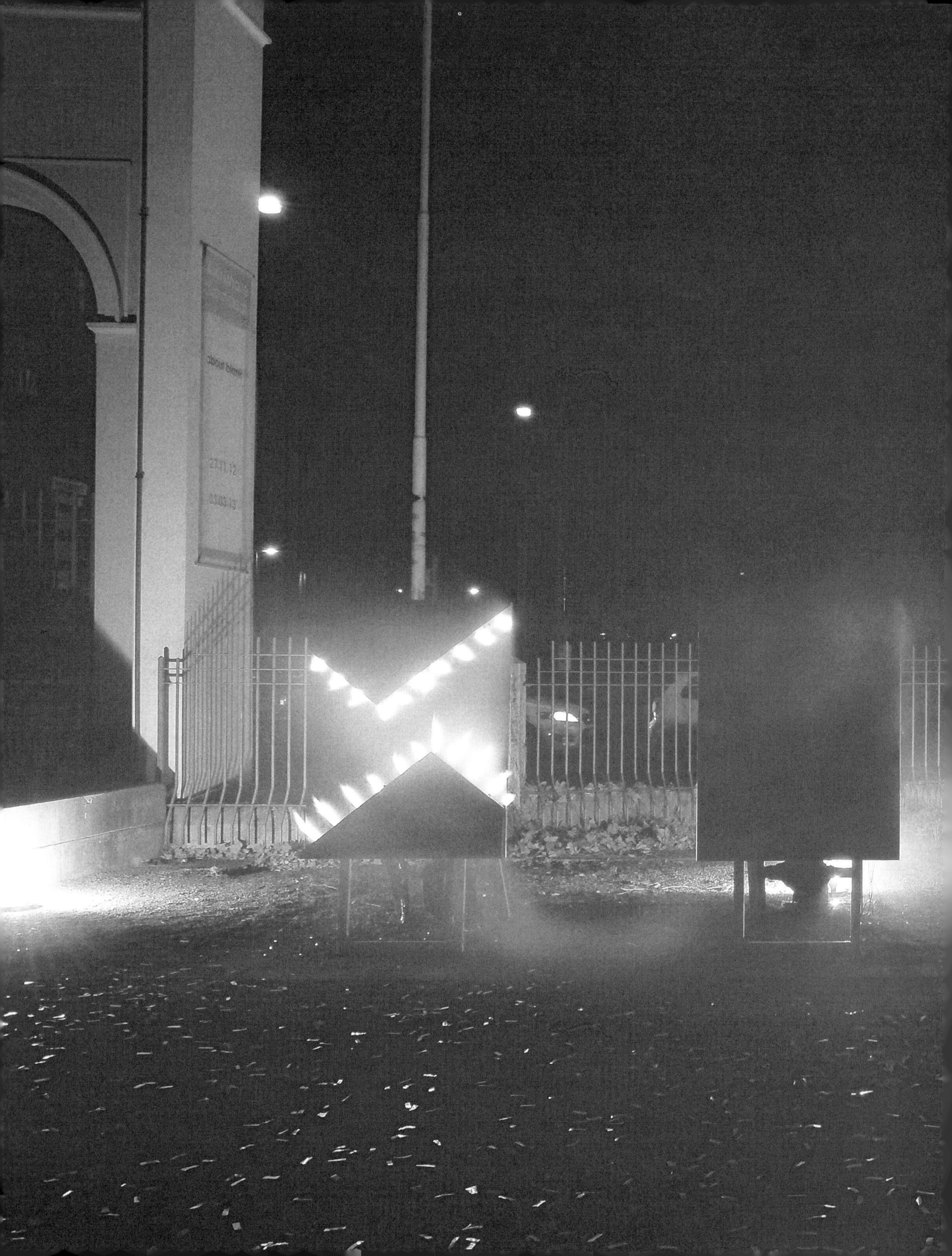

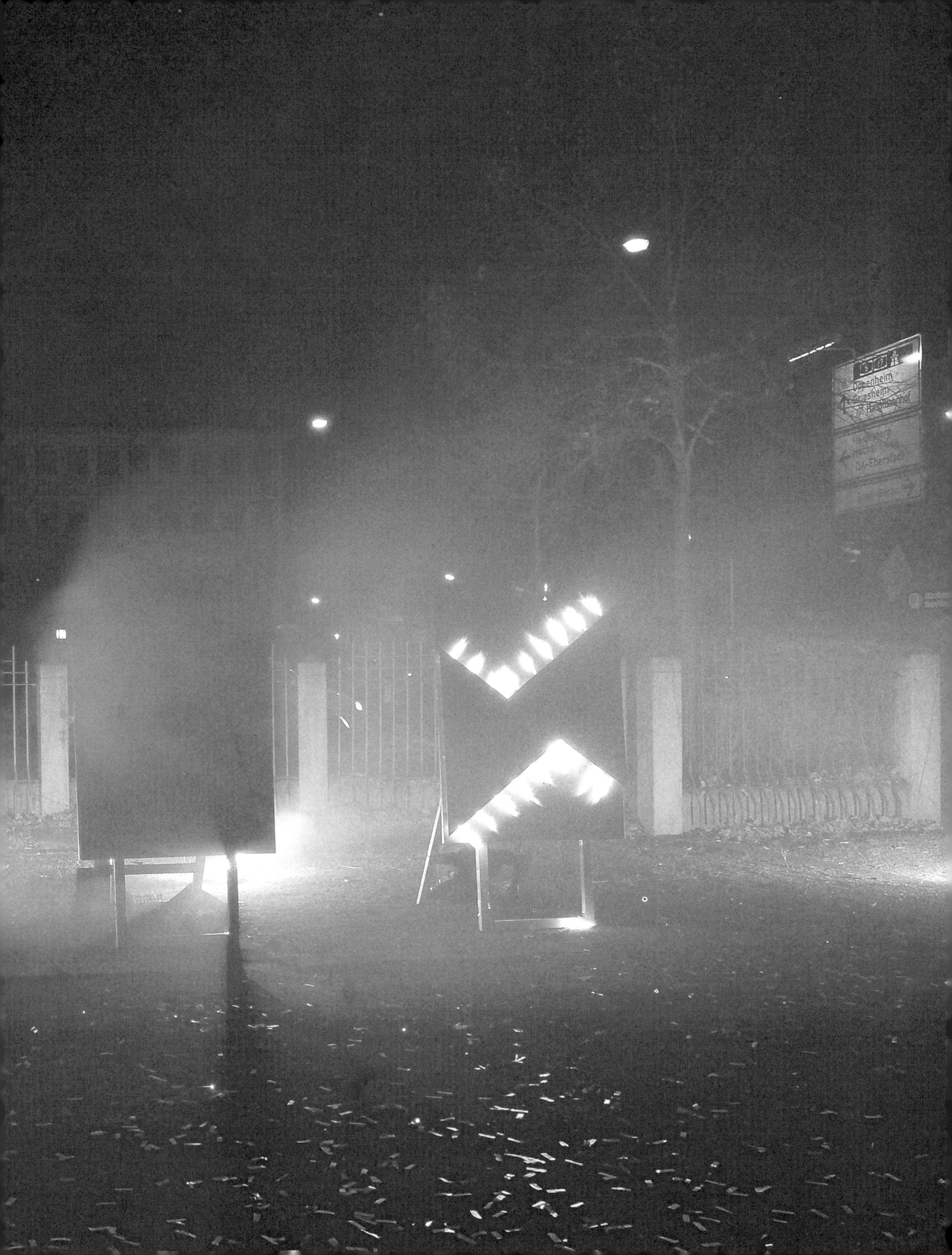

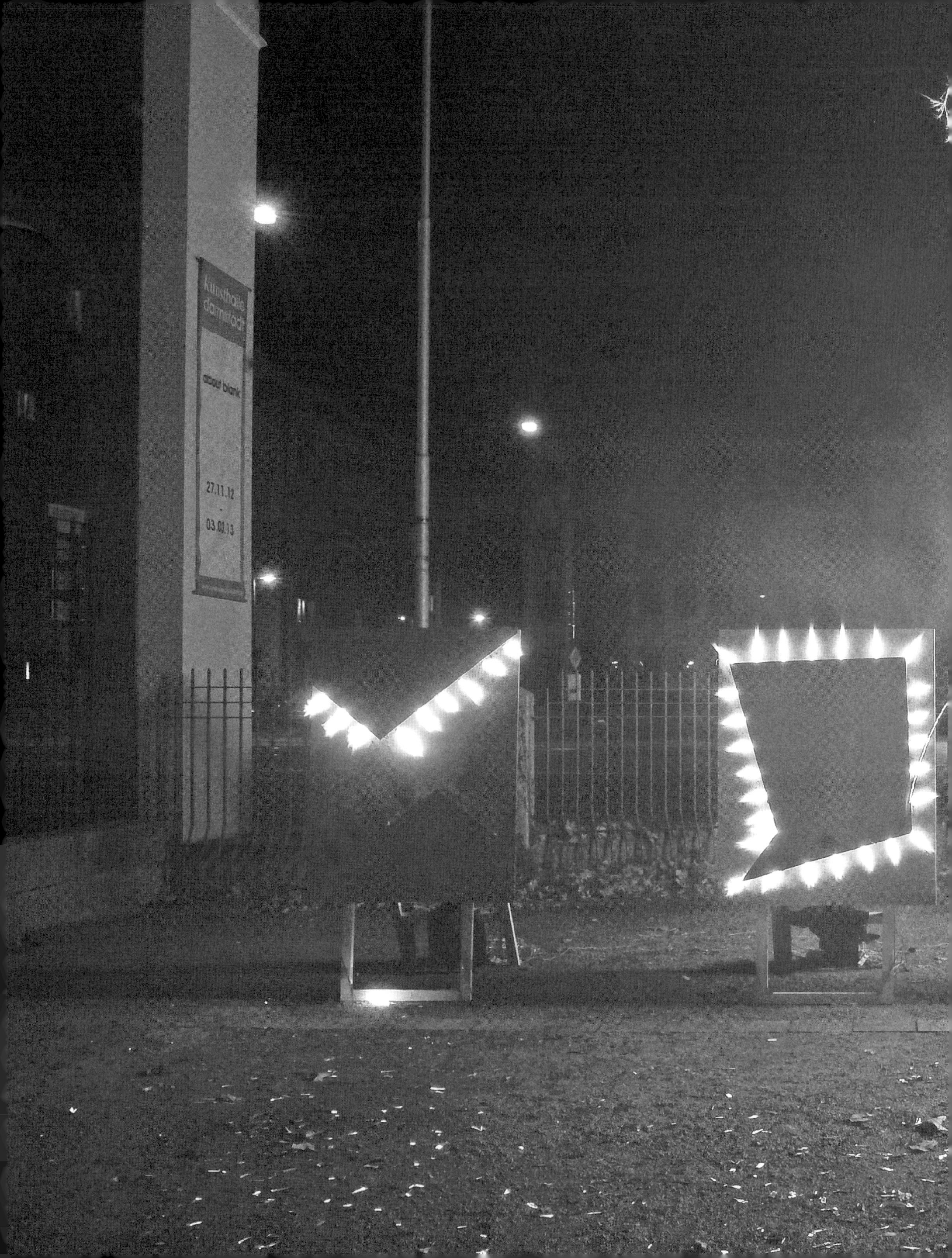

kunsthalle
darmstadt

about blank

27.11.12
–
03.03.13

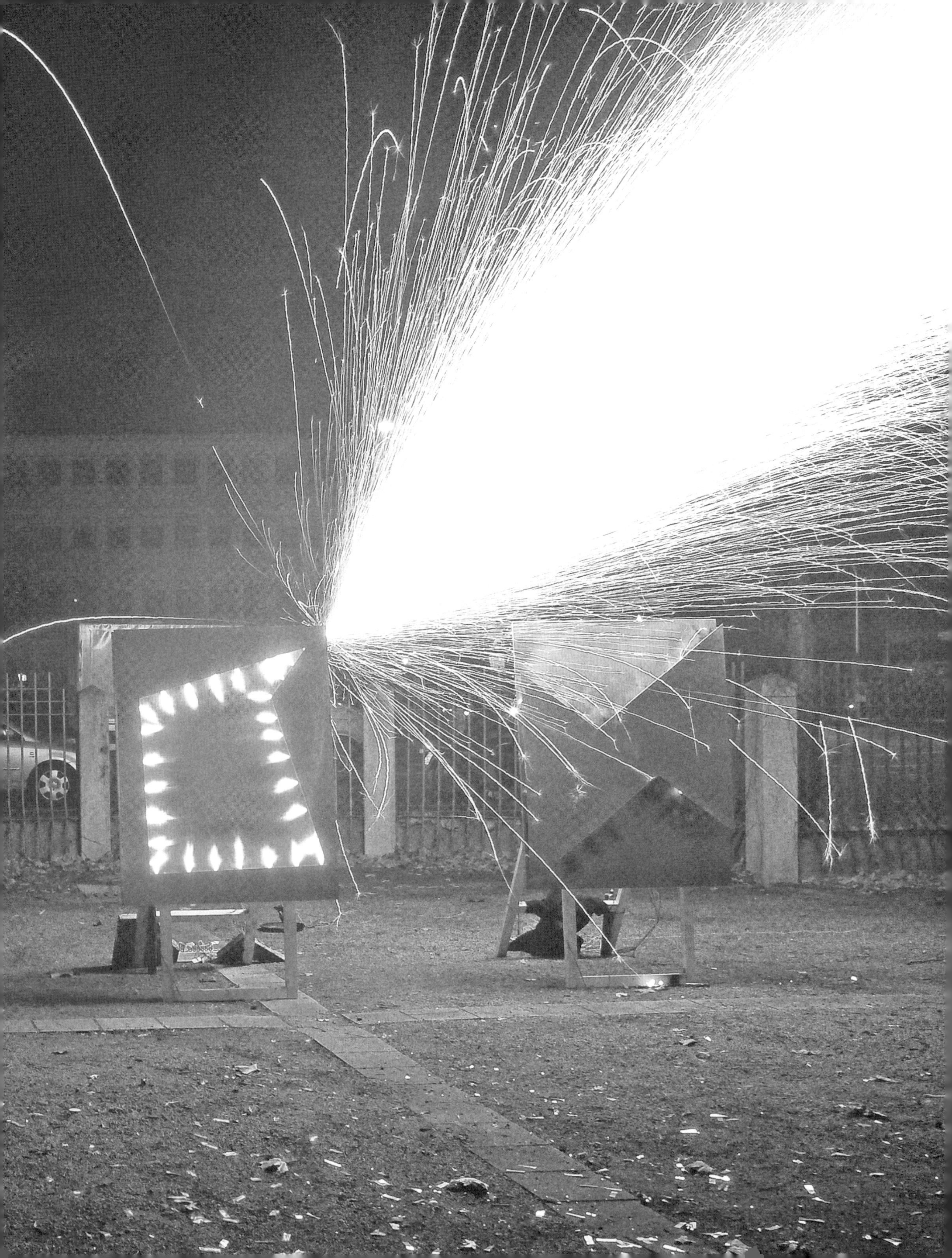

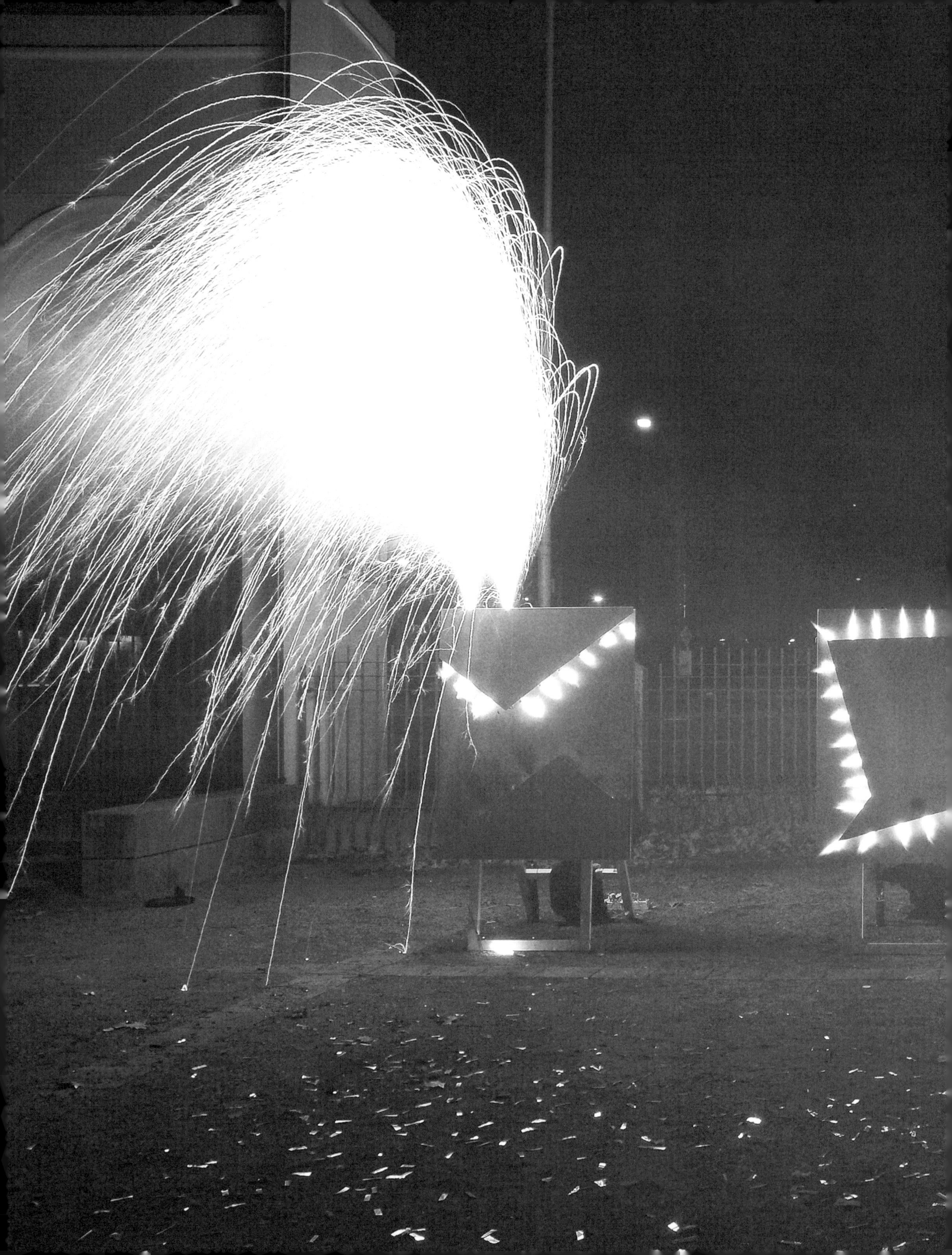

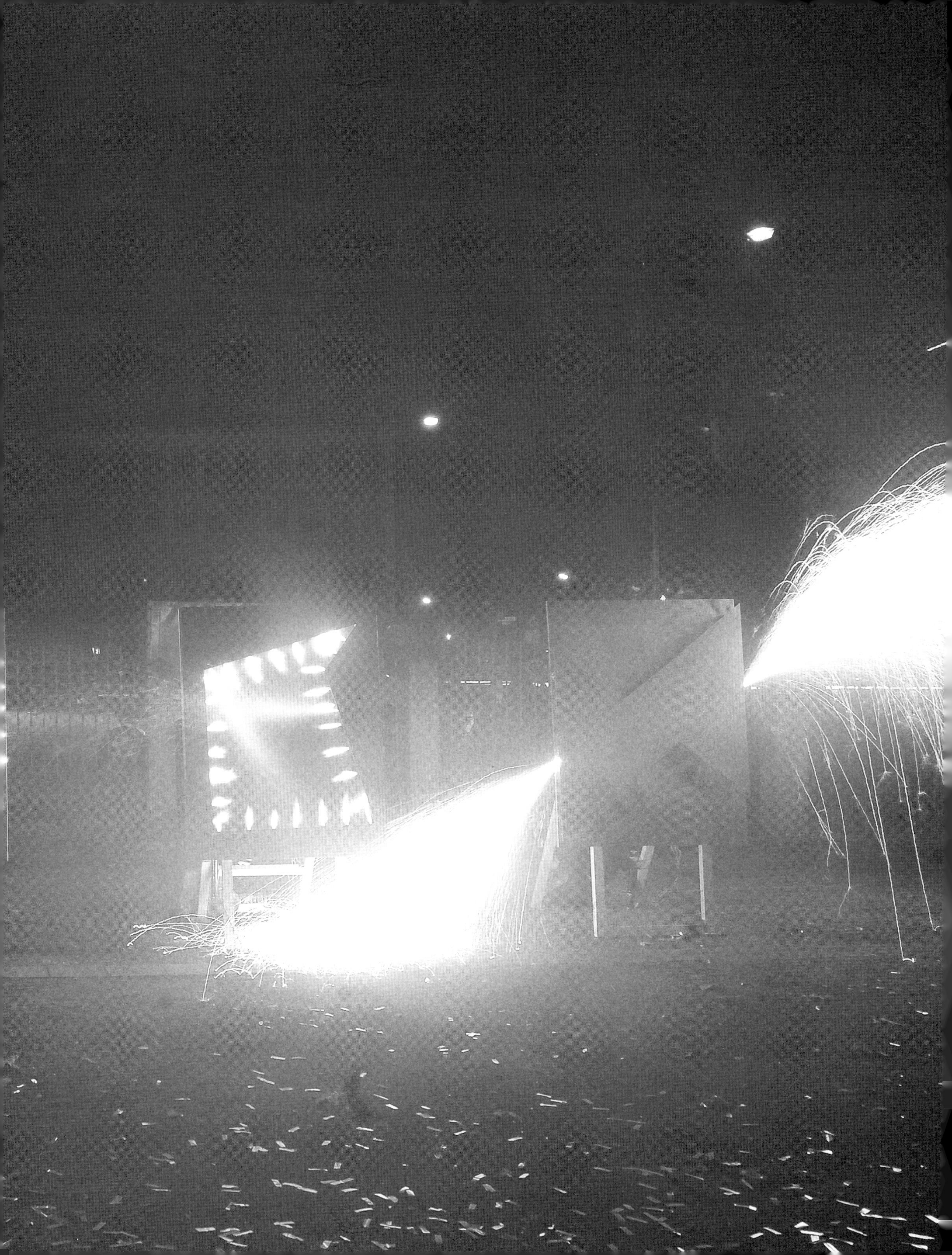

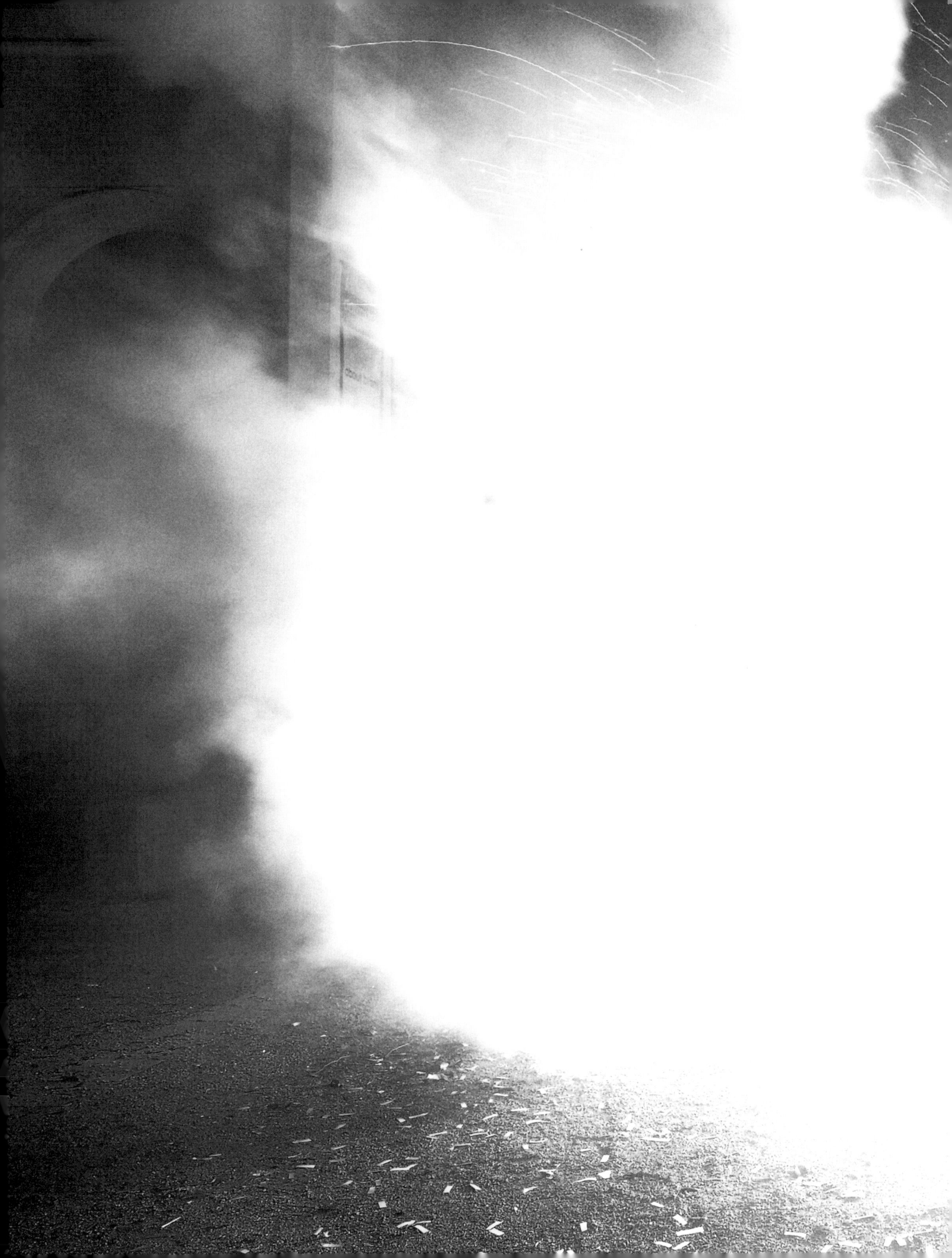

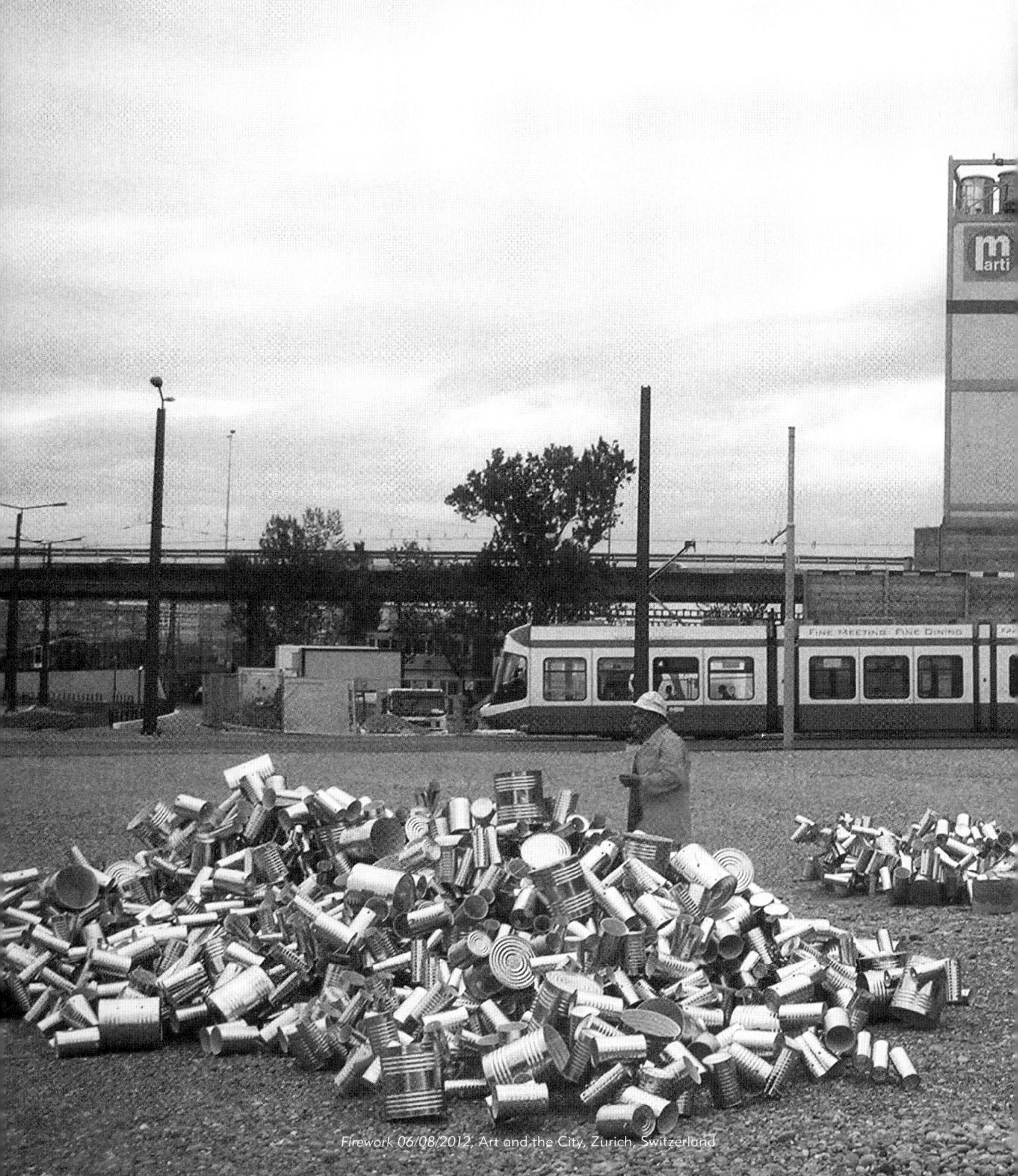

Firework 06/08/2012, Art and the City, Zurich, Switzerland

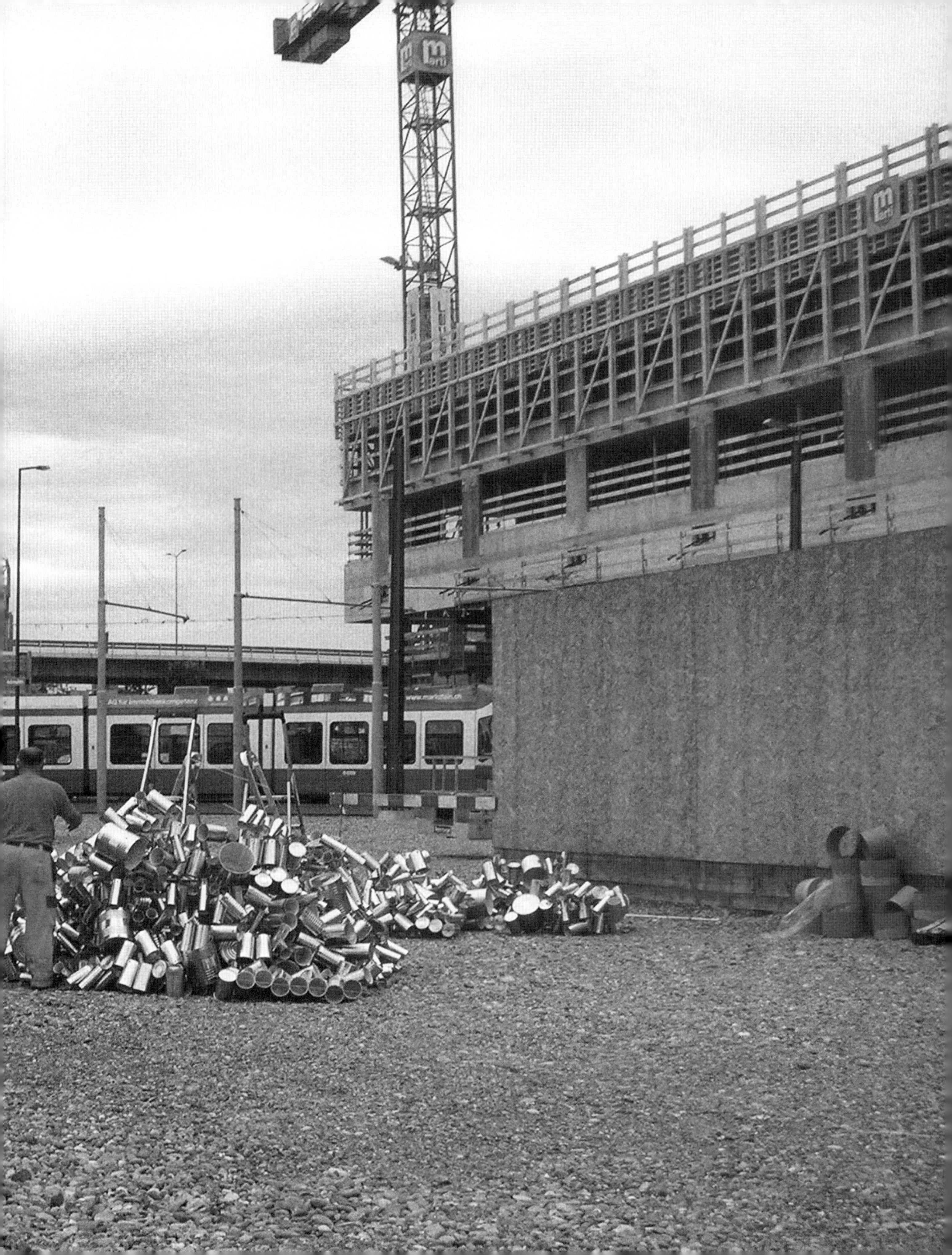

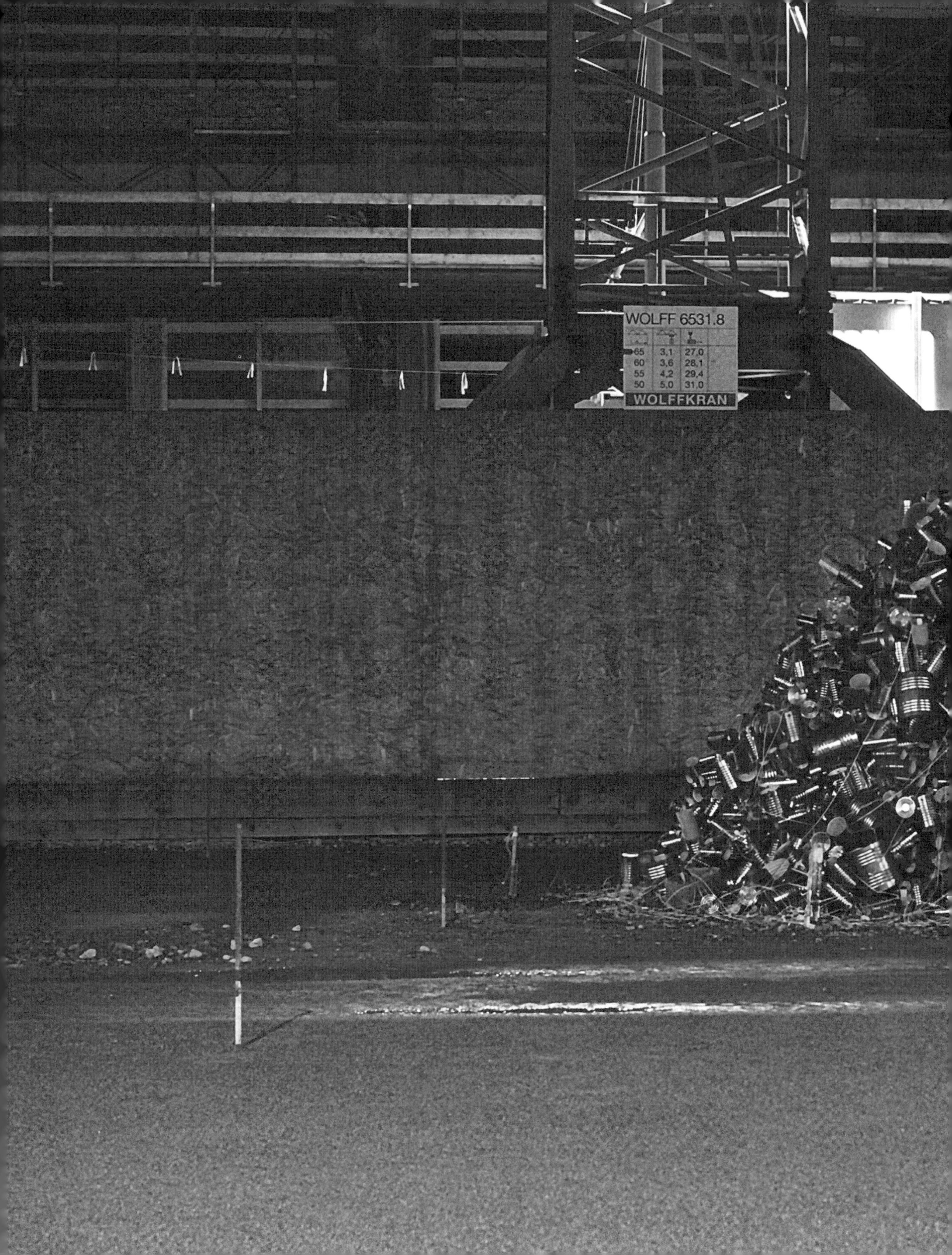
WOLFF 6531.8
65   3,1   27,0
60   3,6   28,1
55   4,2   29,4
50   5,0   31,0
WOLFFKRAN

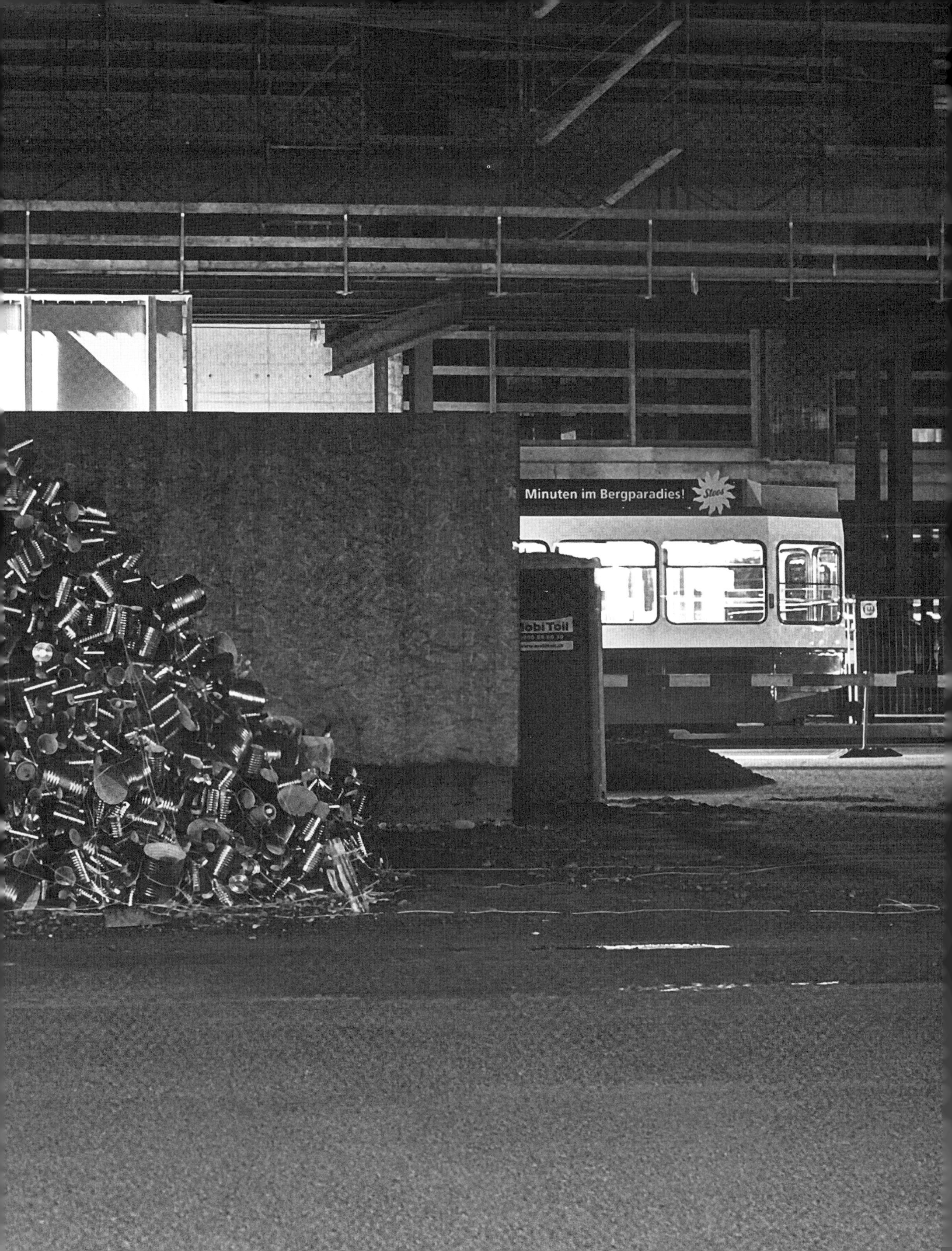

Minuten im Bergparadies!
Stoos
obi Toil

WOLFF 6531.8
65   3.1   27.0
60   3.6   28.1
55   4.2   29.4
50   5.0   31.0
WOLFFKRAN

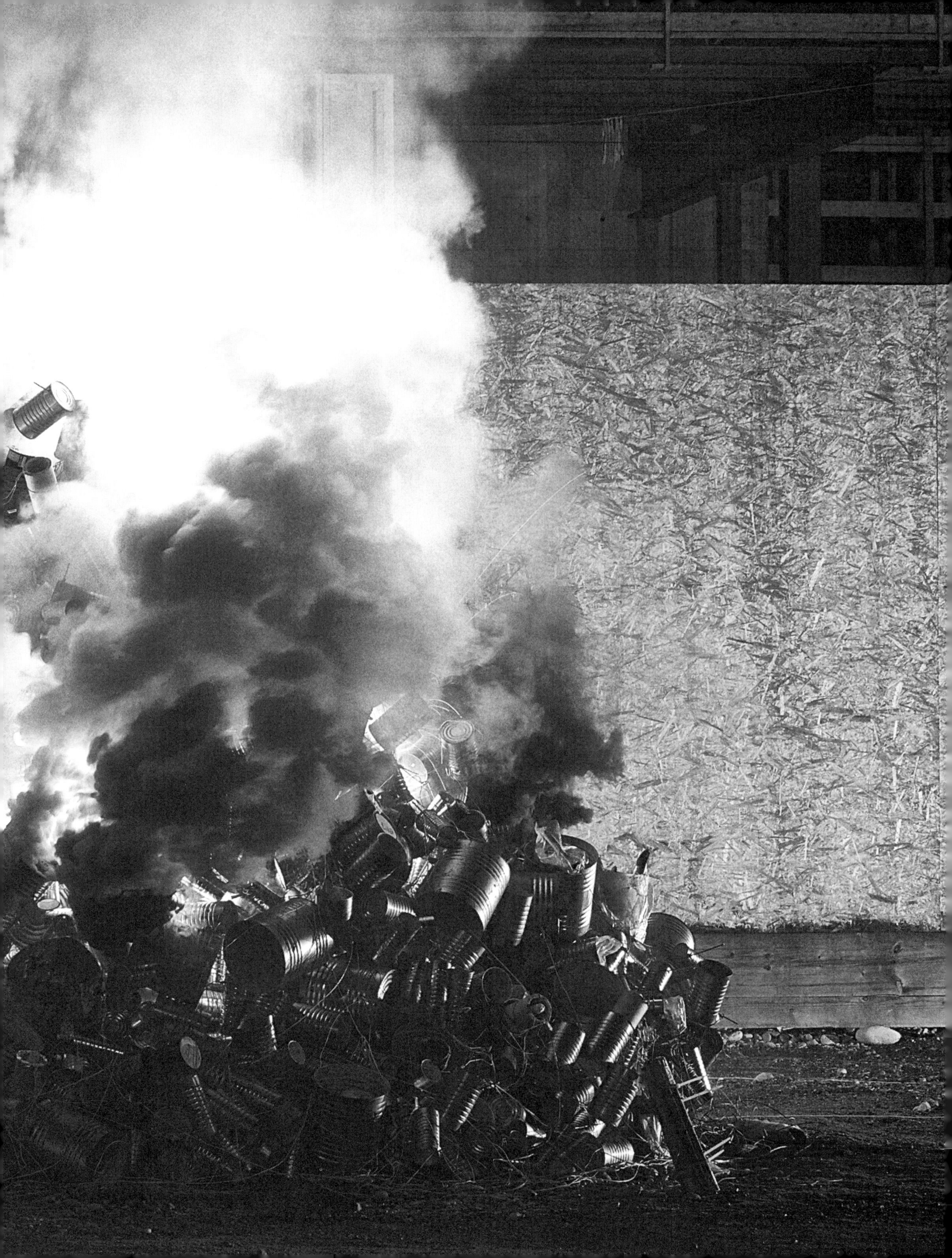

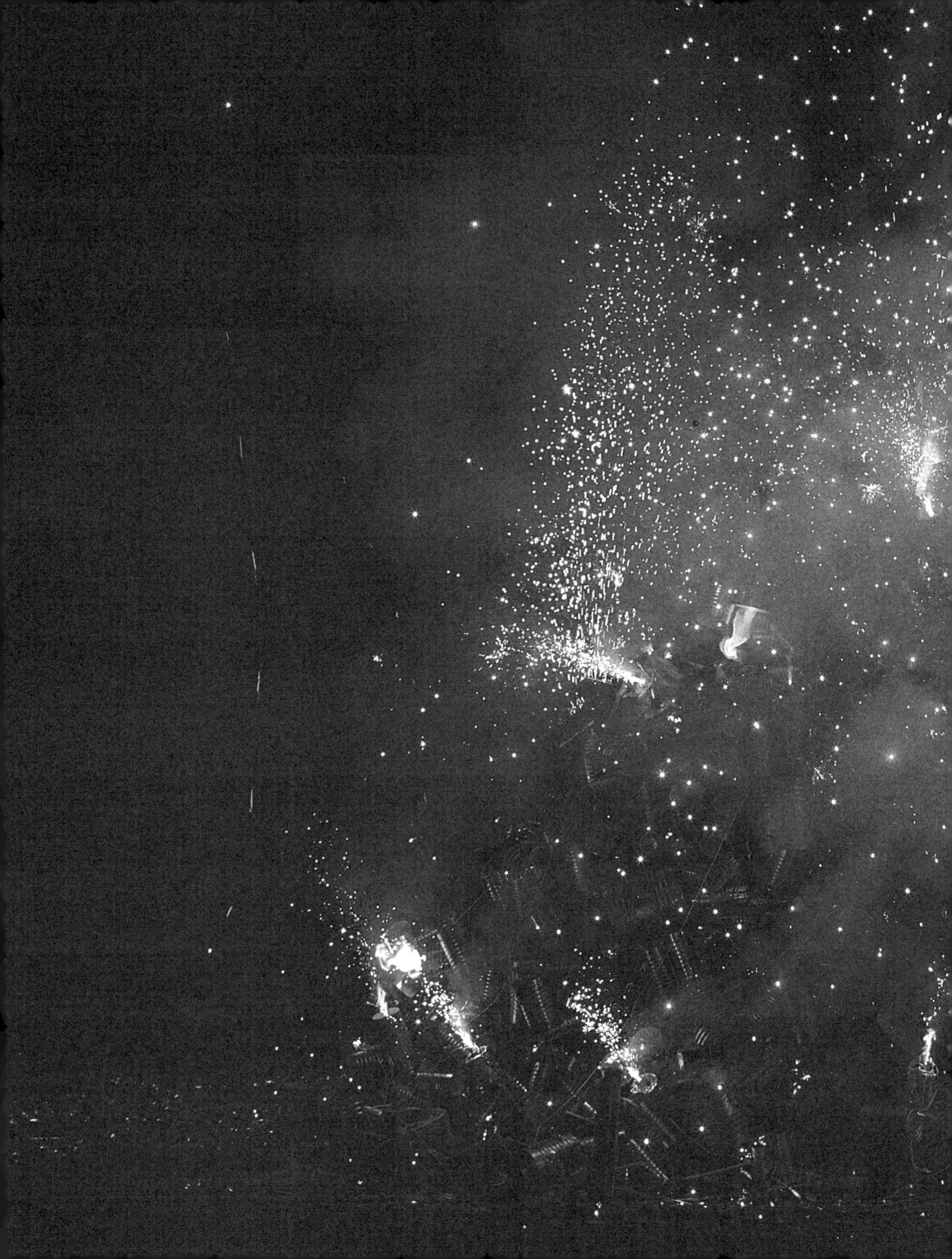

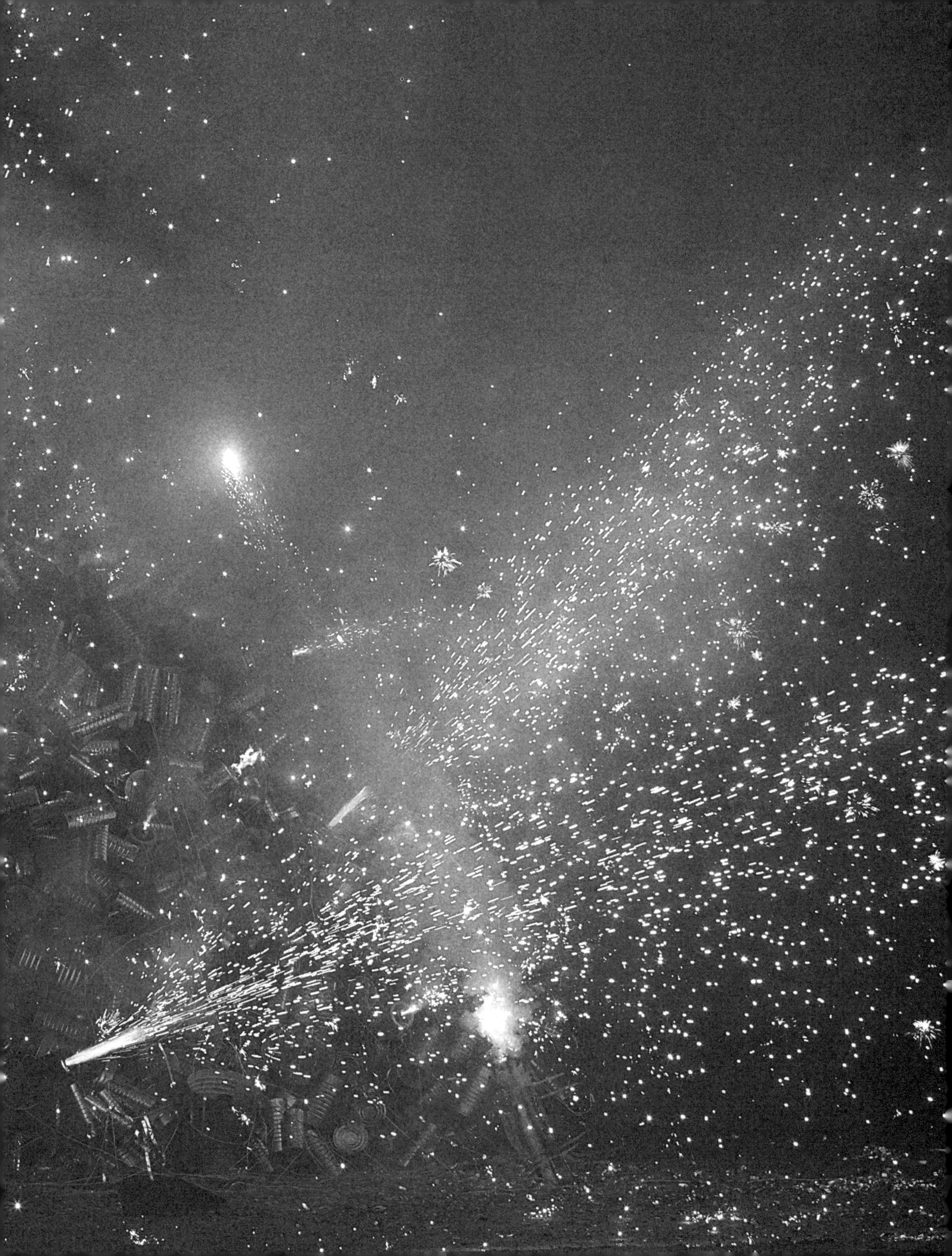

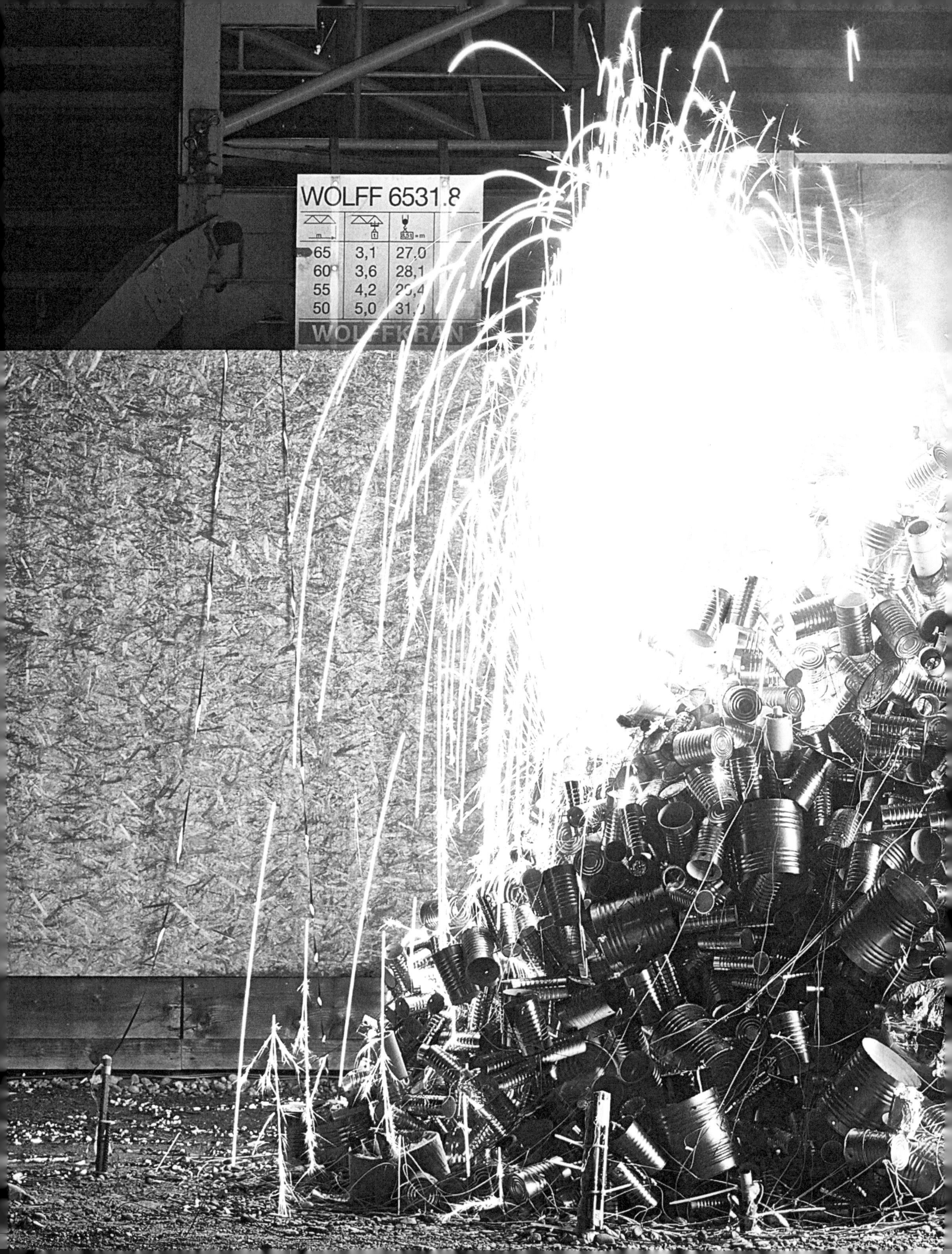

WOLFF 6531.8
65   3,1   27,0
60°   3,6   28,1
55   4,2   29,4
50   5,0   31,0
WOLFFKRAN

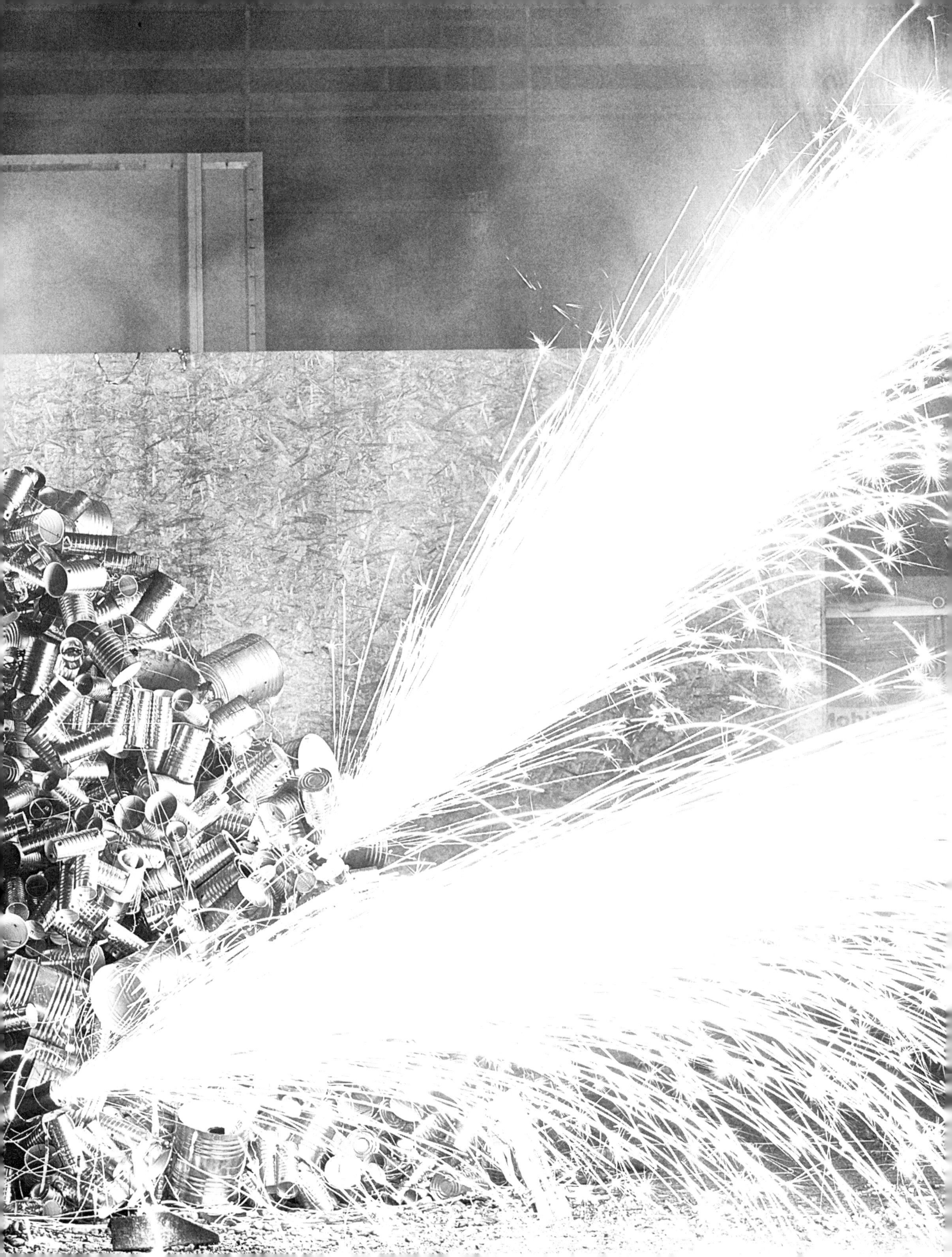

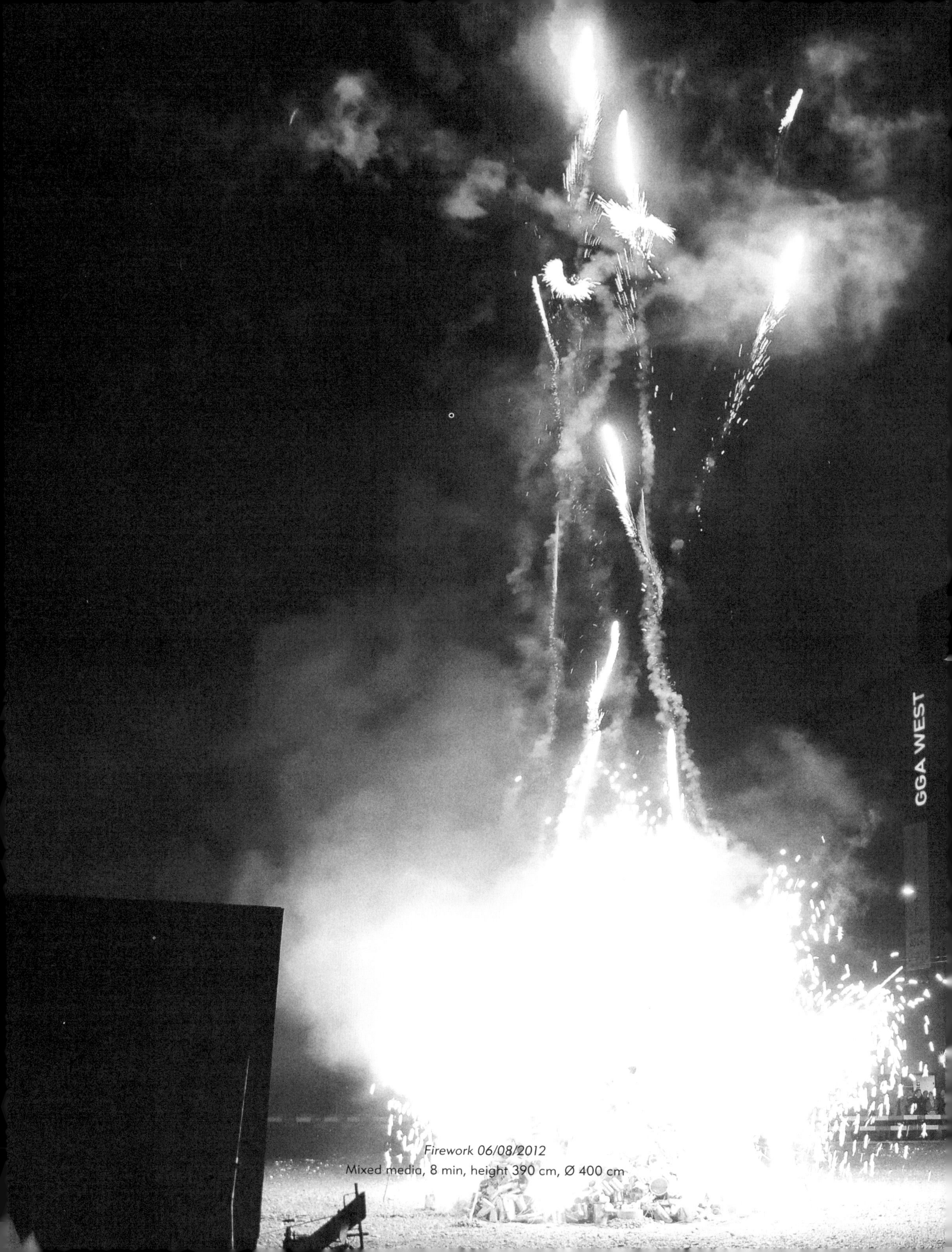

Firework 06/08/2012
Mixed media, 8 min, height 390 cm, Ø 400 cm

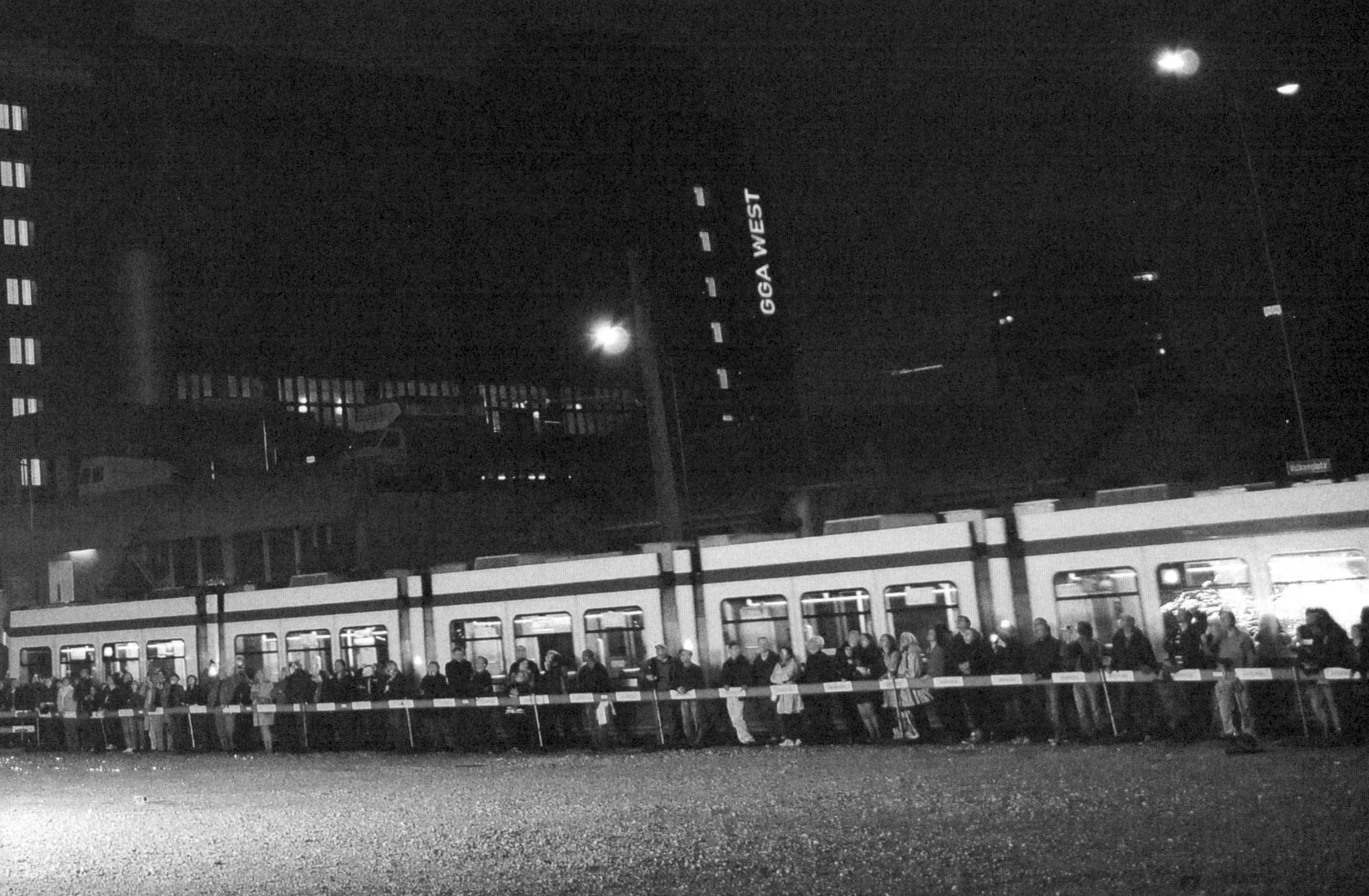
GGA WEST

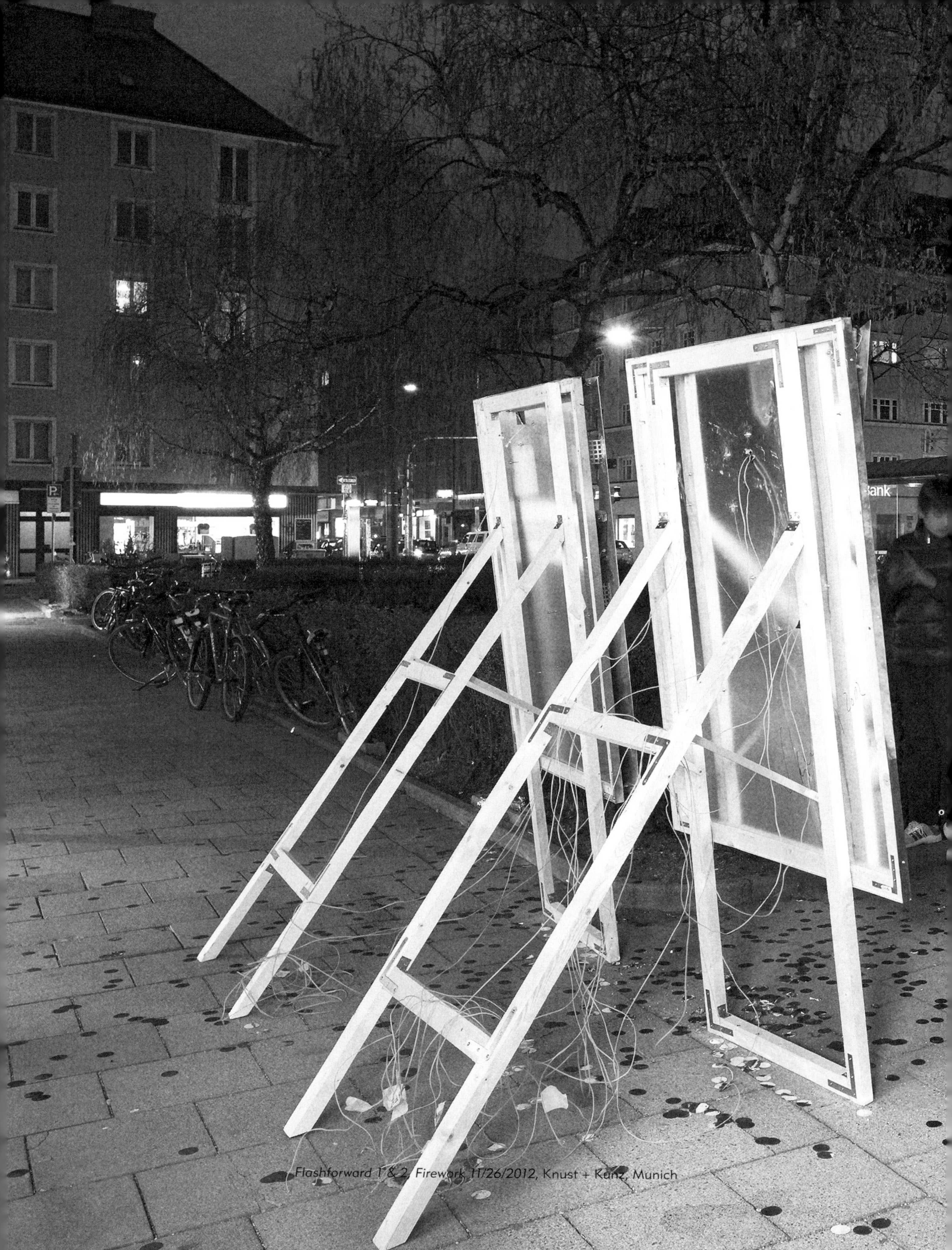

Flashforward 1 & 2, Firework 11/26/2012, Knust + Kunz, Munich

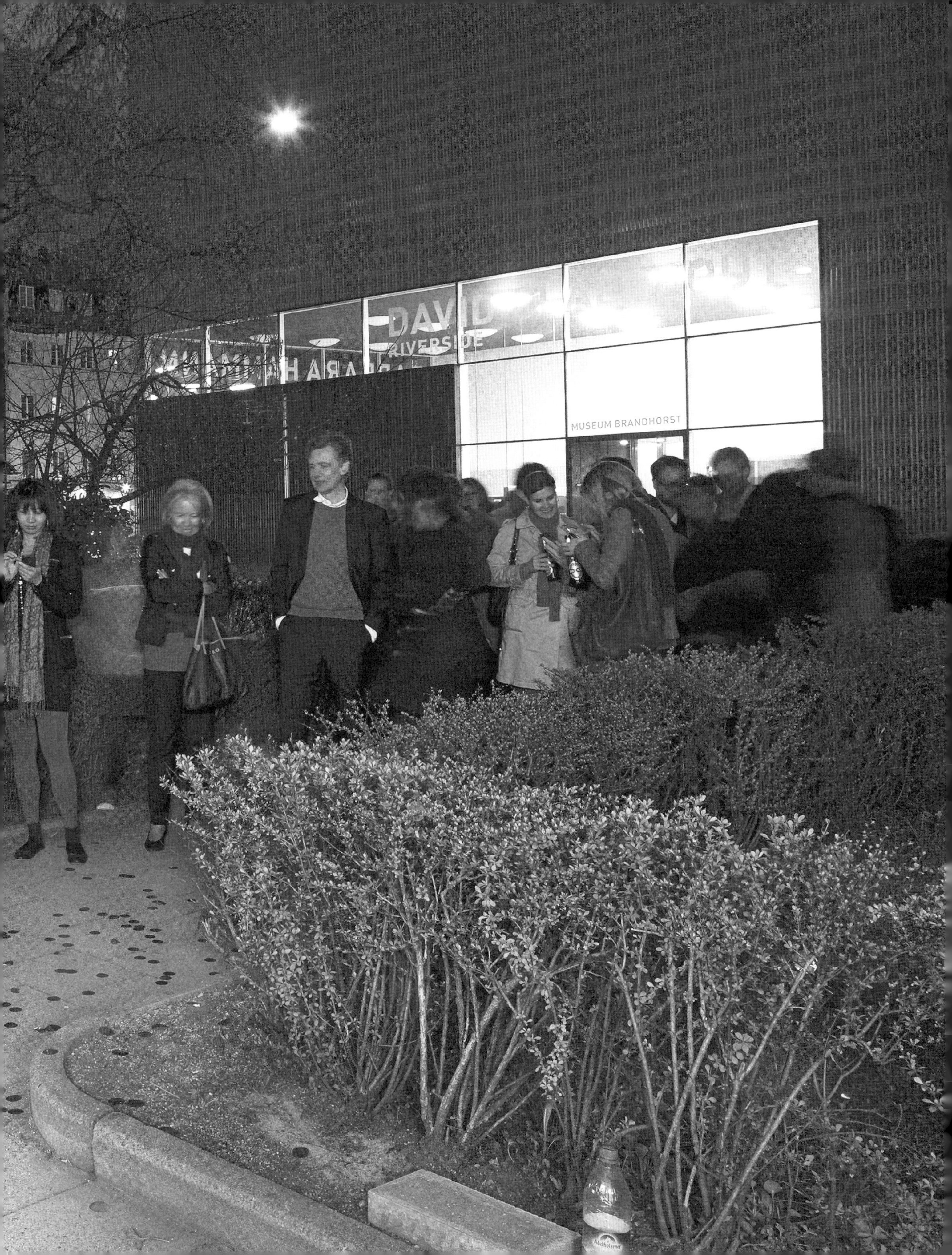
DAVID
RIVERSIDE
MUSEUM BRANDHORST

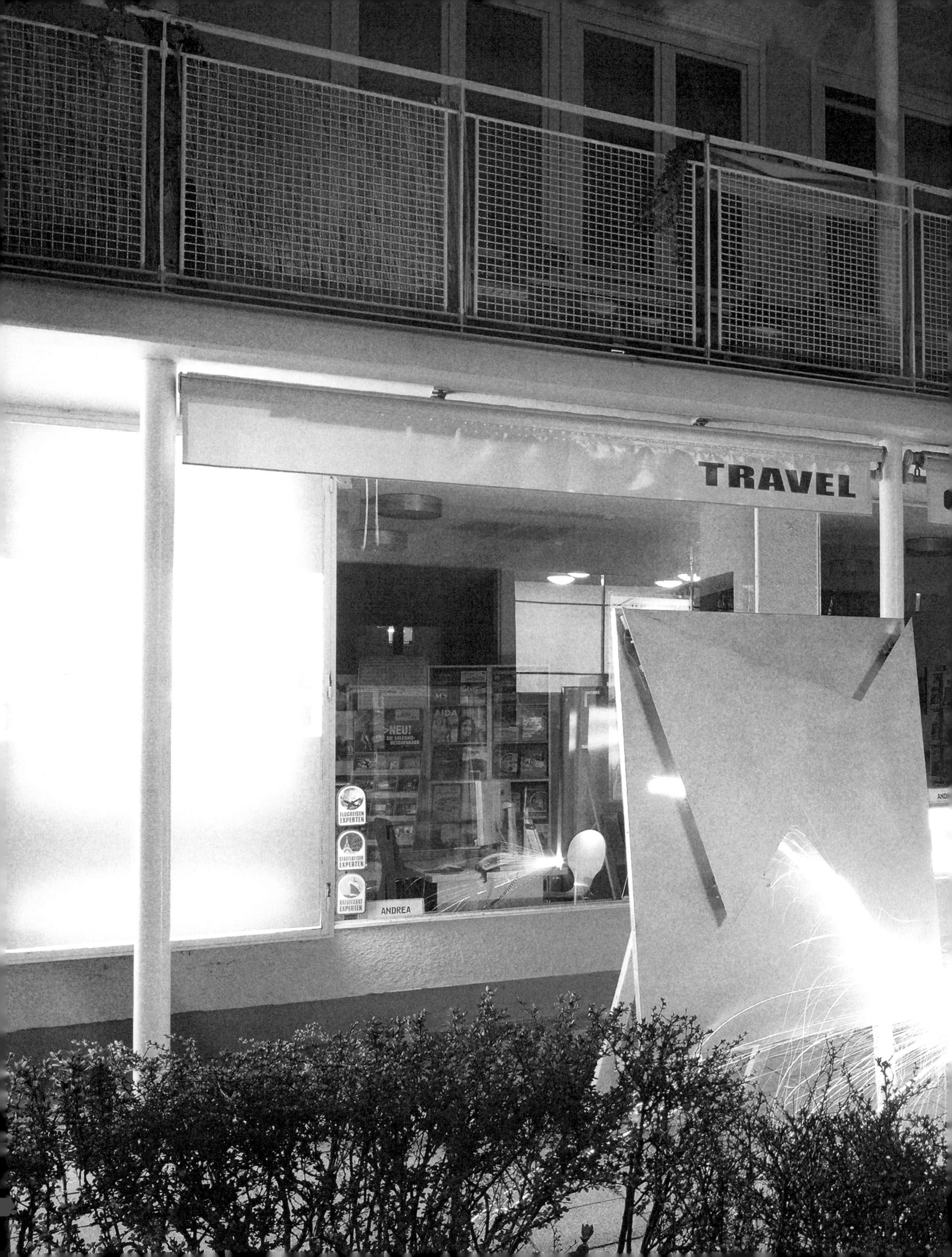

TRAVEL
ANDREA

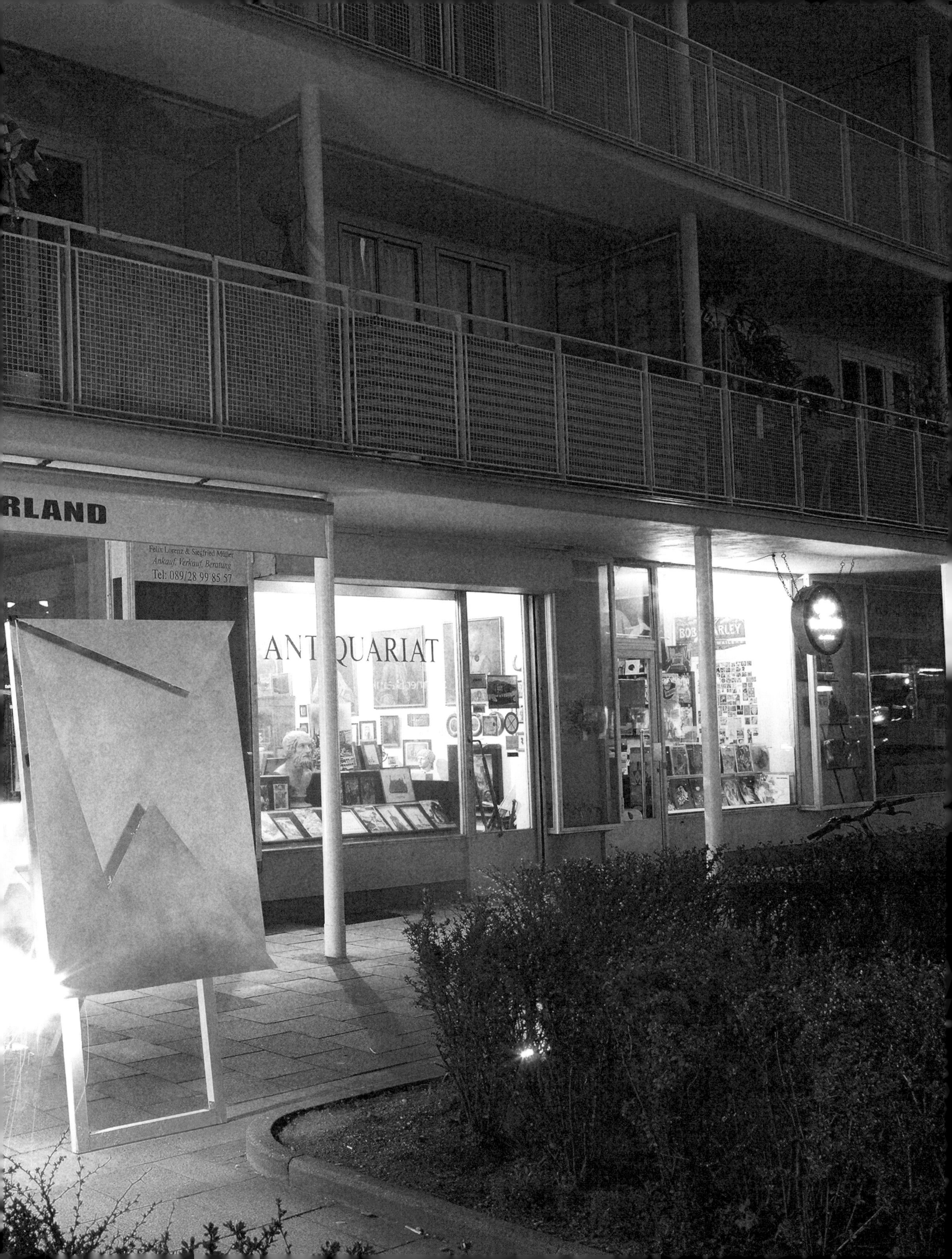
RLAND
Felix Lorenz & Siegfried Mißler
Ankauf, Verkauf, Beratung
Tel: 089/28 99 85 57
ANTIQUARIAT
BOB MARLEY

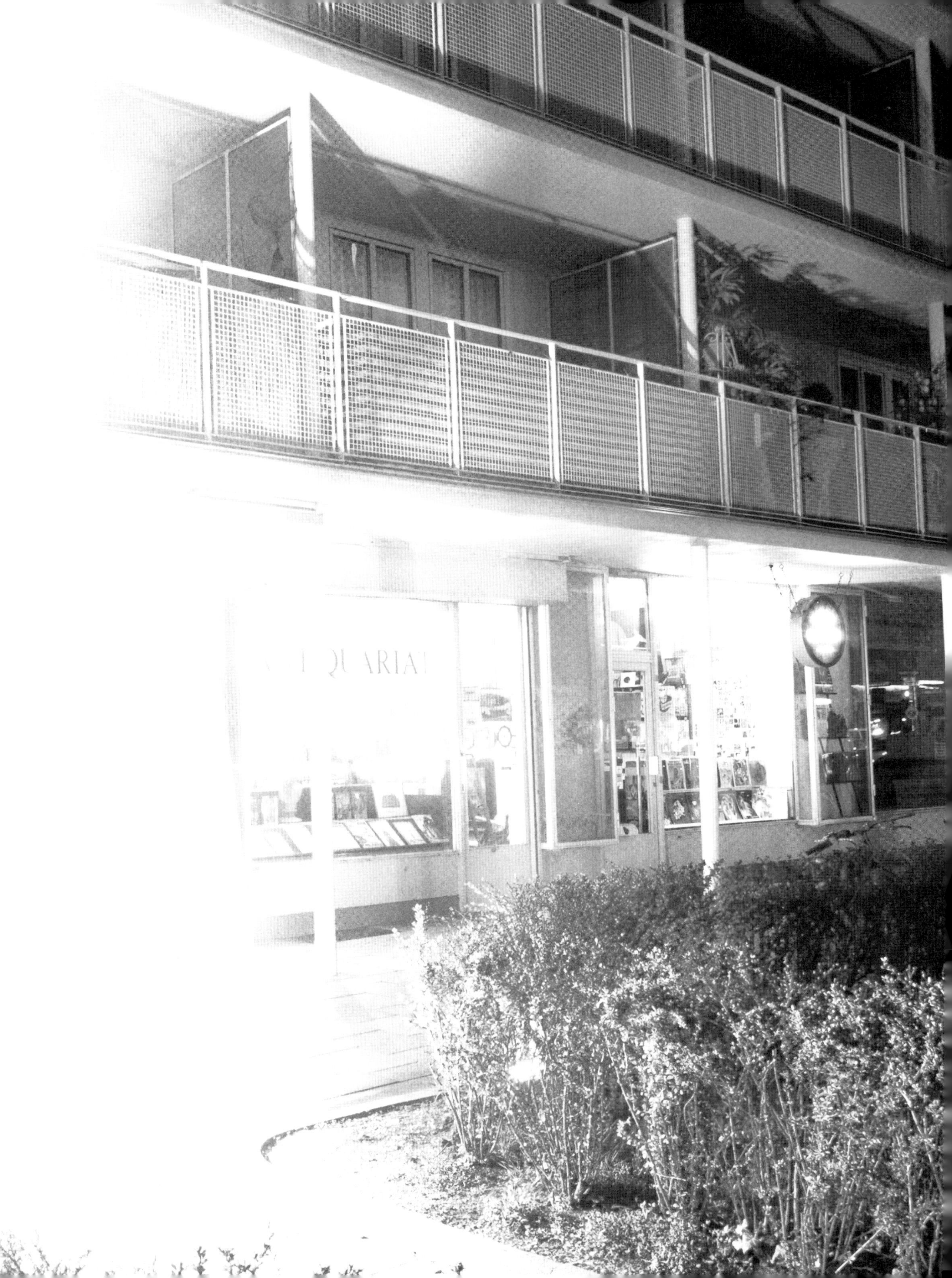

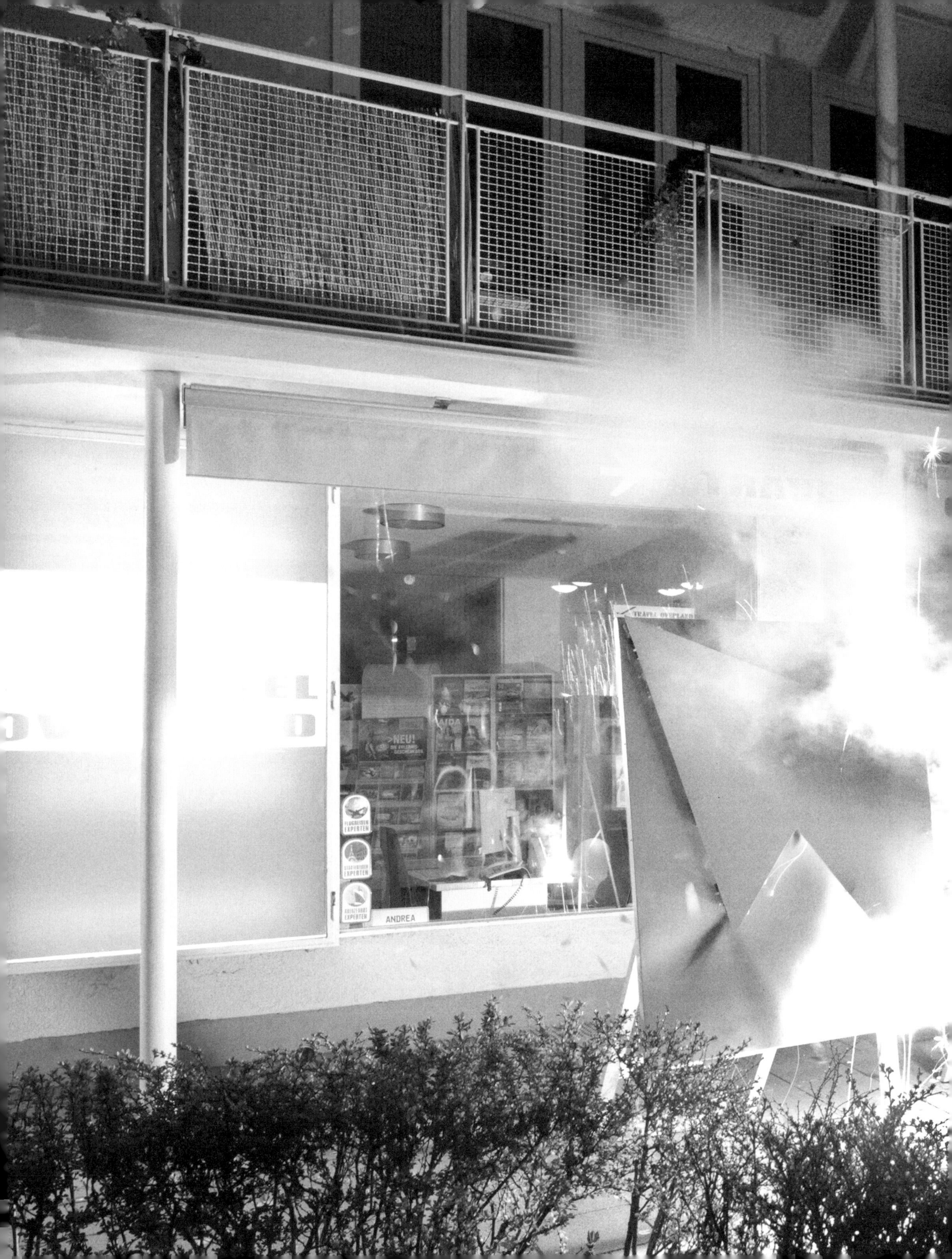

NEU!
FLUGREISEN EXPERTEN
STÄDTEREISEN EXPERTEN
KREUZFAHRT EXPERTEN
ANDREA
AIDA

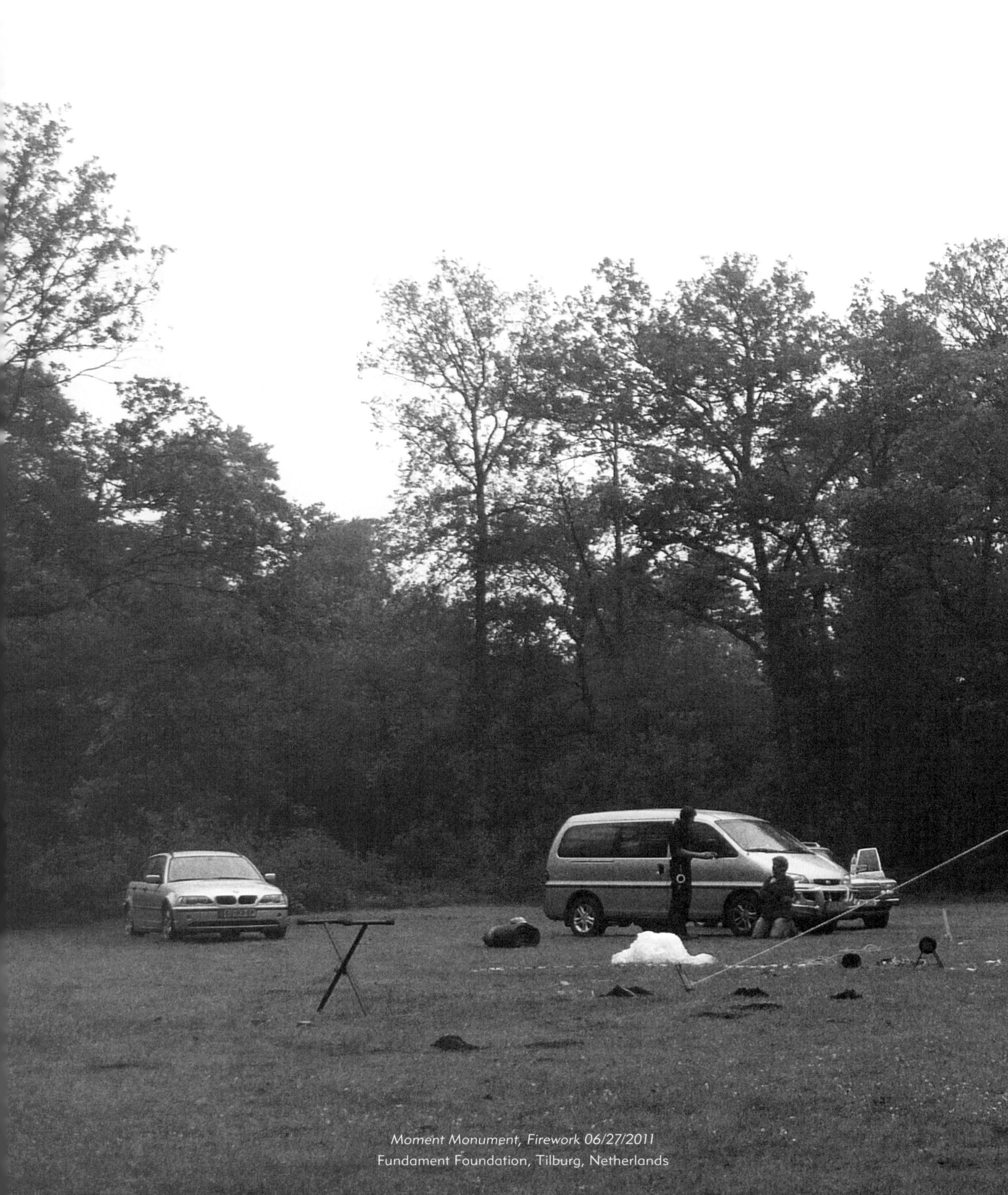

Moment Monument, Firework 06/27/2011
Fundament Foundation, Tilburg, Netherlands

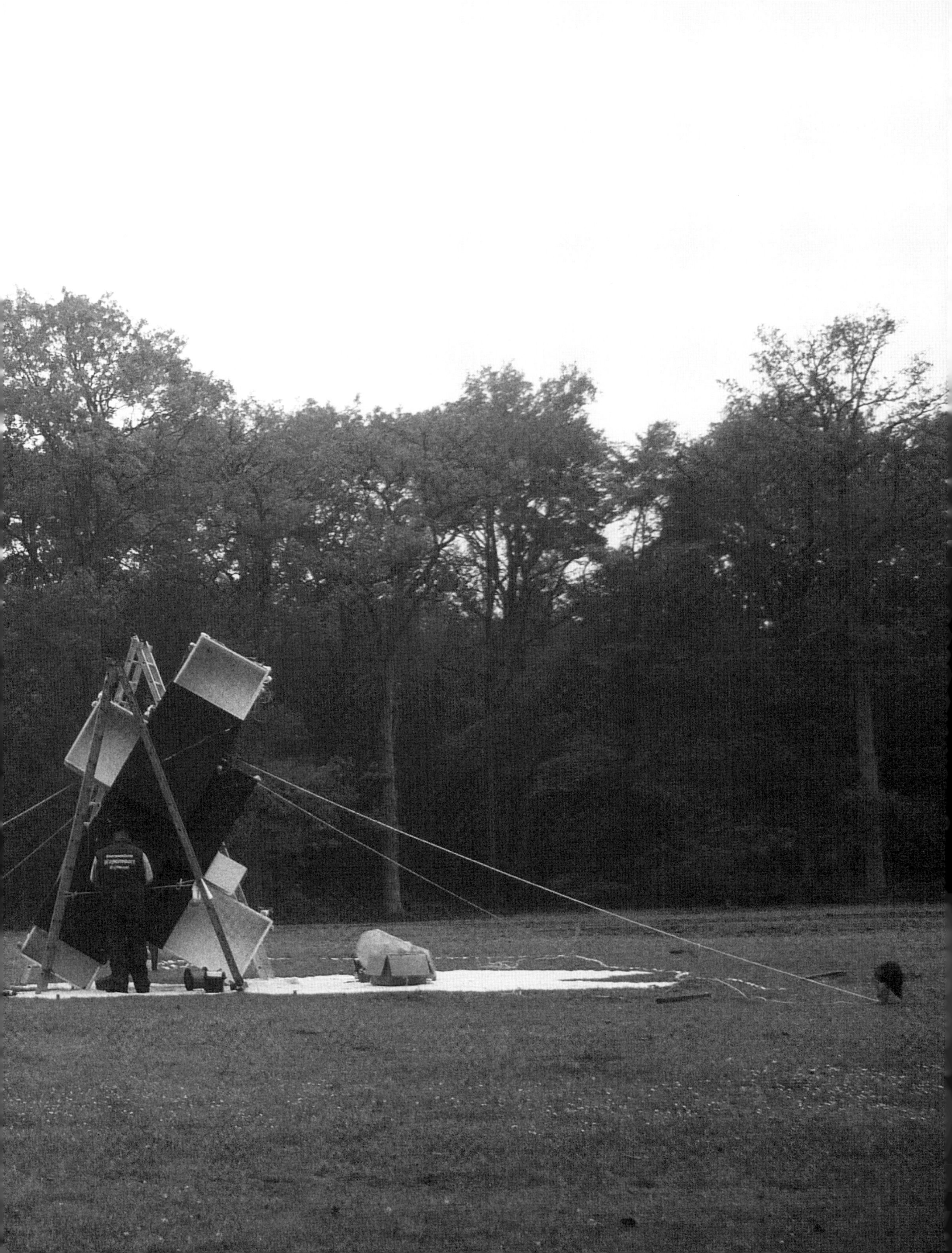

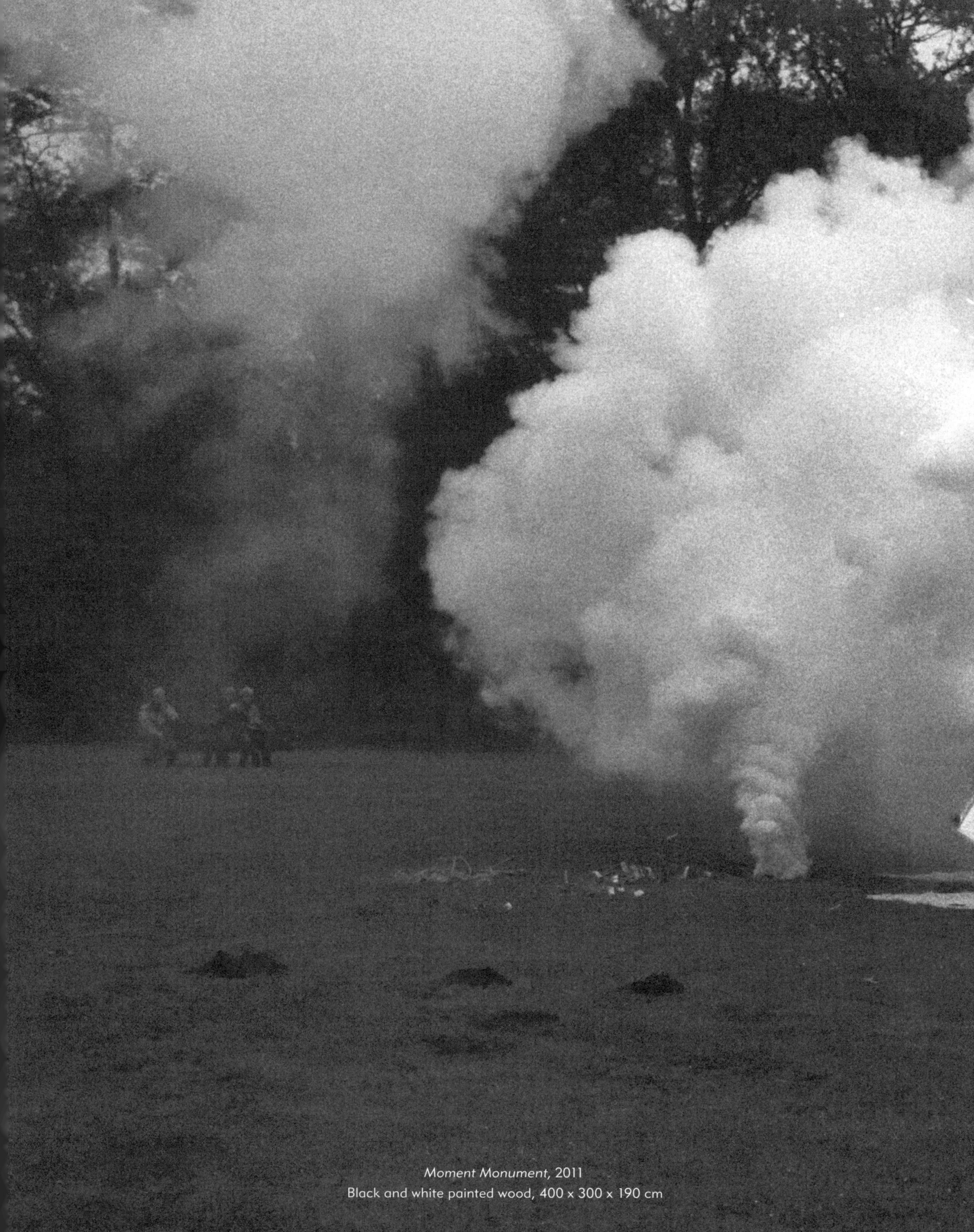

Moment Monument, 2011
Black and white painted wood, 400 x 300 x 190 cm

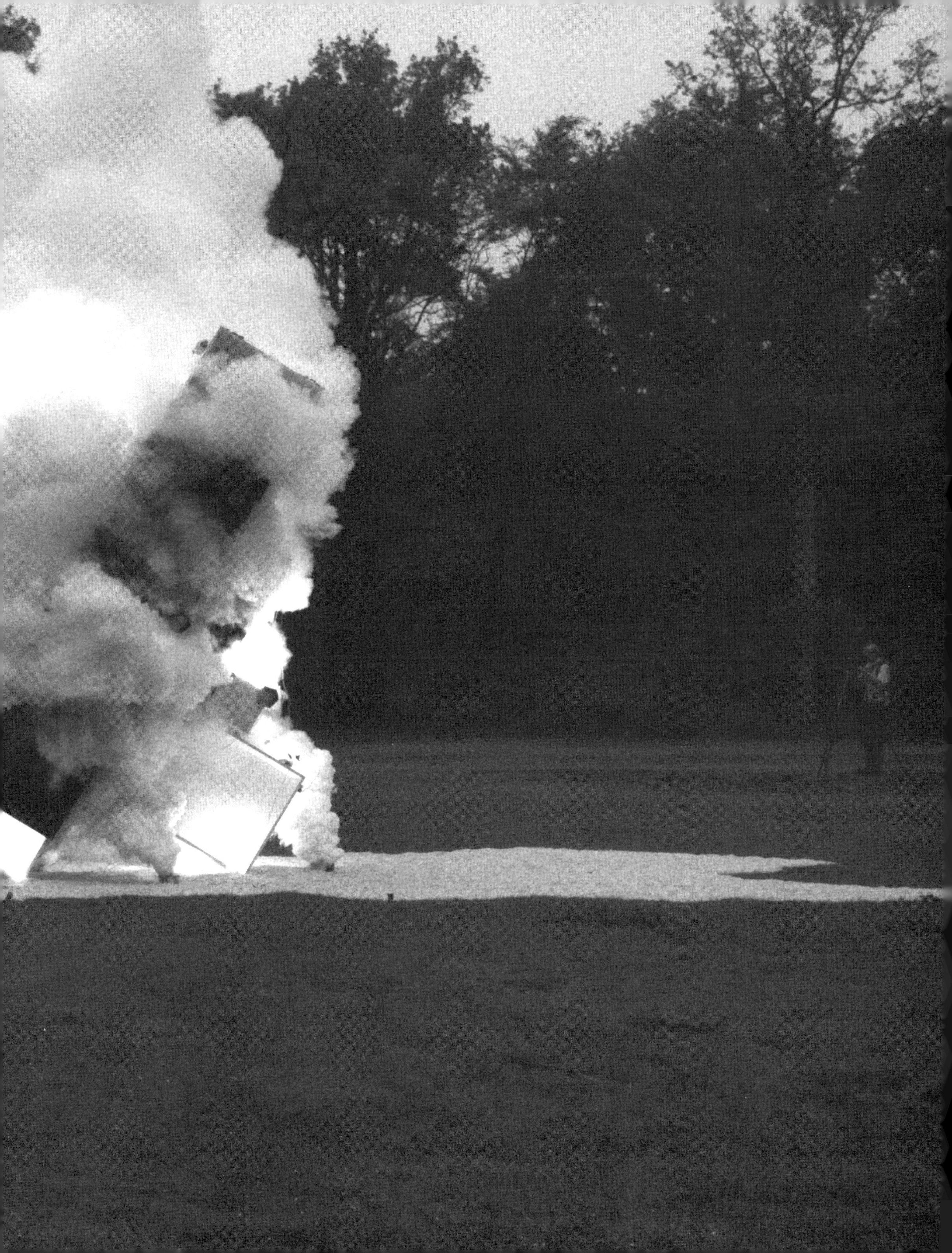

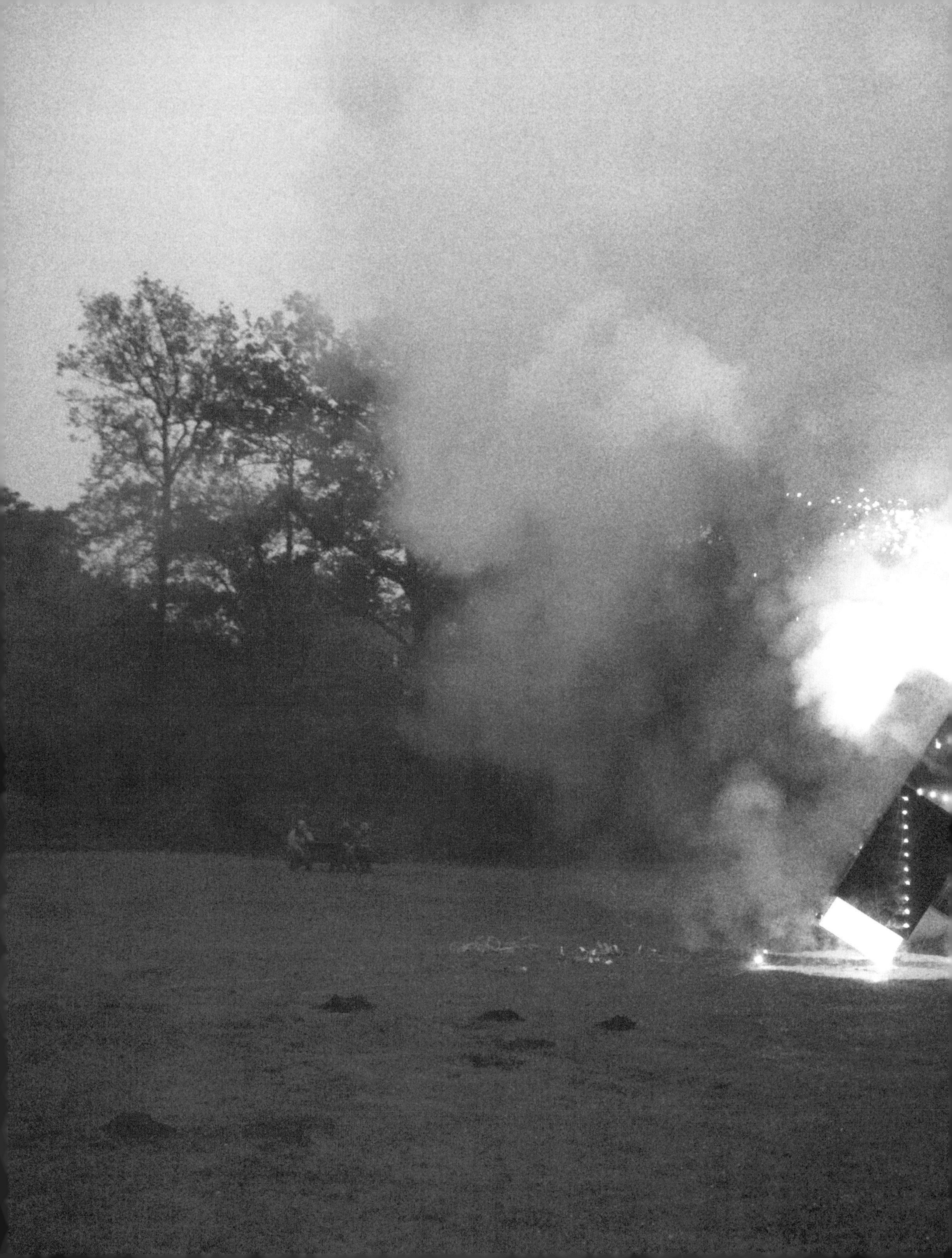

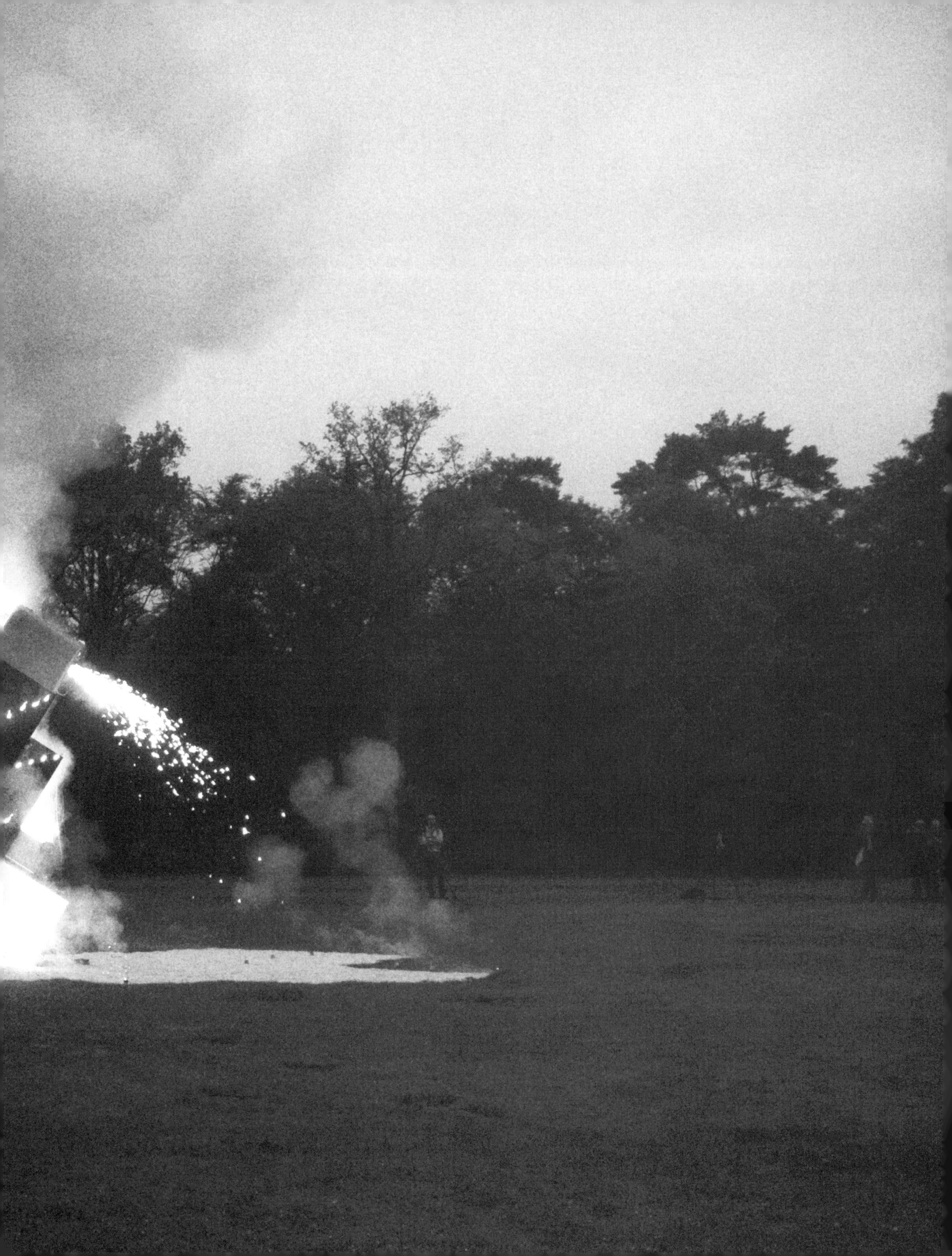

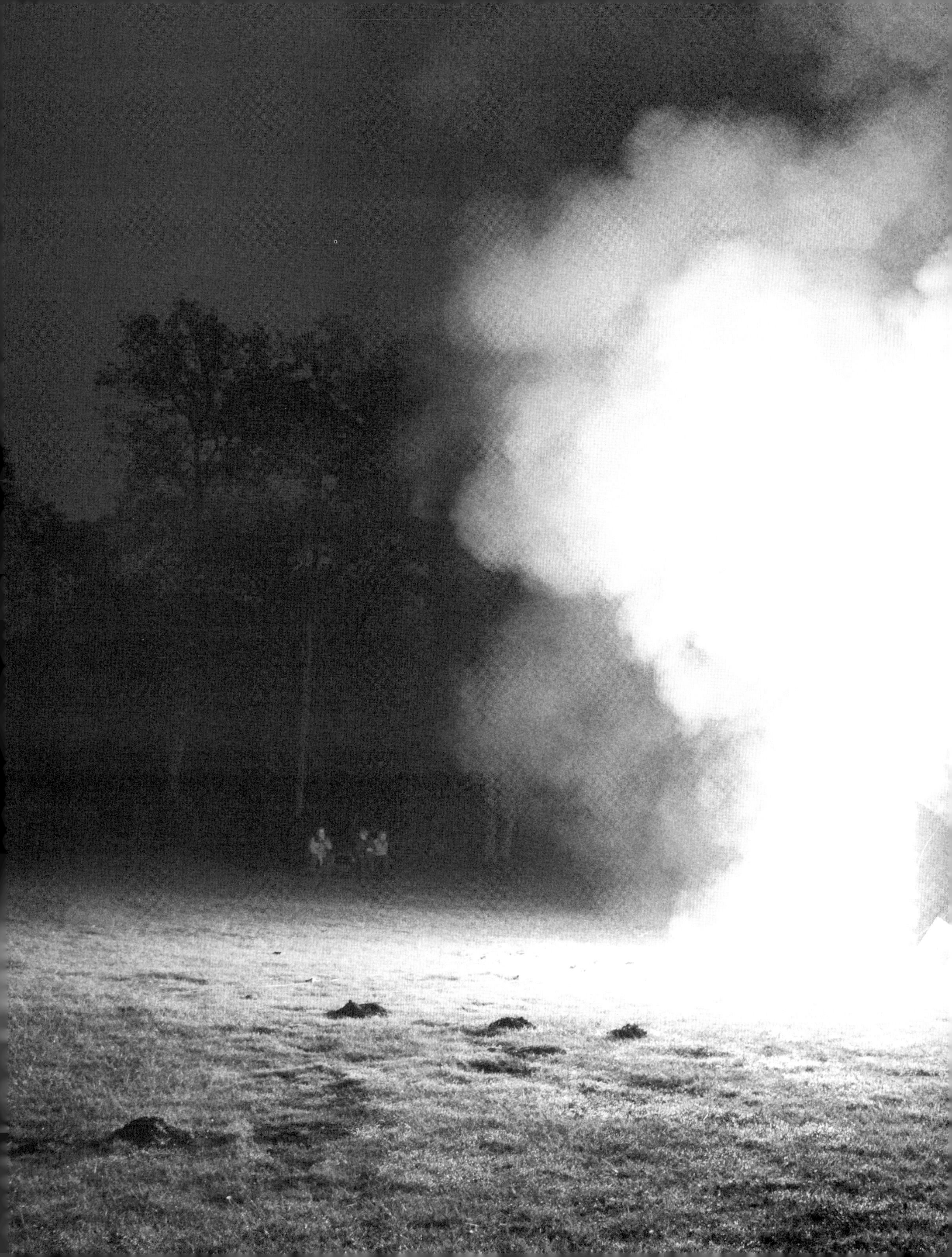

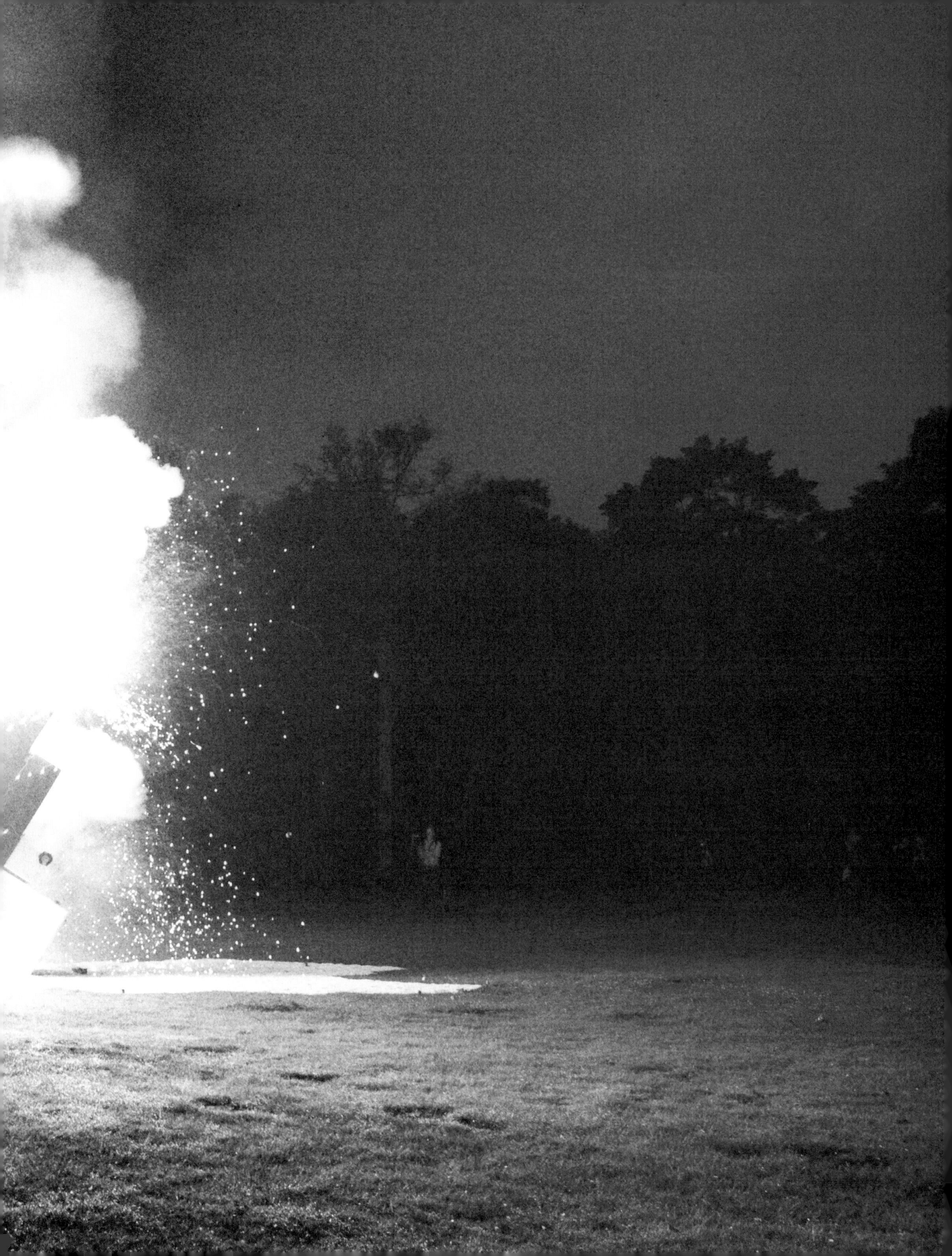

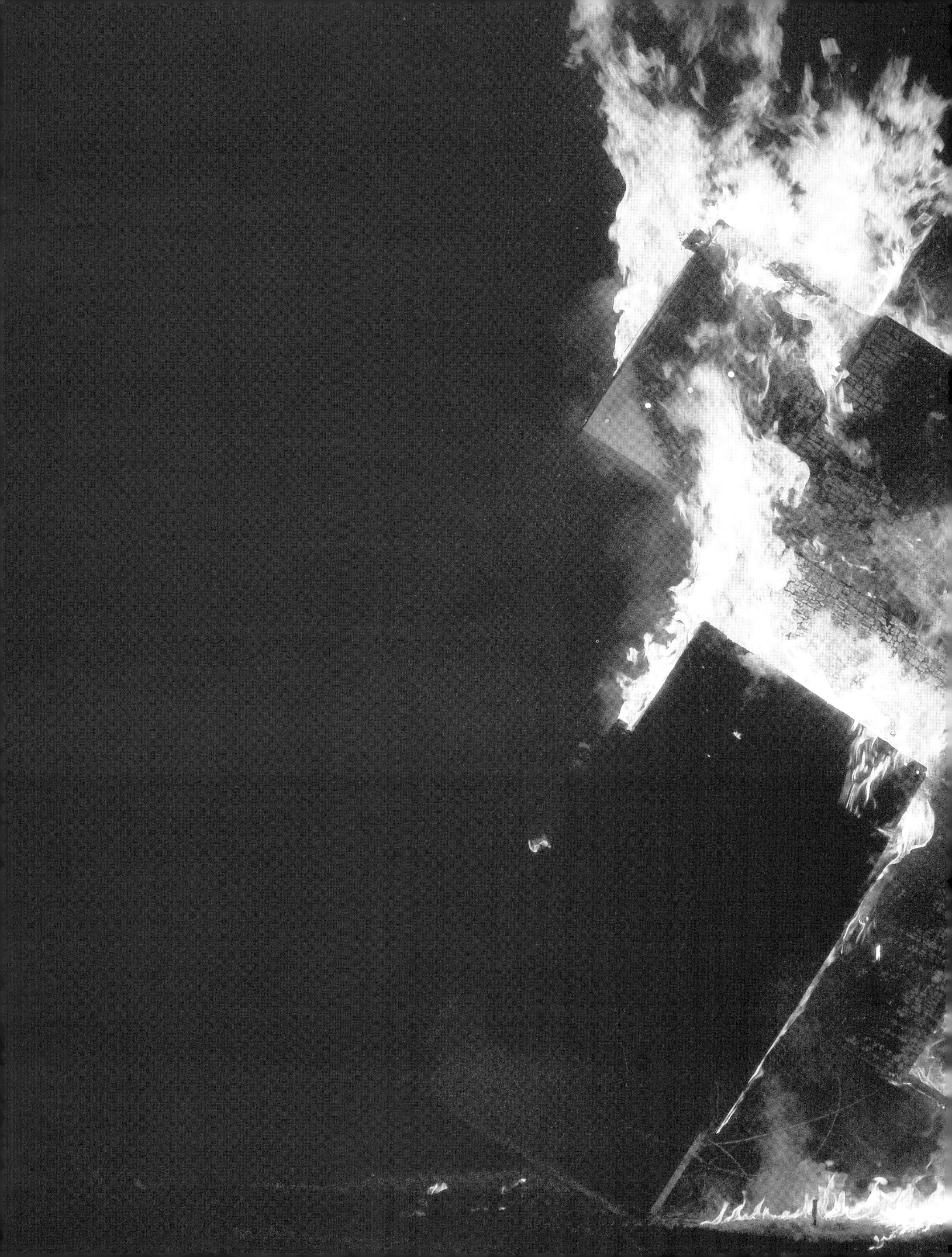

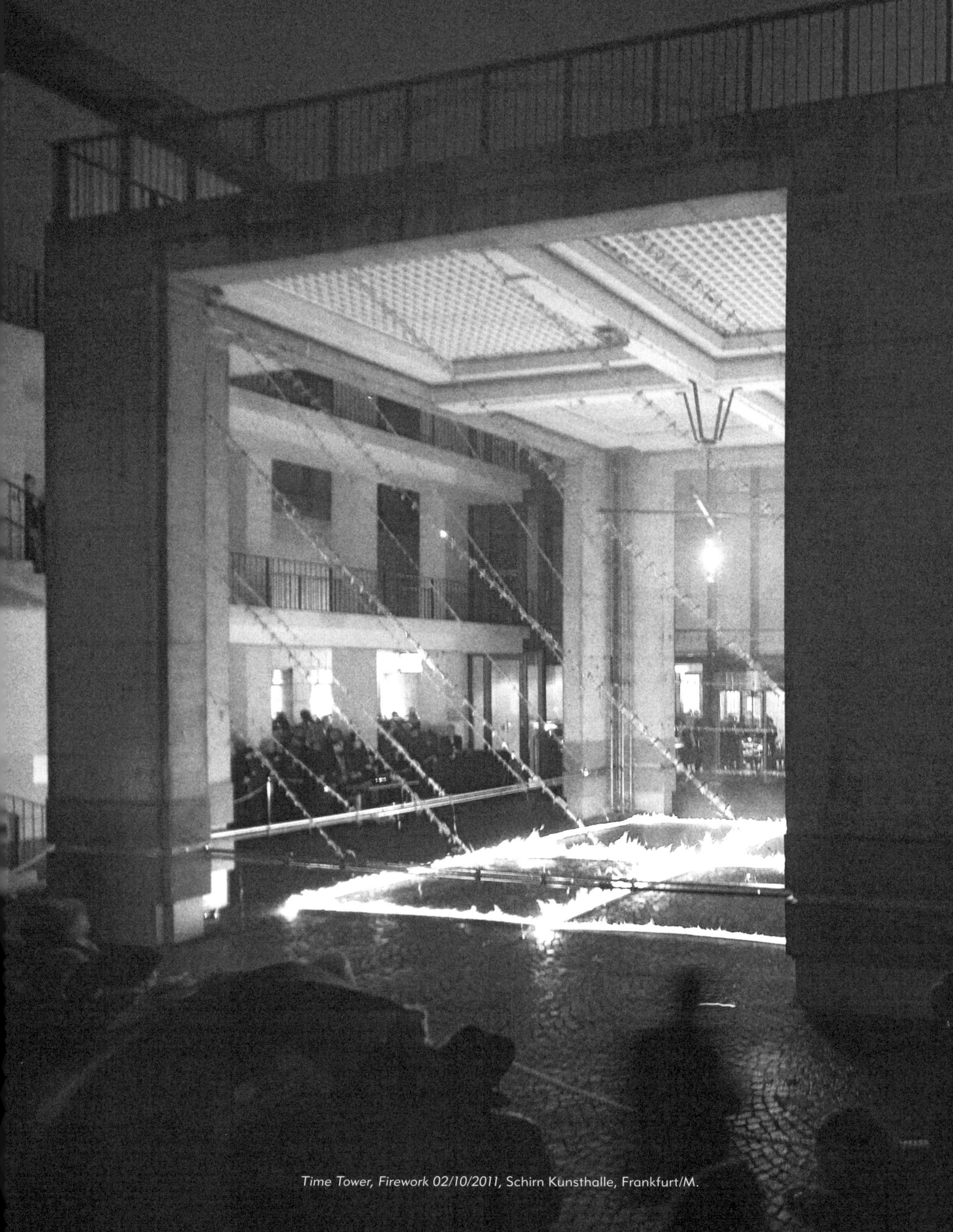

Time Tower, Firework 02/10/2011, Schirn Kunsthalle, Frankfurt/M.

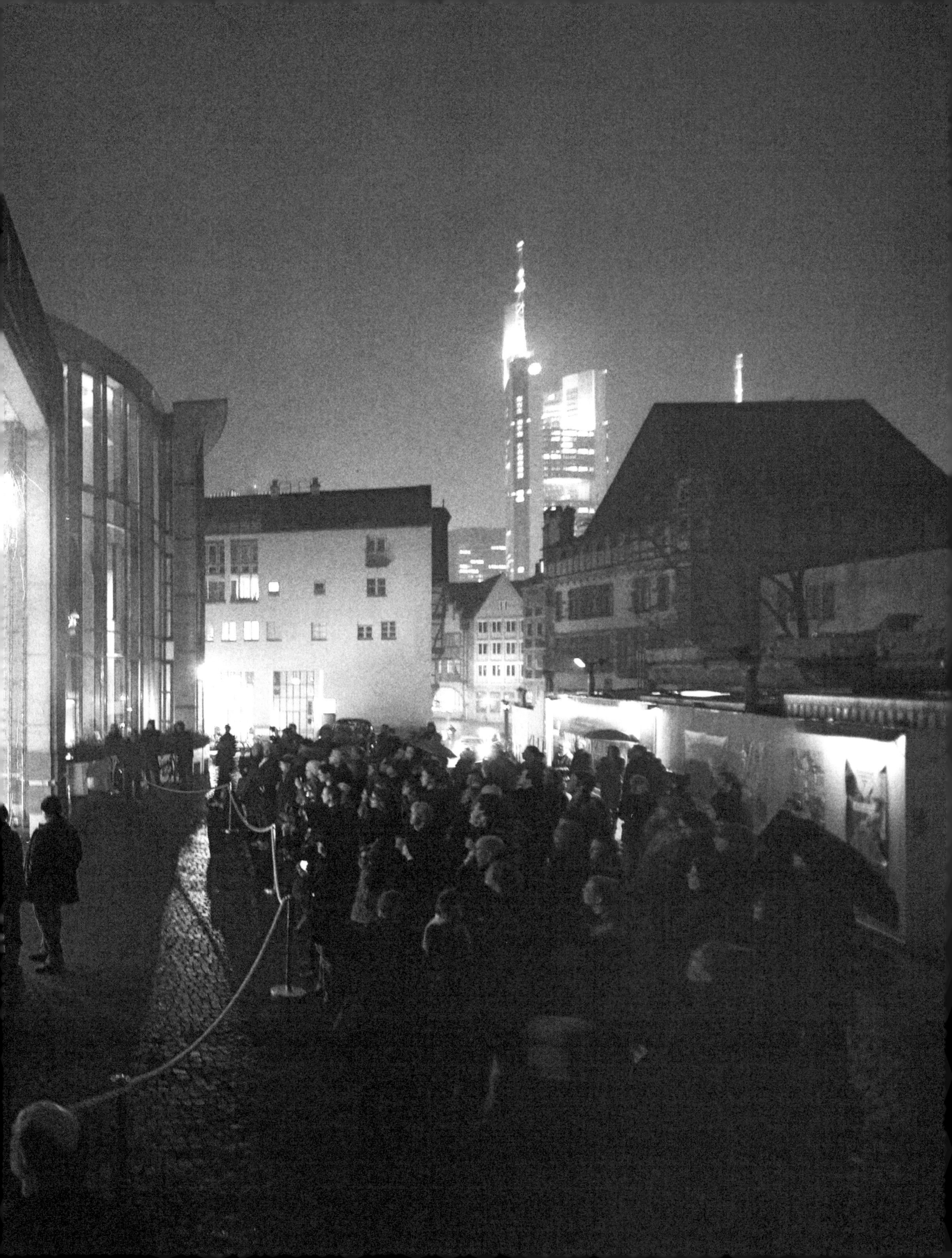

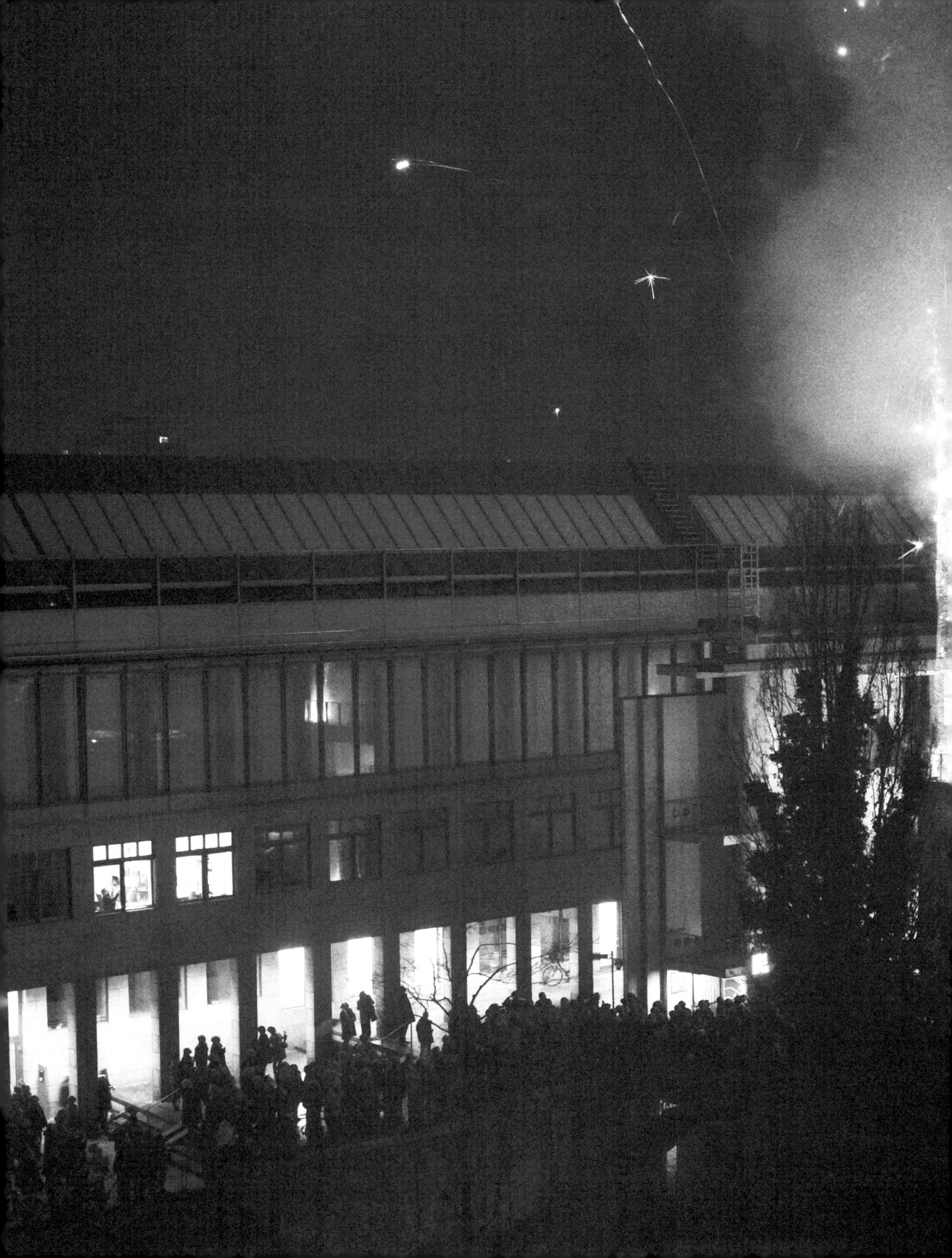

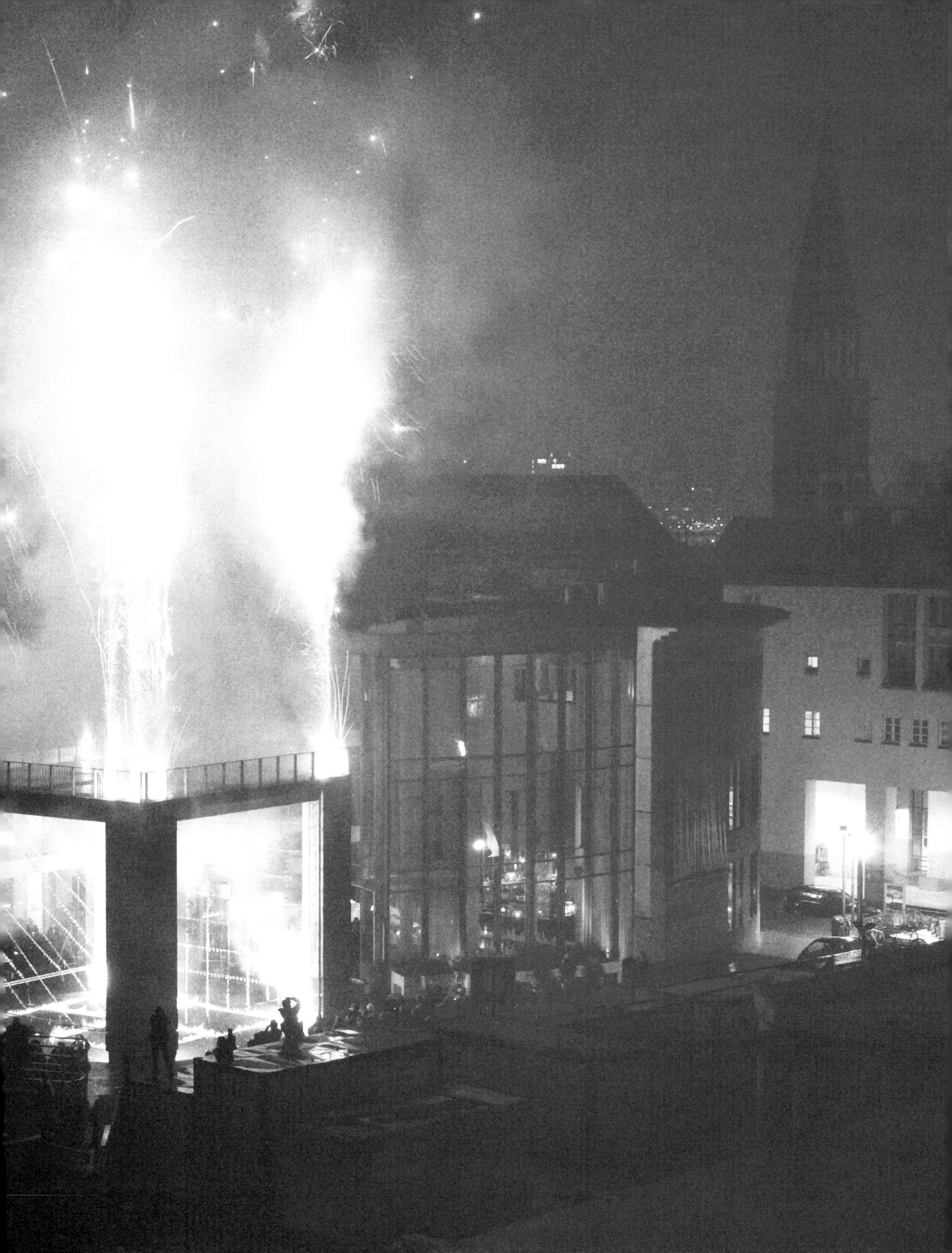

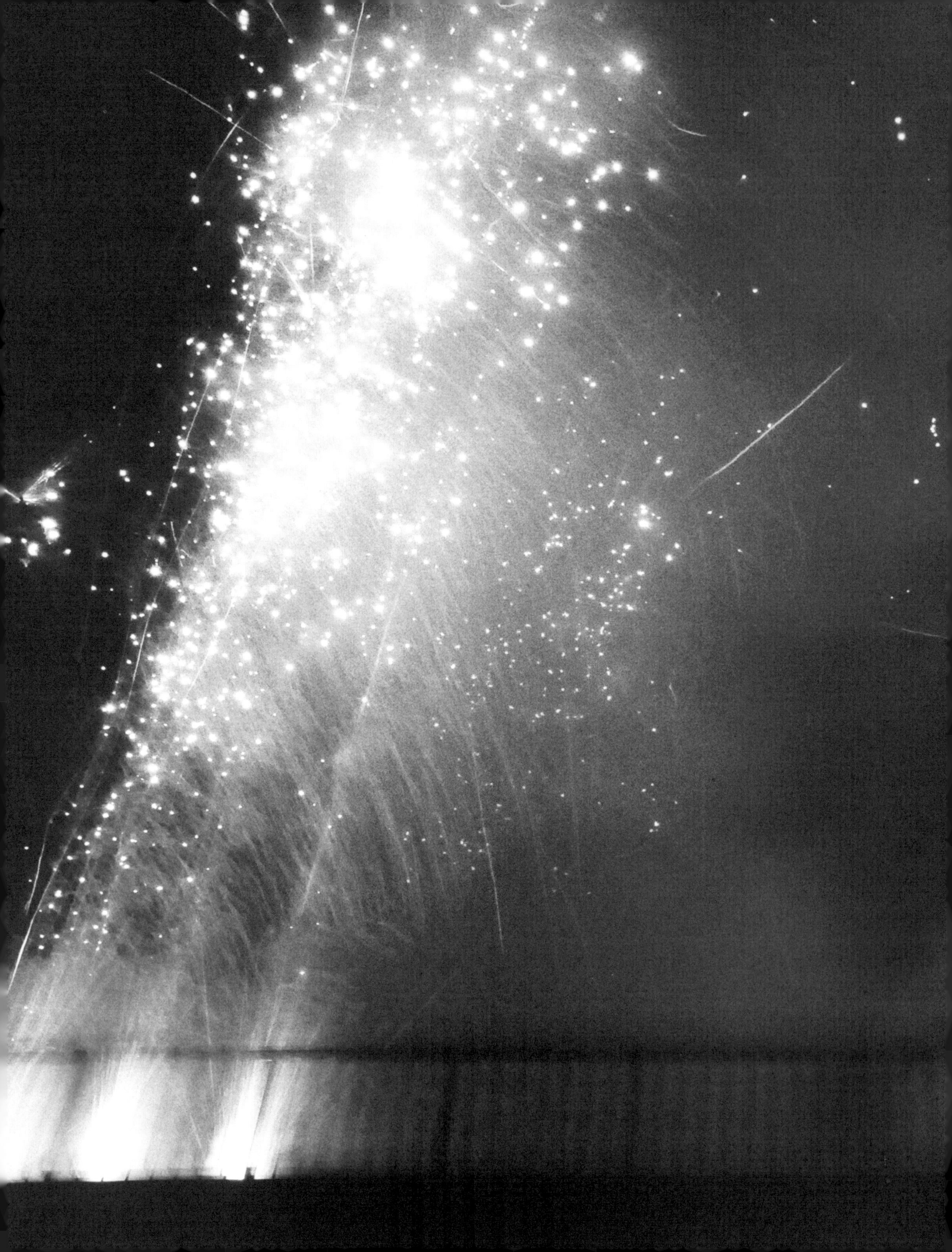

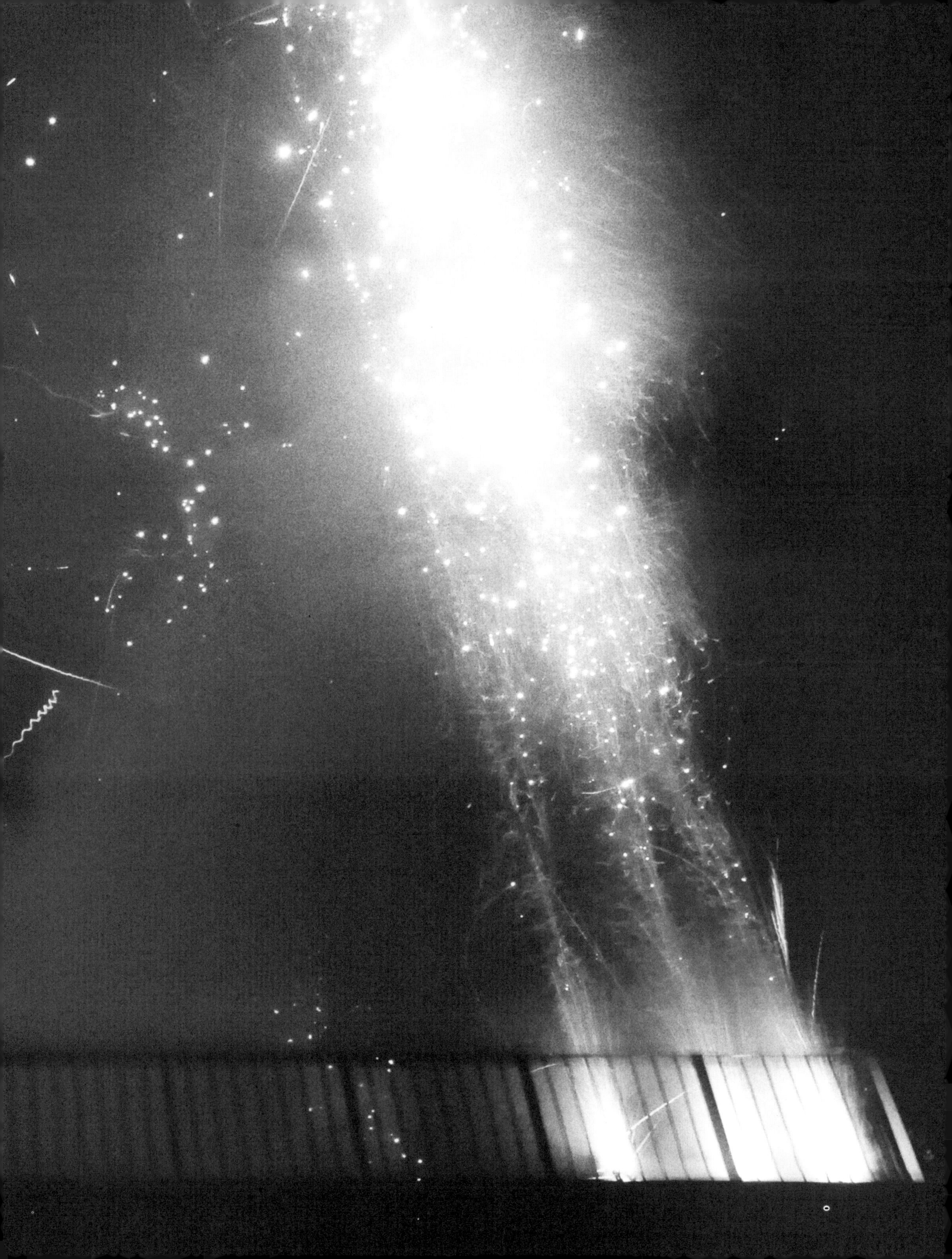

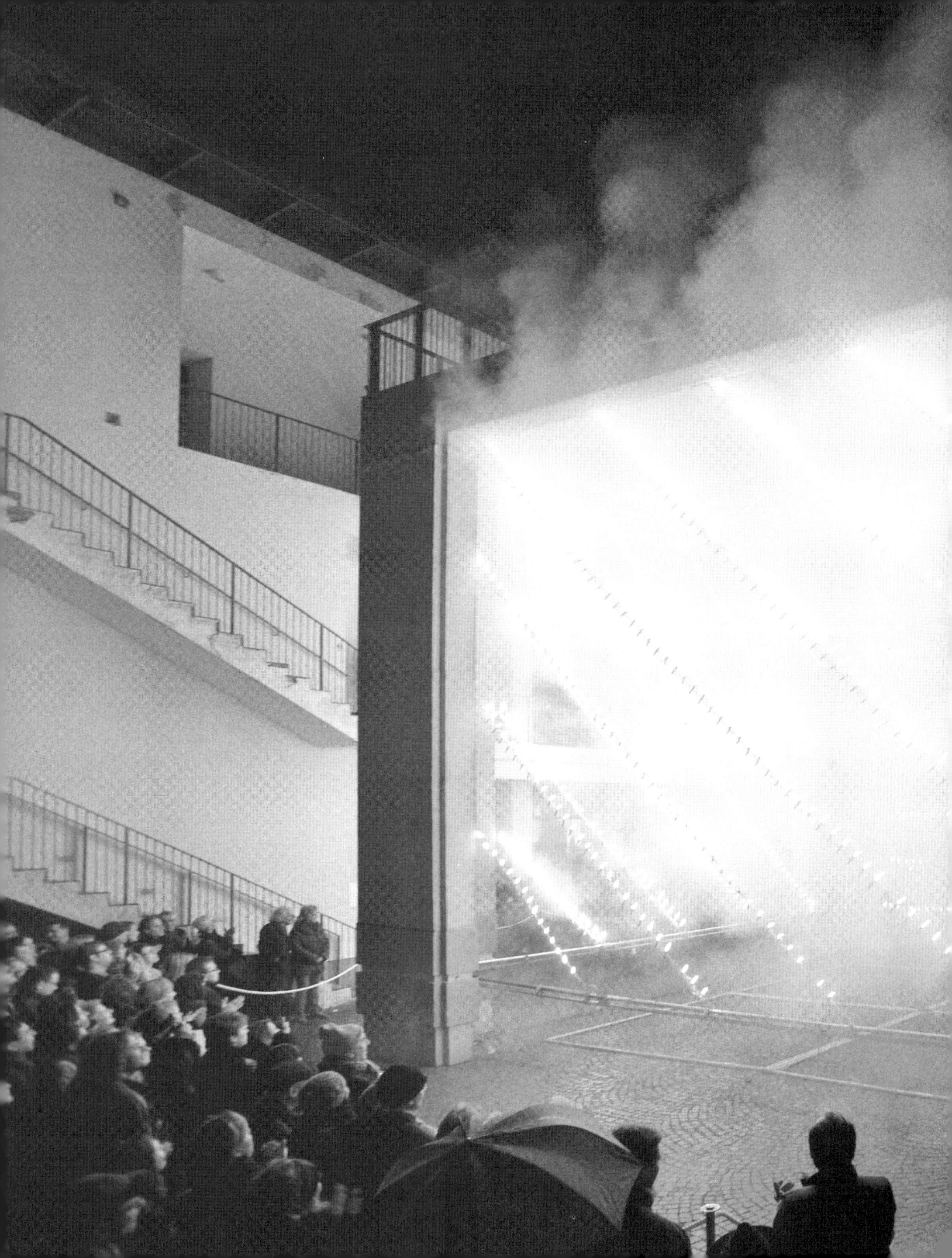

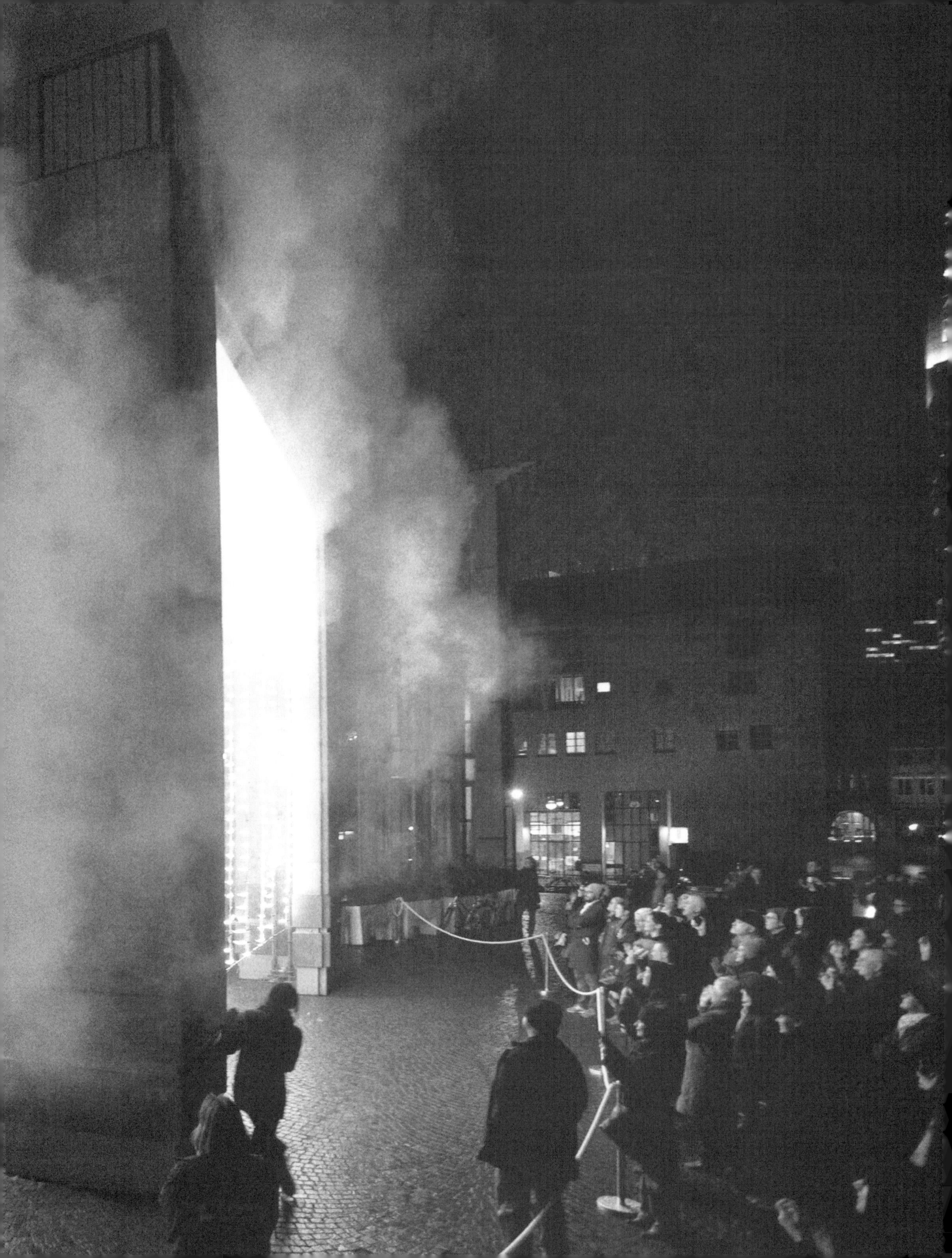

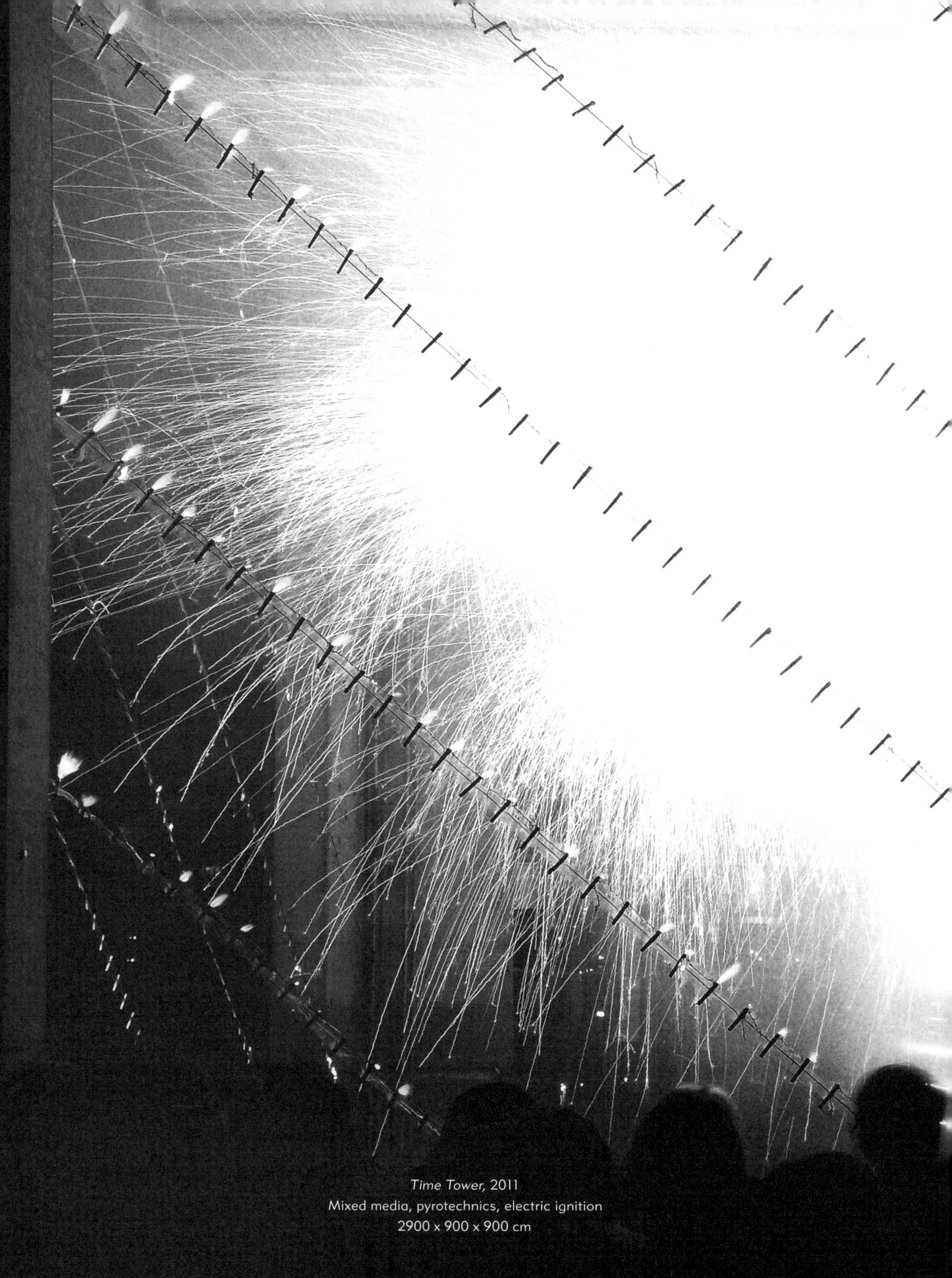

Time Tower, 2011
Mixed media, pyrotechnics, electric ignition
2900 x 900 x 900 cm

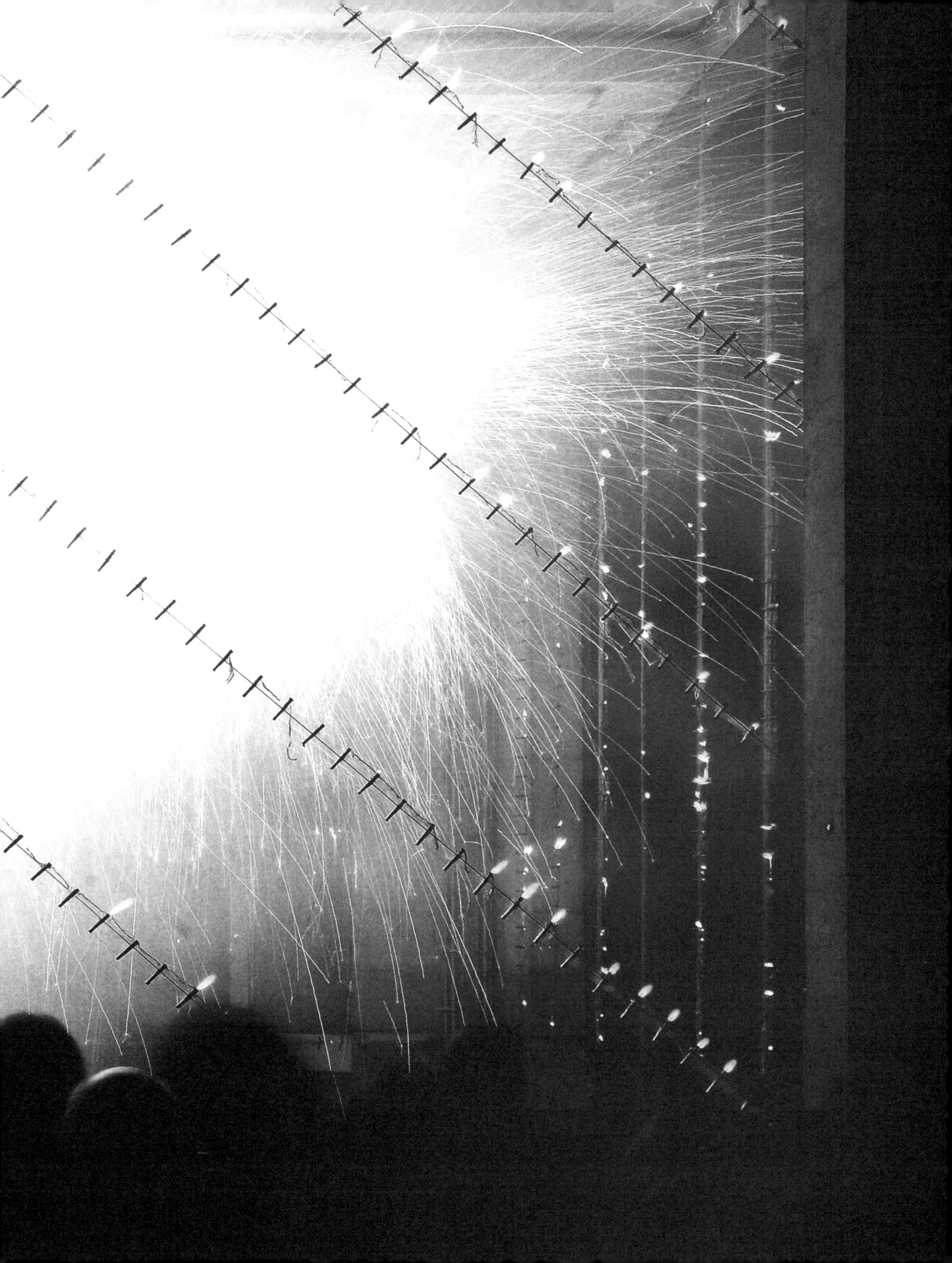

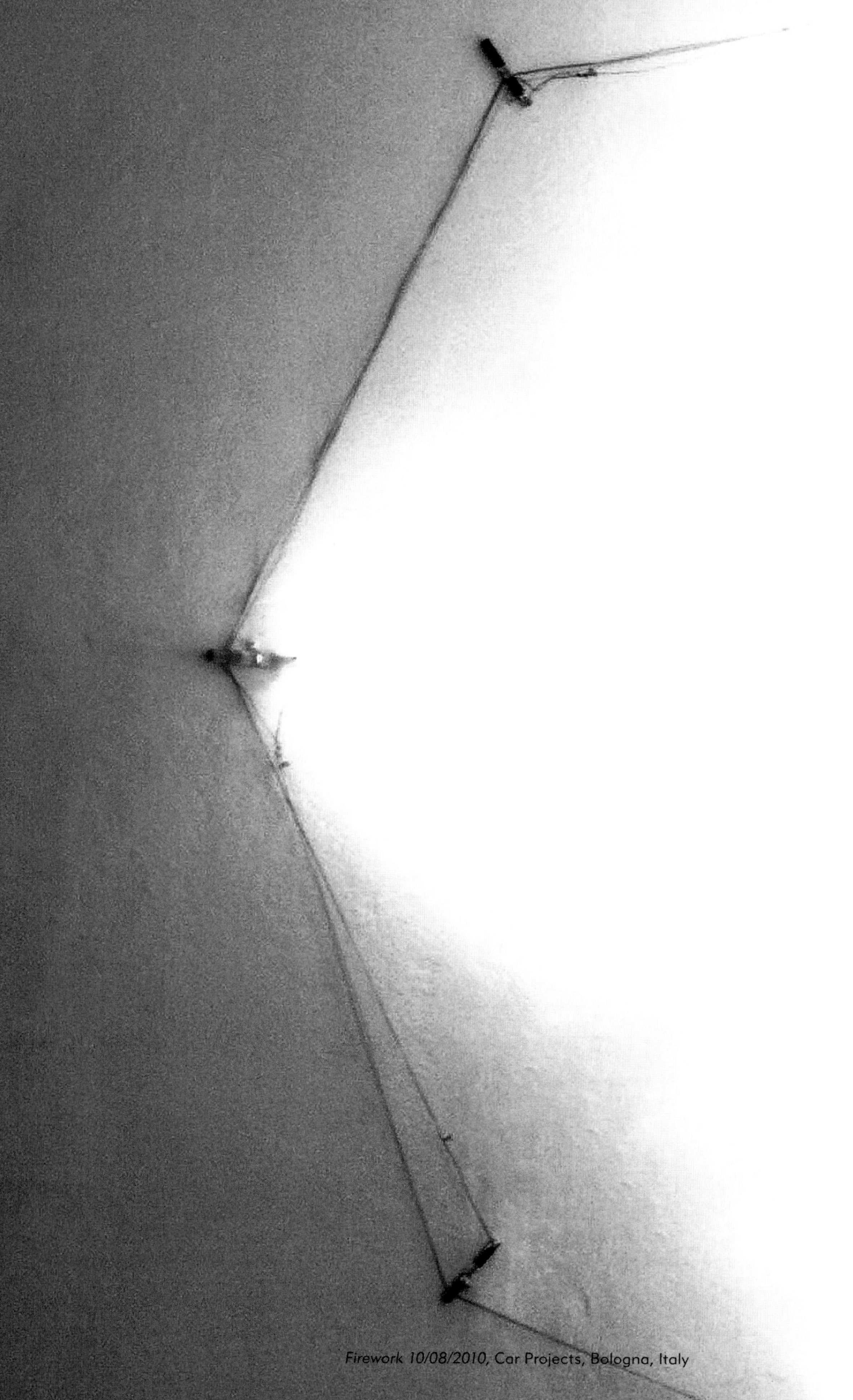

Firework 10/08/2010, Car Projects, Bologna, Italy

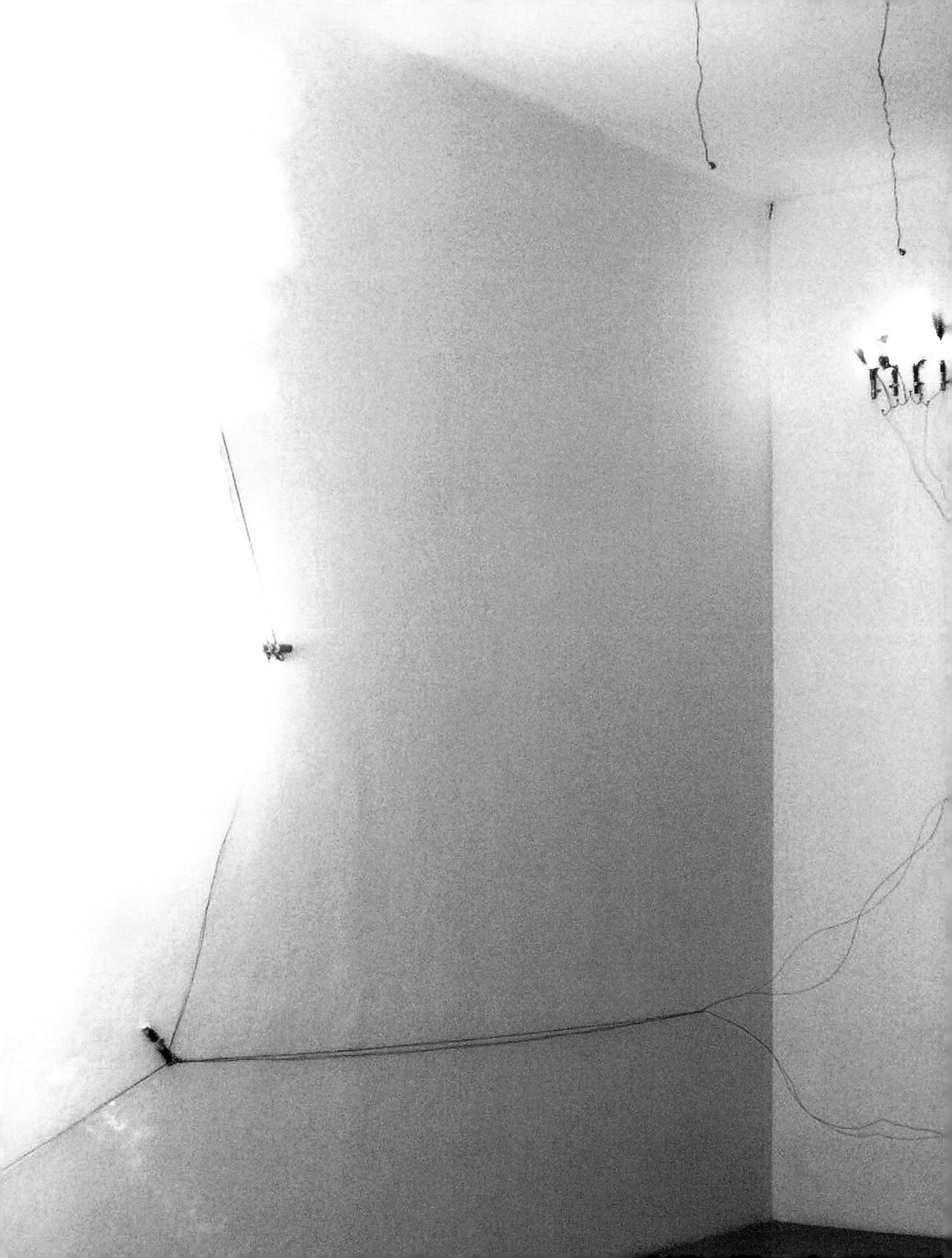

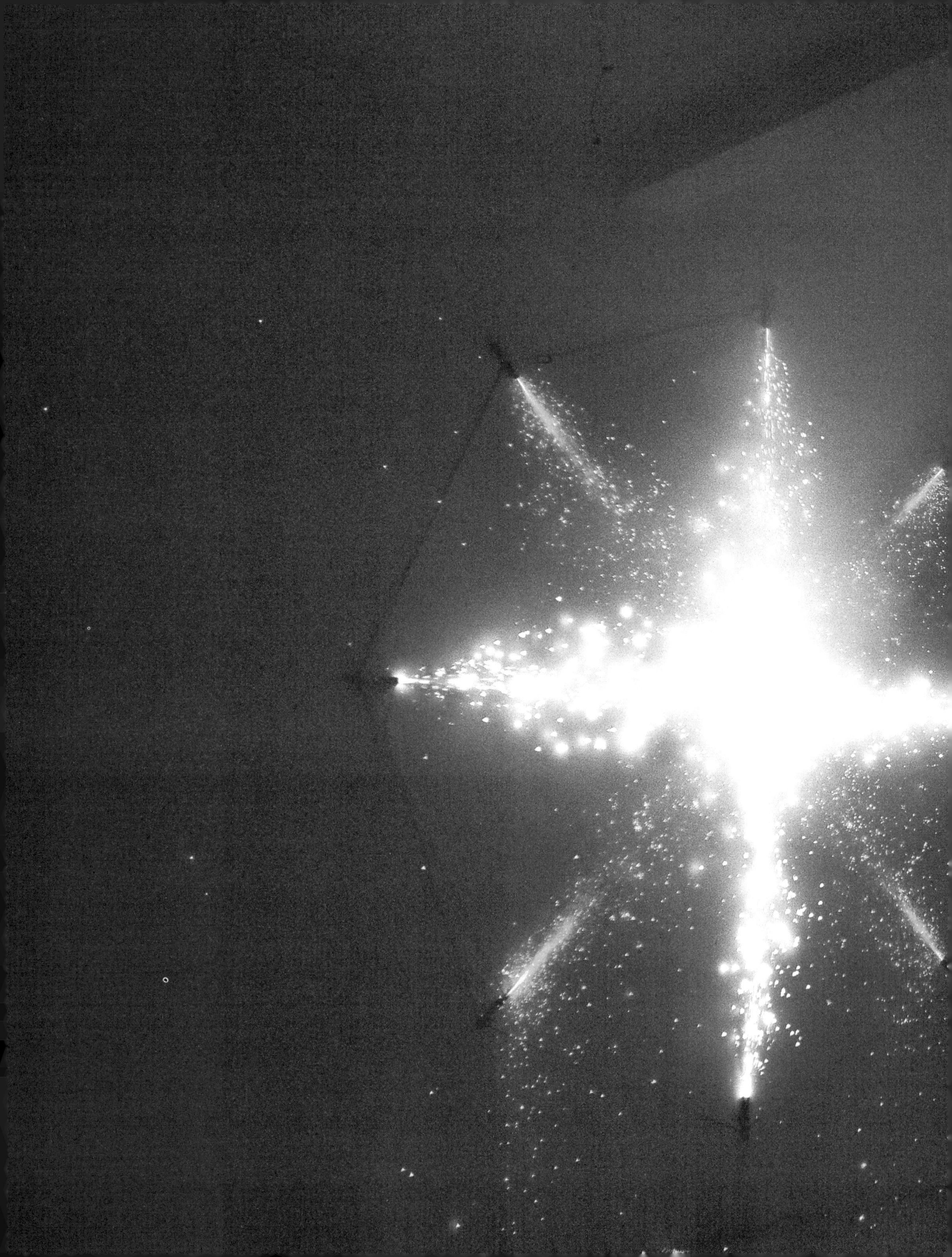

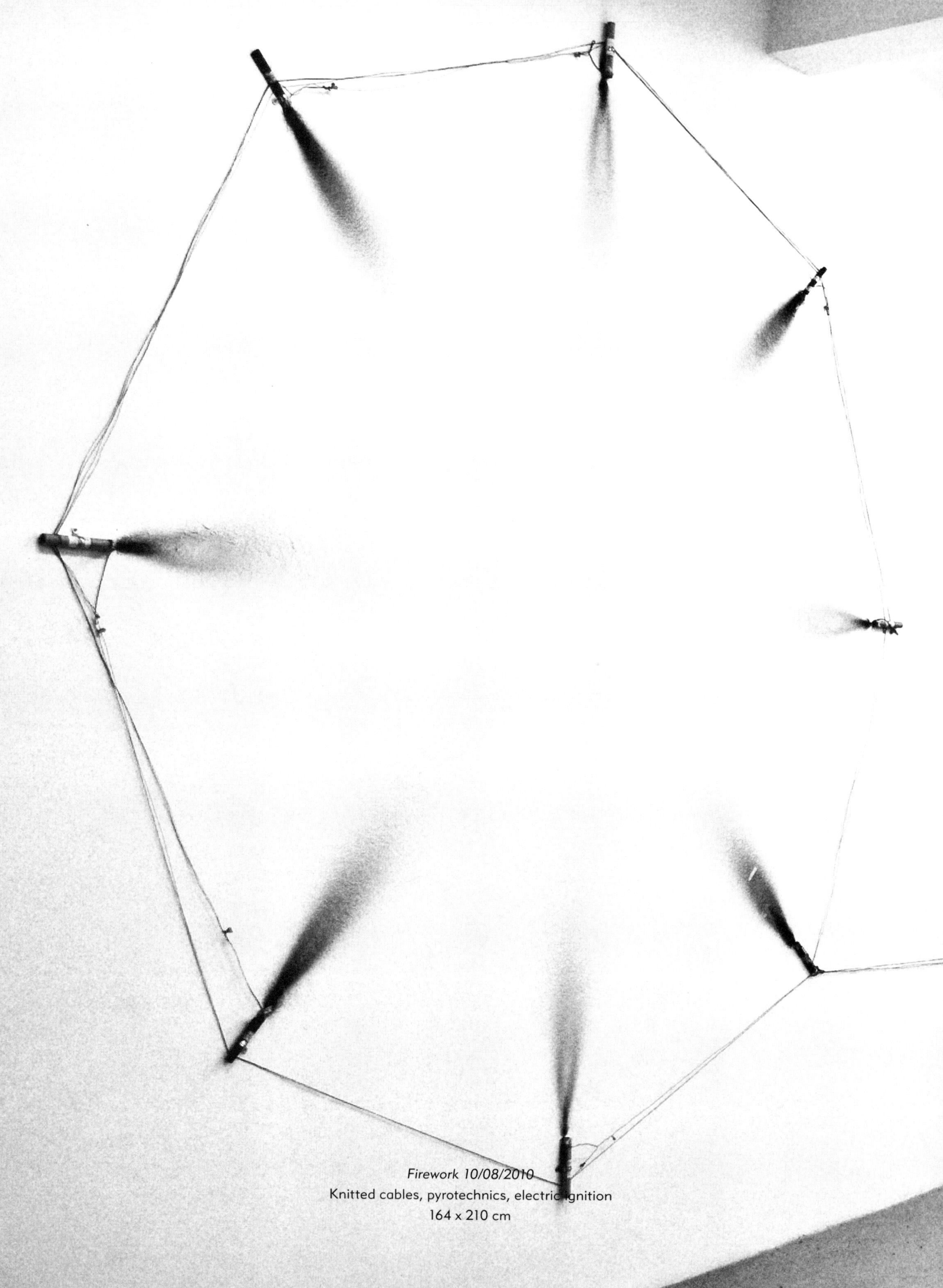

Firework 10/08/2010
Knitted cables, pyrotechnics, electric ignition
164 x 210 cm

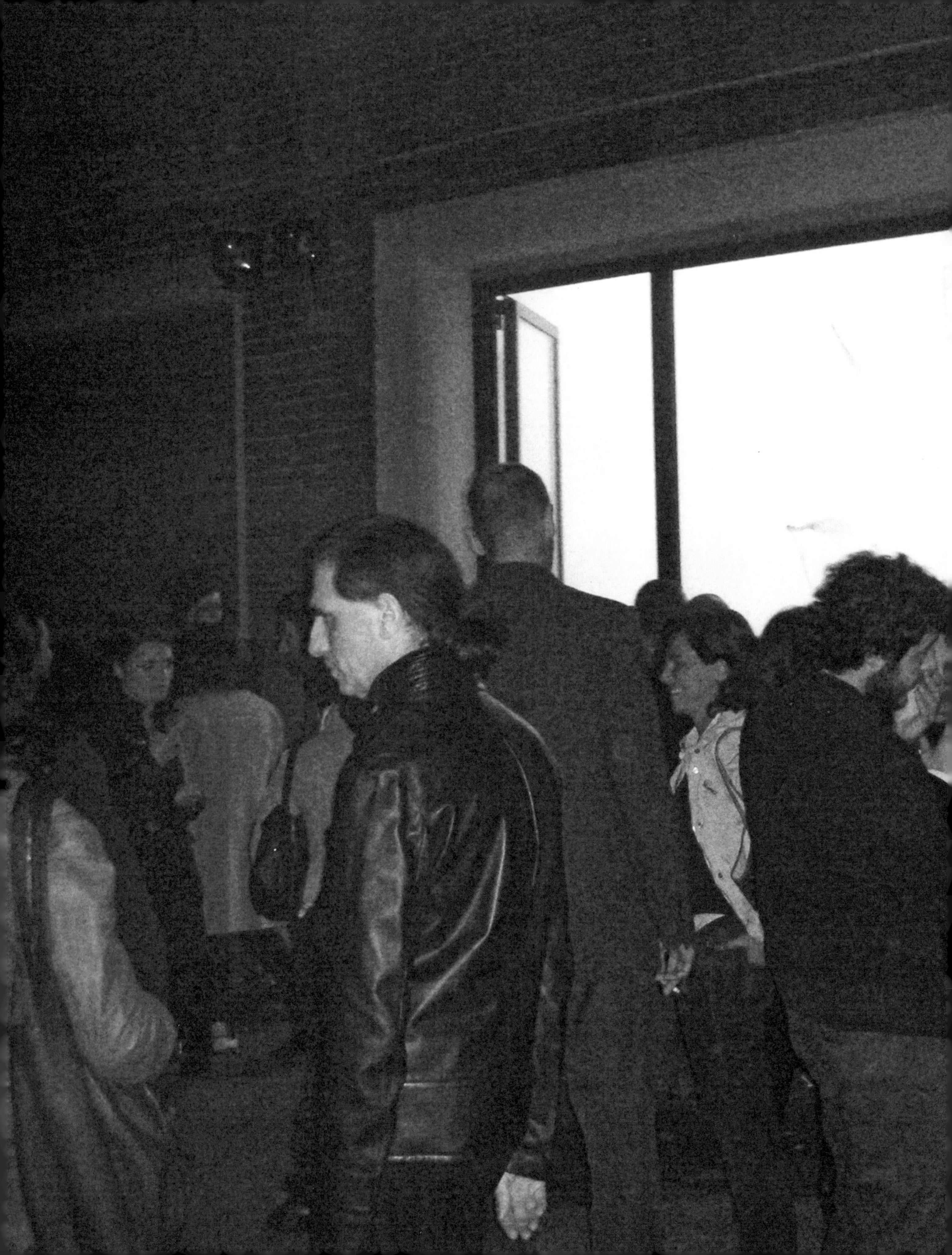

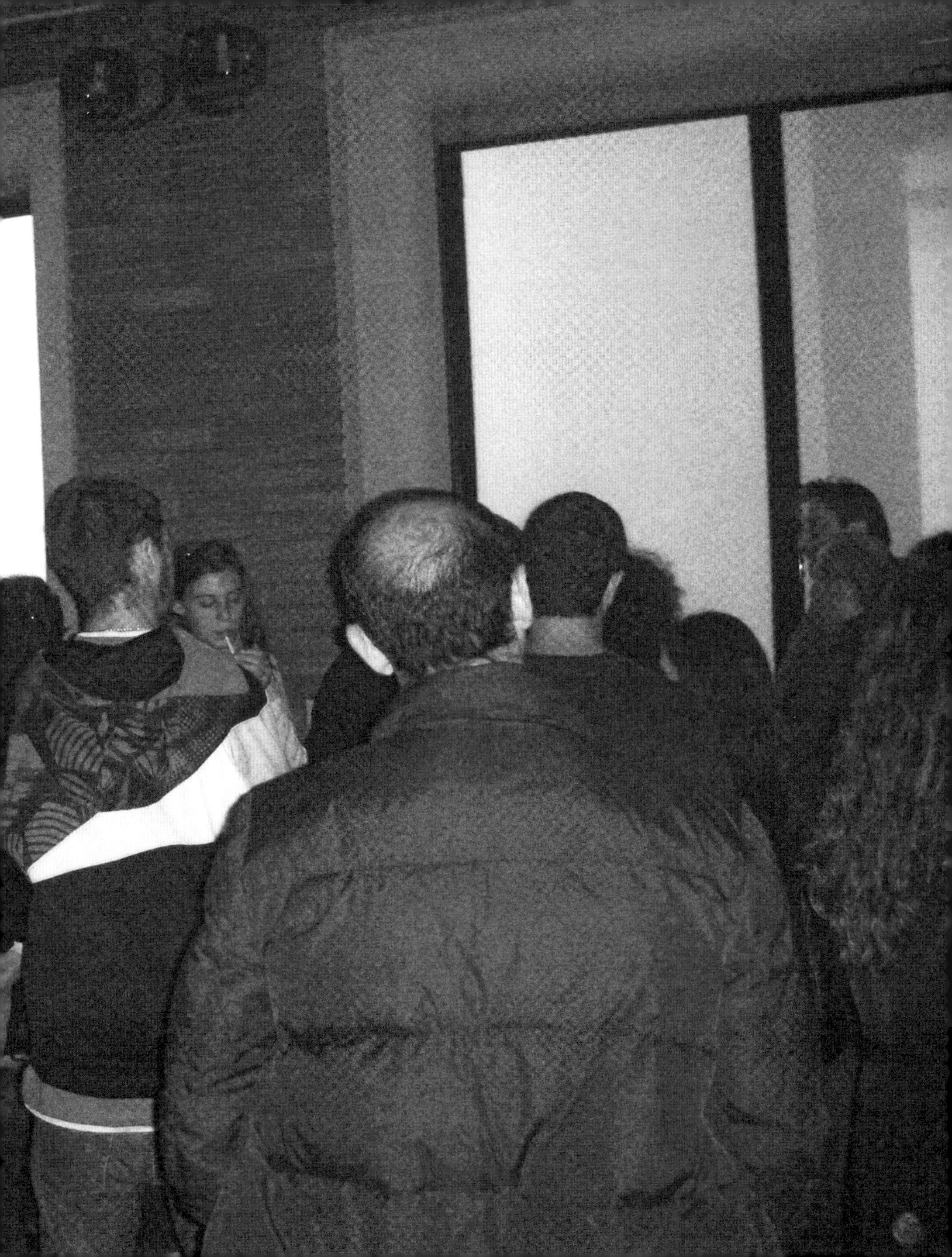

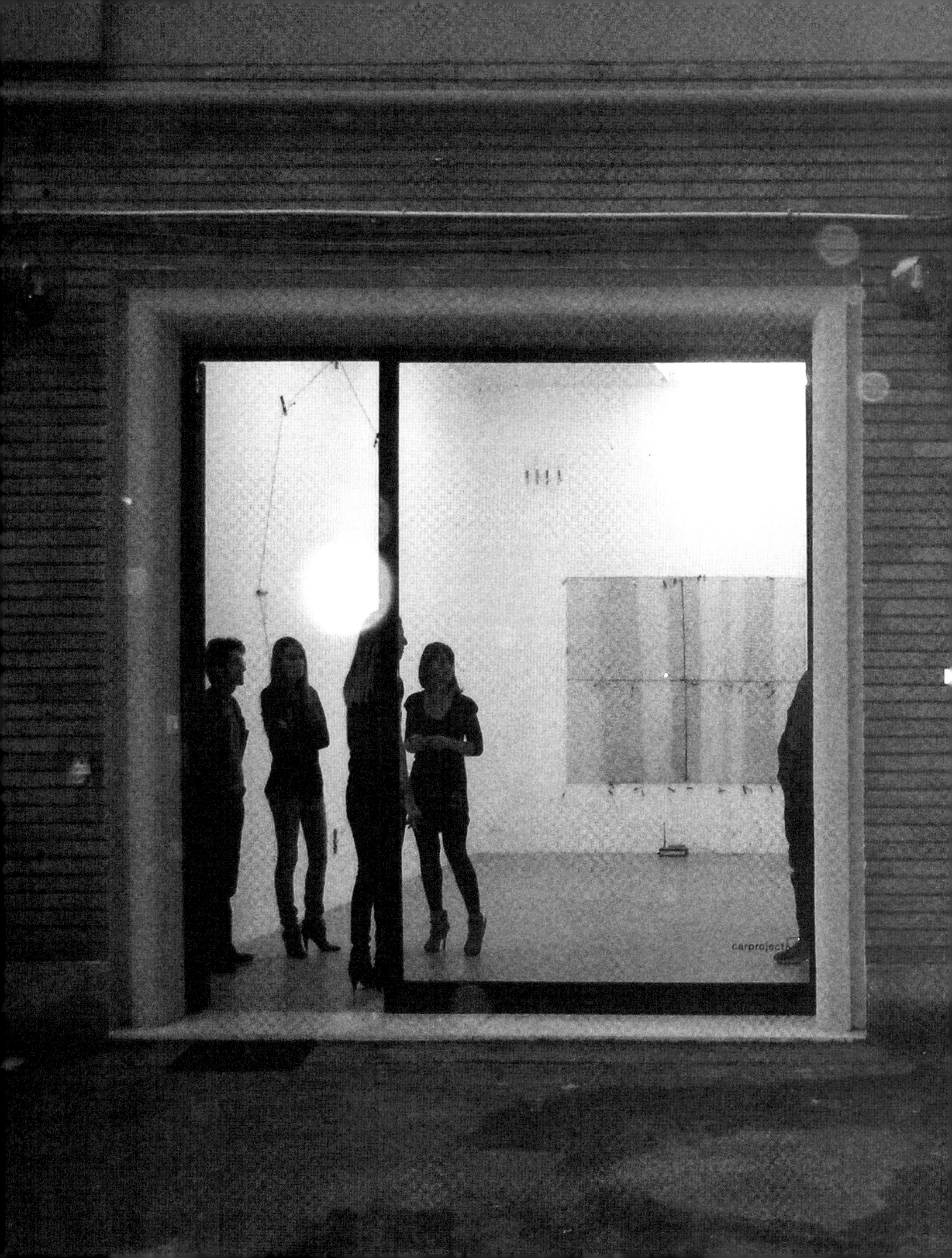

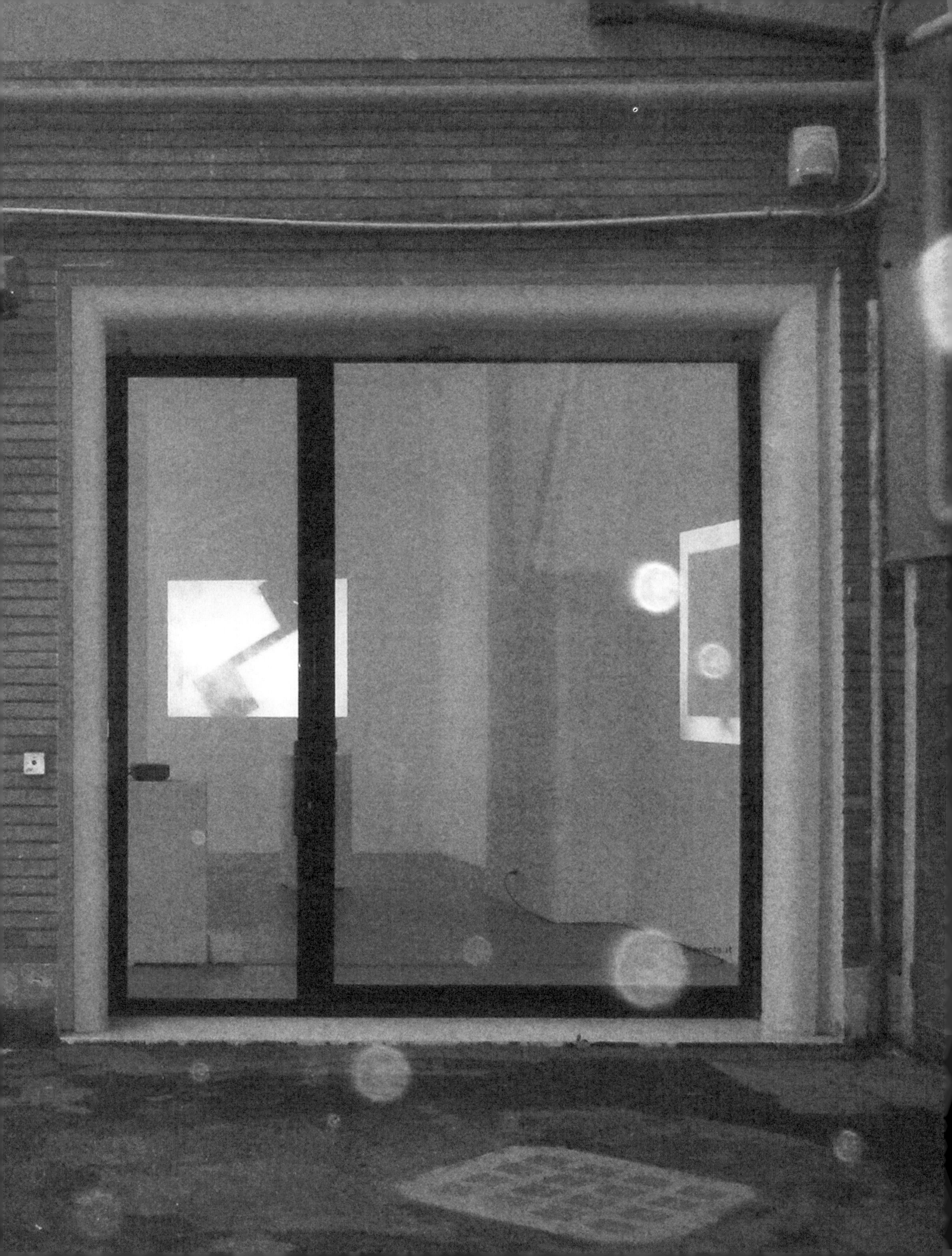

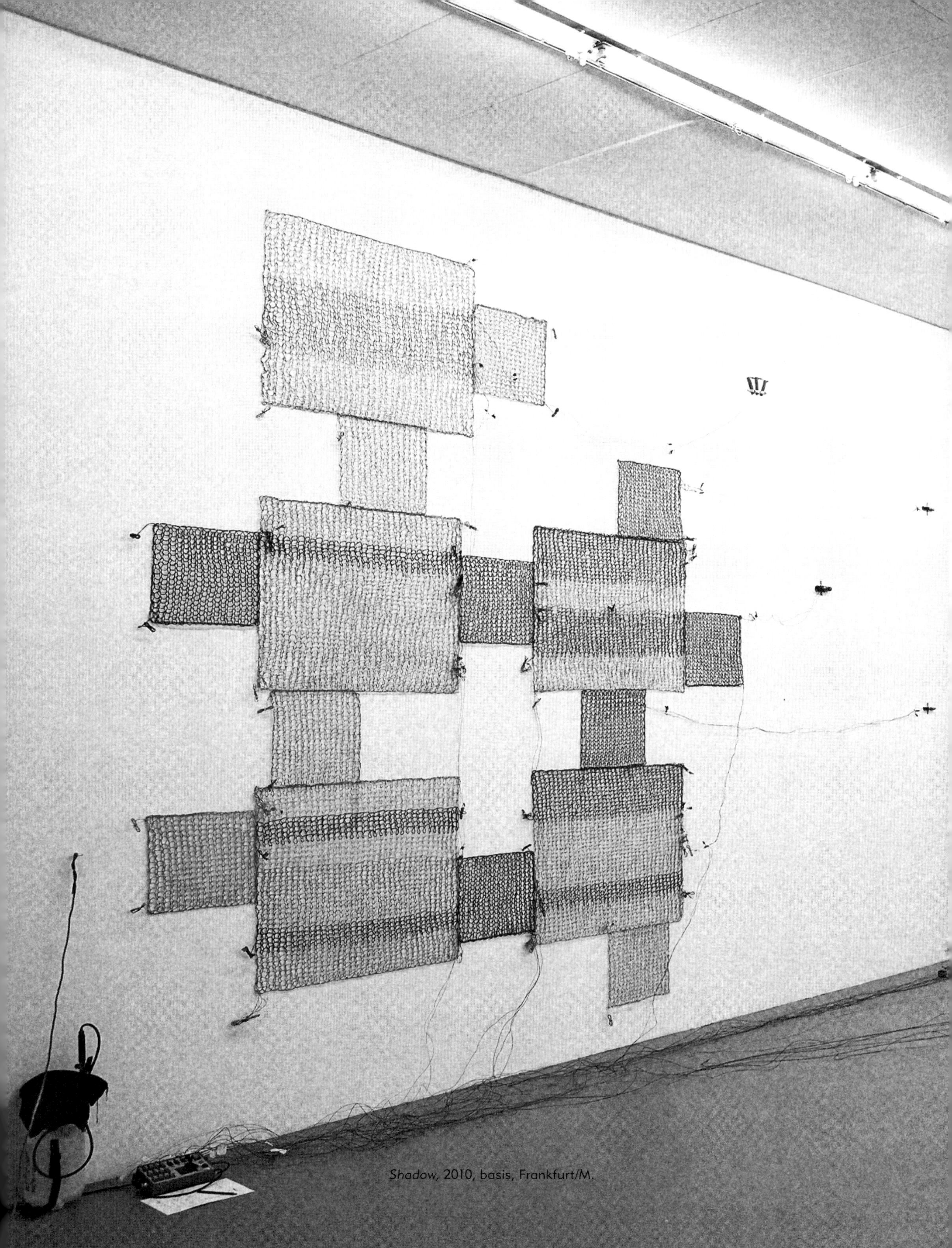

Shadow, 2010, basis, Frankfurt/M.

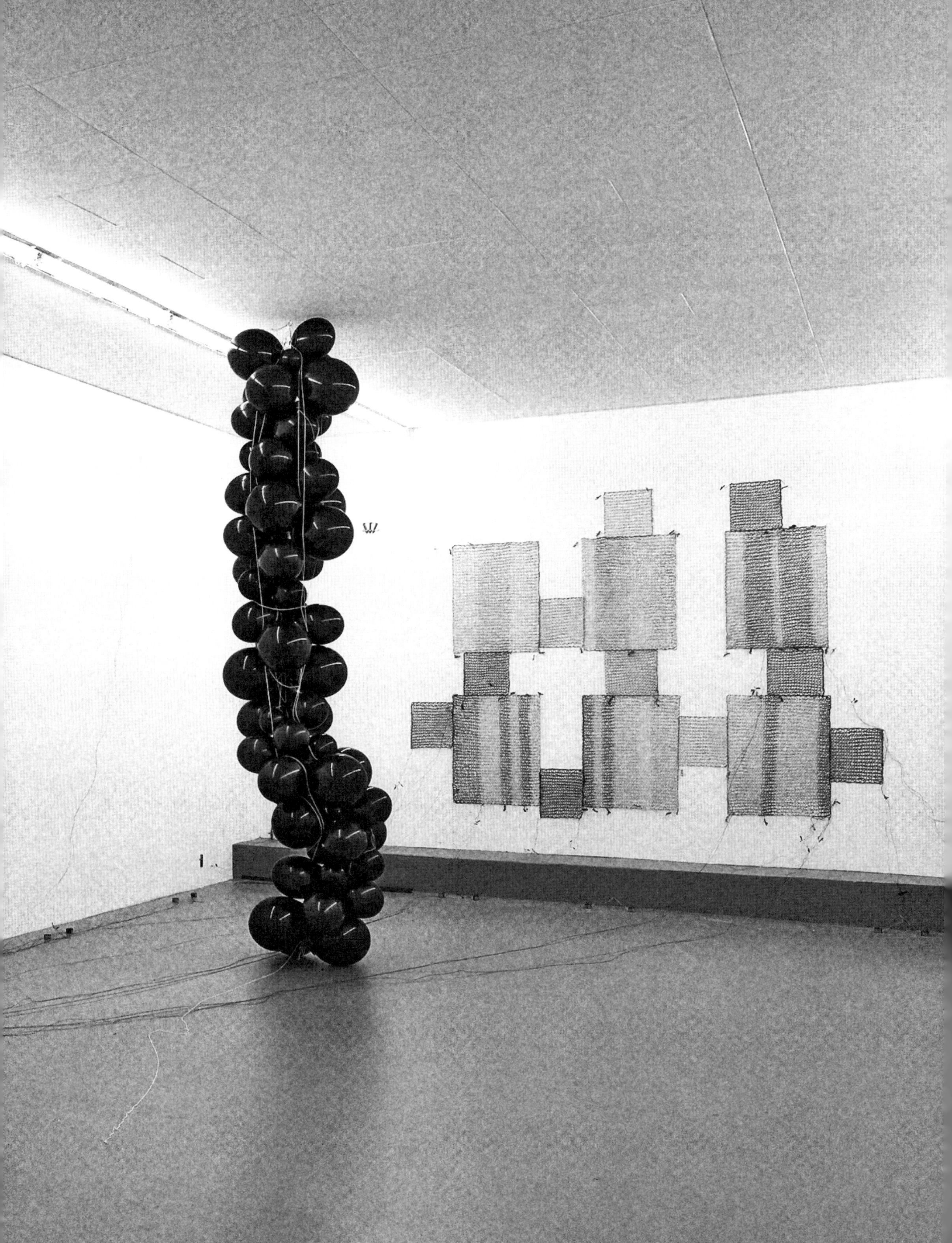

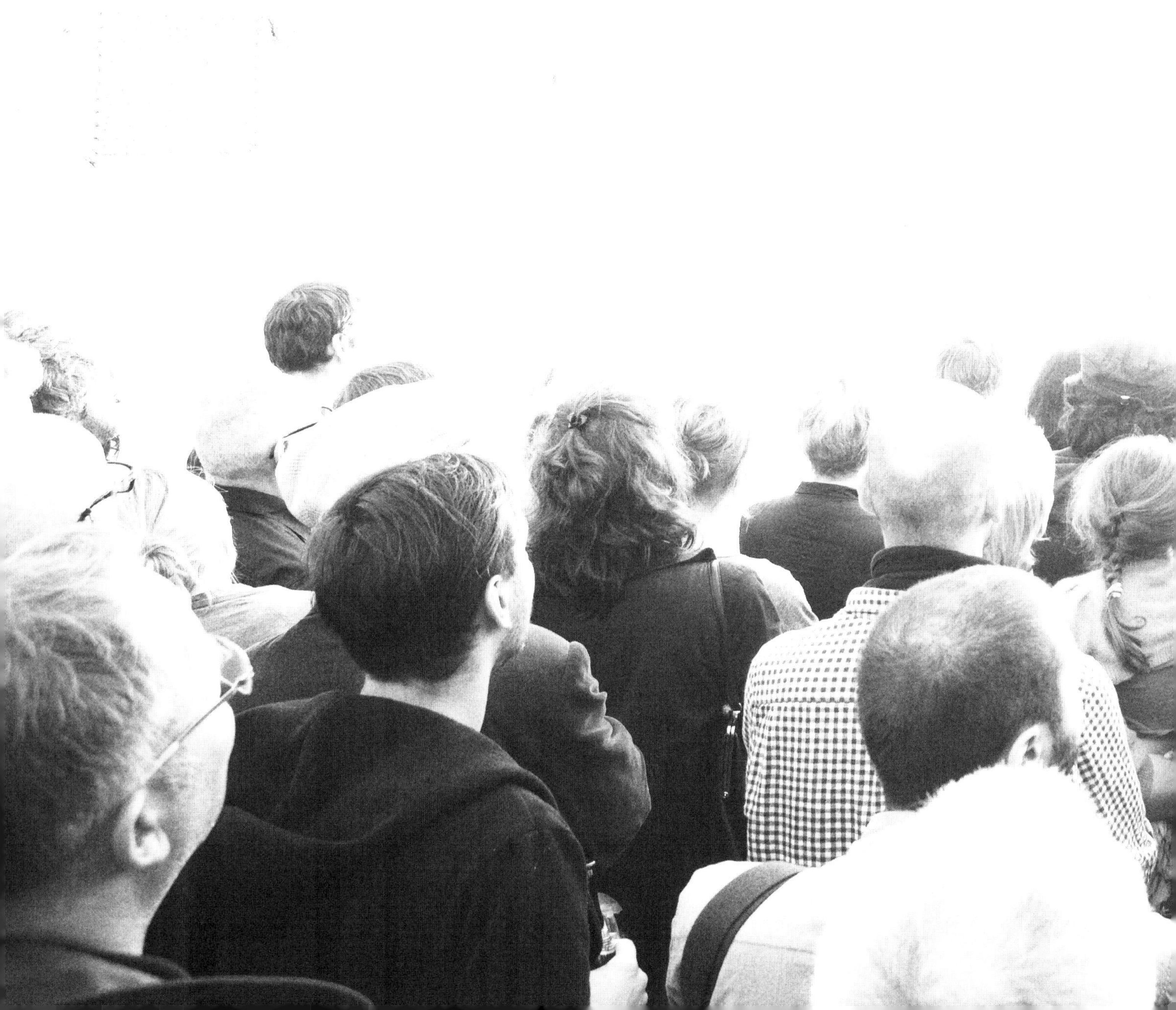

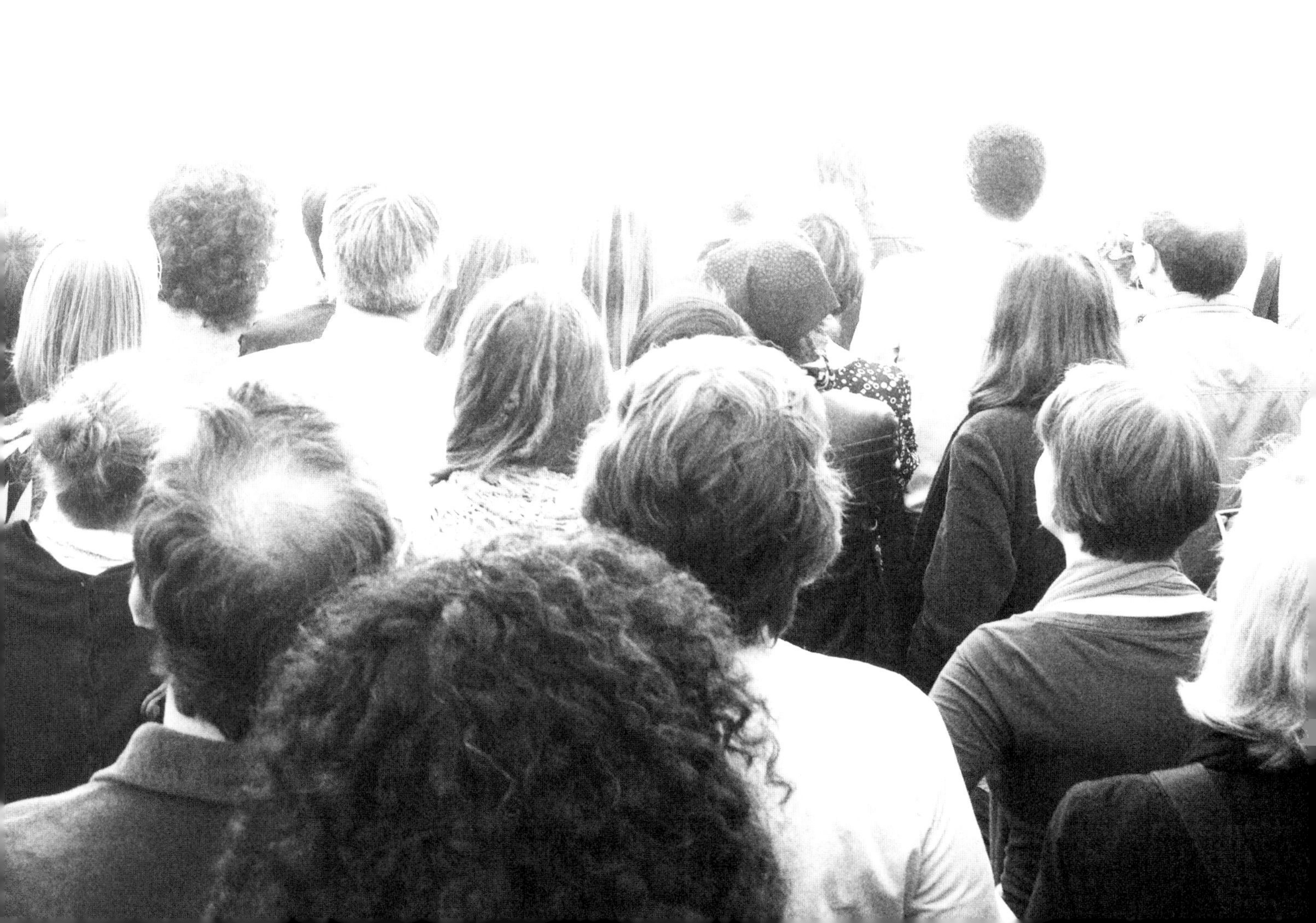

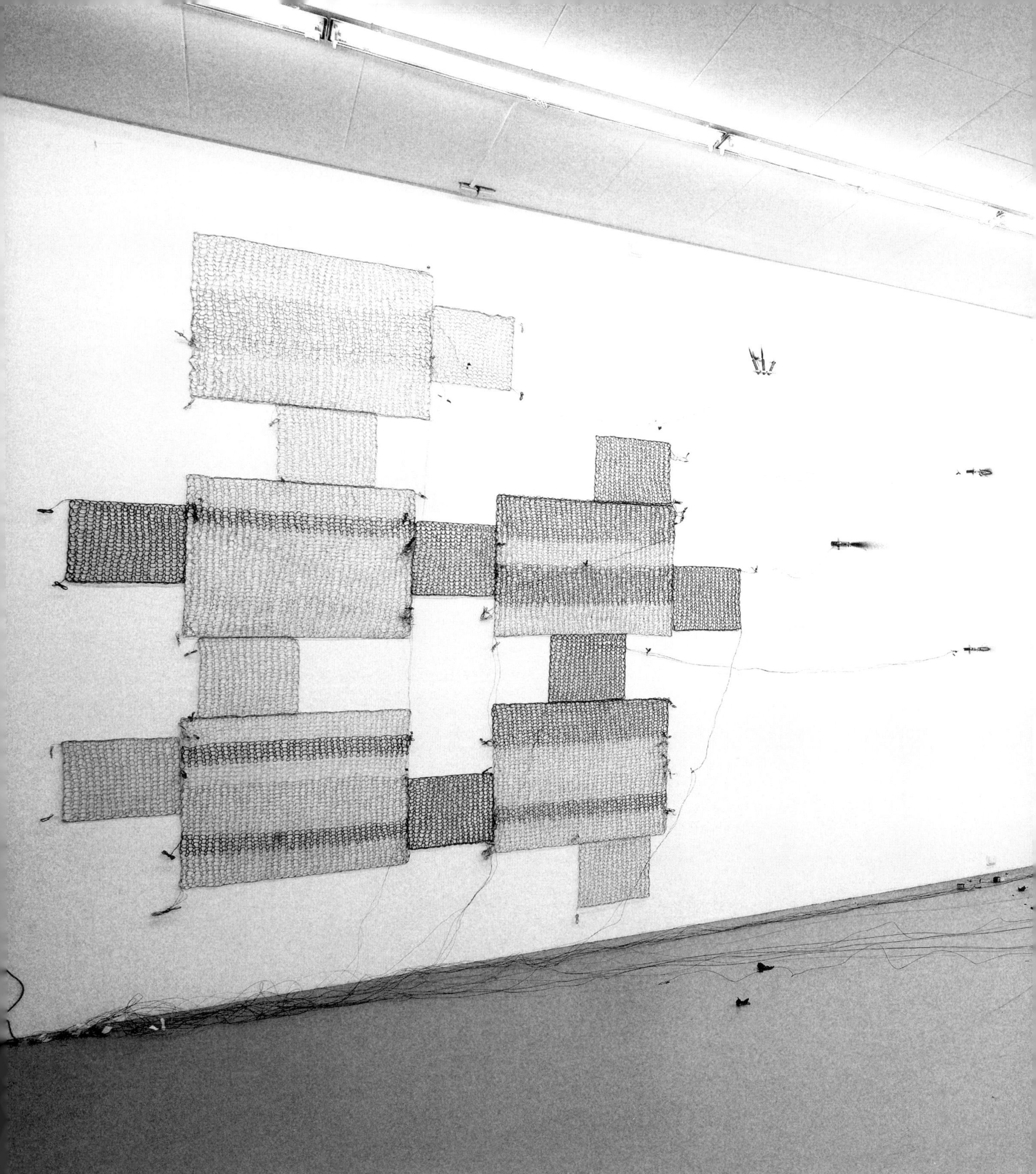

Shadow, 2010
Knitted cables, pyrotechnics, electric ignition
dimensions variable

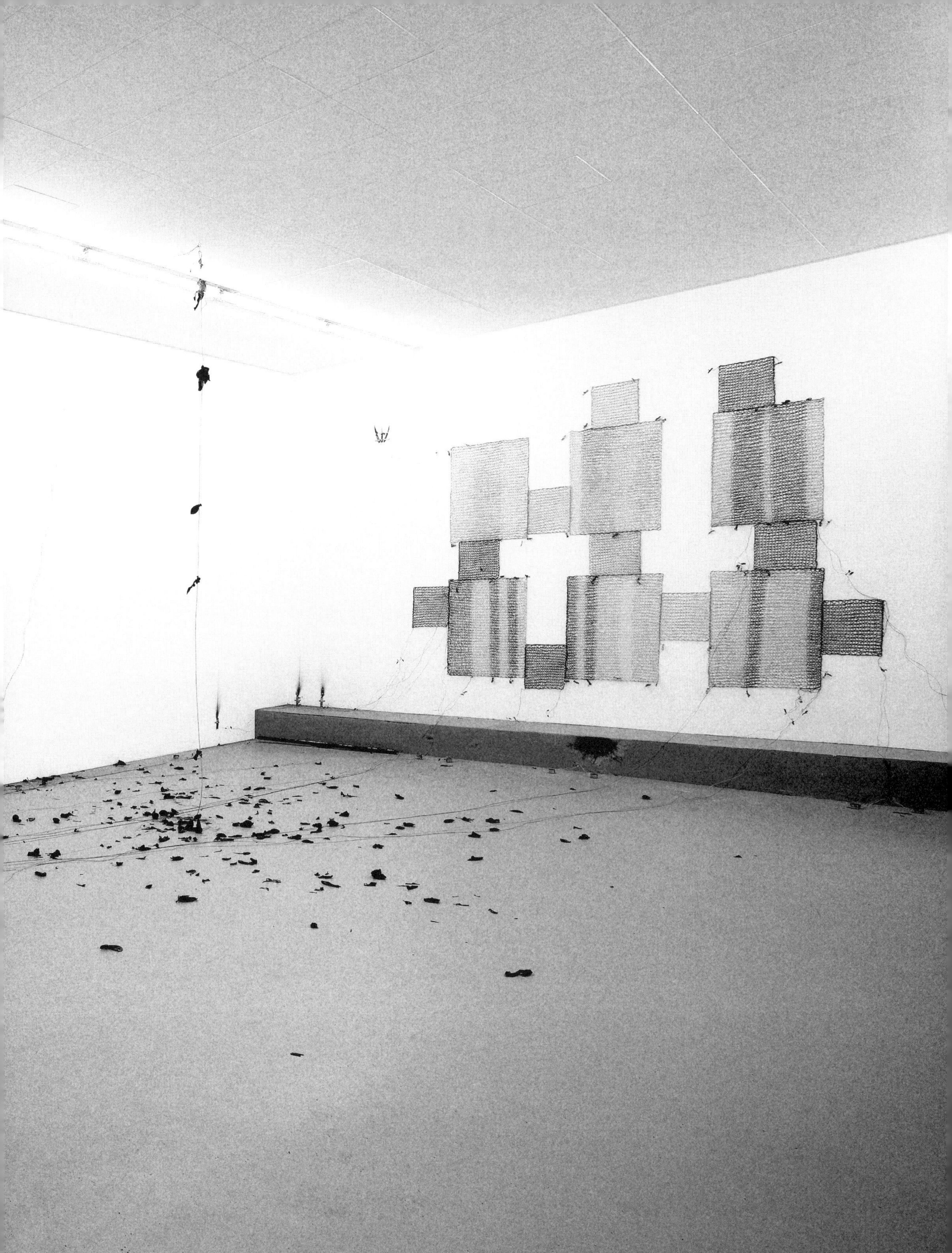

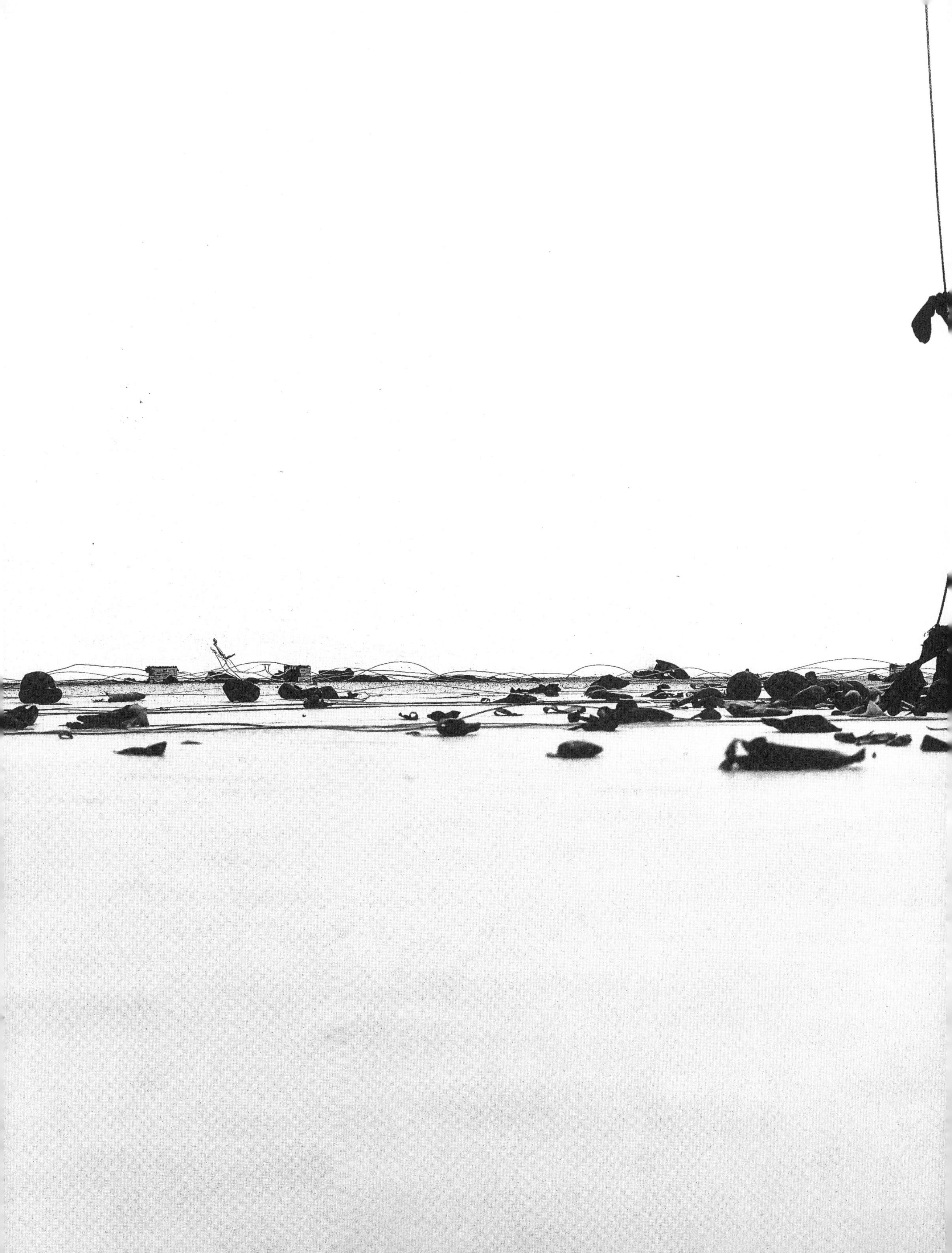

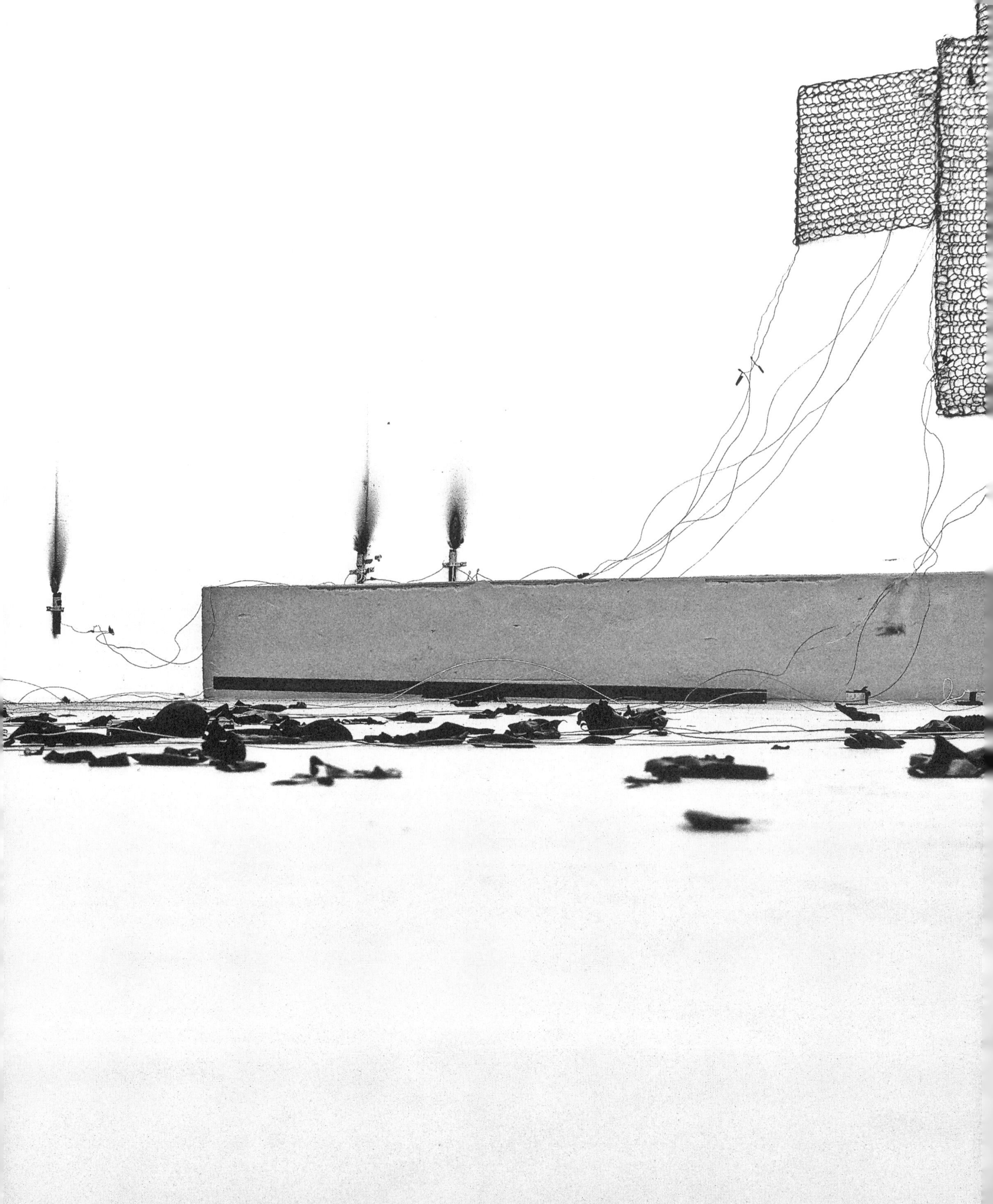

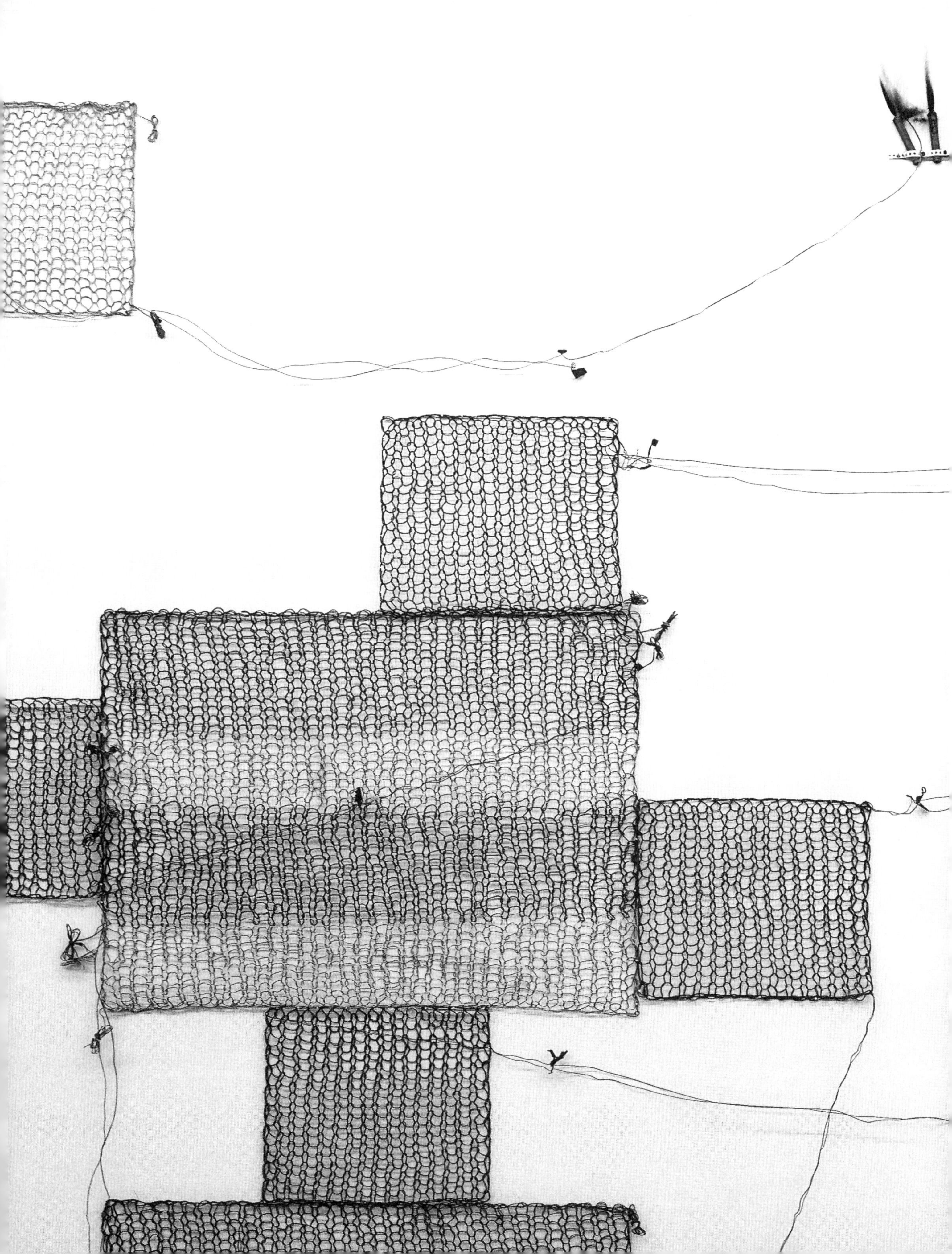

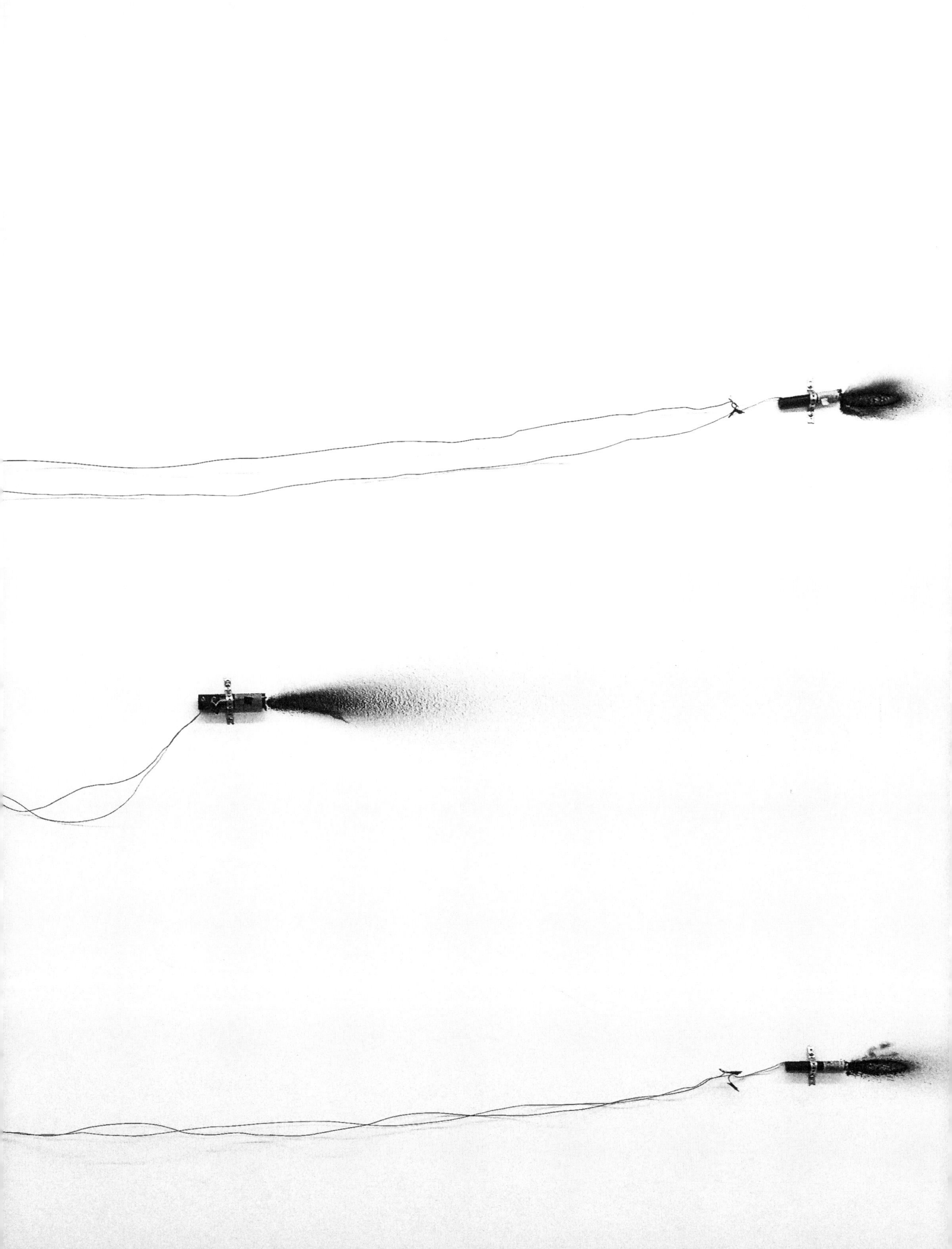

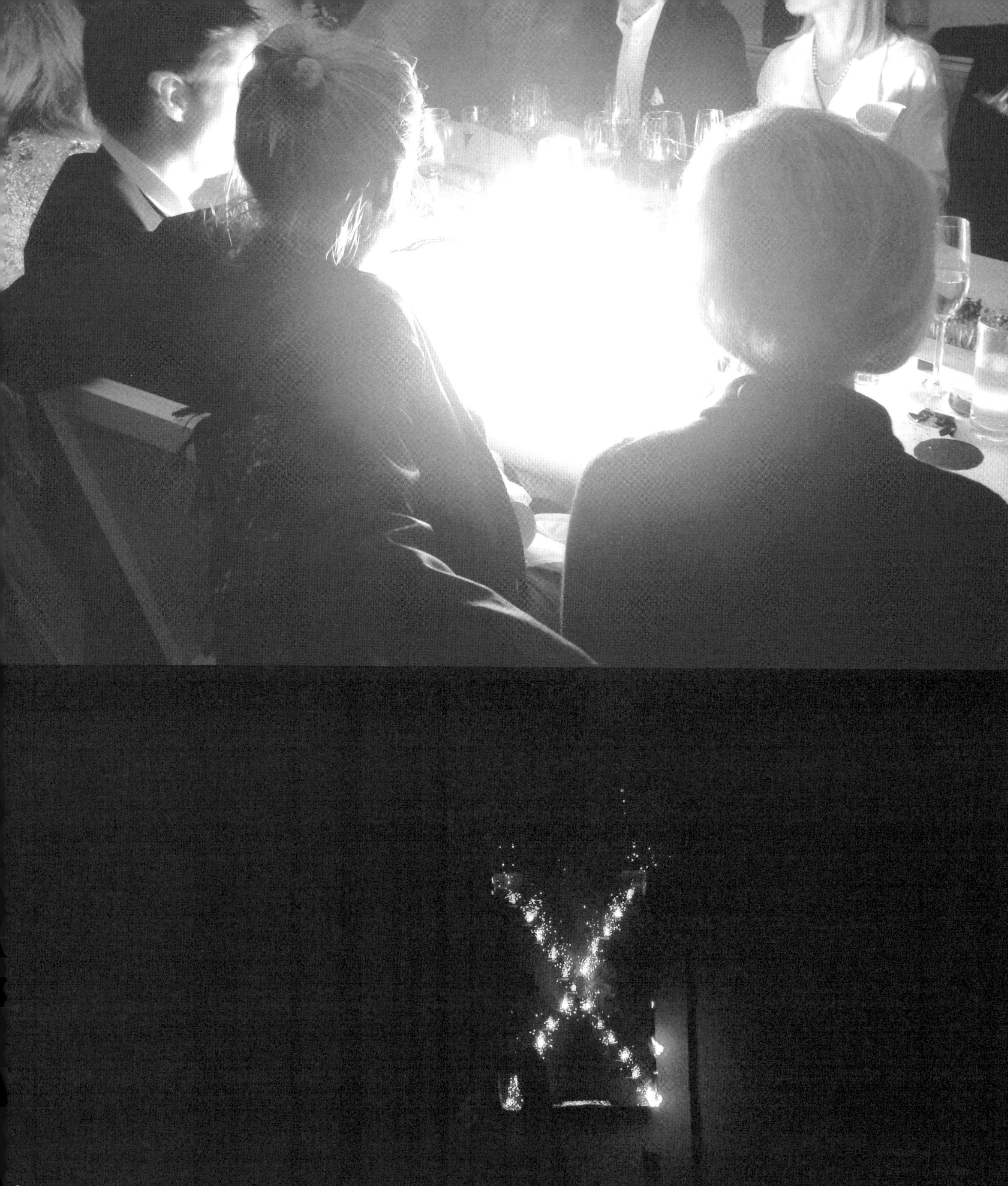

Firework 06/02/2010
Kunstverein Assenheim and Ursula Blickle Stiftung, Assenheim

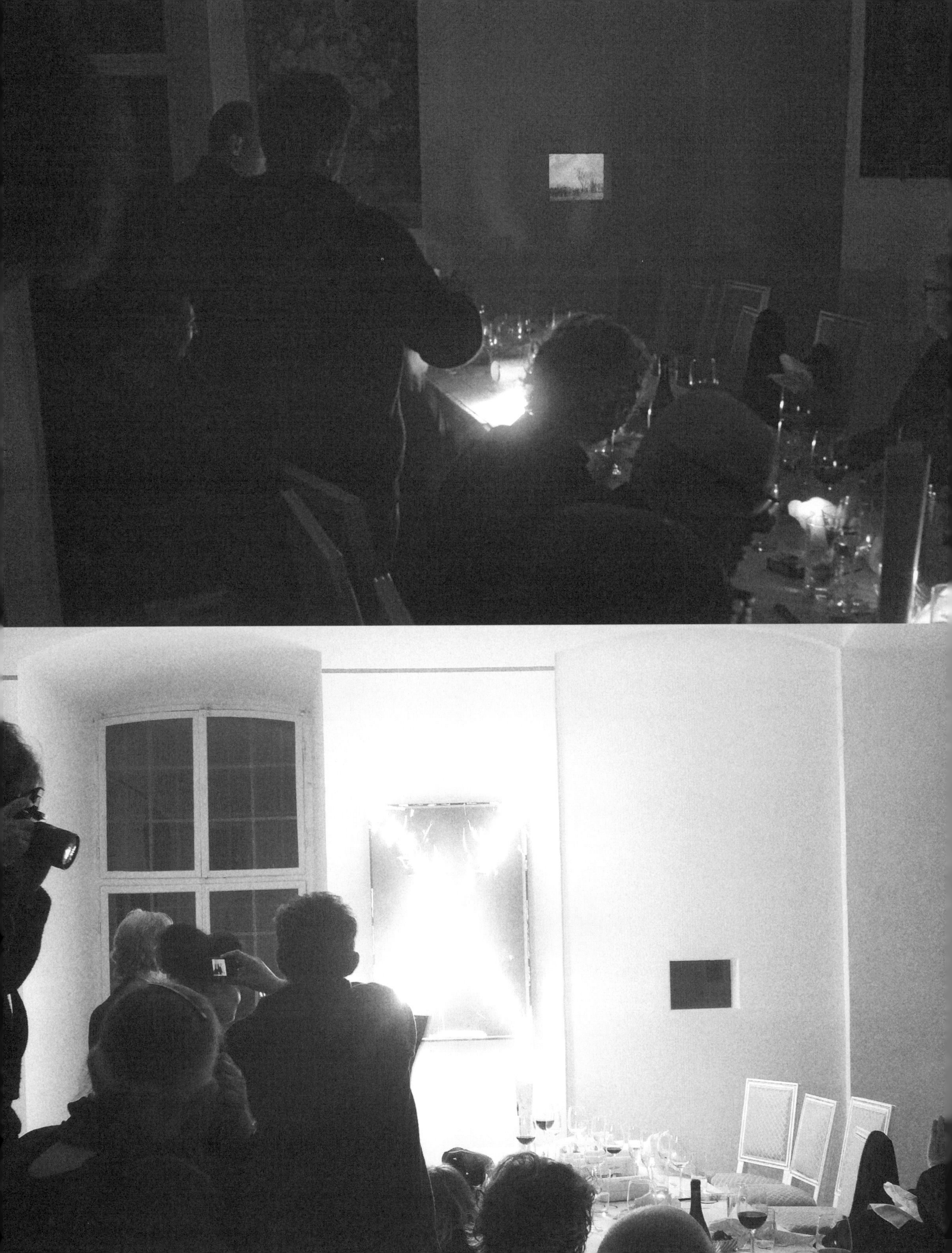

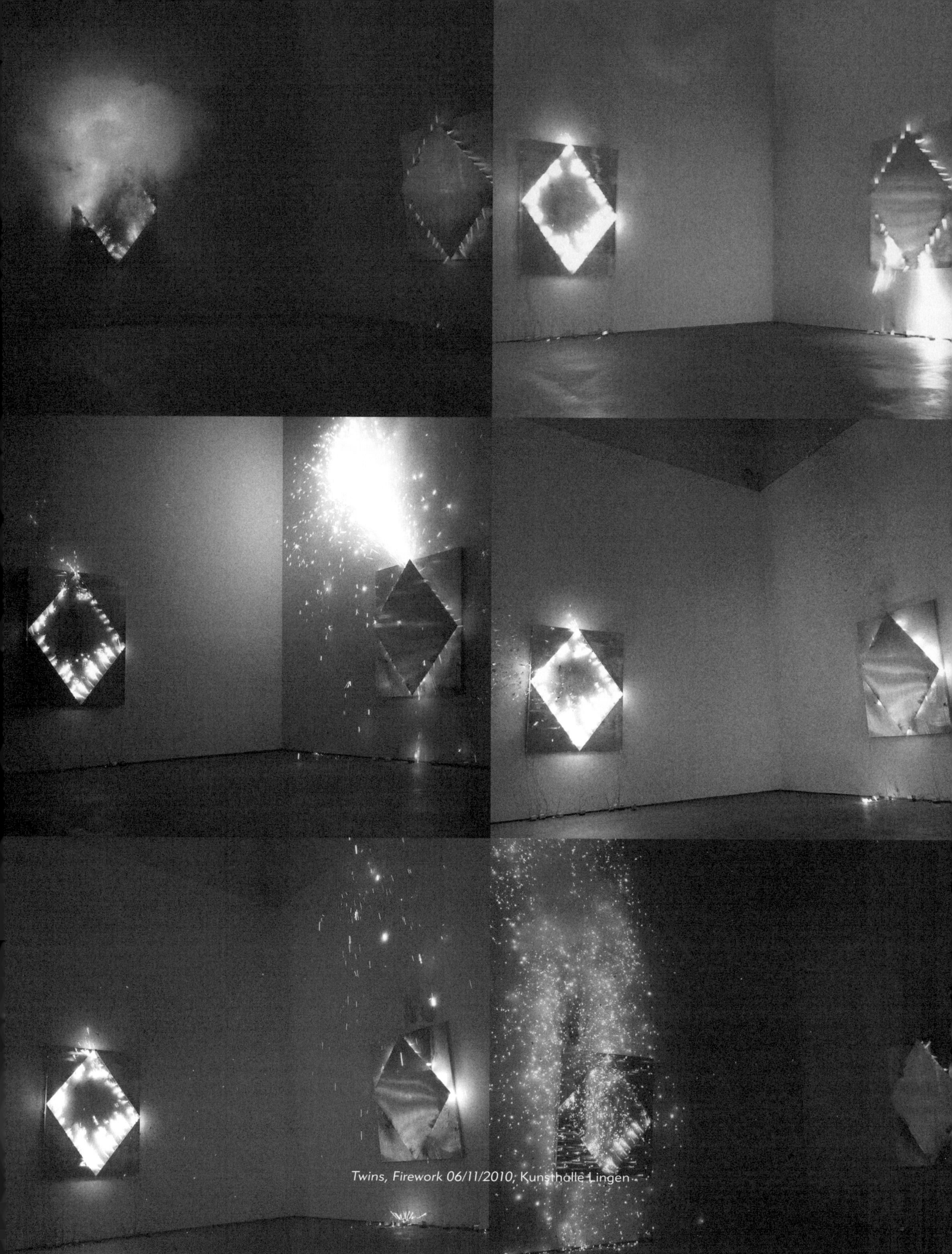

Twins, Firework 06/11/2010, Kunsthalle Lingen

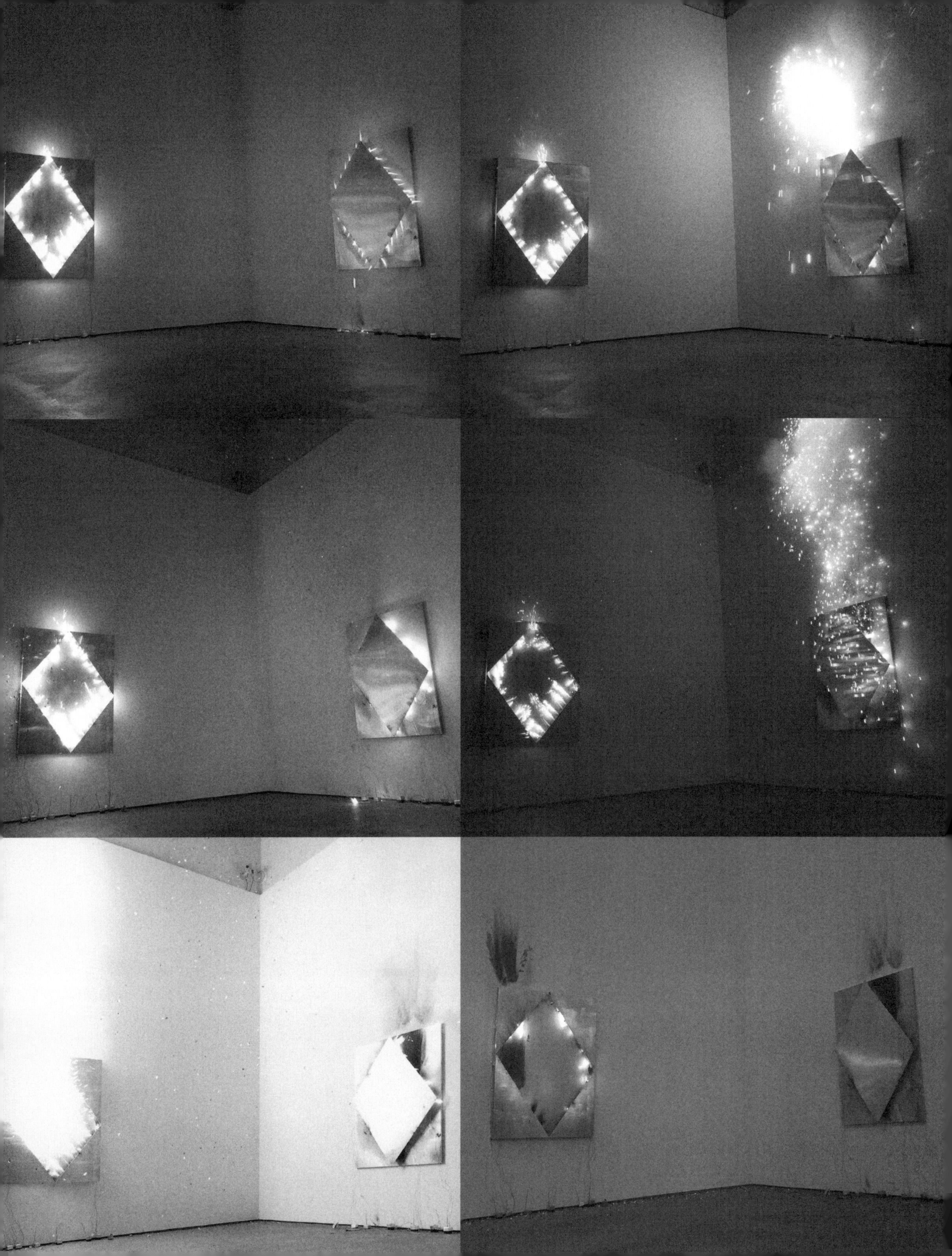

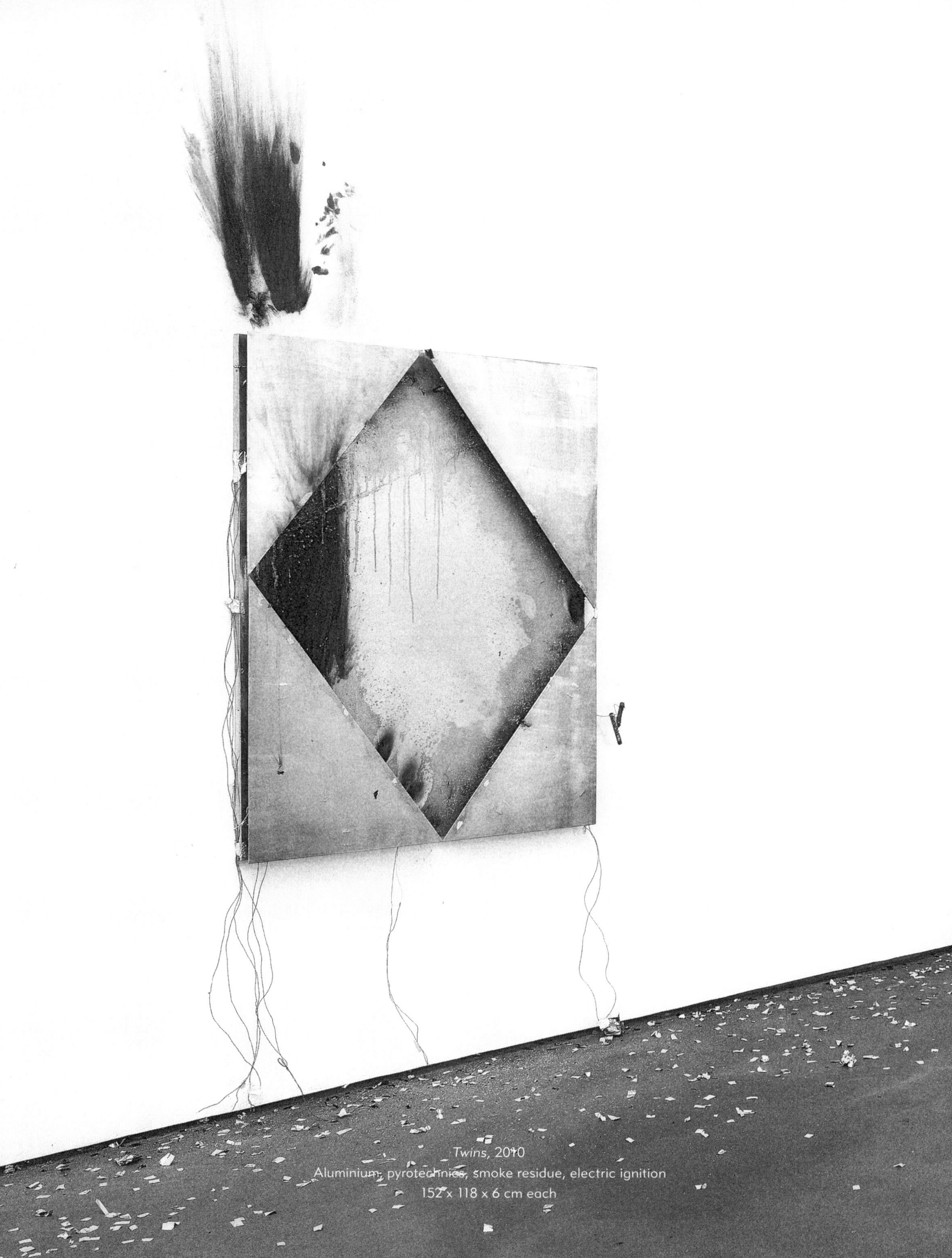

Twins, 2010
Aluminium, pyrotechnics, smoke residue, electric ignition
152 x 118 x 6 cm each

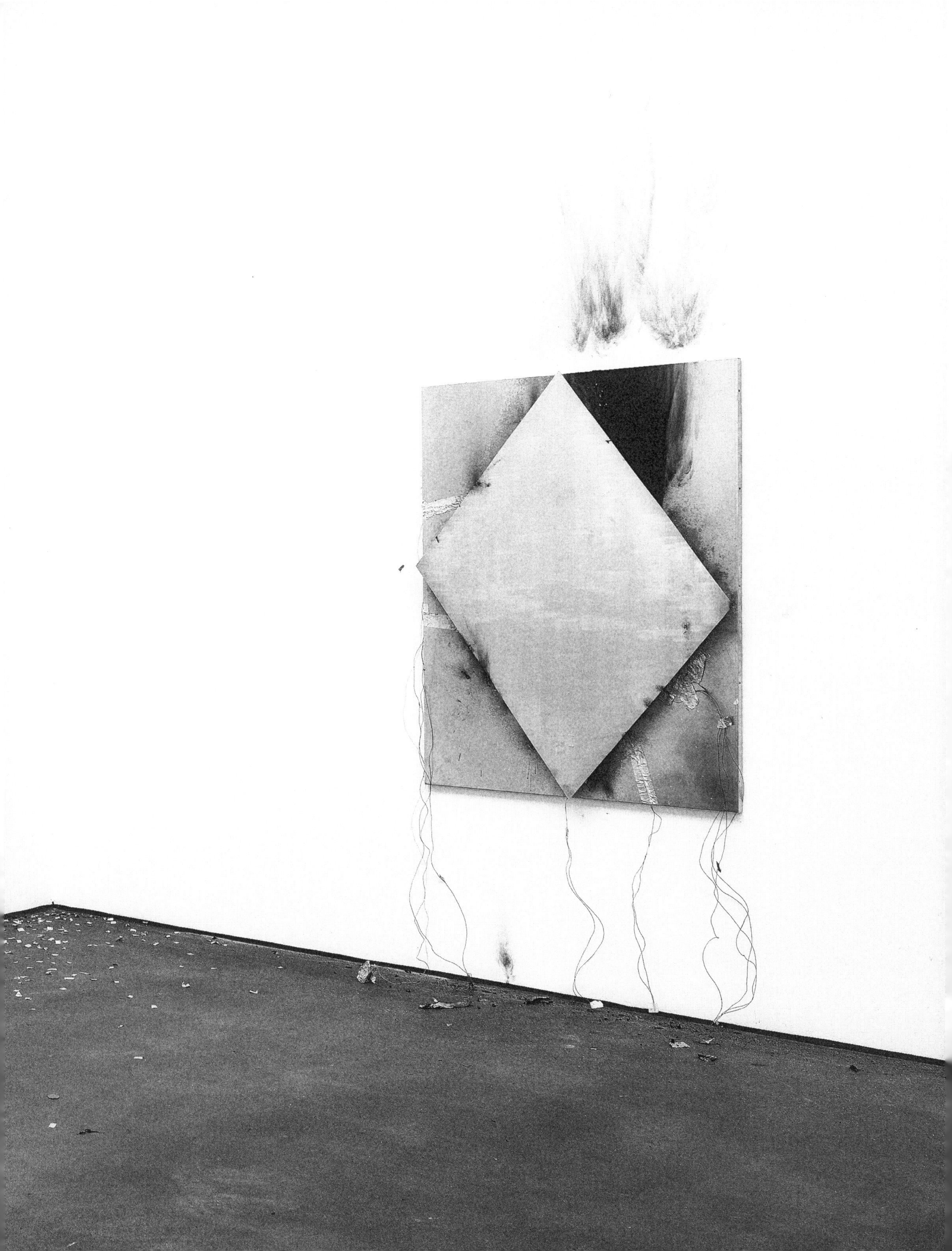

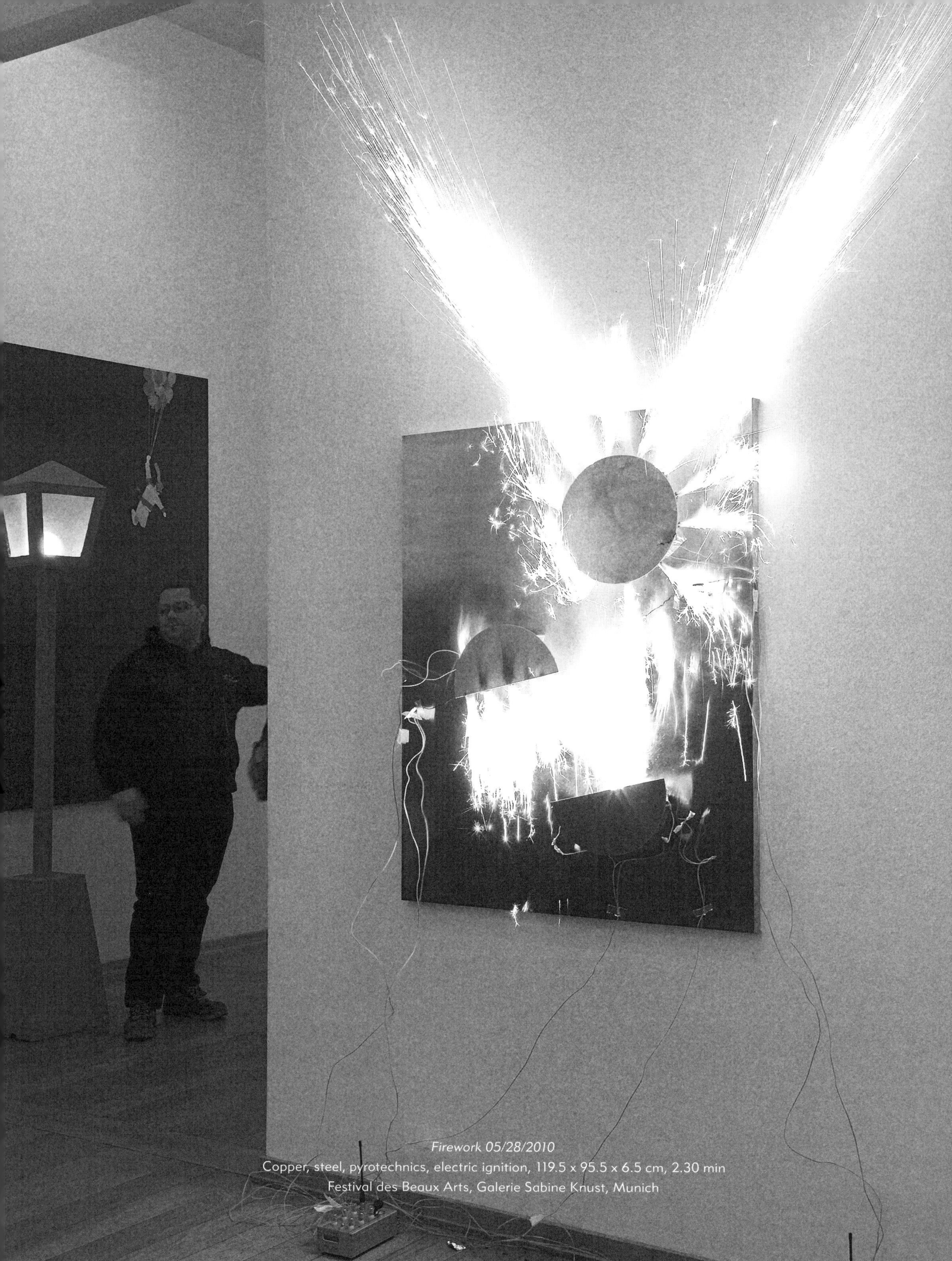

Firework 05/28/2010
Copper, steel, pyrotechnics, electric ignition, 119.5 x 95.5 x 6.5 cm, 2.30 min
Festival des Beaux Arts, Galerie Sabine Knust, Munich

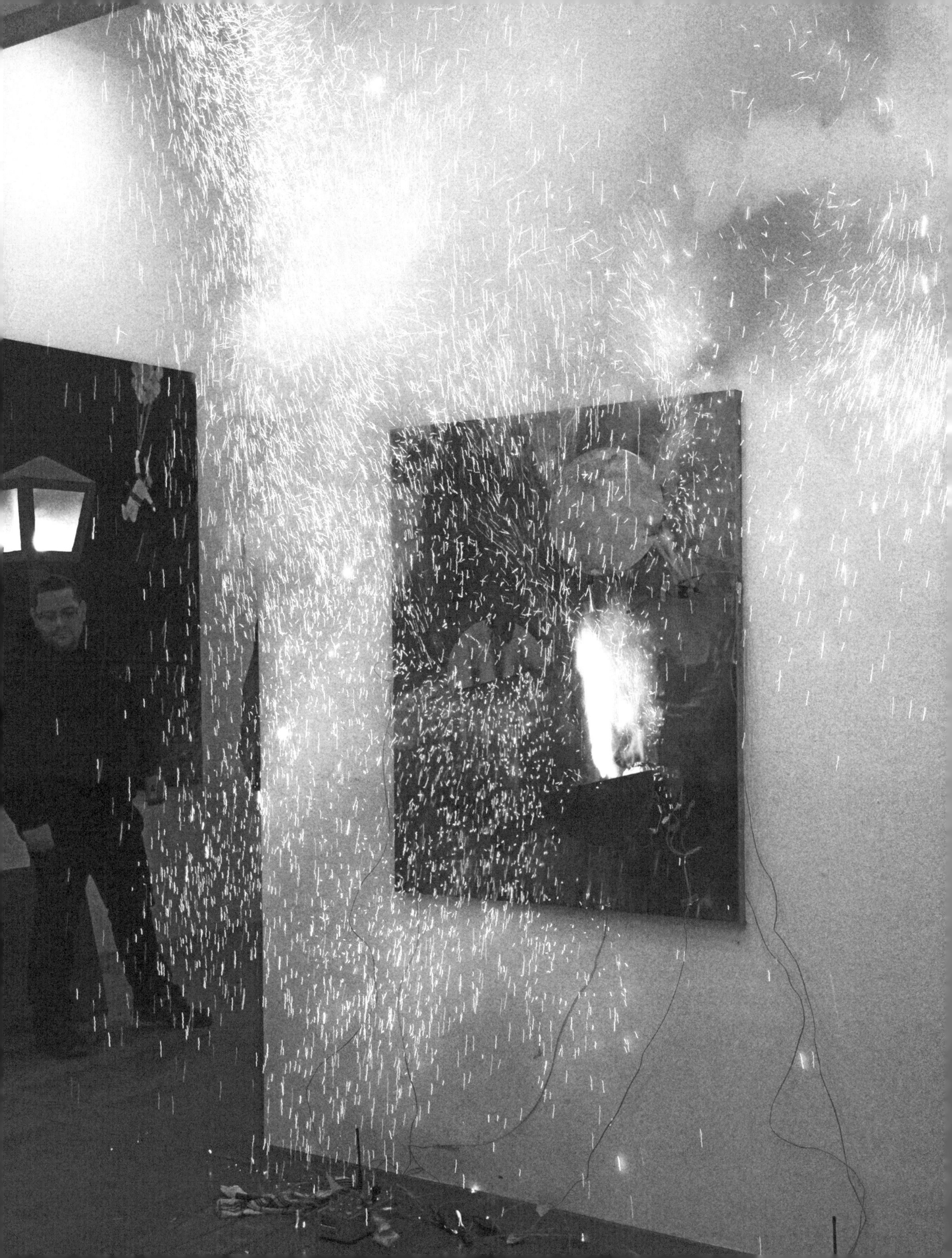

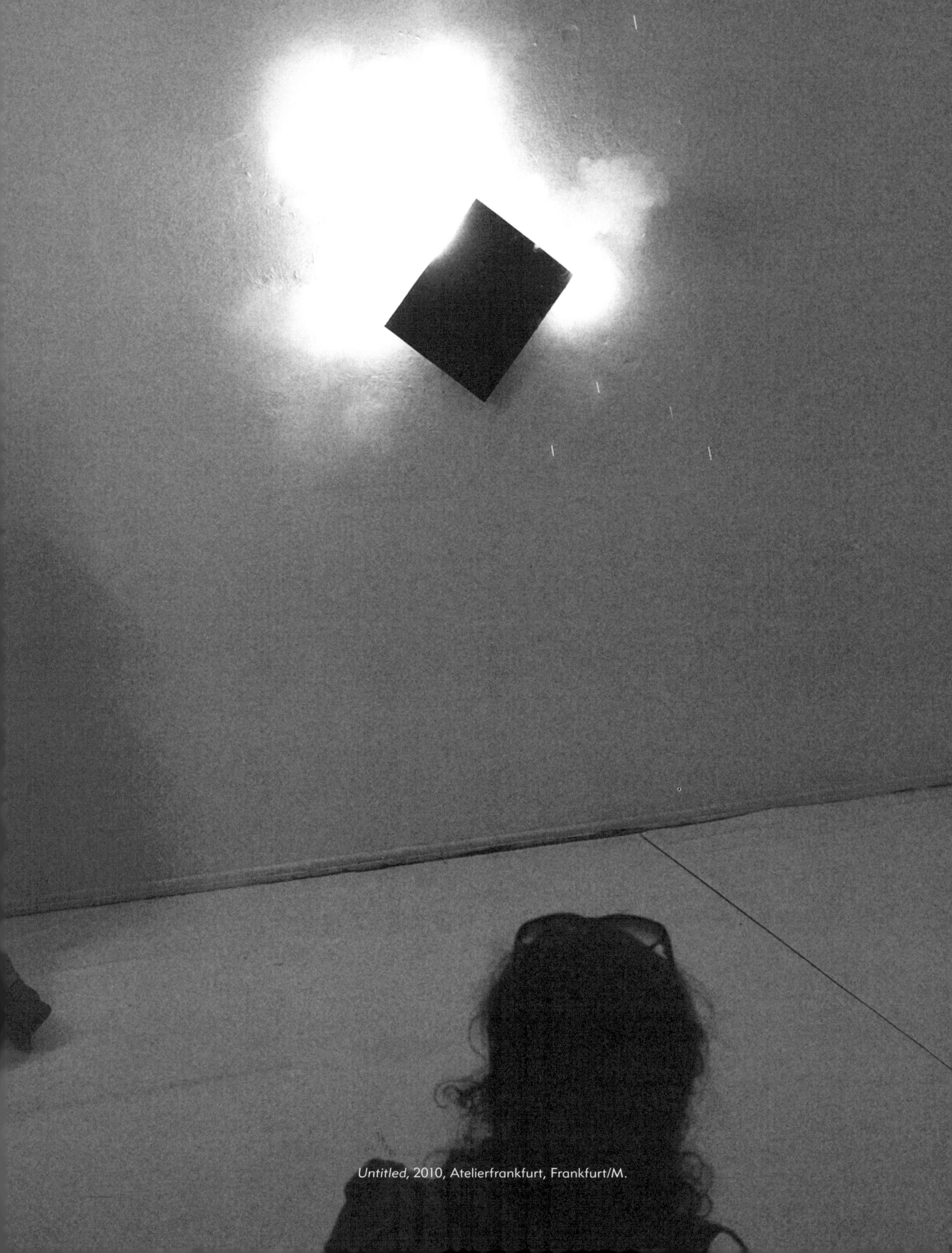

Untitled, 2010, Atelierfrankfurt, Frankfurt/M.

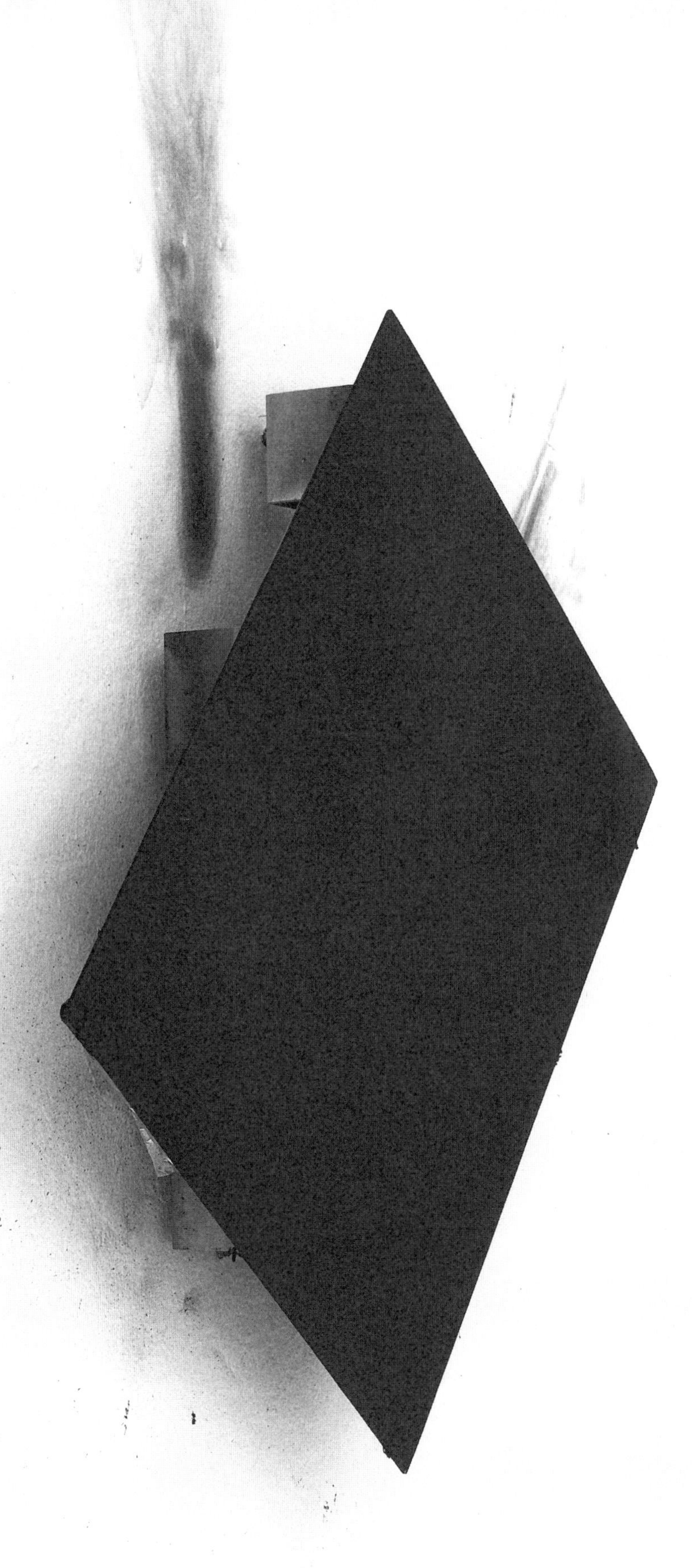

Untitled, 2010
Black painted steel relief, pyrotechnics, electric ignition, 0.40 min
49 x 39 x 6,3 cm

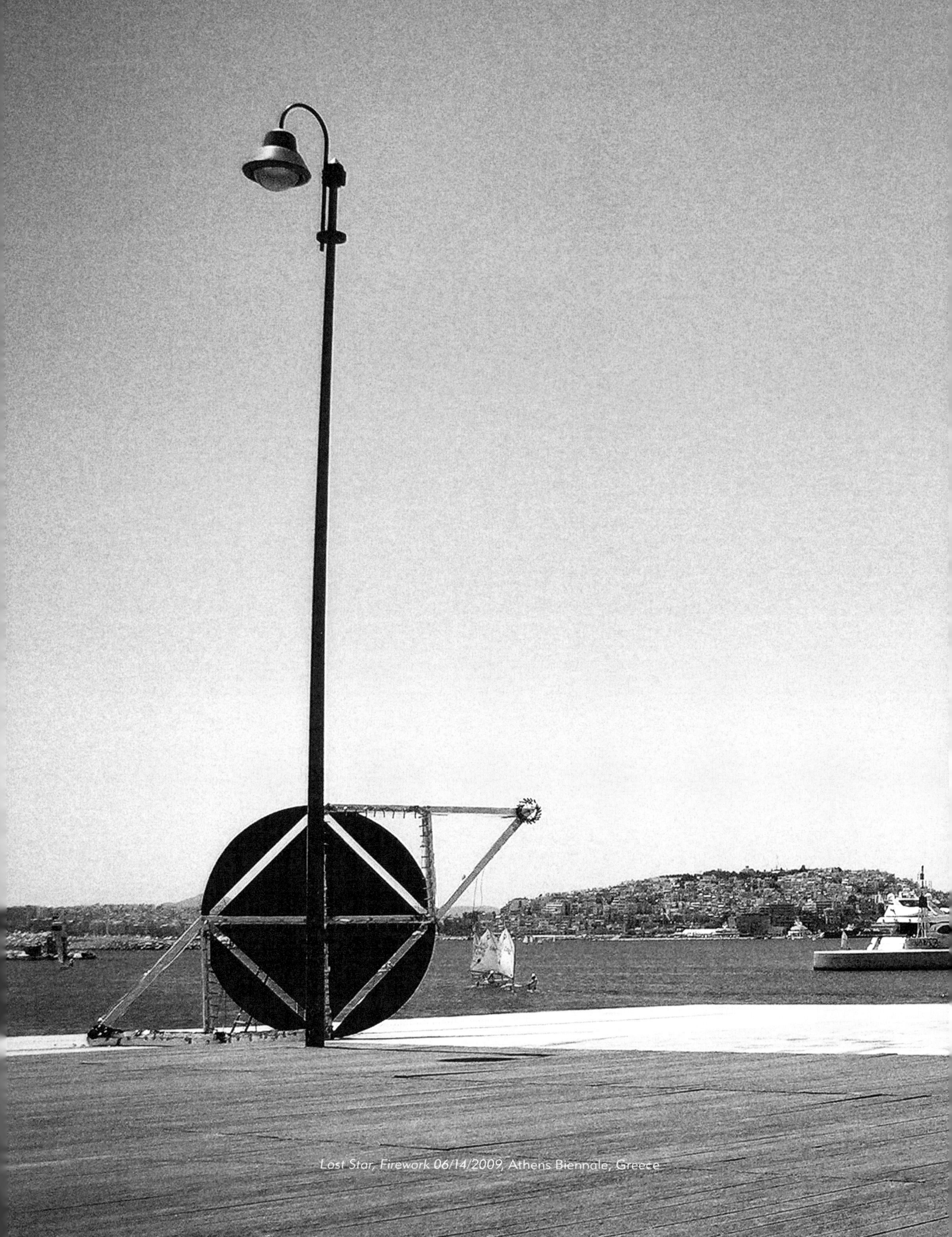

Lost Star, Firework 06/14/2009, Athens Biennale, Greece

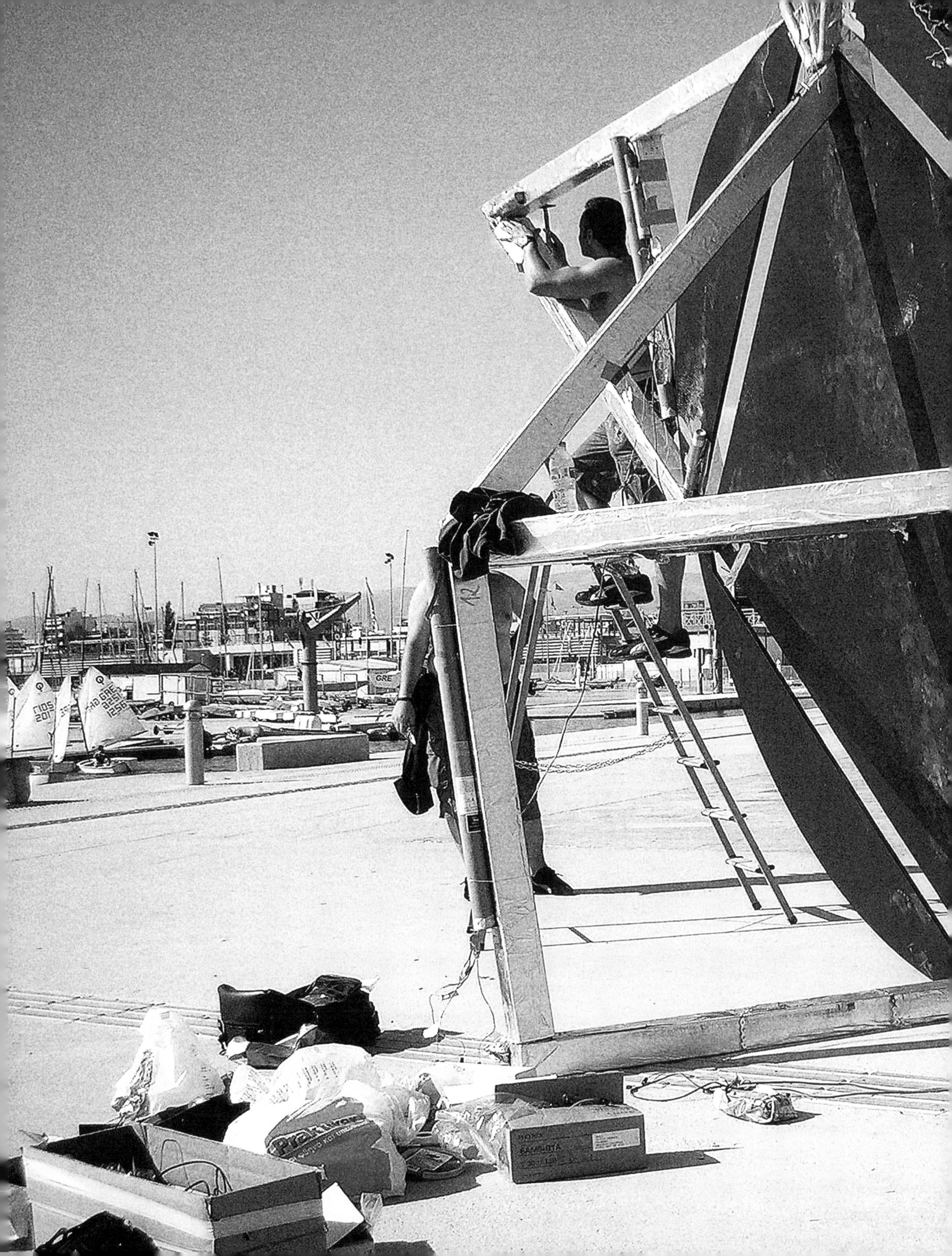

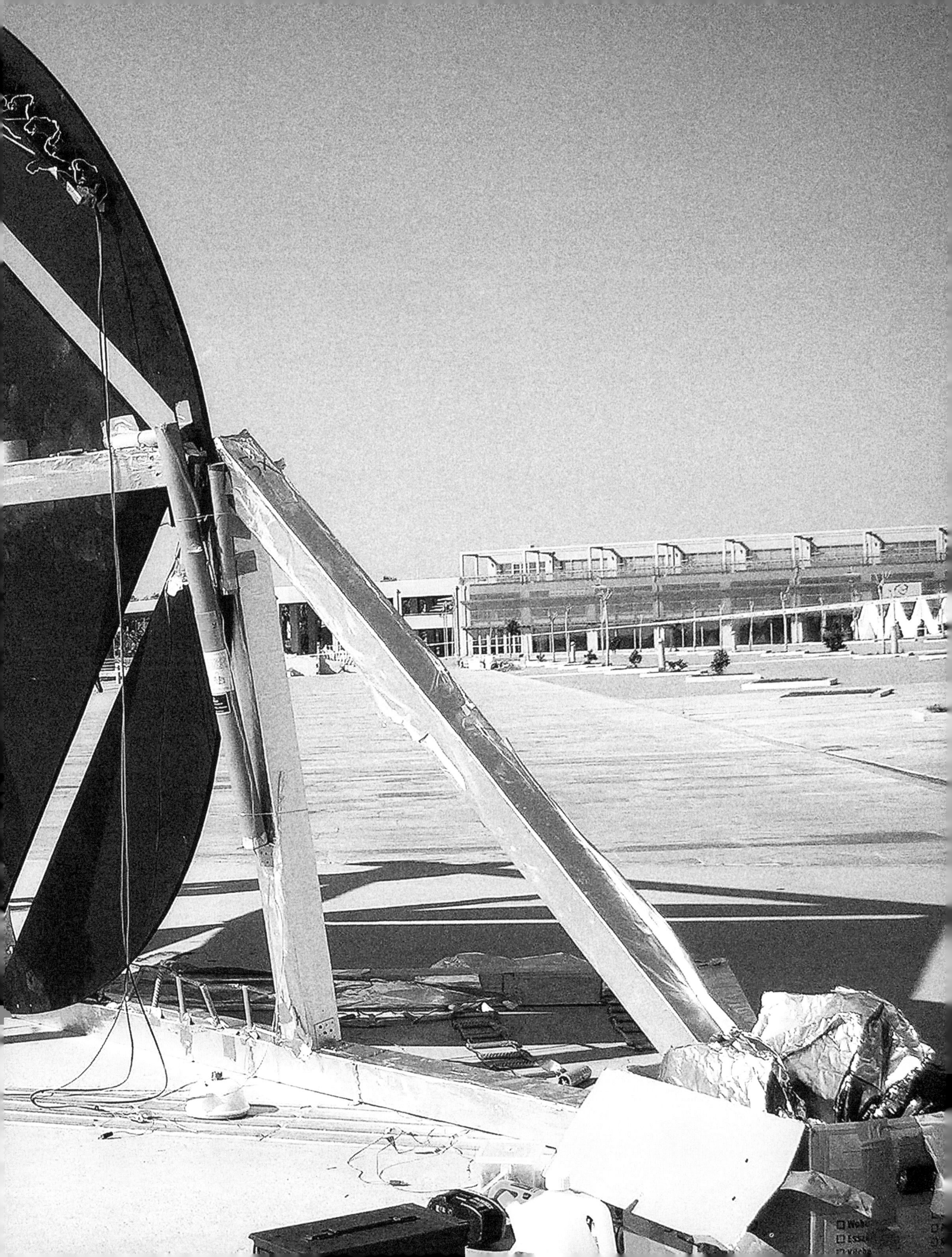

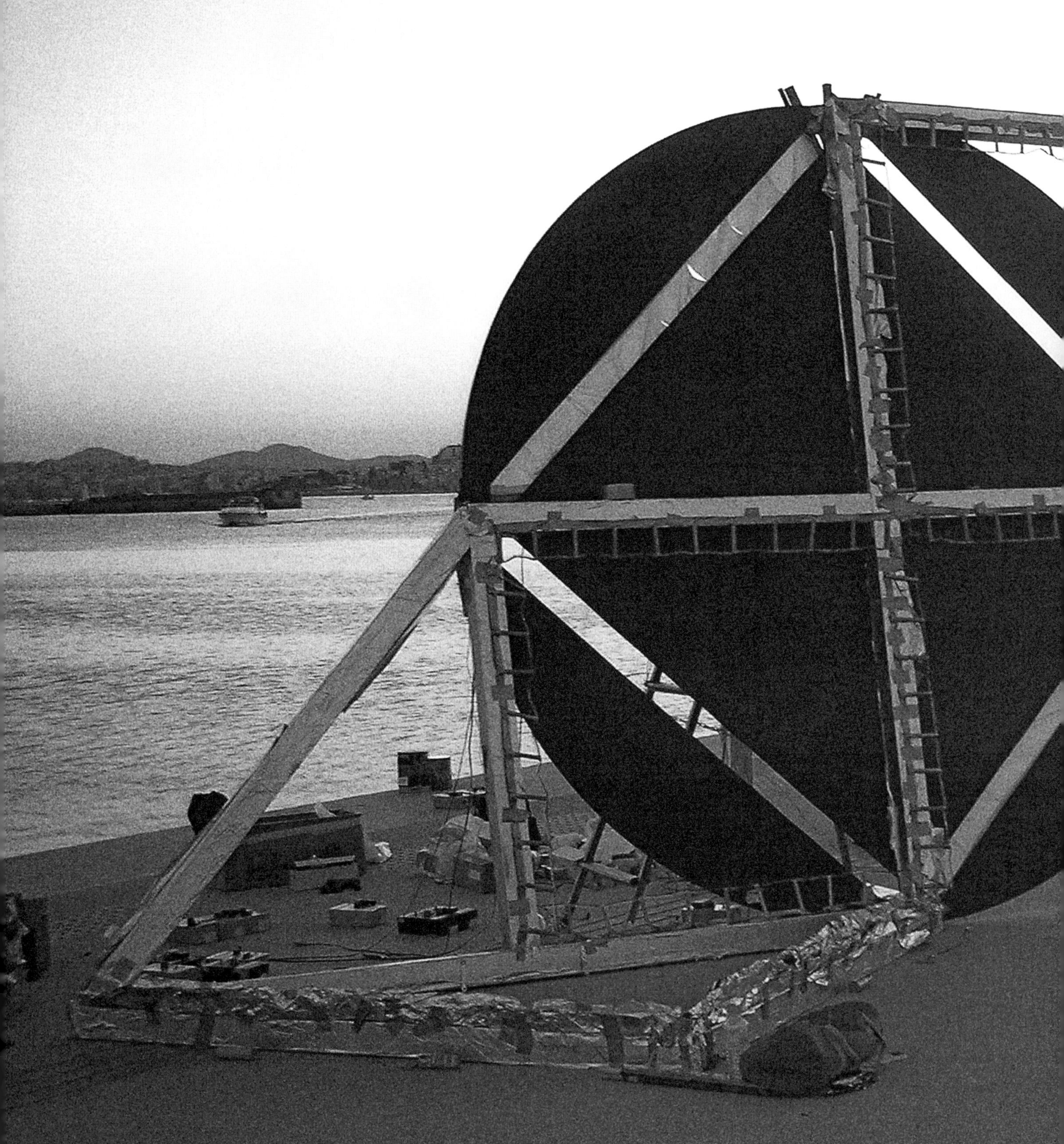

Lost Star, 2009
Black painted wood, pyrotechnics, electric ignition
300 x 600 x 300 cm

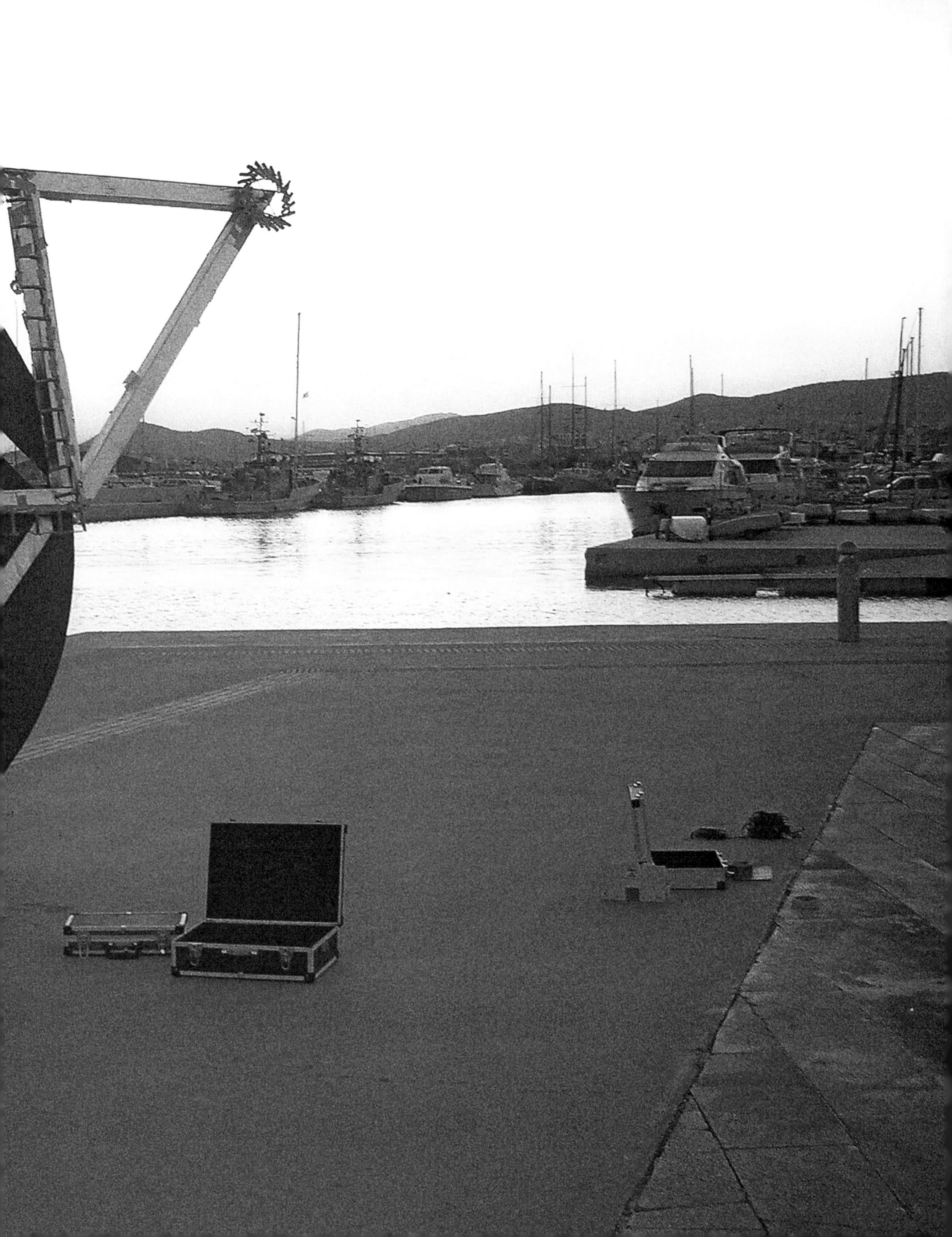

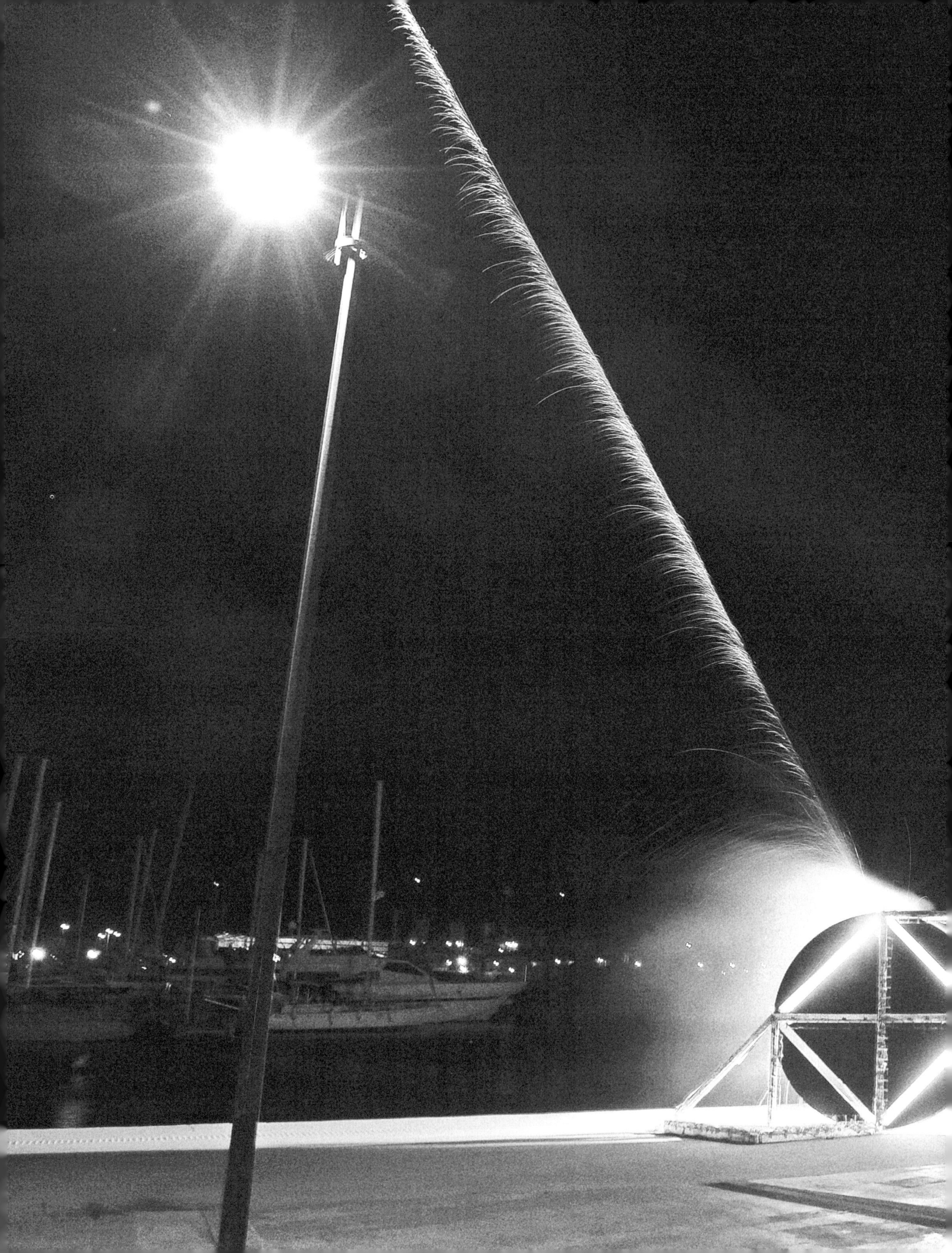

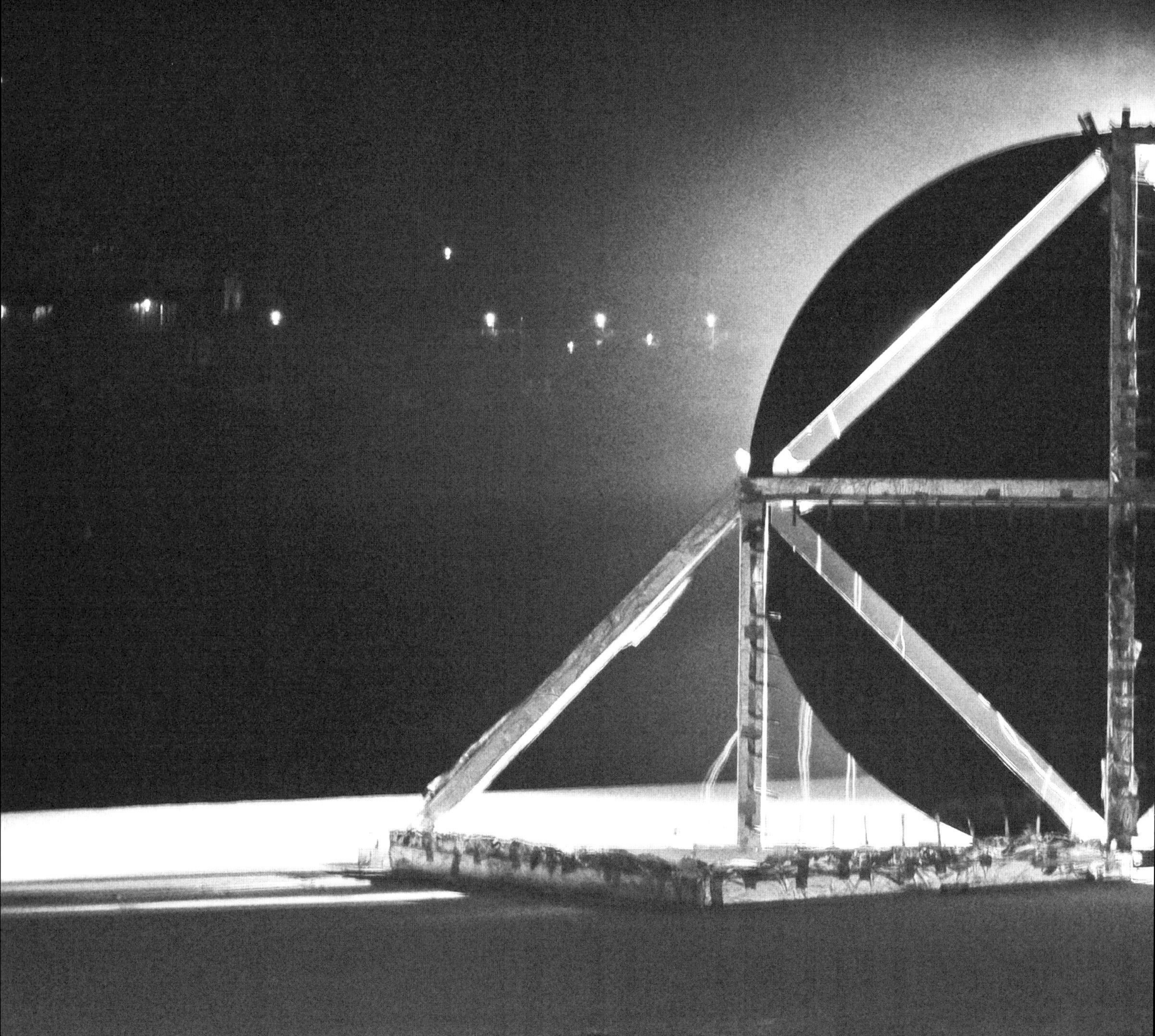

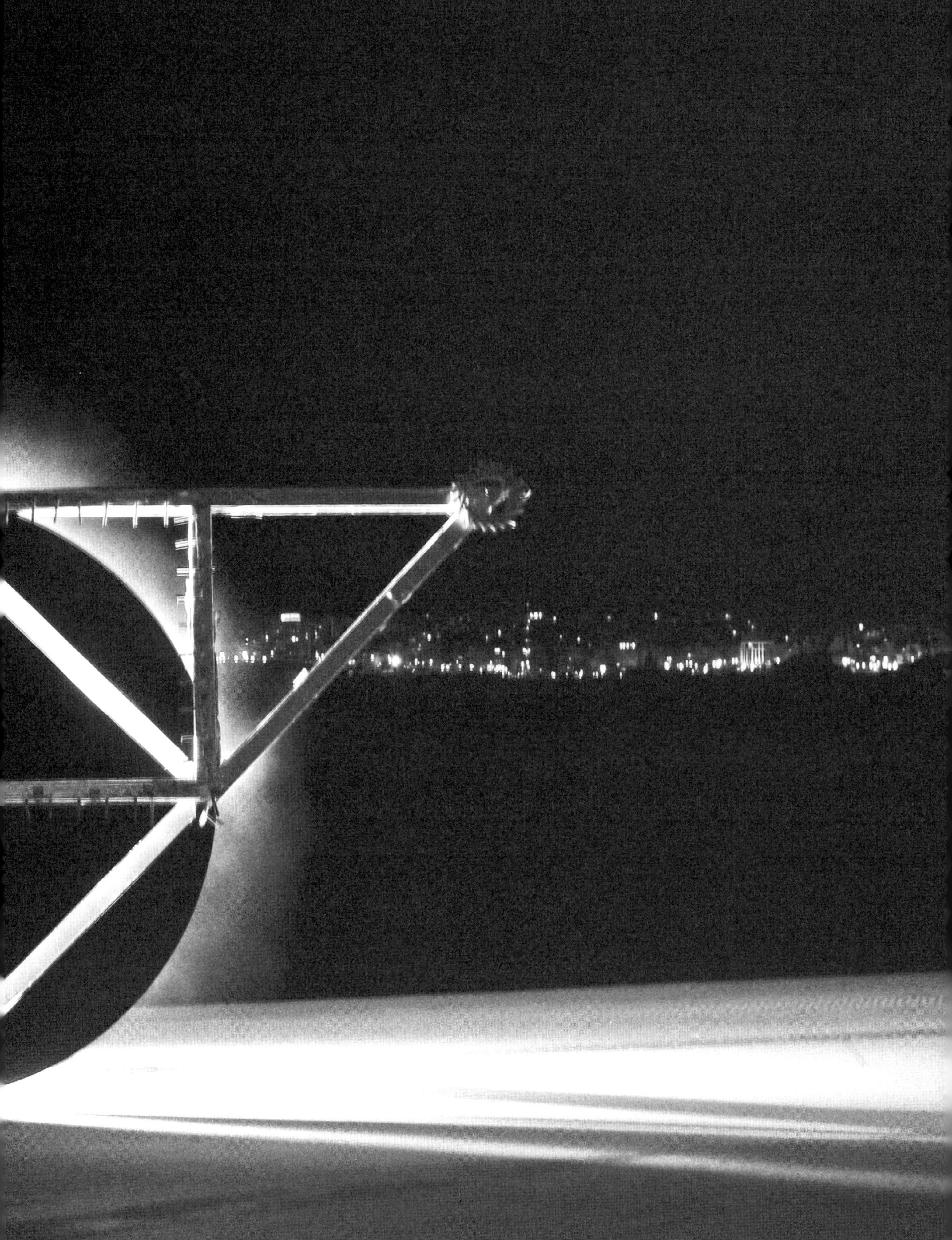

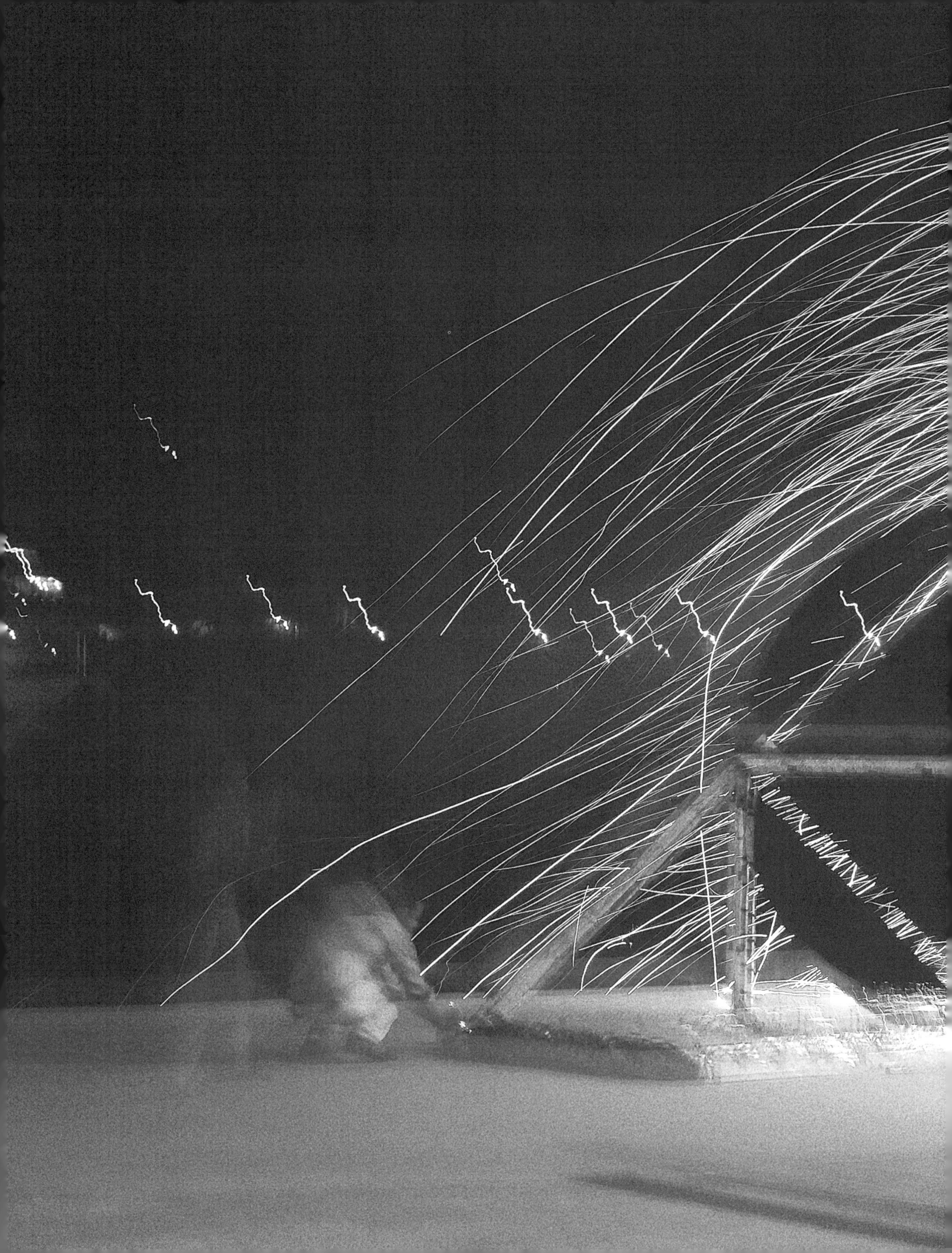

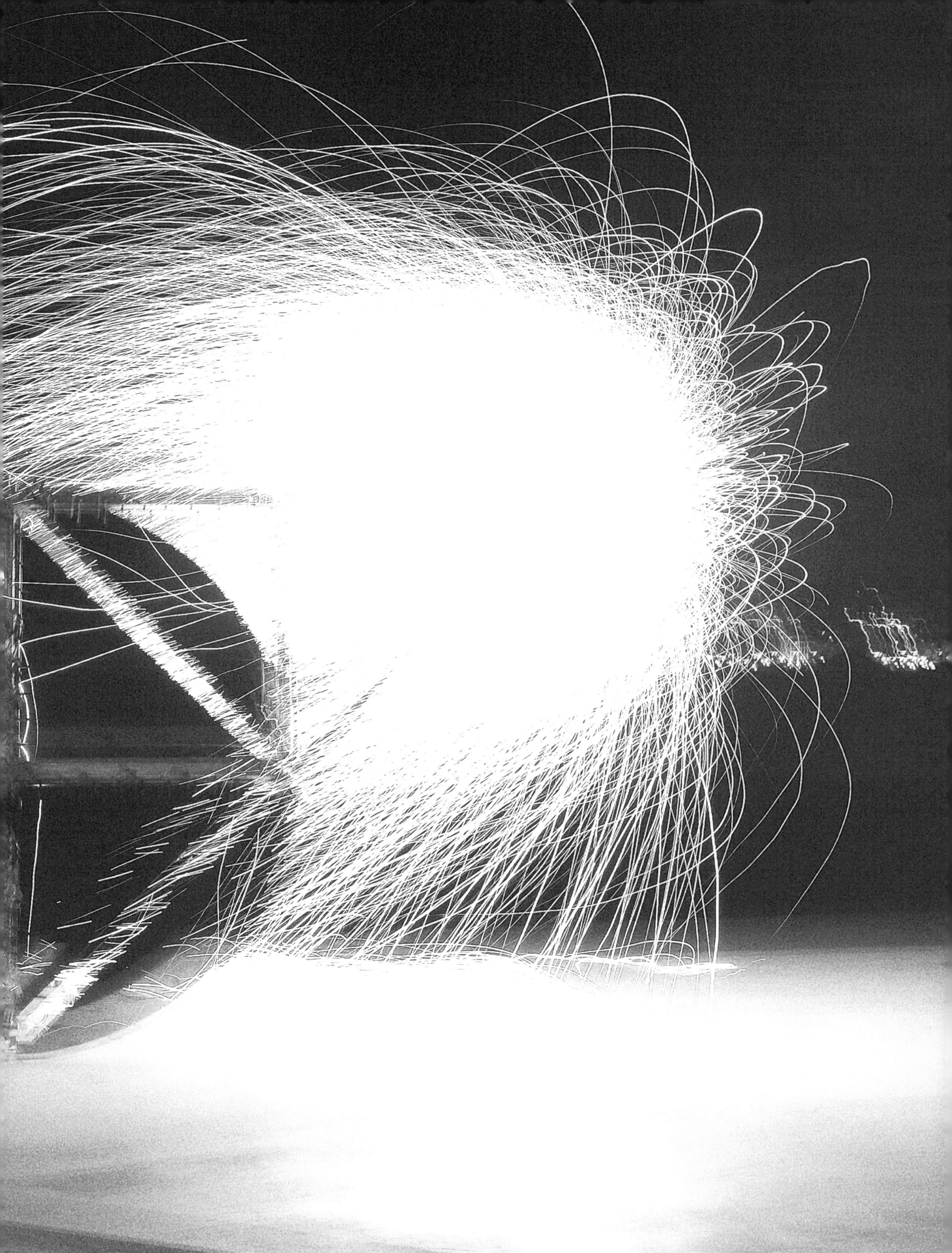

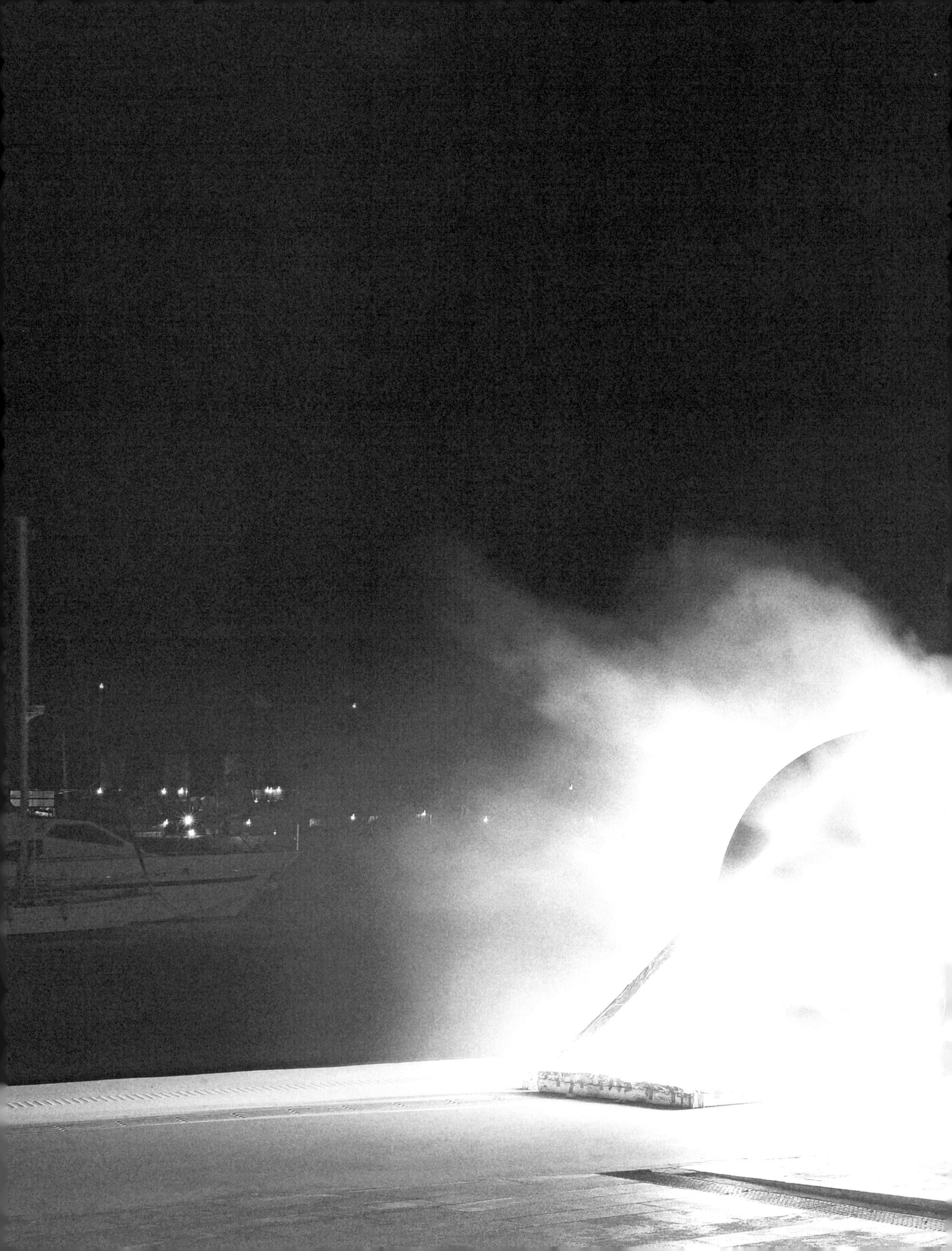

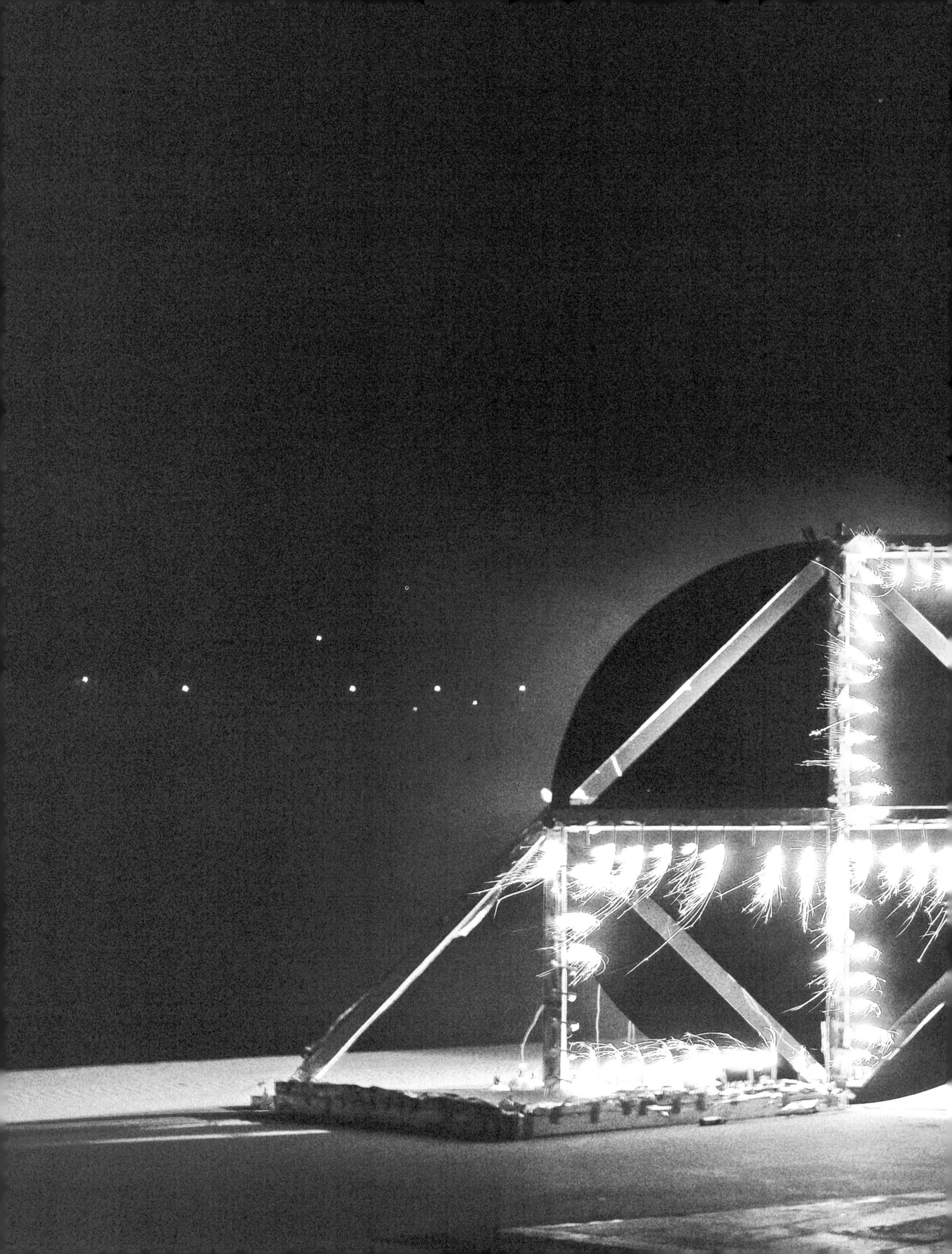

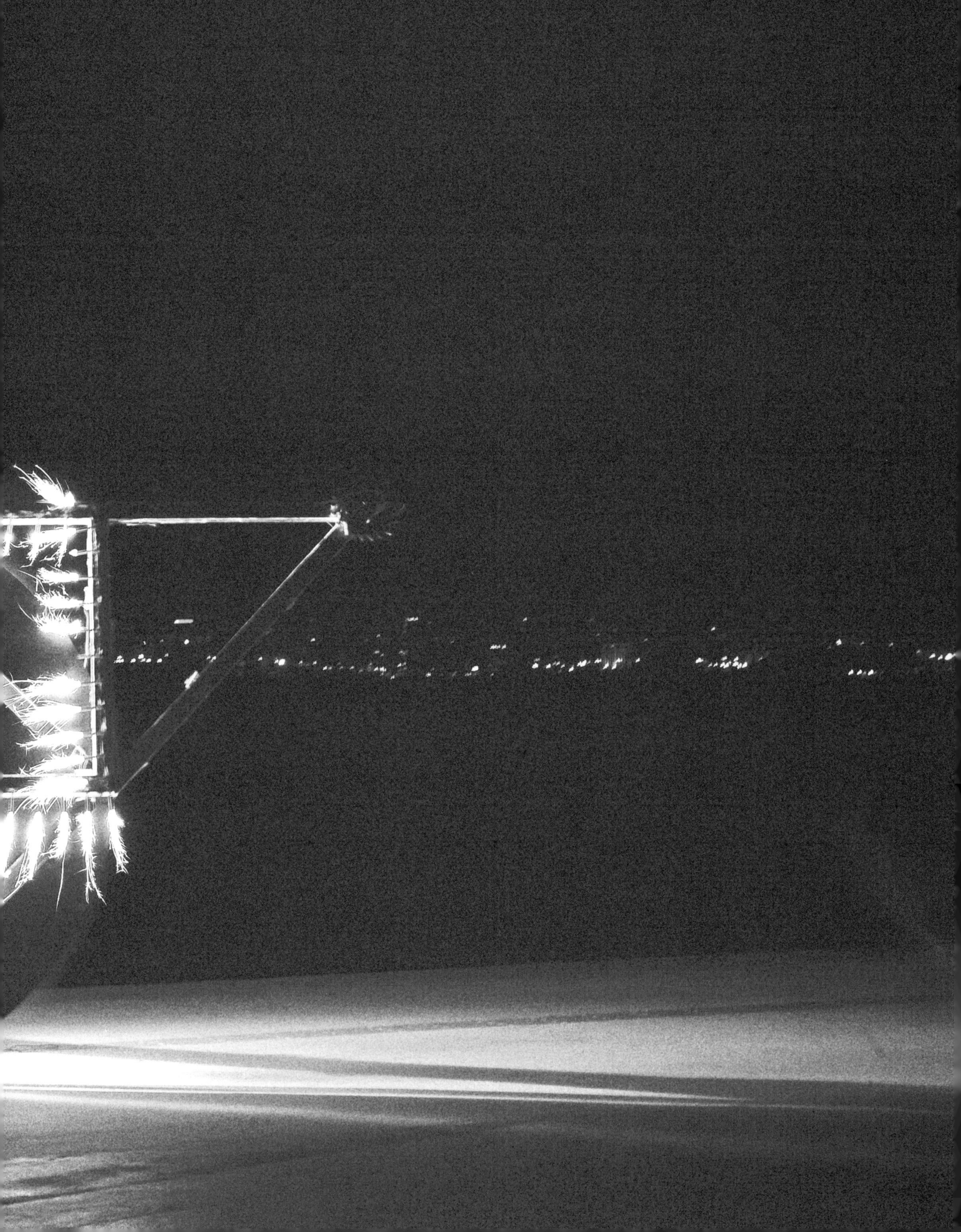

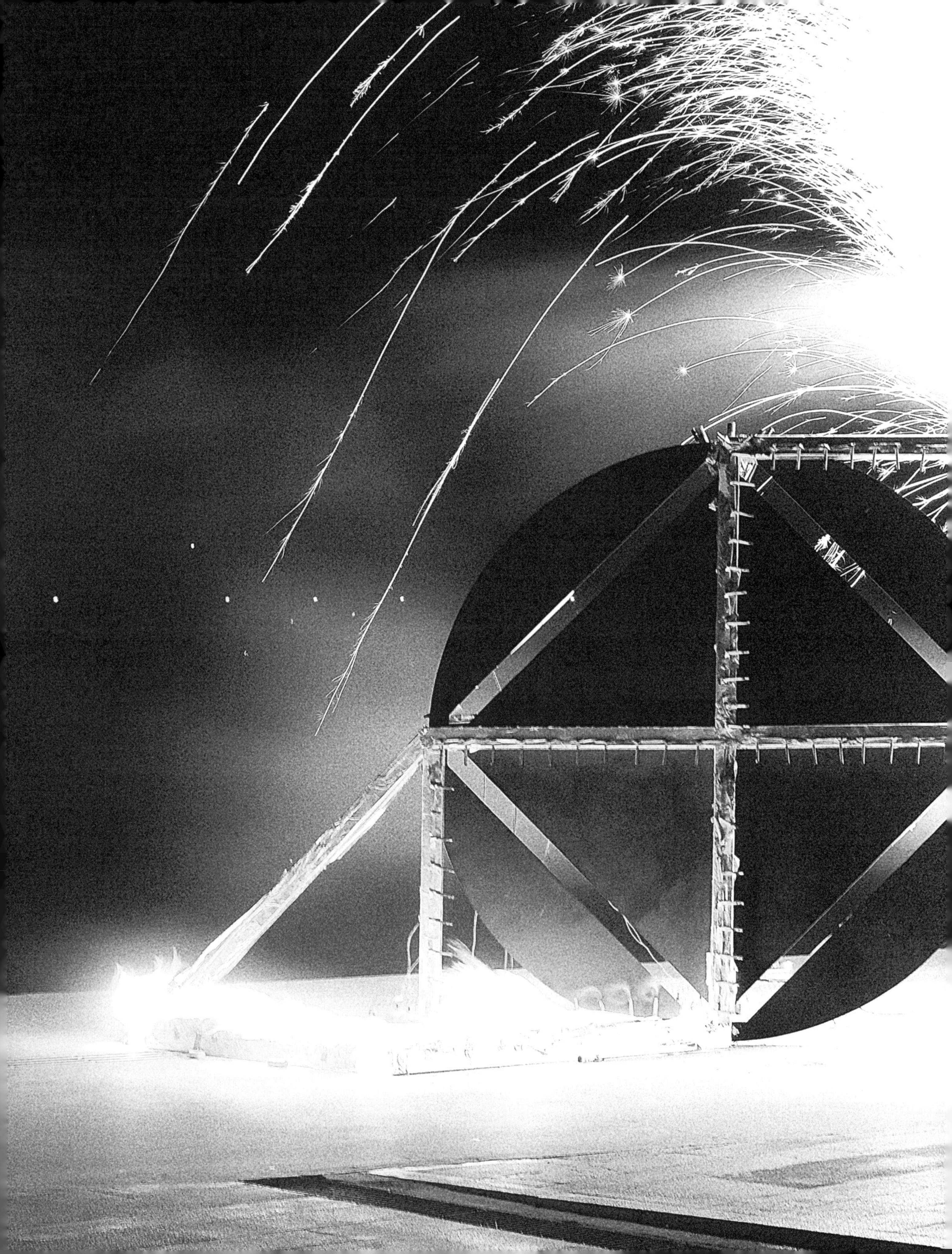

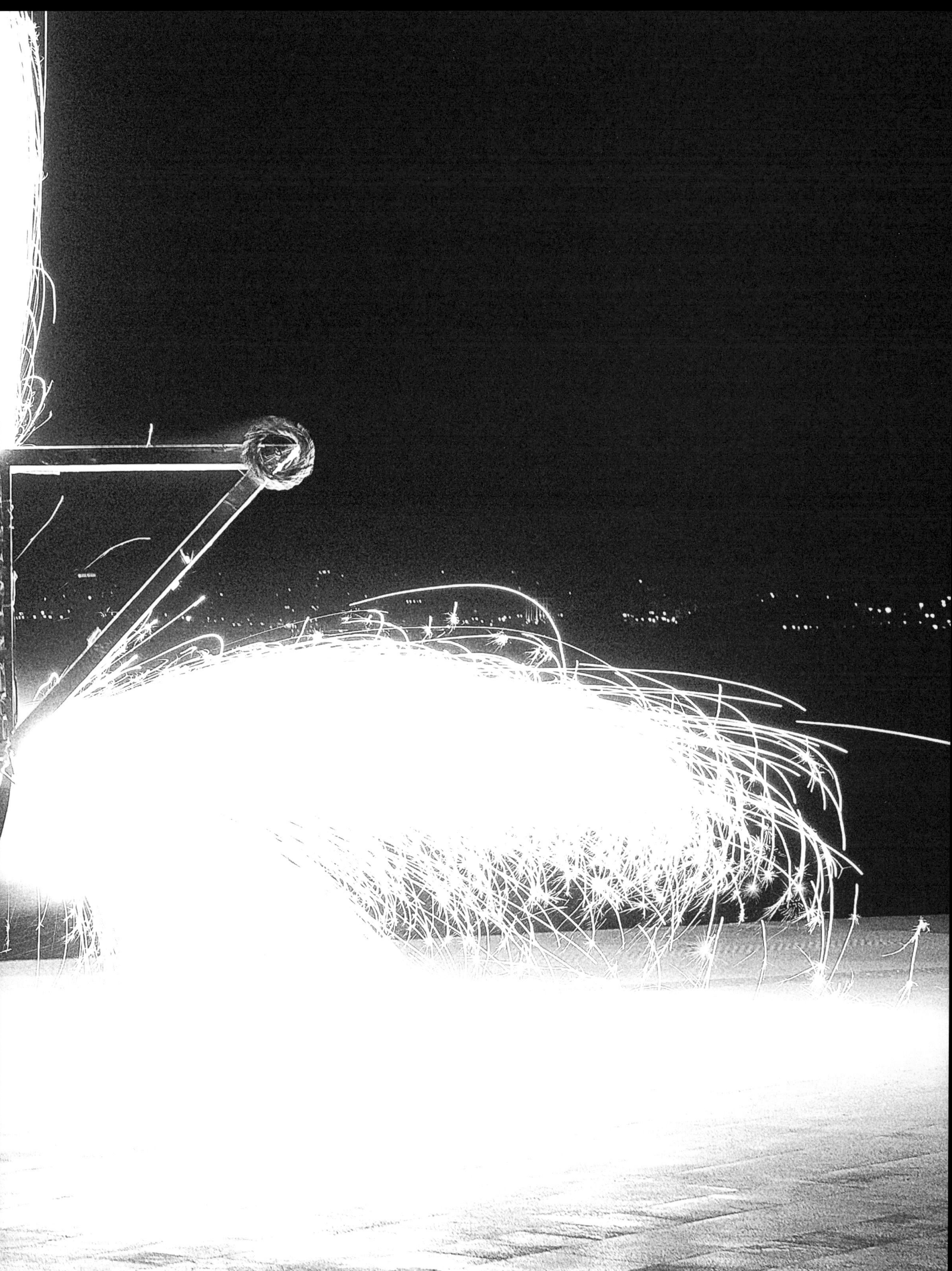

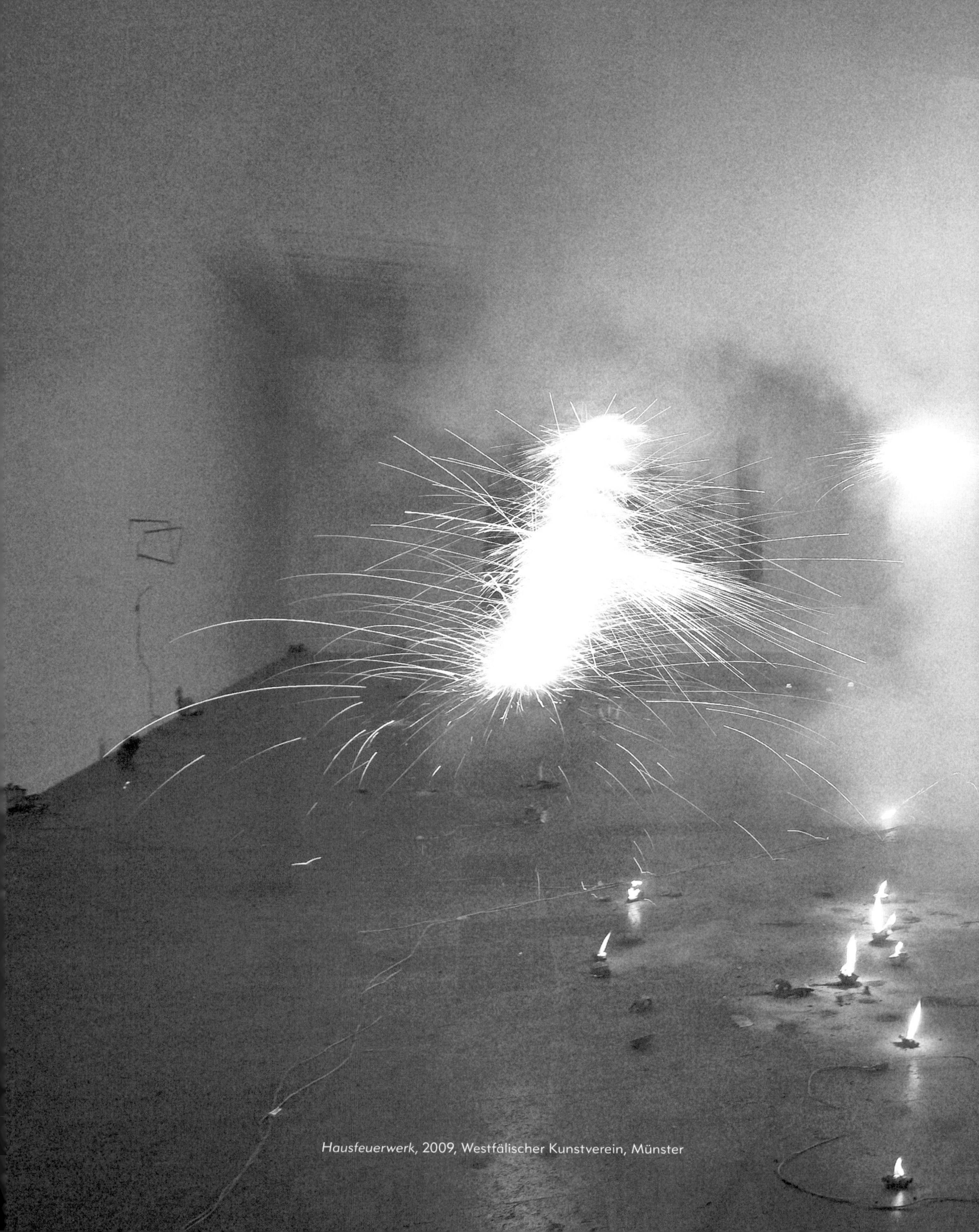

Hausfeuerwerk, 2009, Westfälischer Kunstverein, Münster

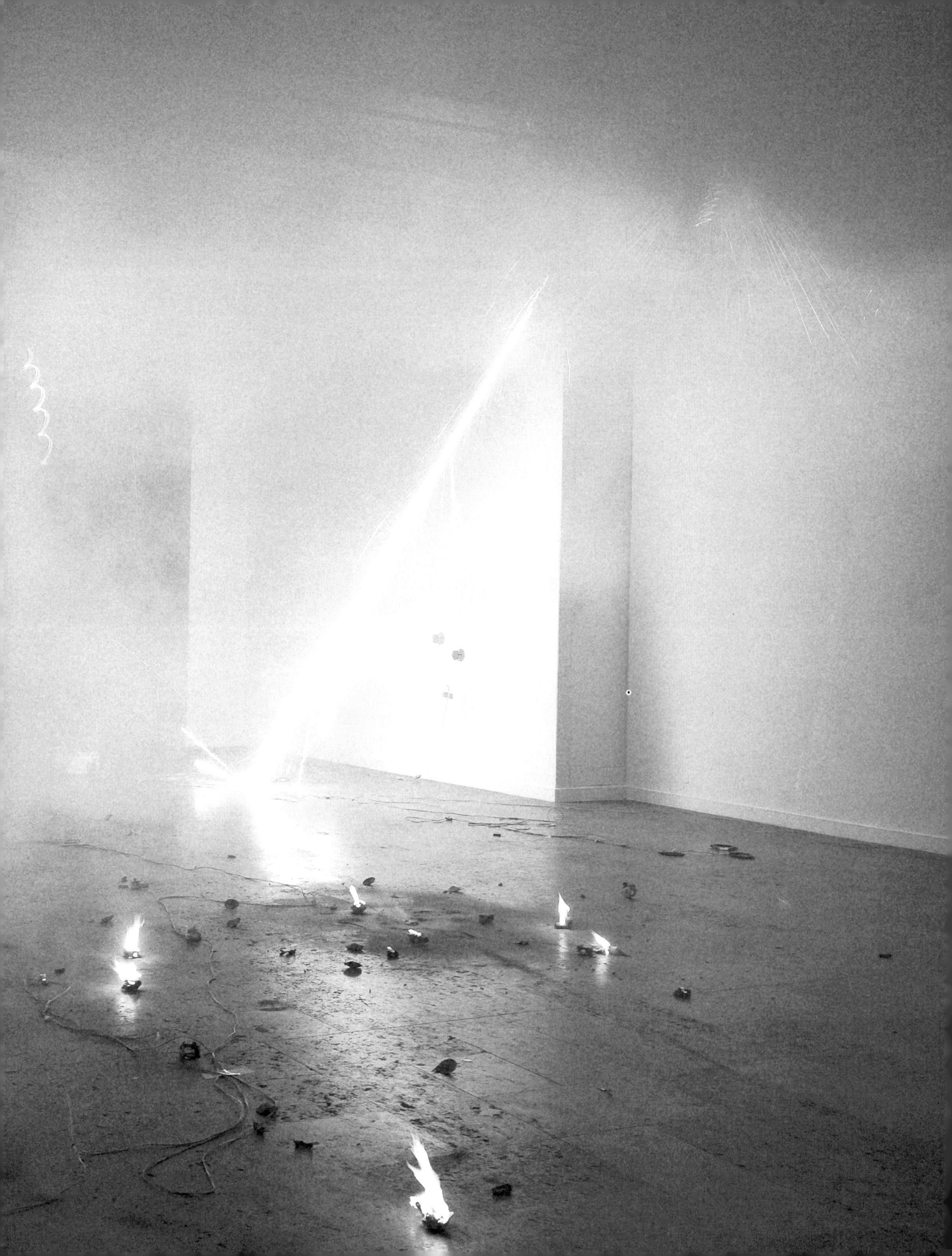

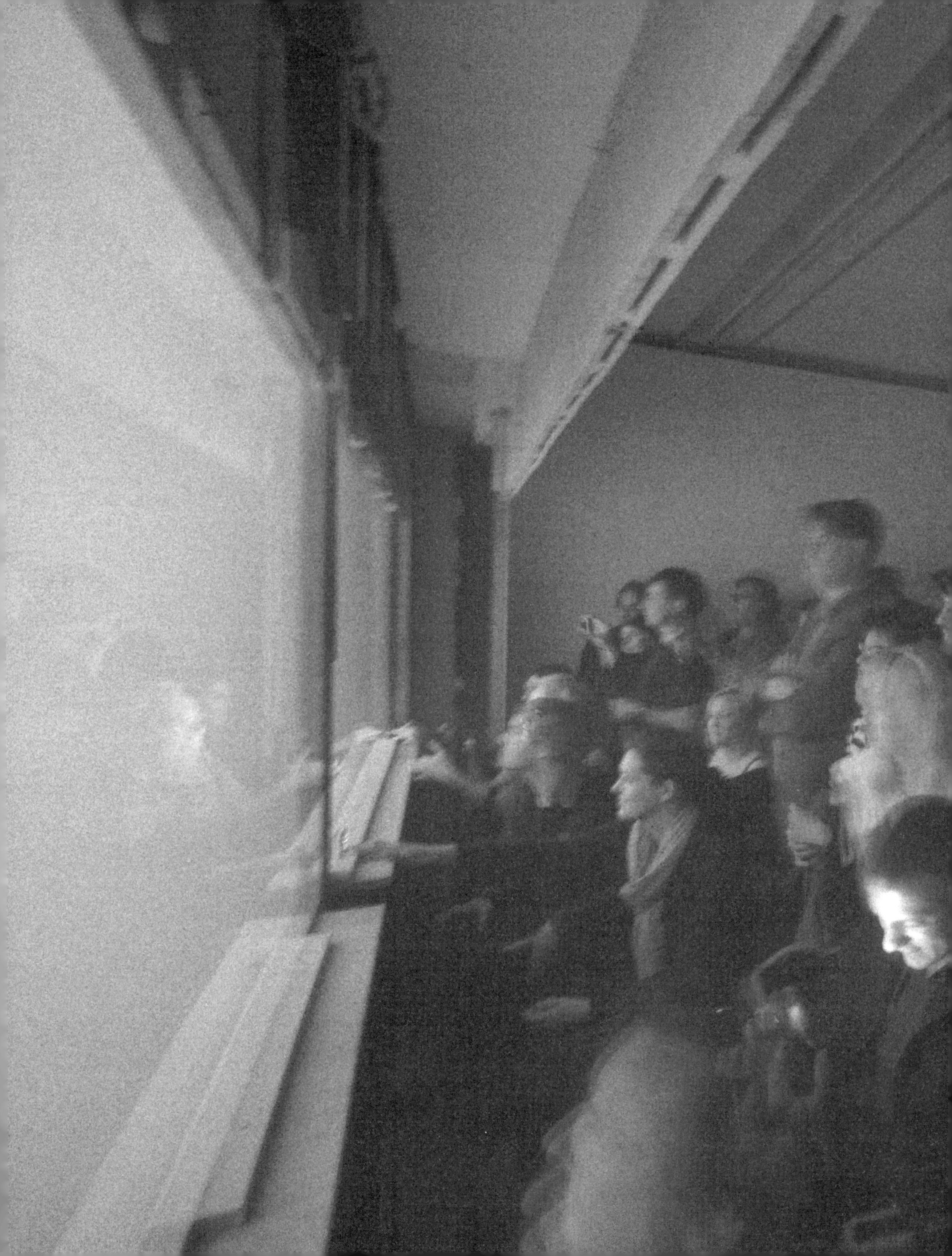

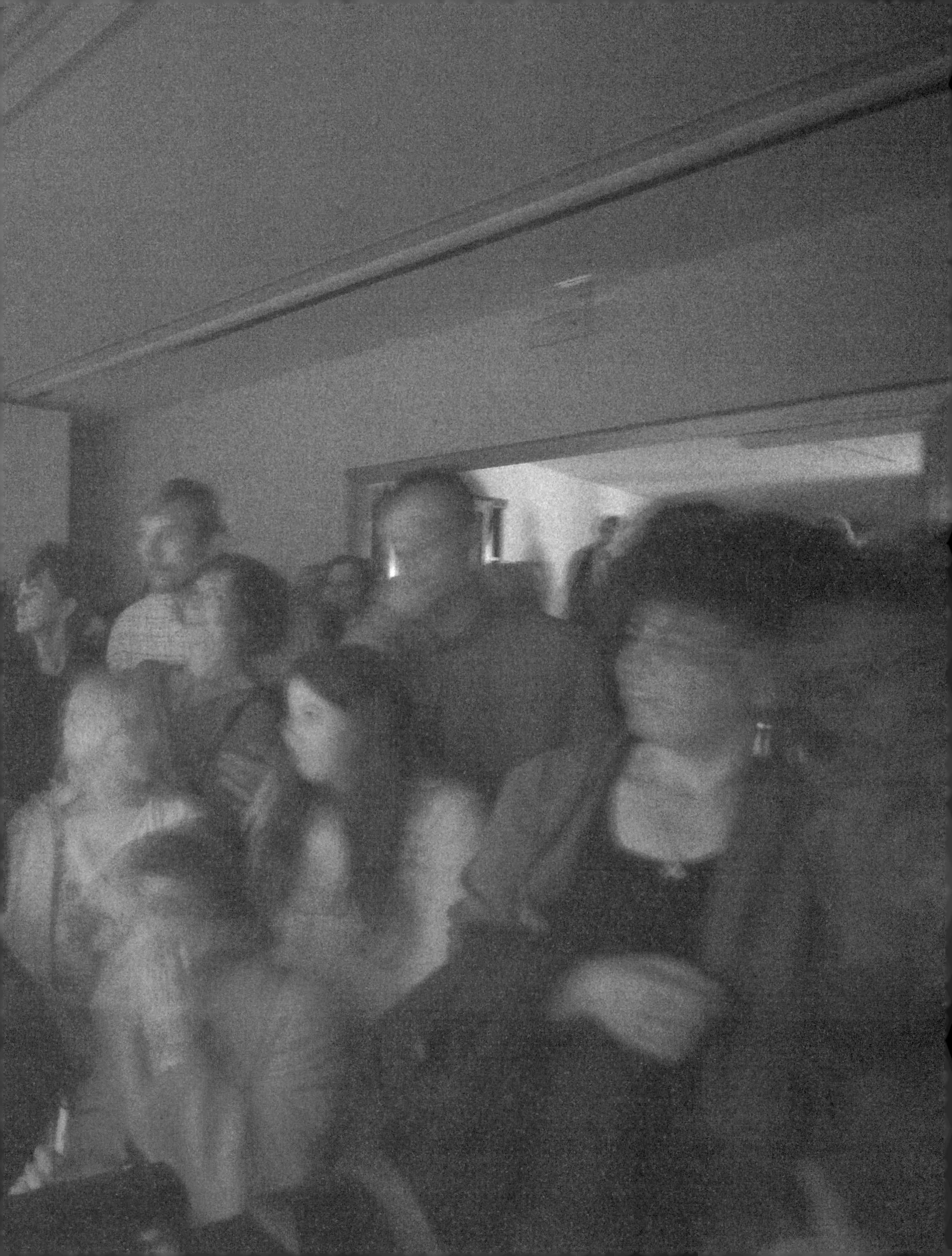

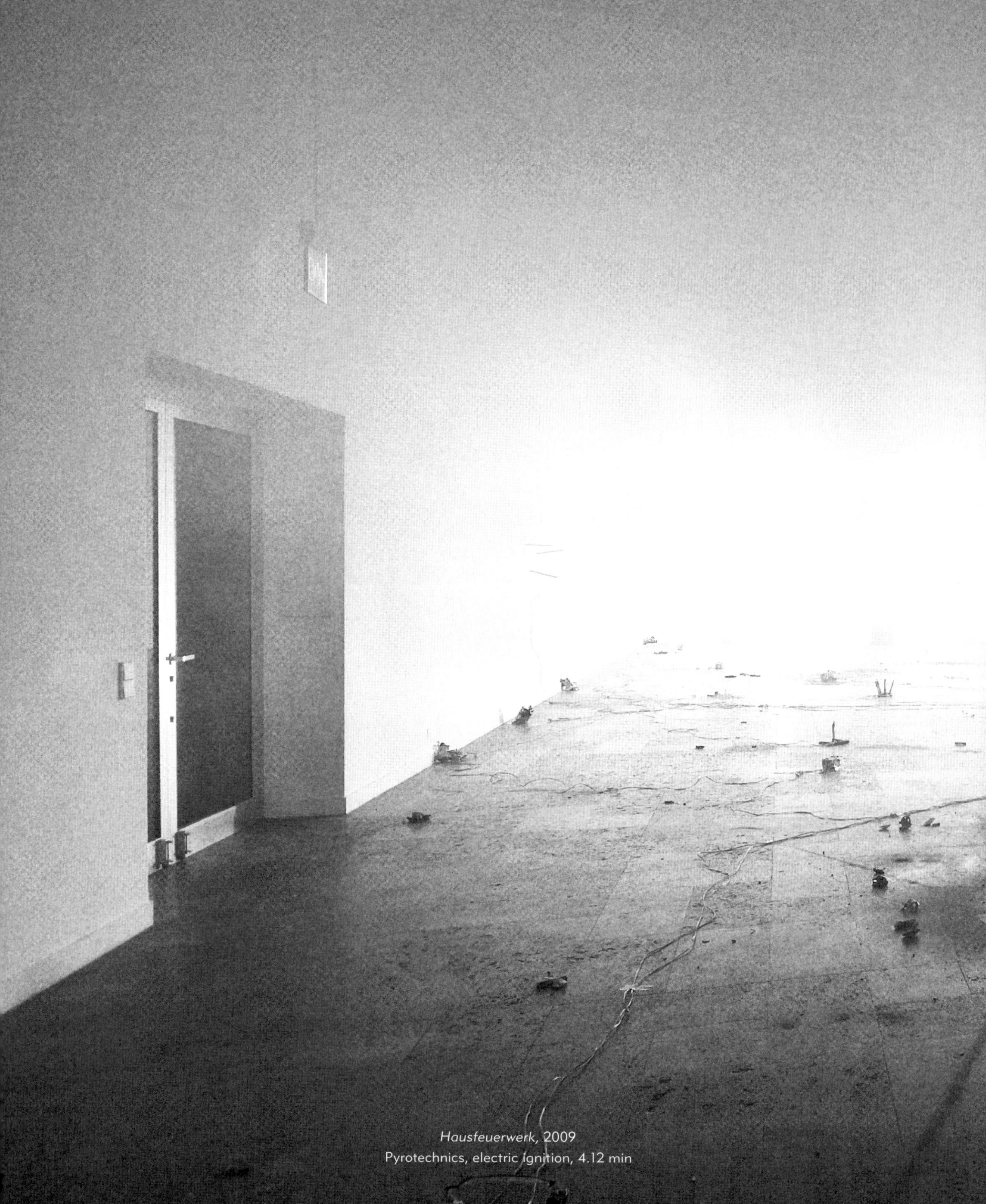

Hausfeuerwerk, 2009
Pyrotechnics, electric ignition, 4.12 min

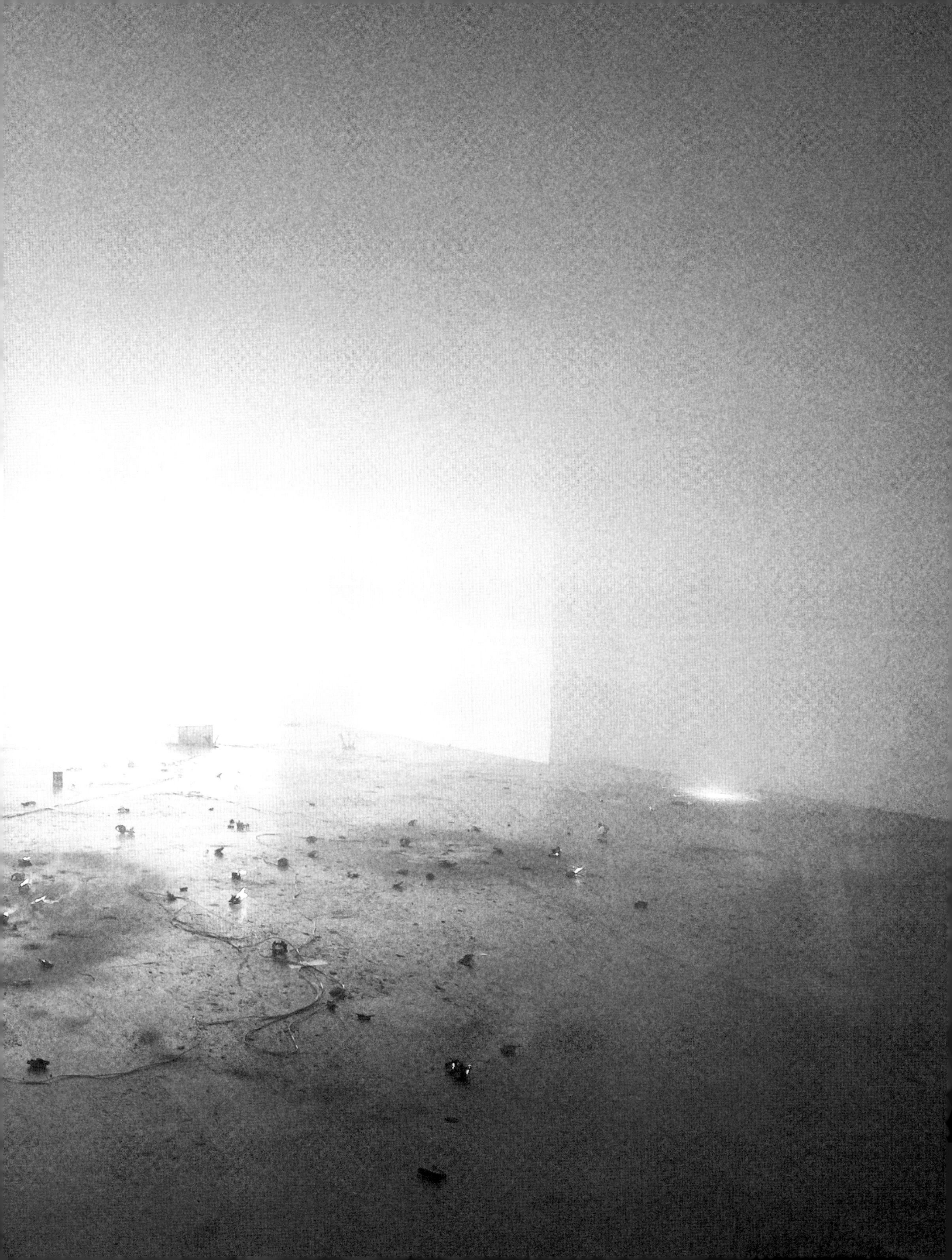

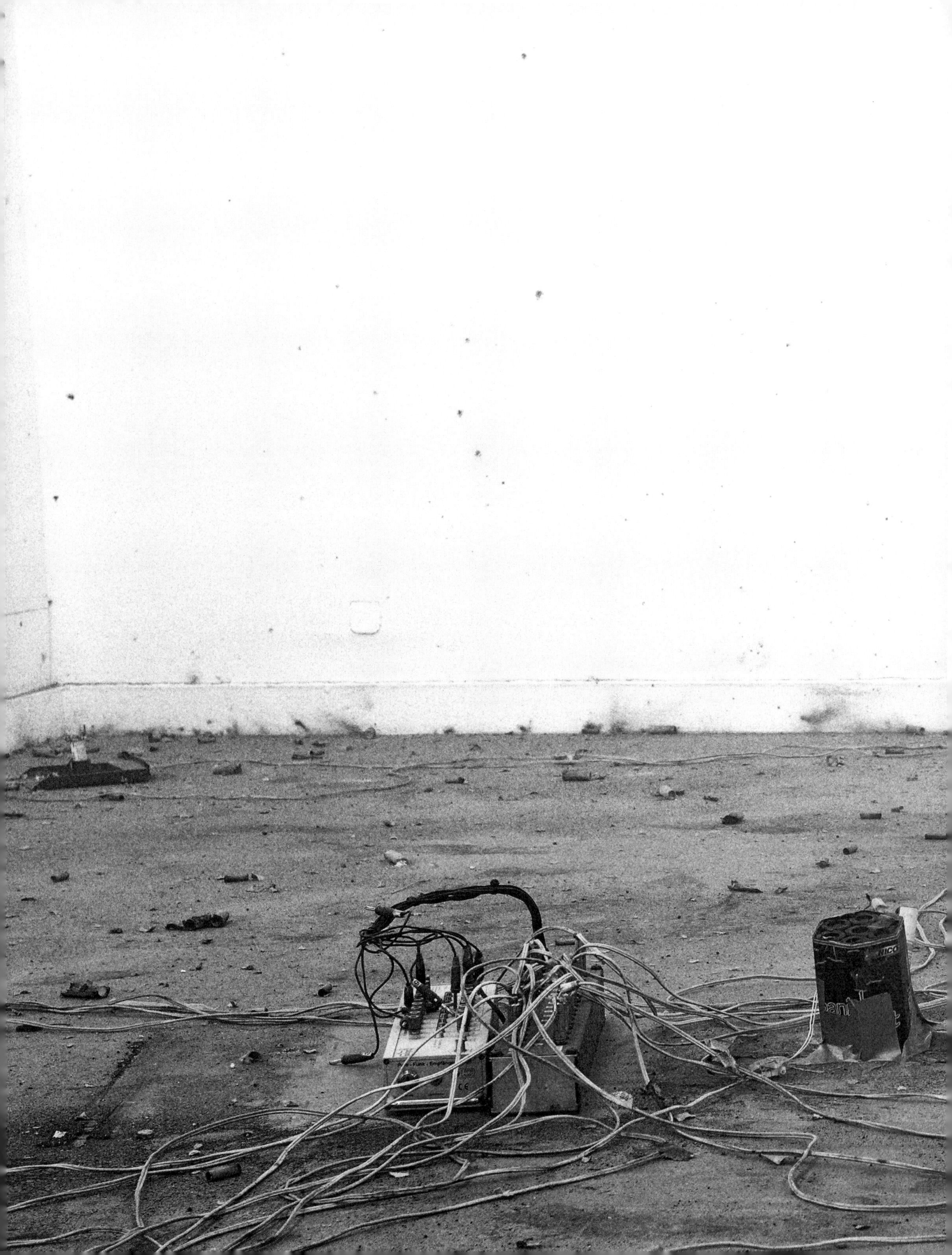

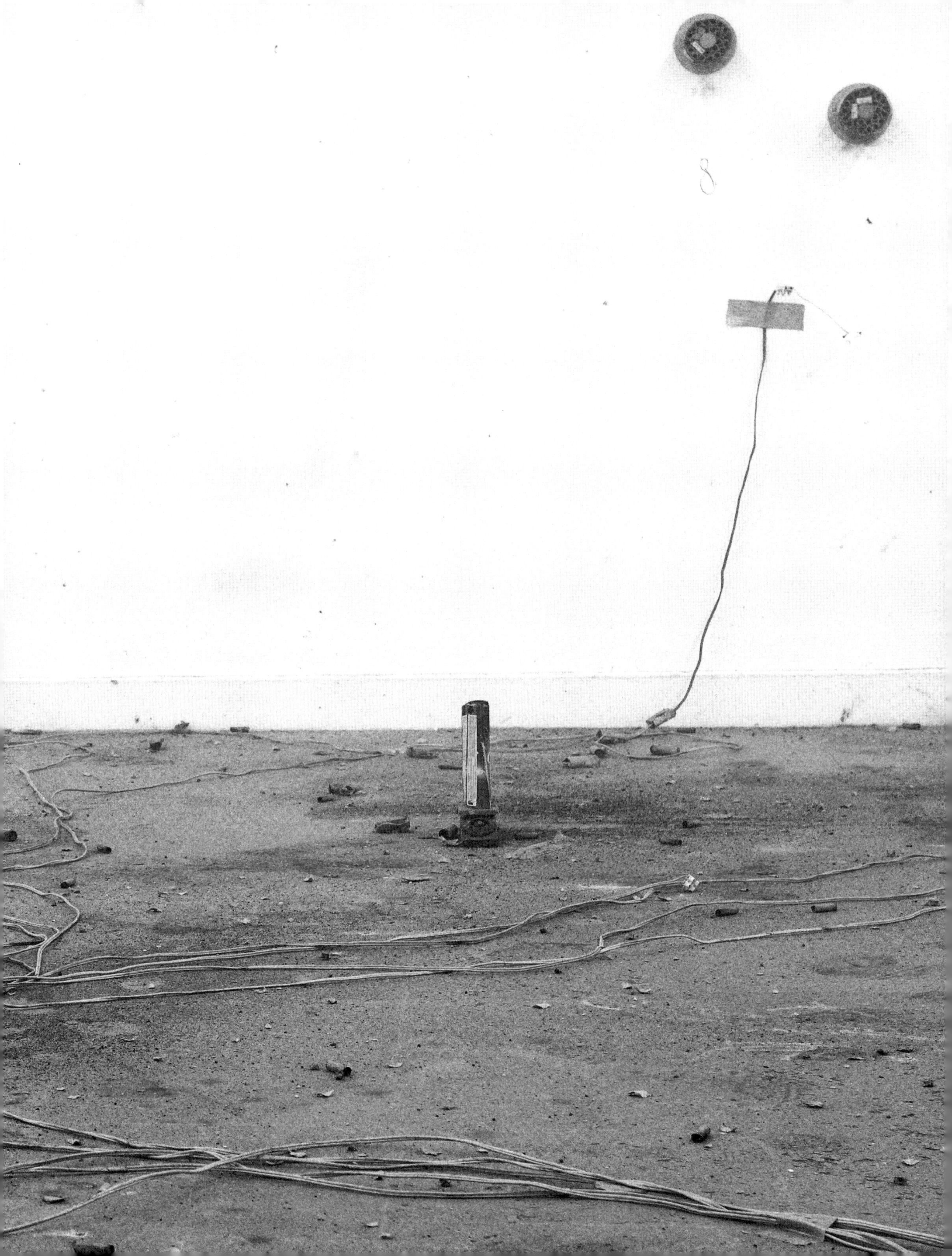

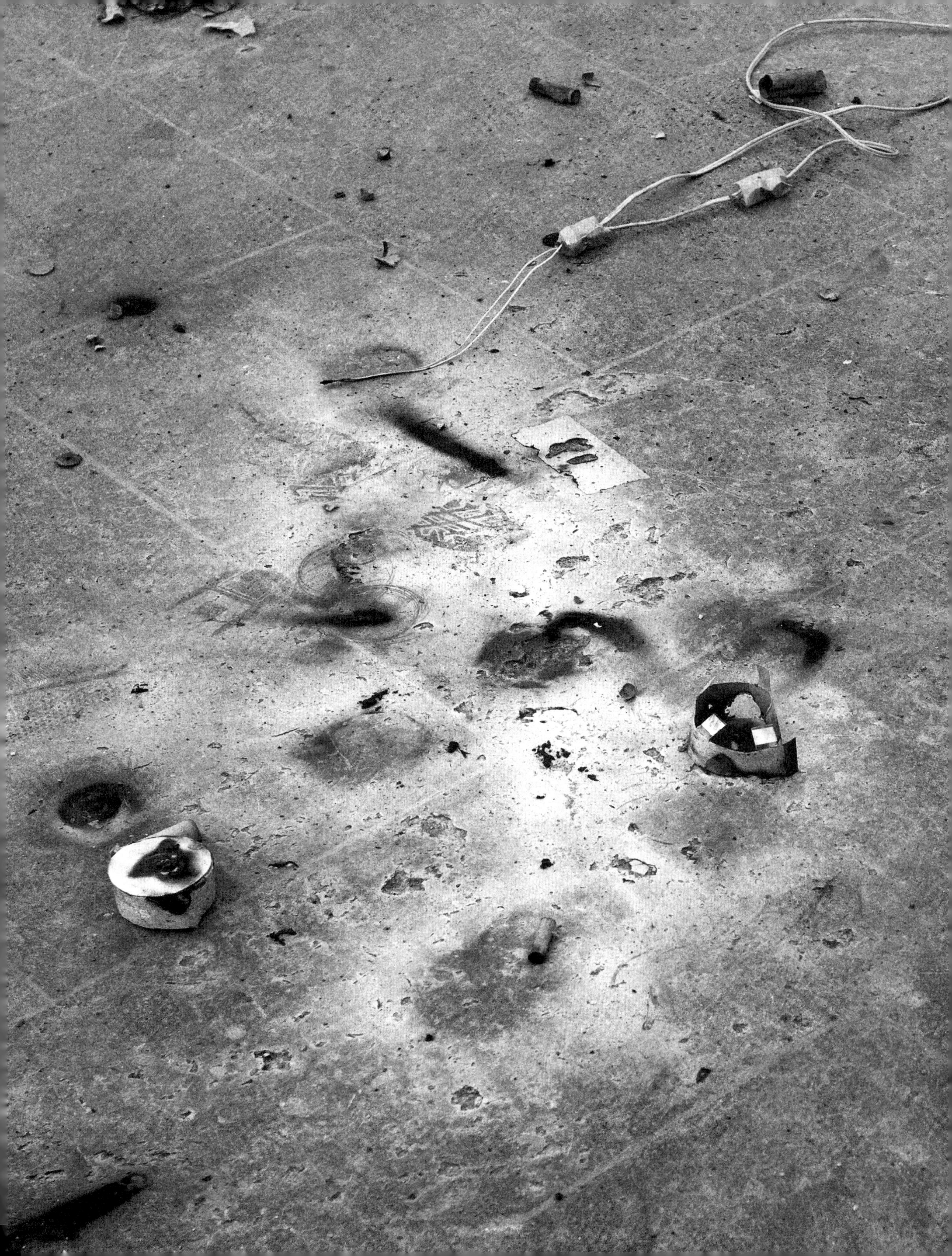

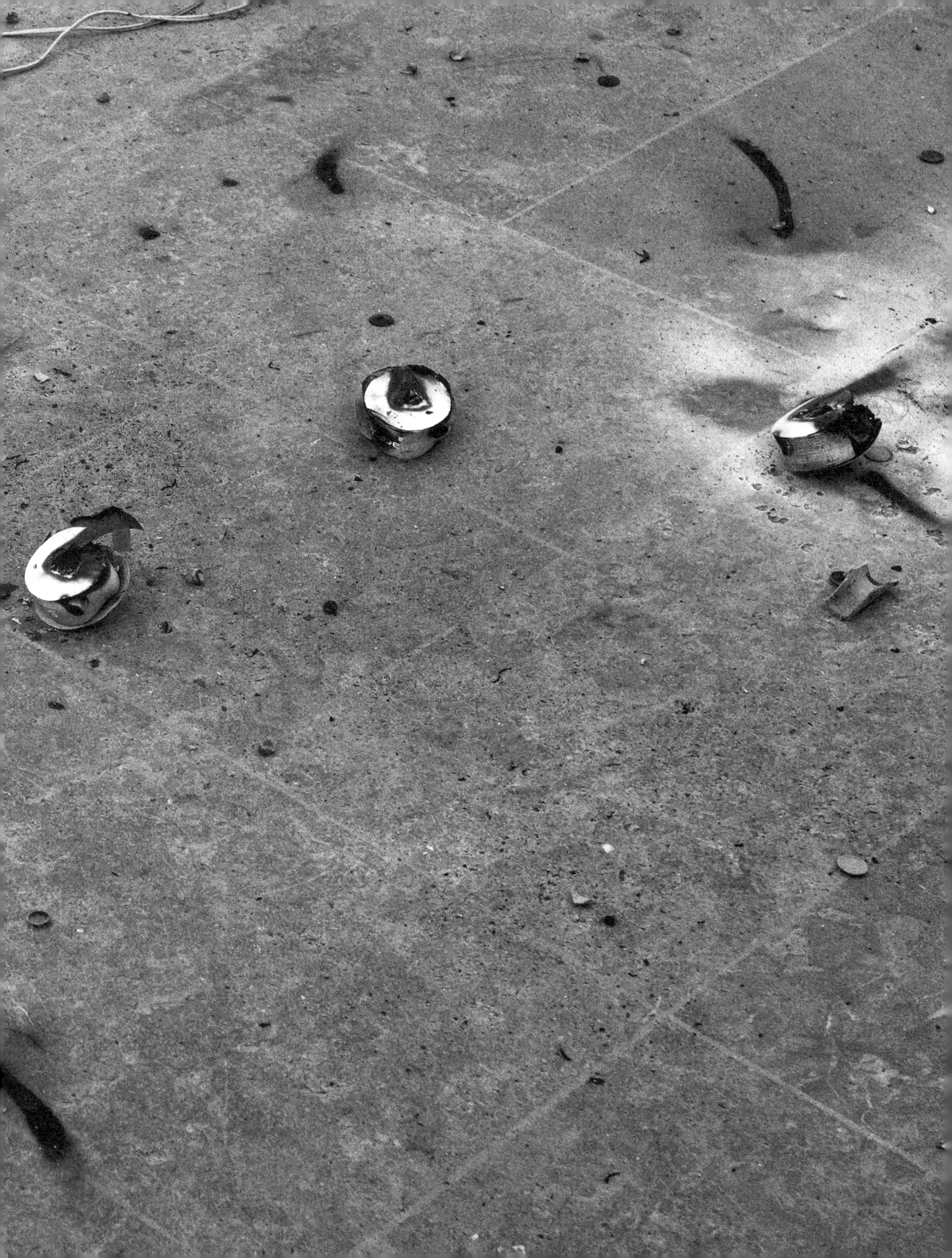

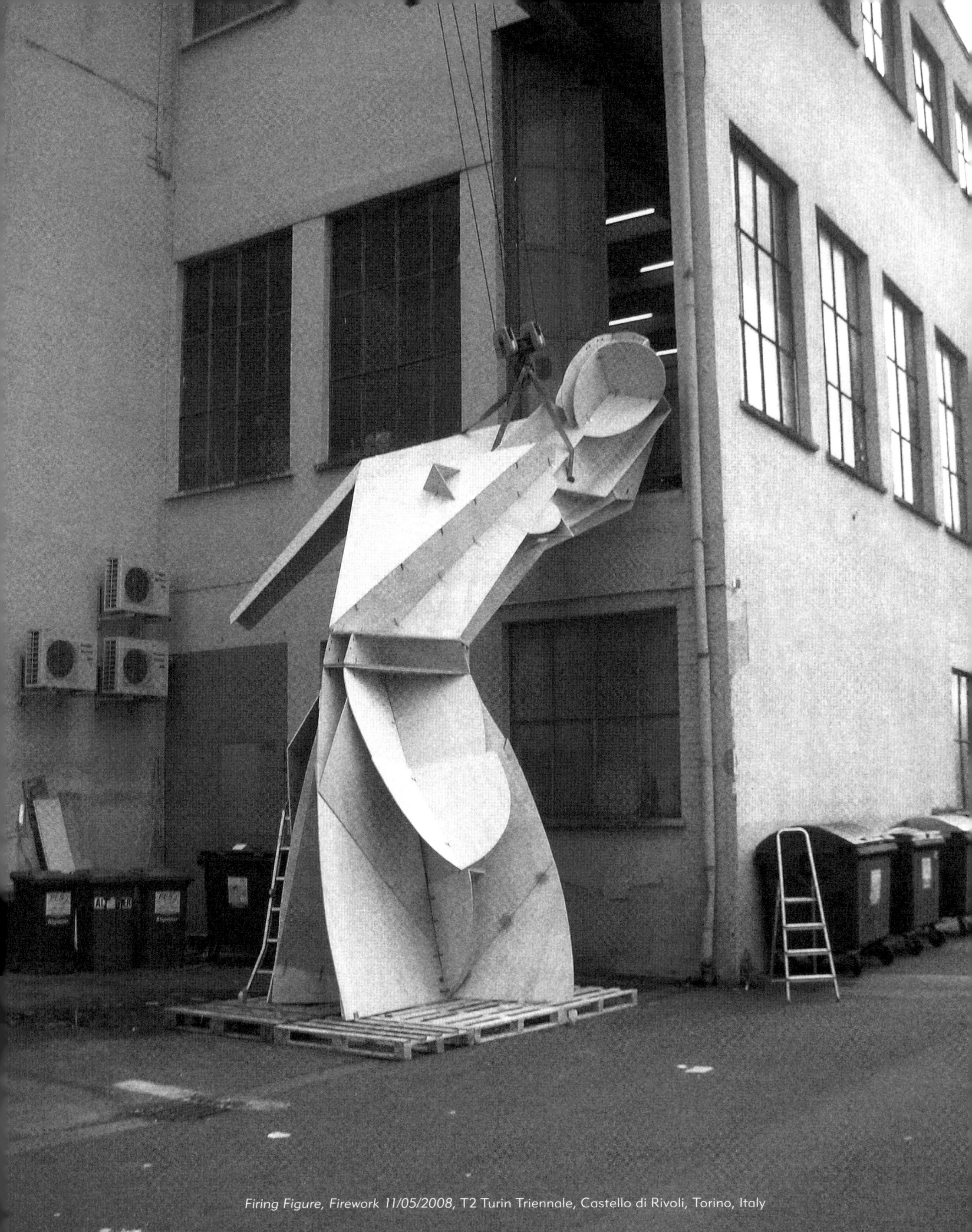

Firing Figure, Firework 11/05/2008, T2 Turin Triennale, Castello di Rivoli, Torino, Italy

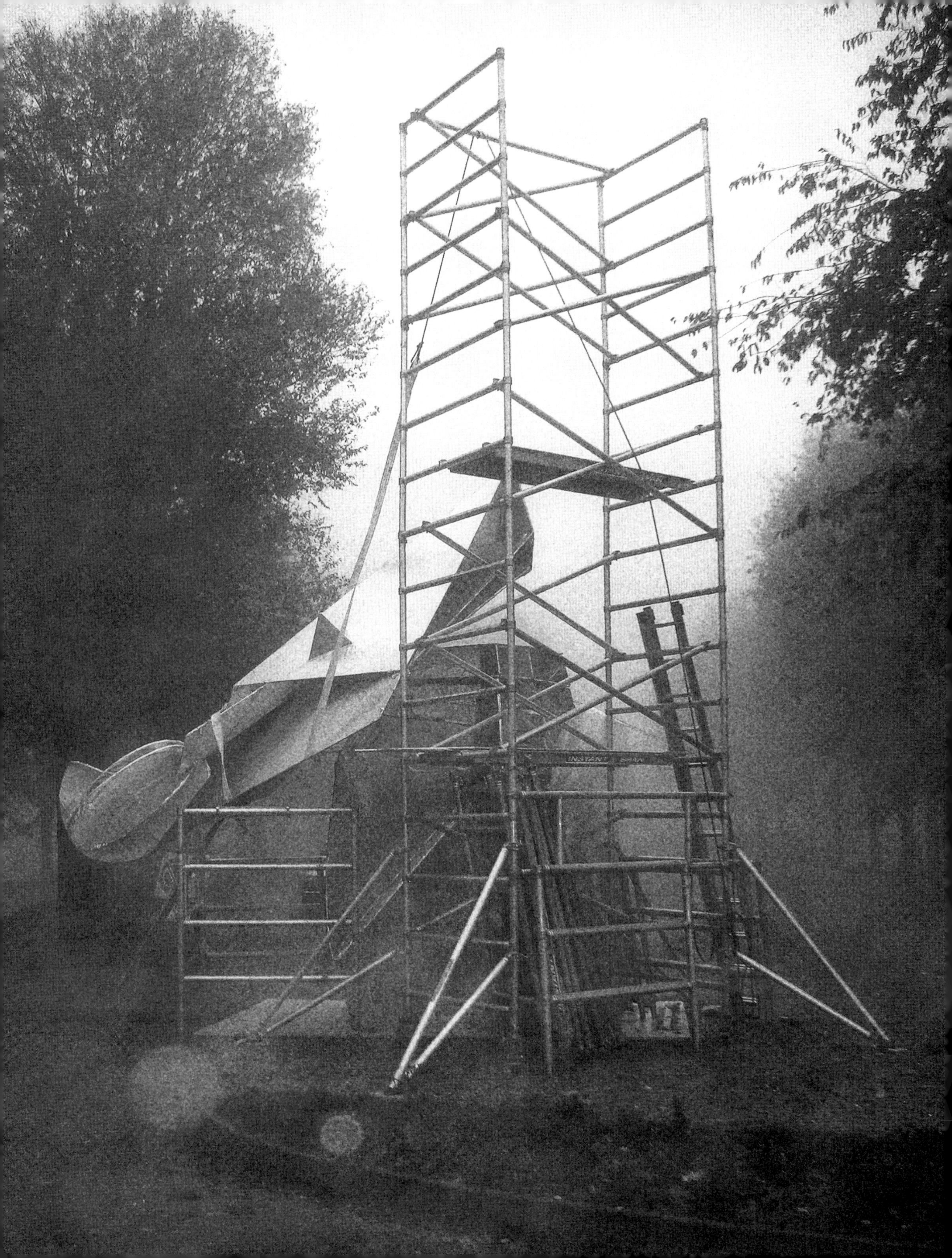

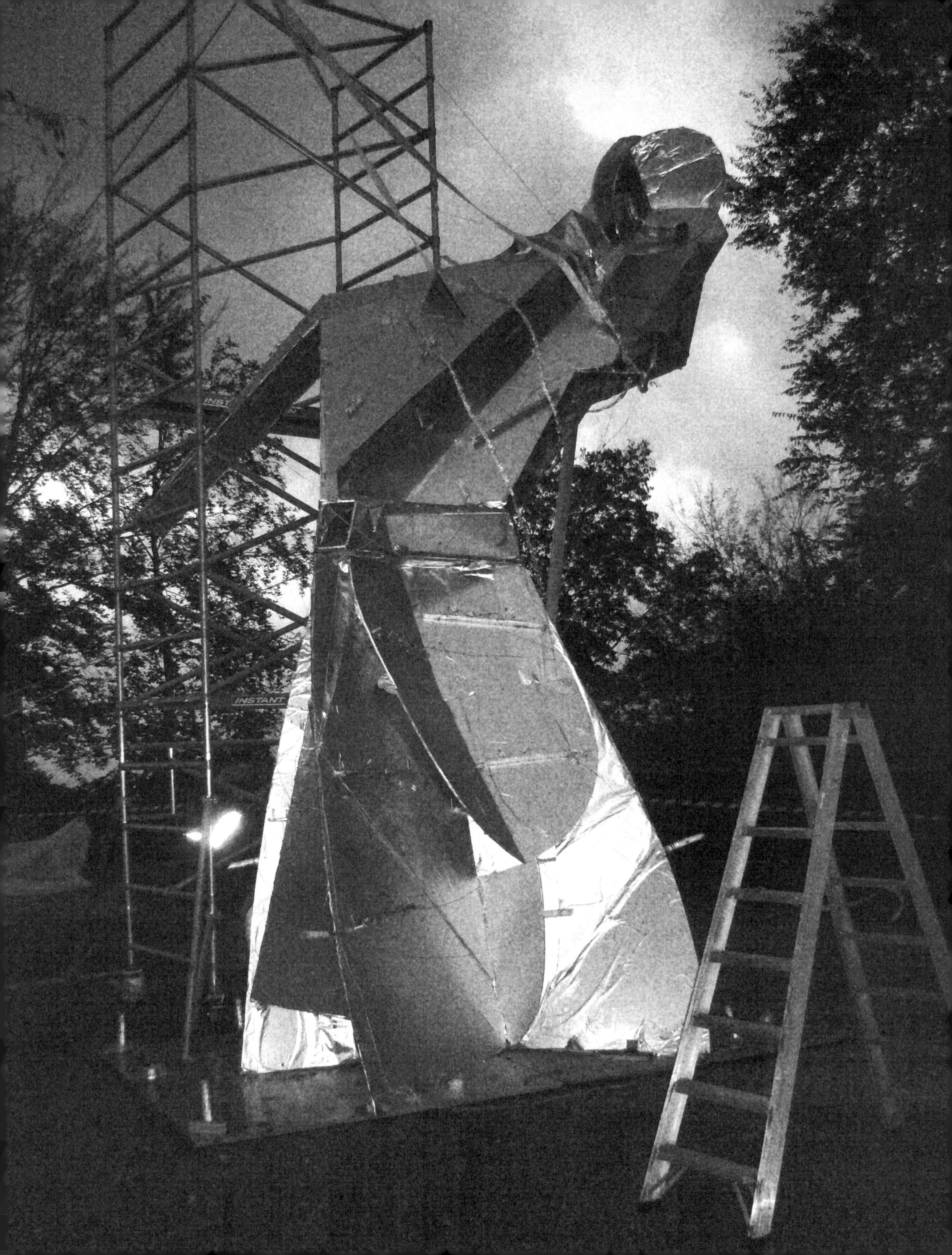

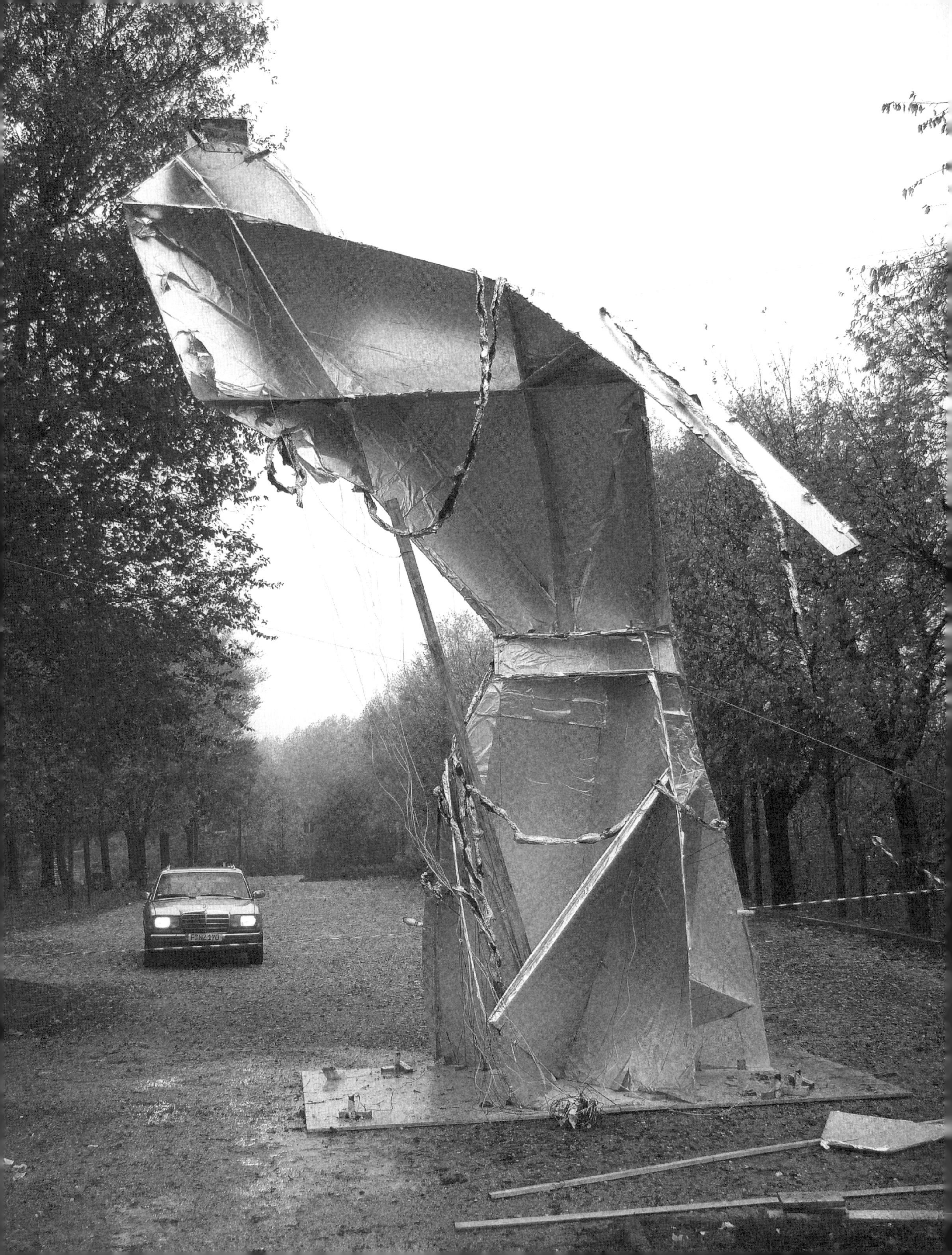

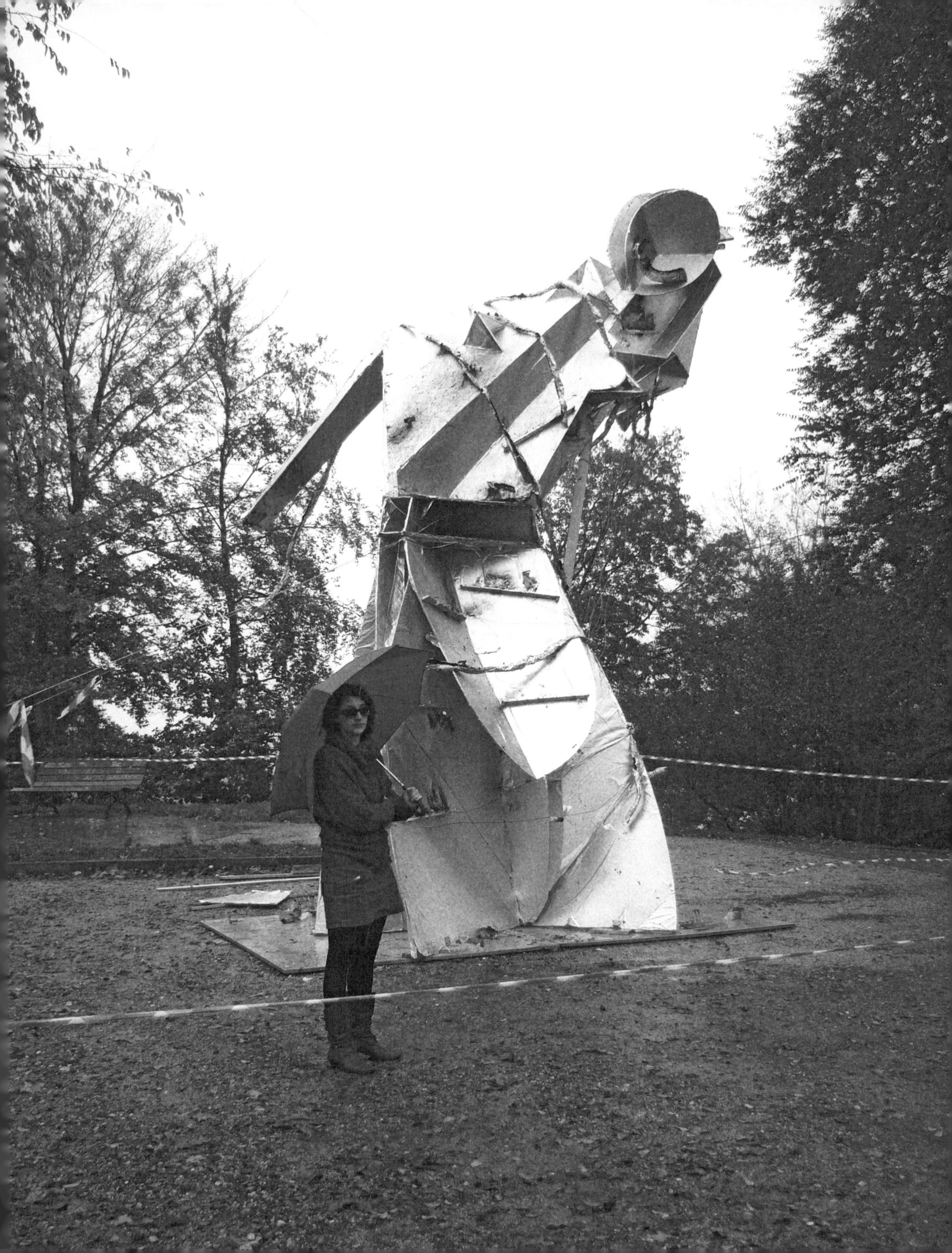

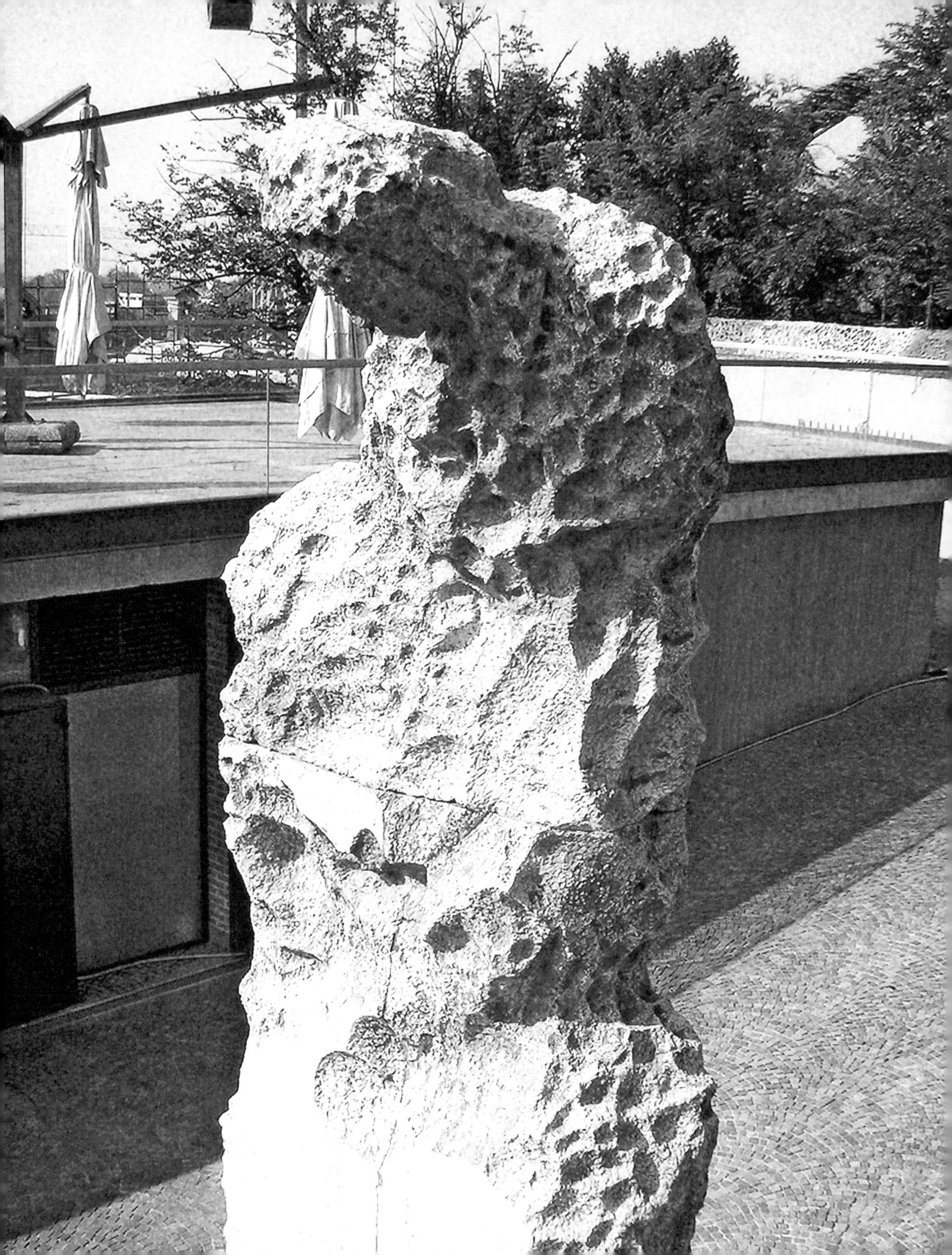

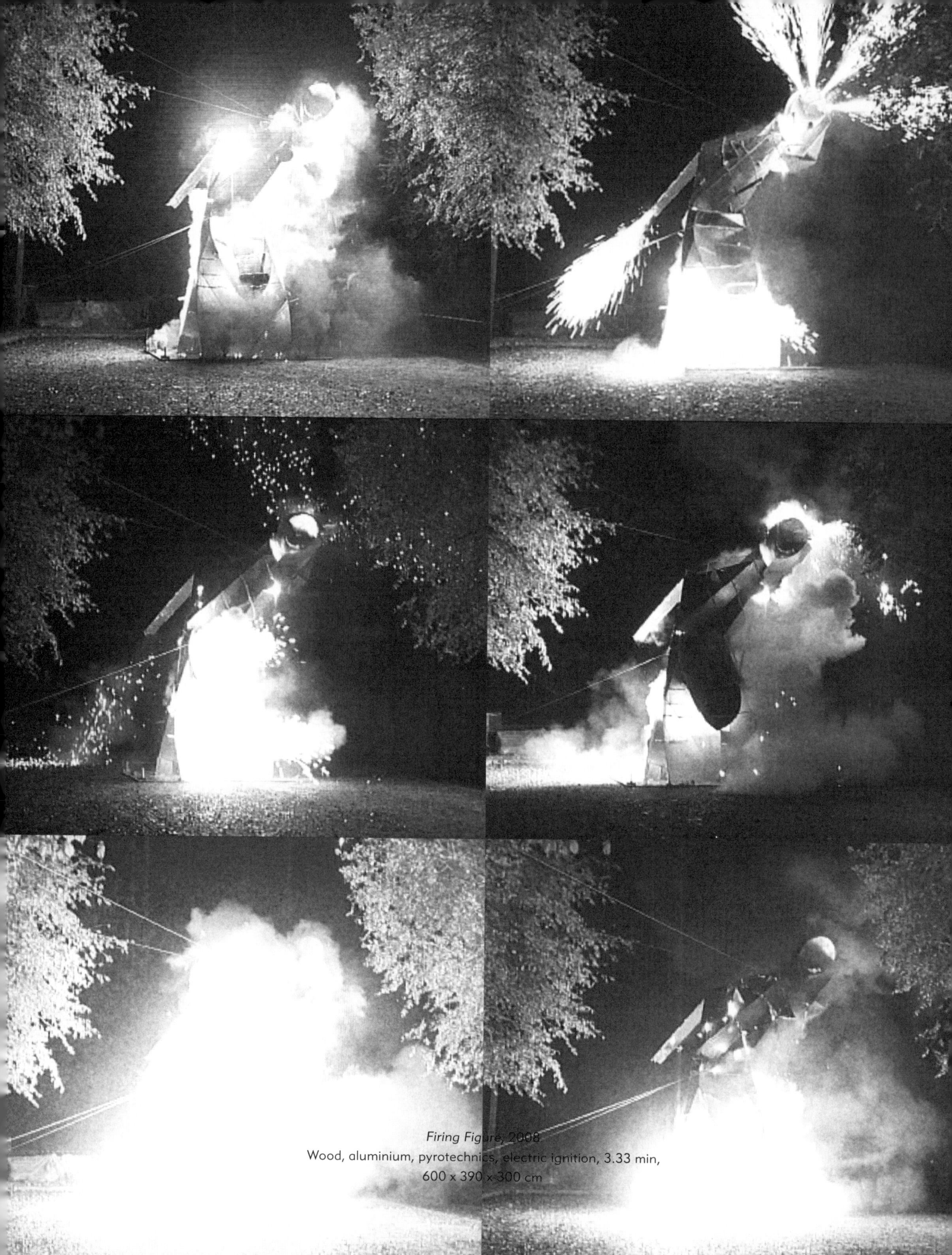

Firing Figure, 2008
Wood, aluminium, pyrotechnics, electric ignition, 3.33 min,
600 x 390 x 300 cm

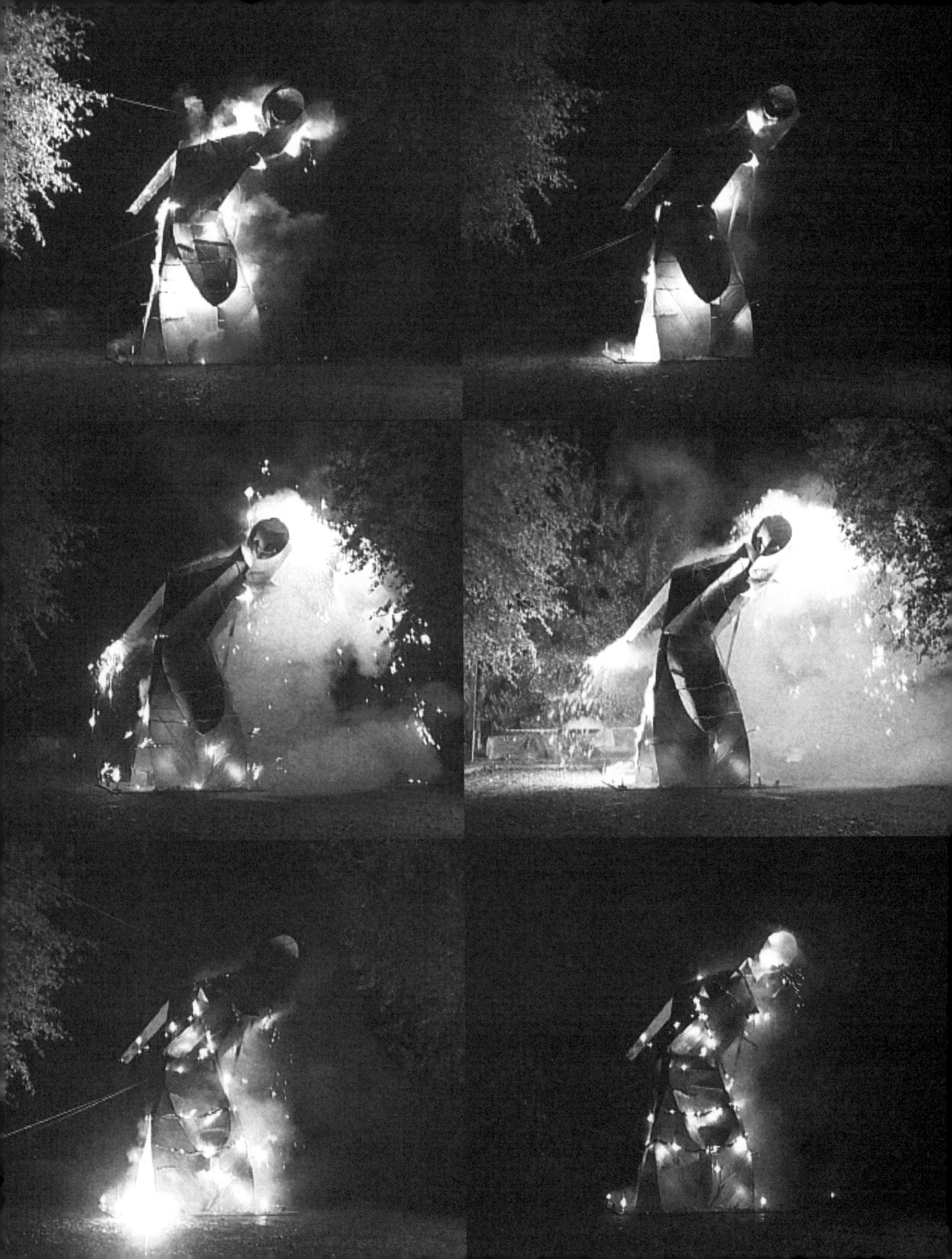

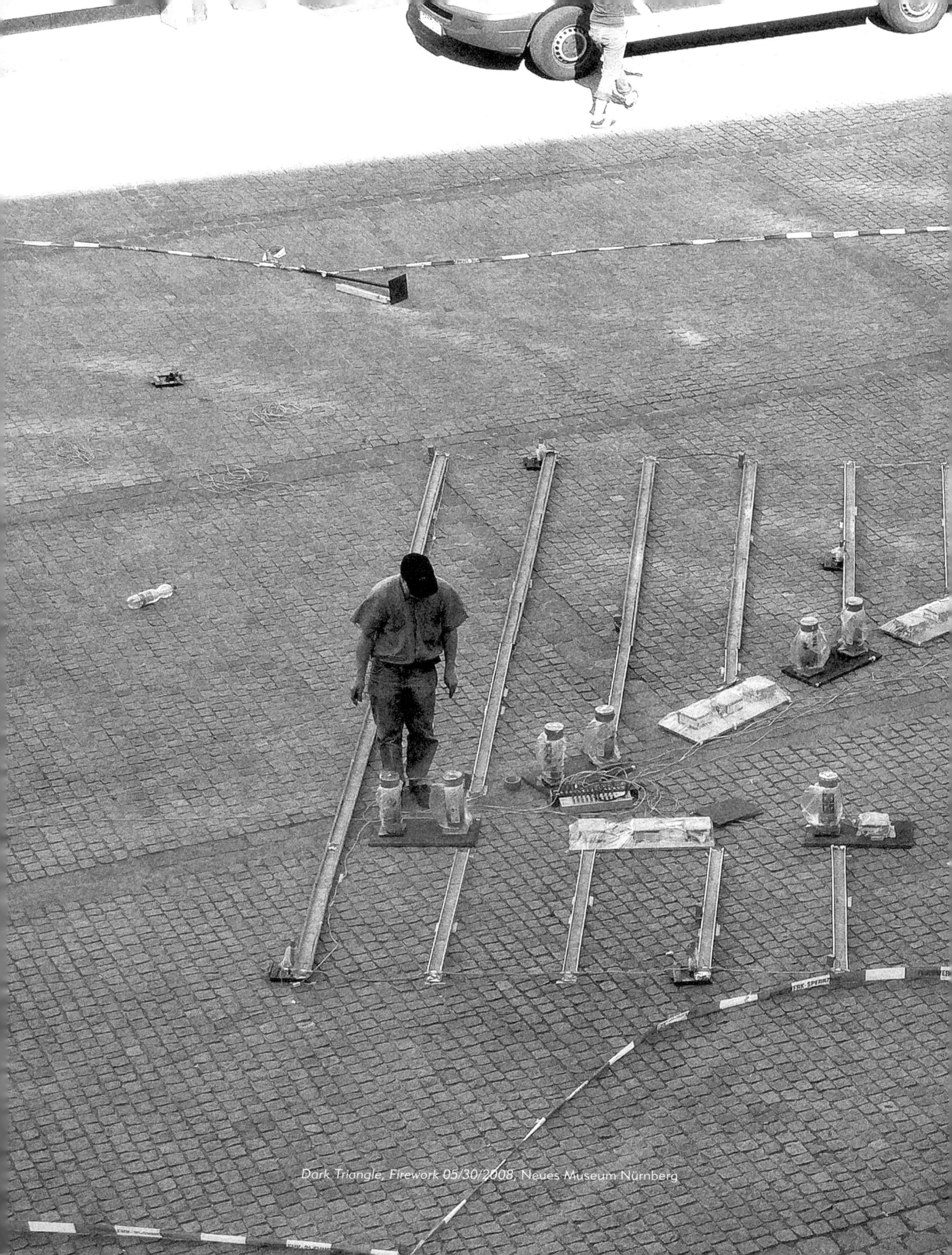

Dark Triangle, Firework 05/30/2008, Neues Museum Nürnberg

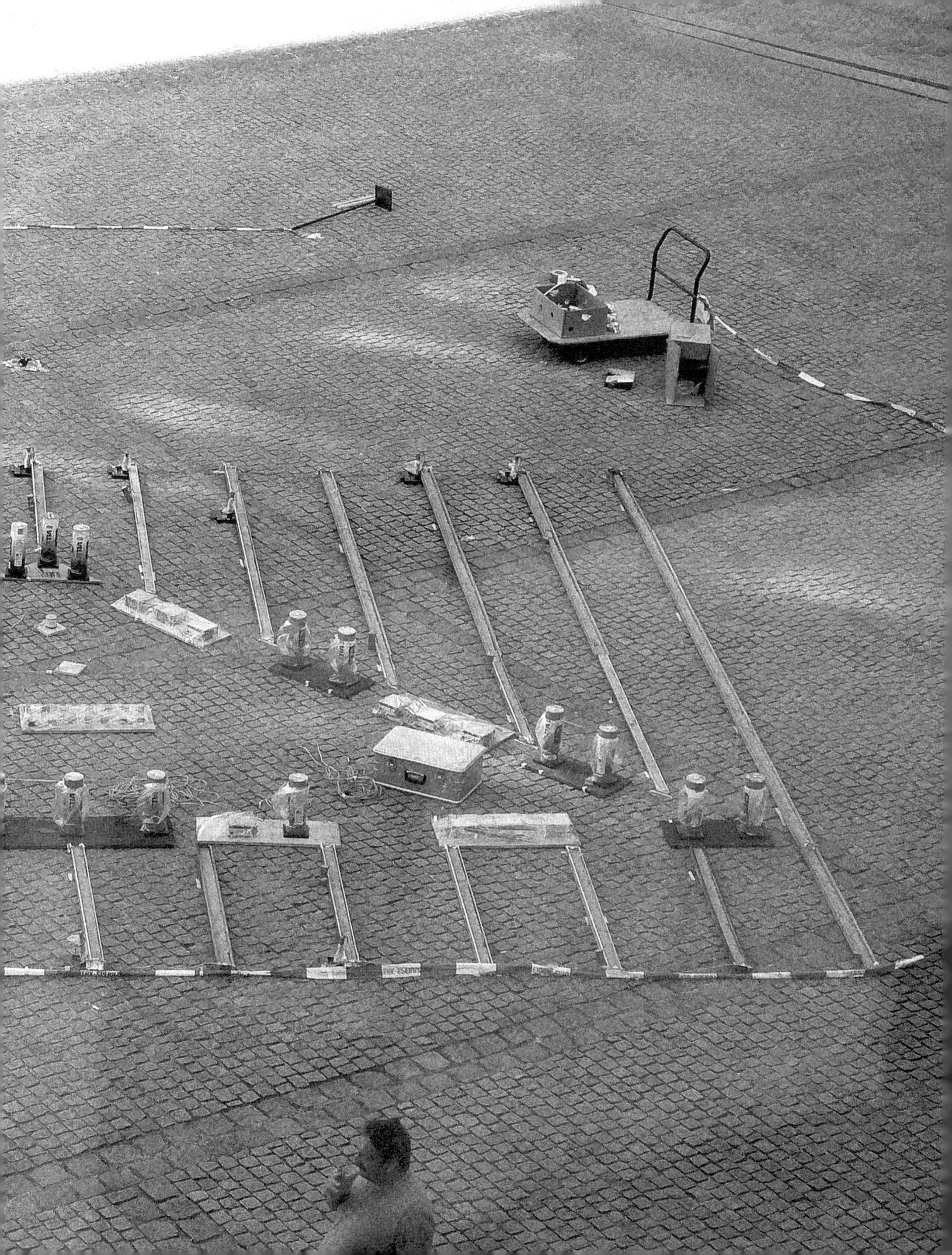

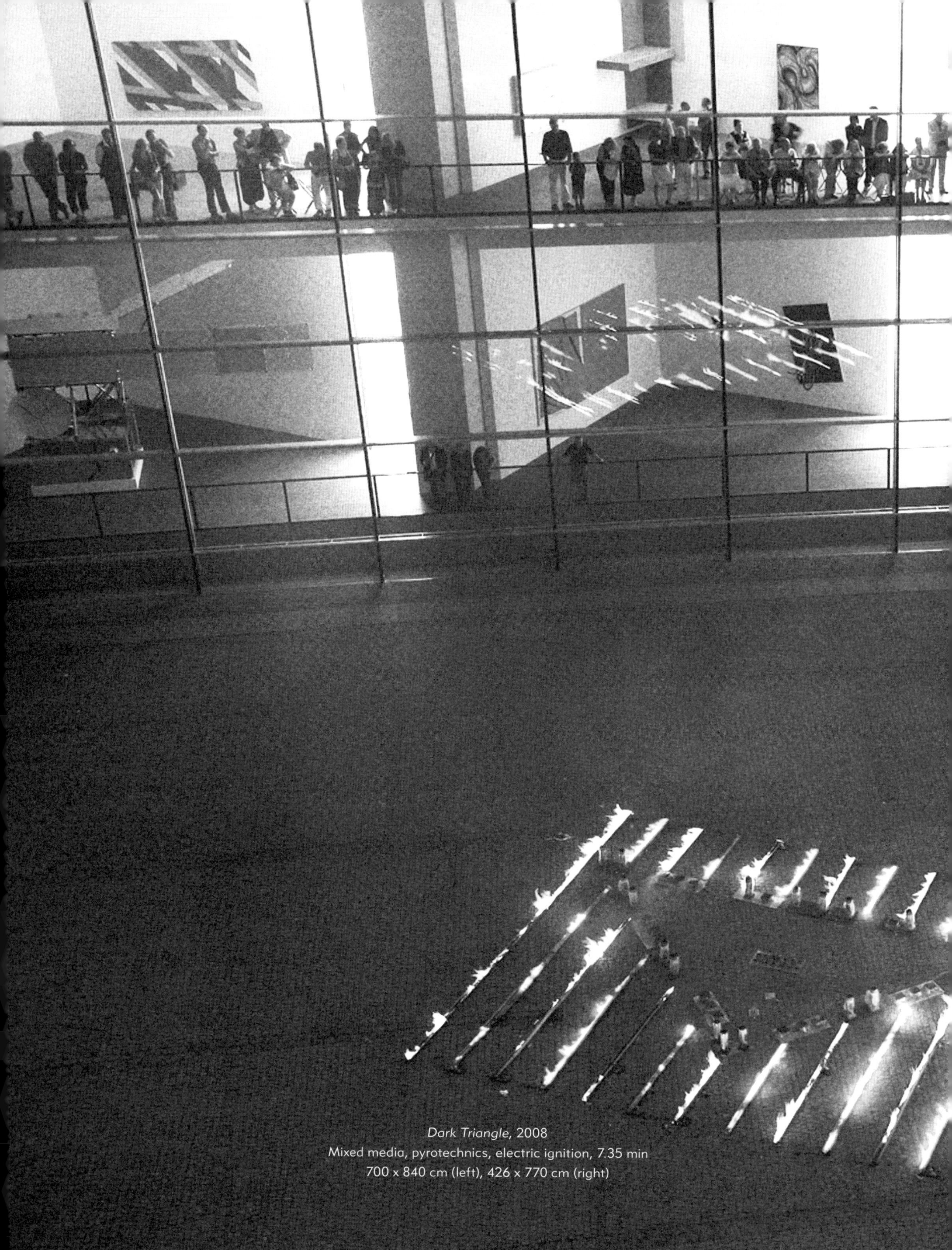

Dark Triangle, 2008
Mixed media, pyrotechnics, electric ignition, 7.35 min
700 x 840 cm (left), 426 x 770 cm (right)

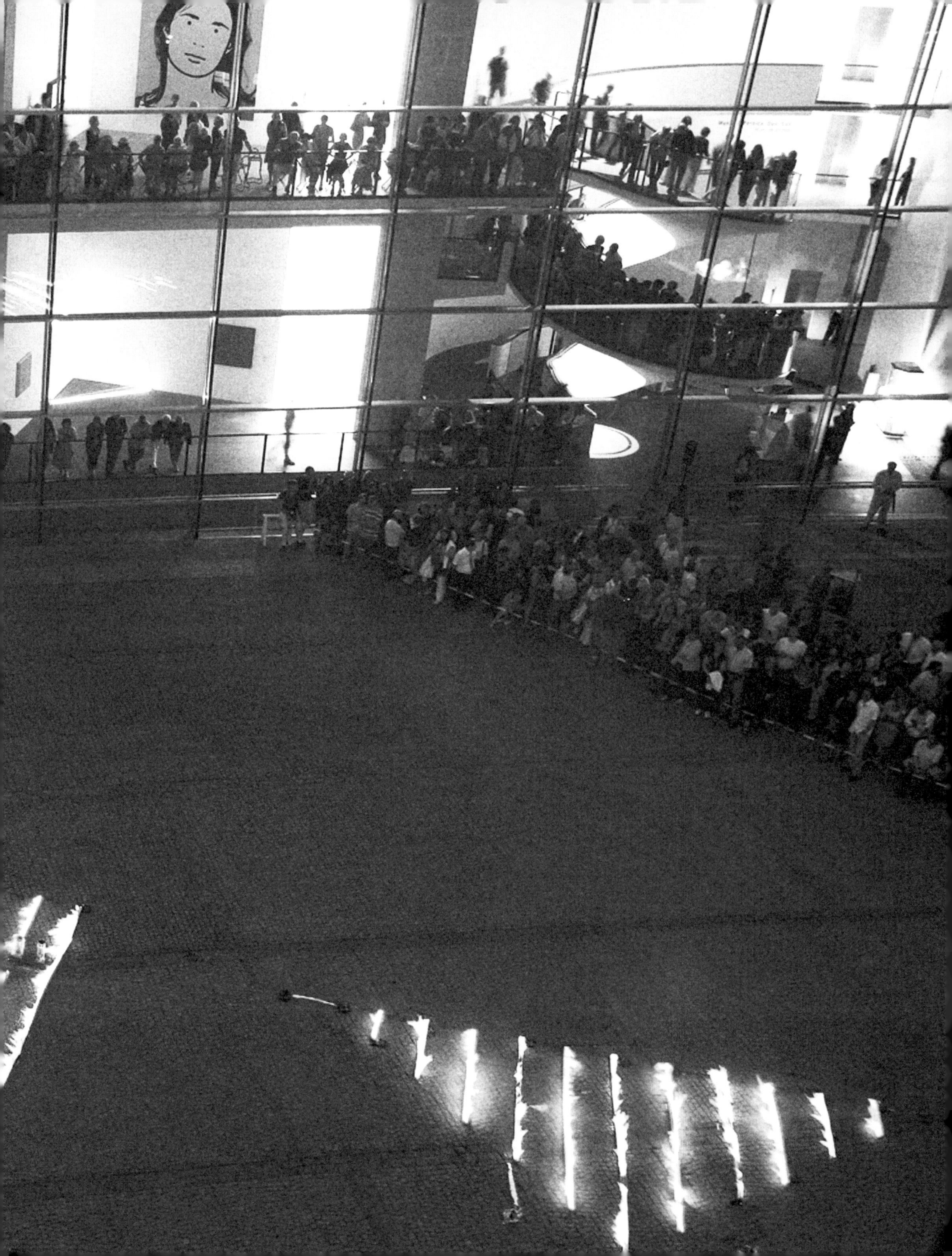

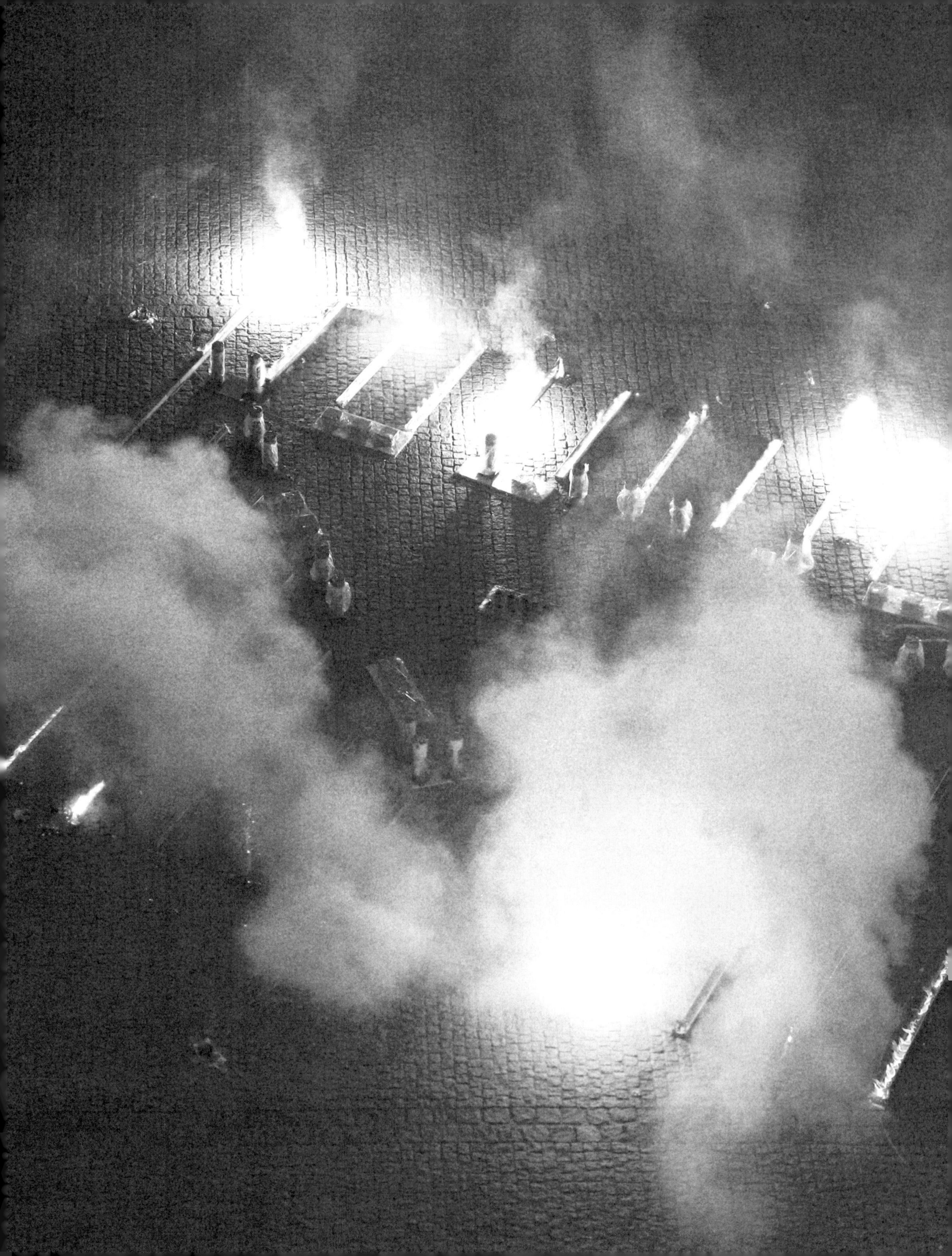

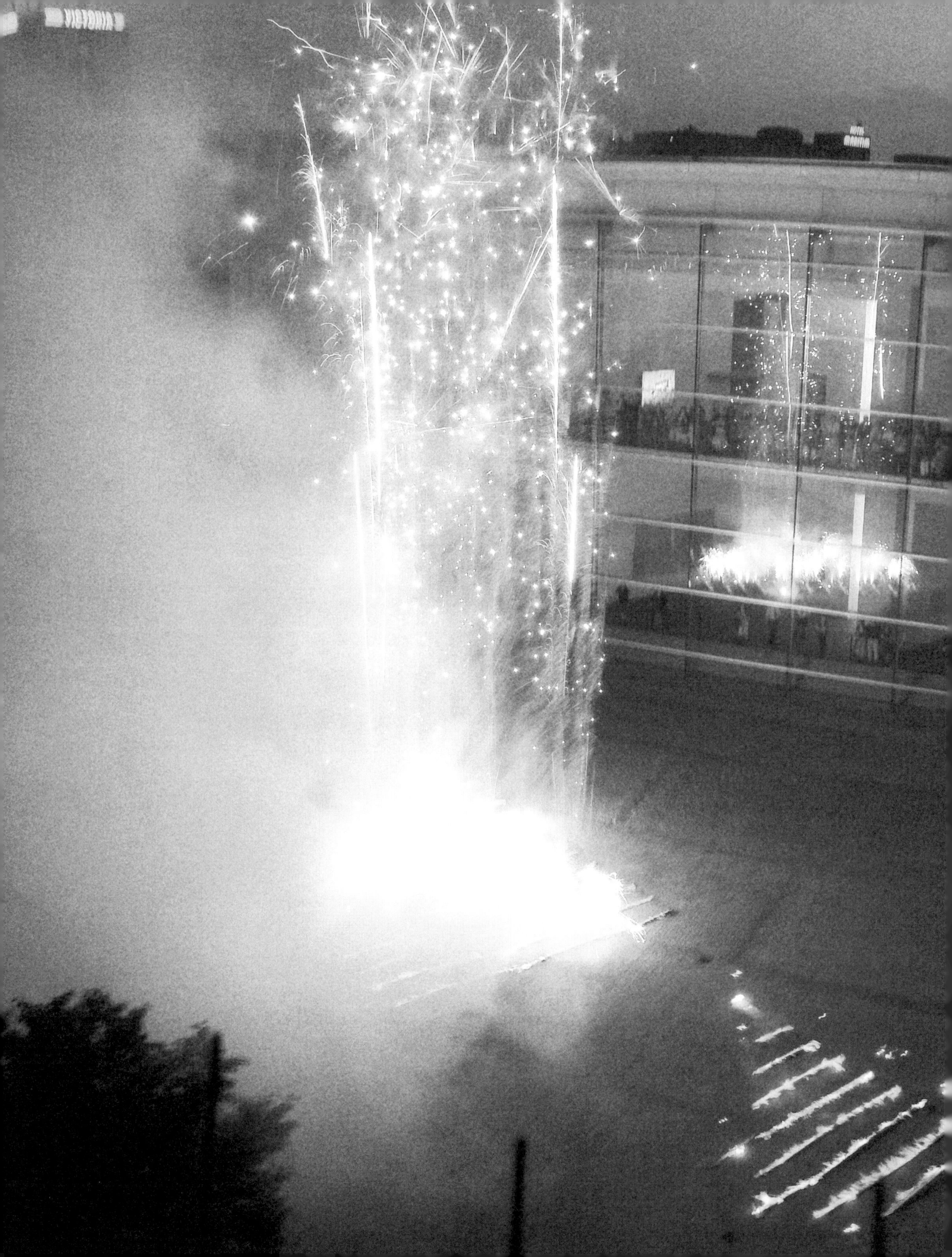

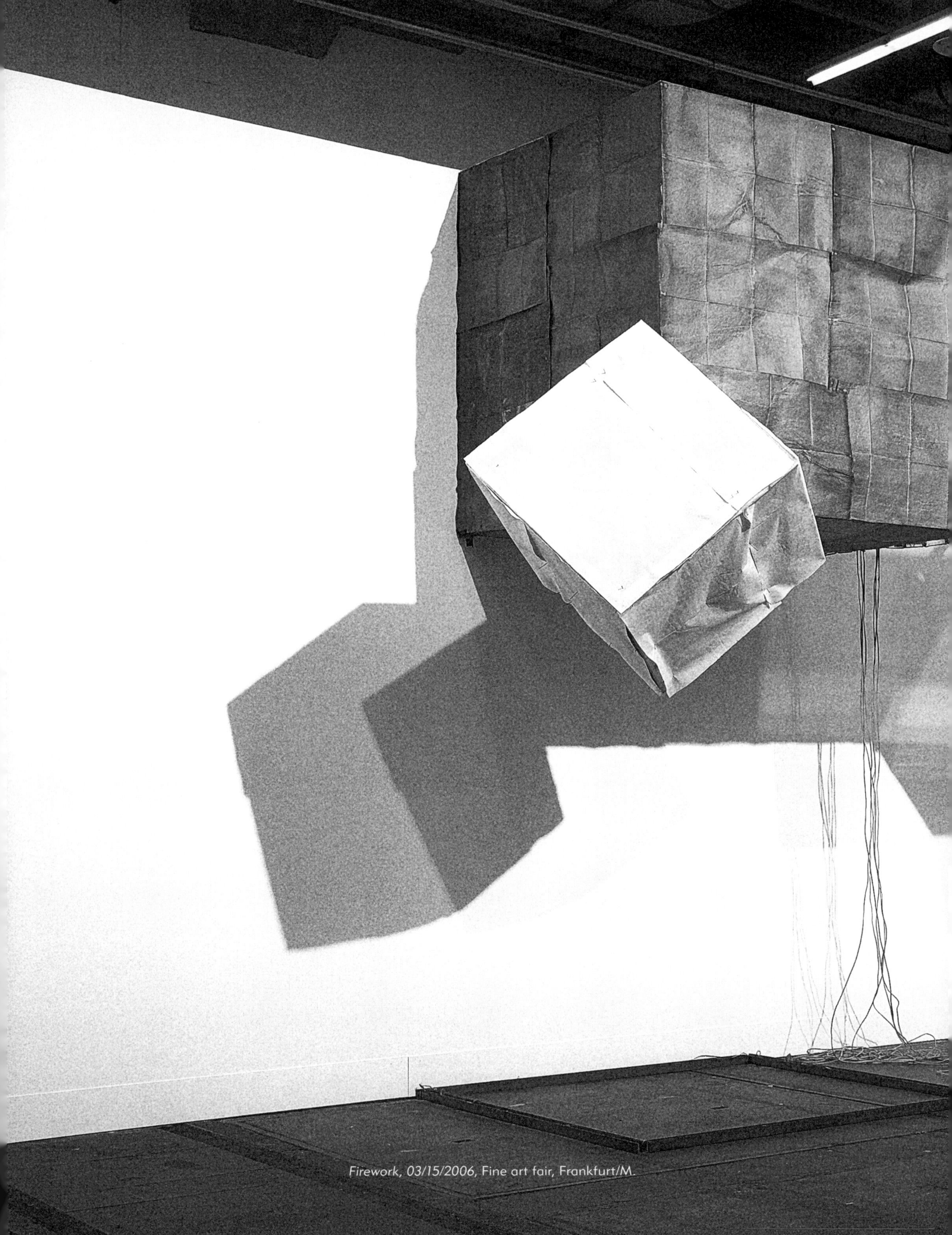

Firework, 03/15/2006, Fine art fair, Frankfurt/M.

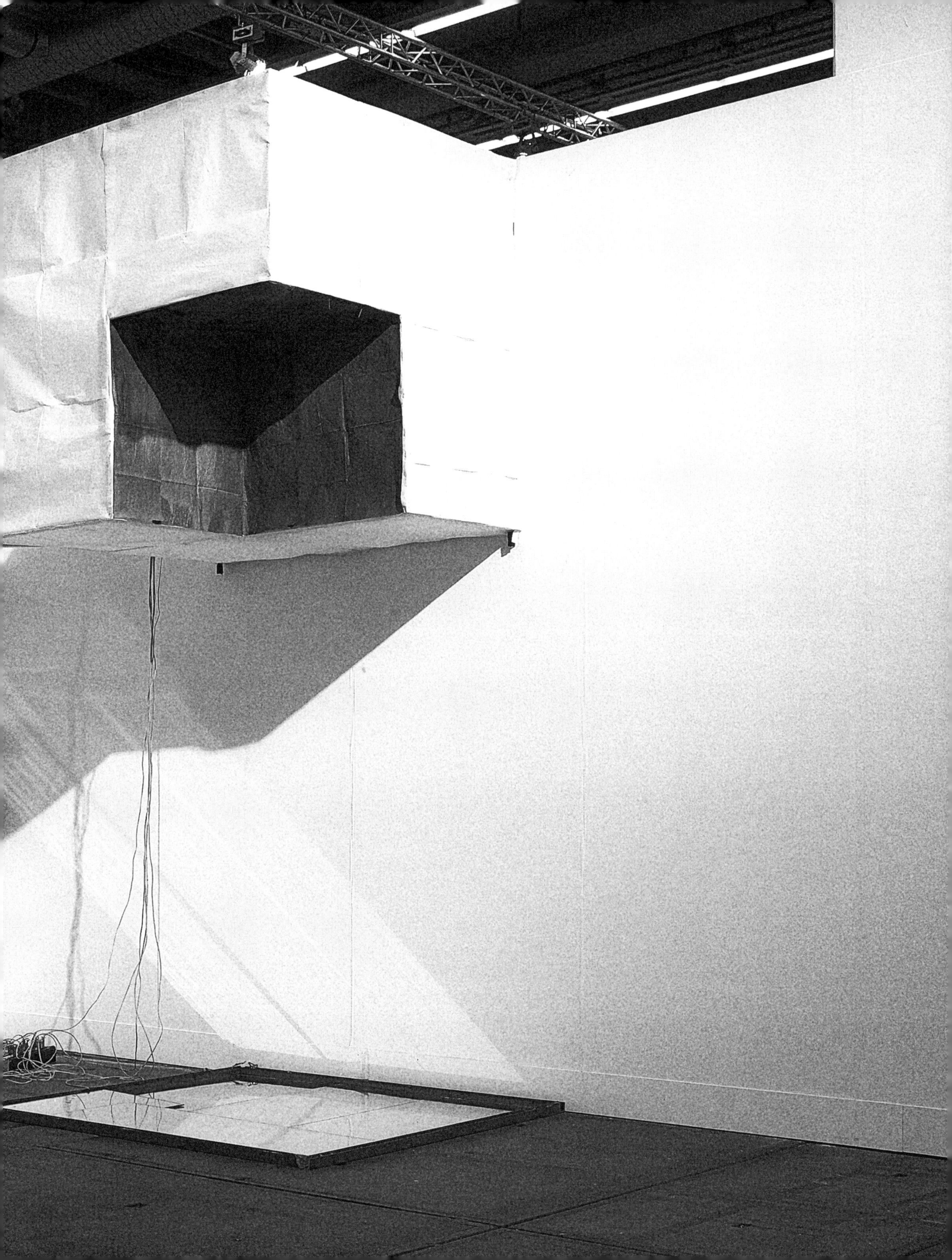

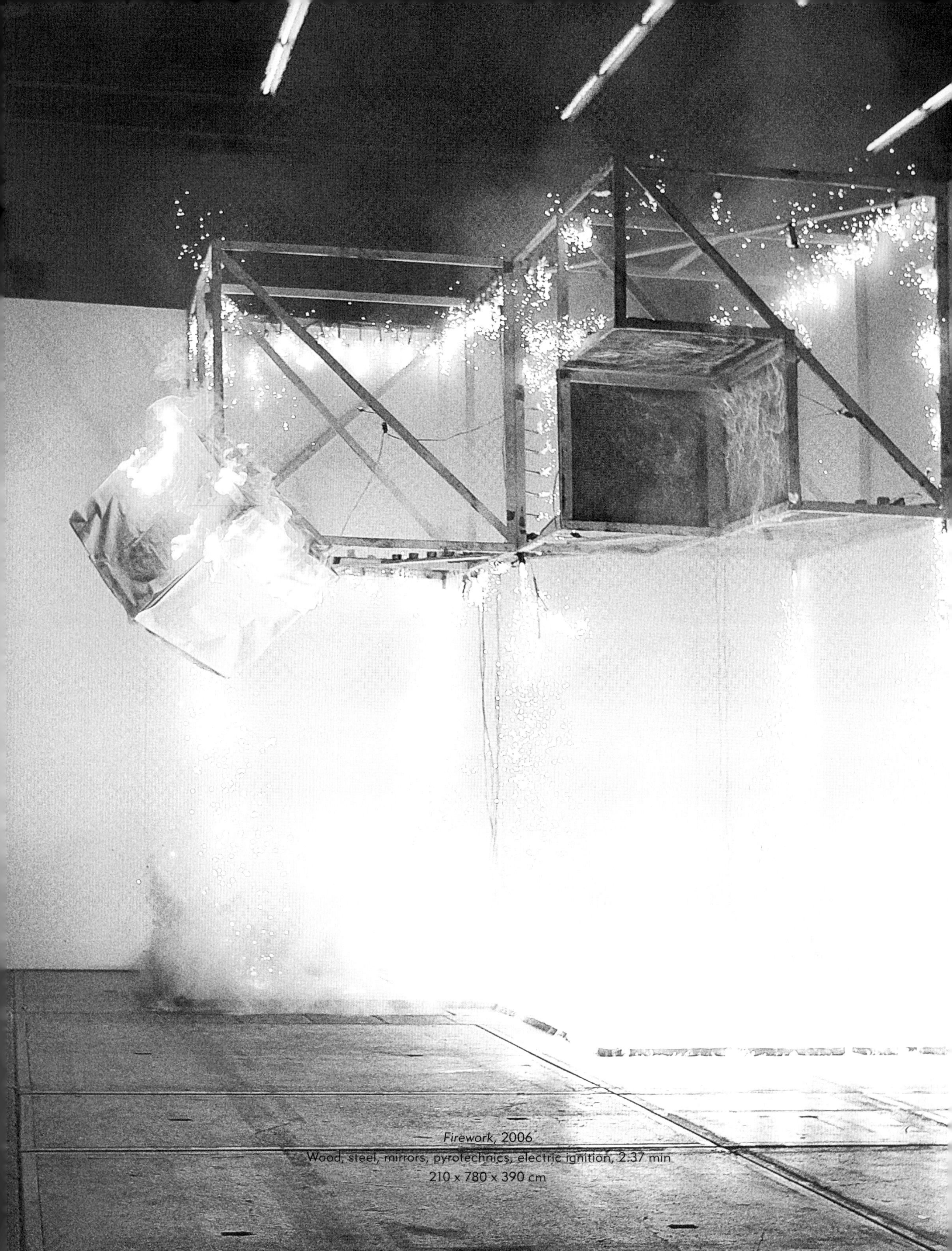

— Firework, 2006
Wood, steel, mirrors, pyrotechnics, electric ignition, 2:37 min
210 x 780 x 390 cm

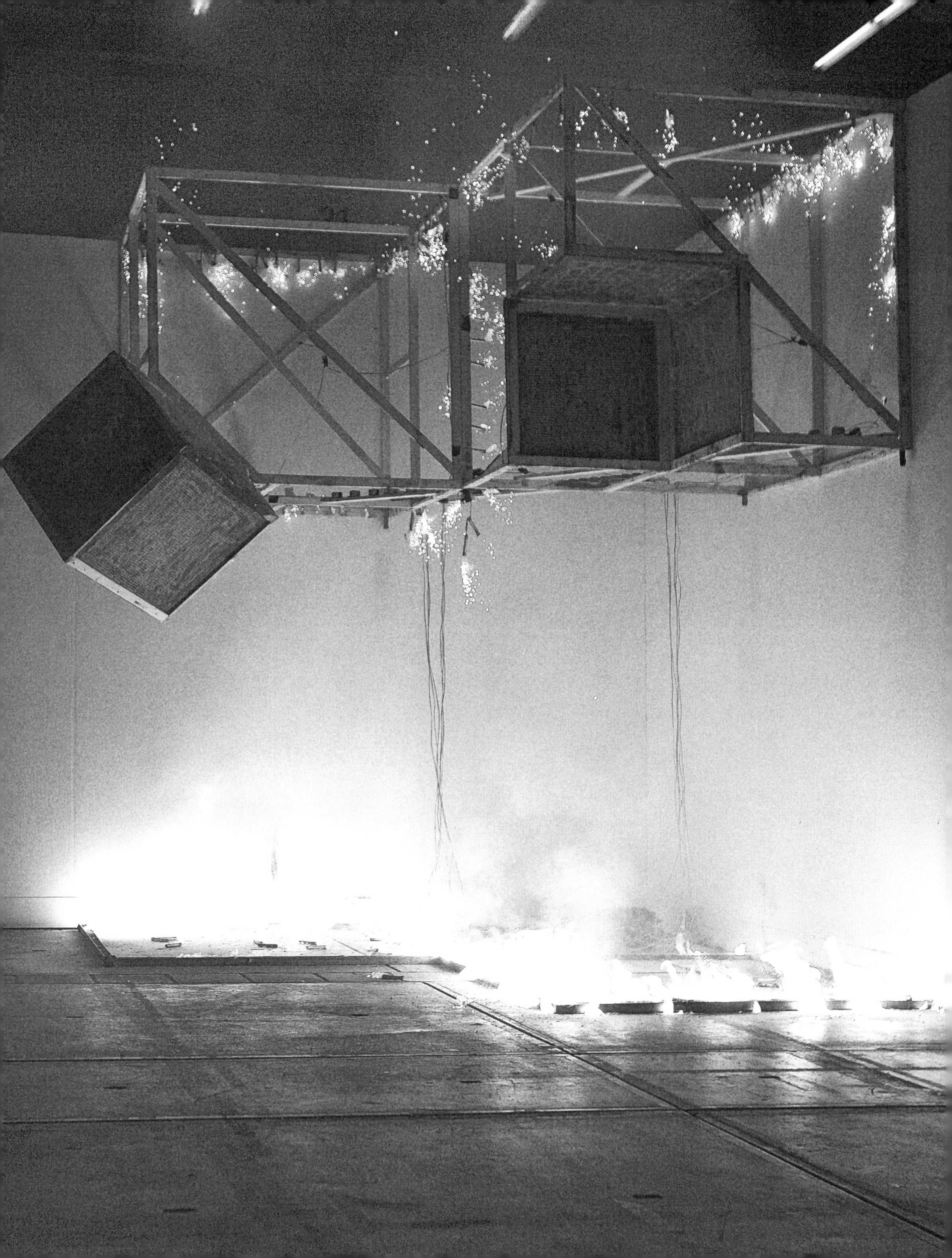

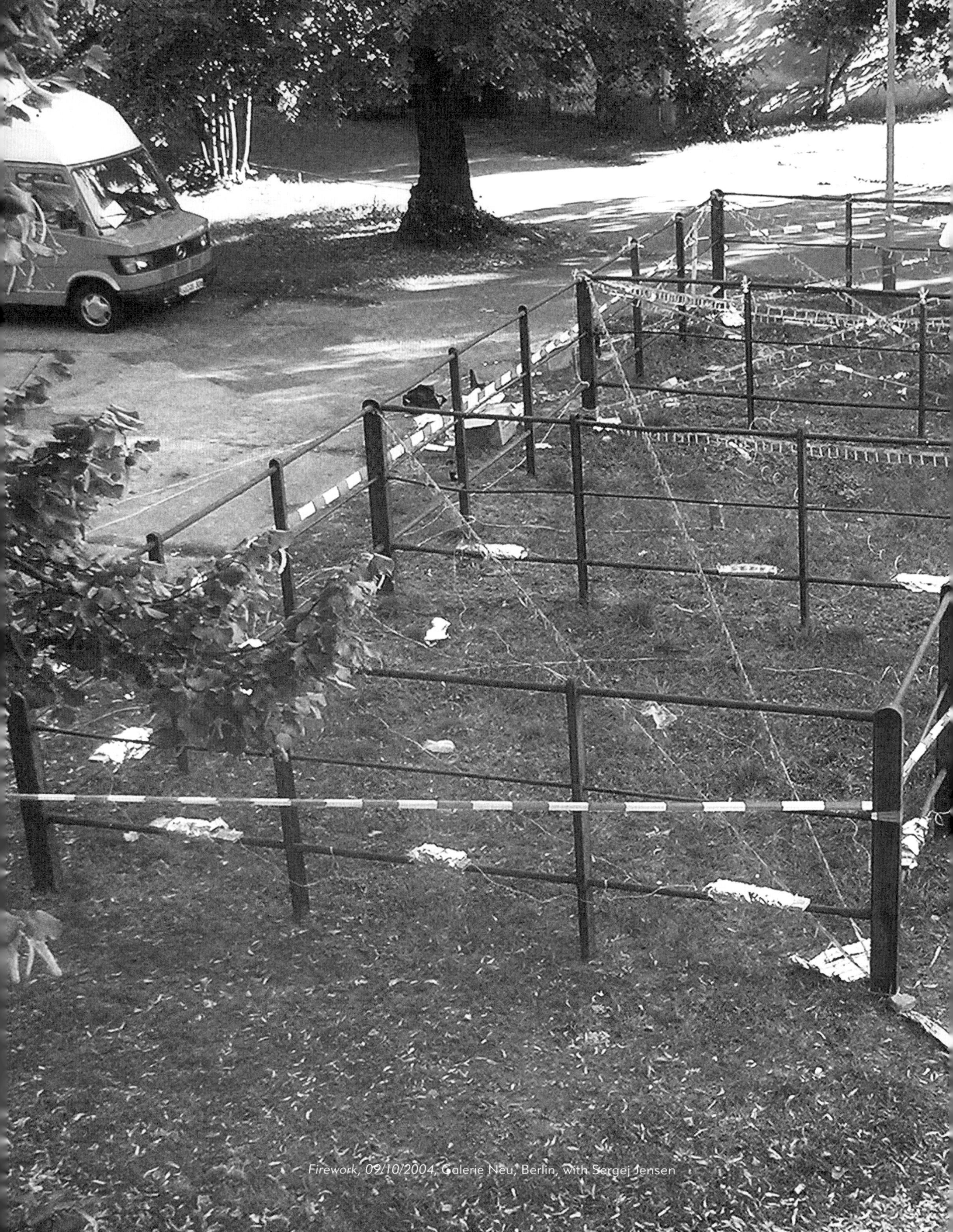

Firework, 09/10/2004, Galerie Neu, Berlin, with Sergej Jensen

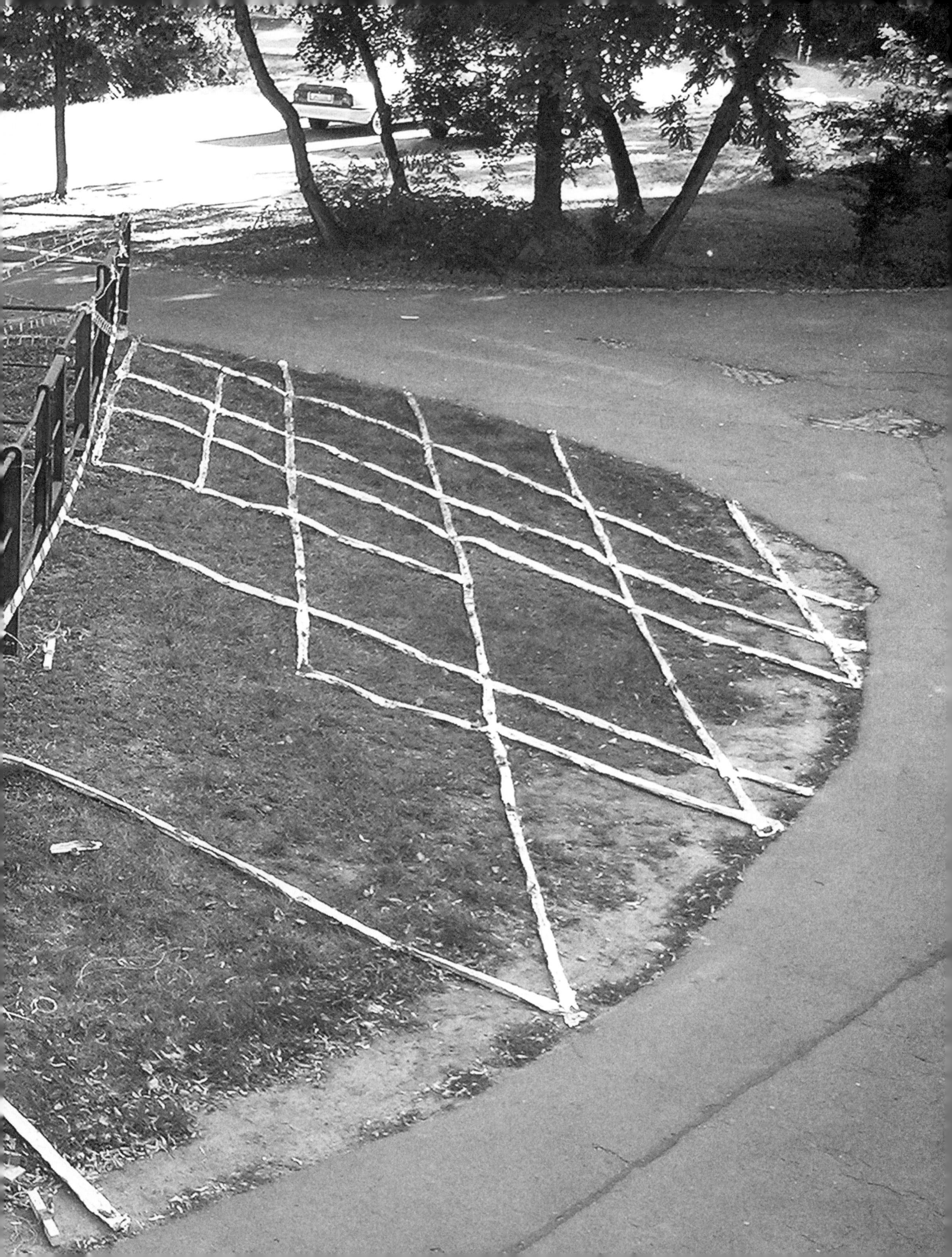

Firework, 09/10/2004
Installation, steel rack, pyrotechnics, electric ignition, 5.21 min
160 x 1500 x 500 cm

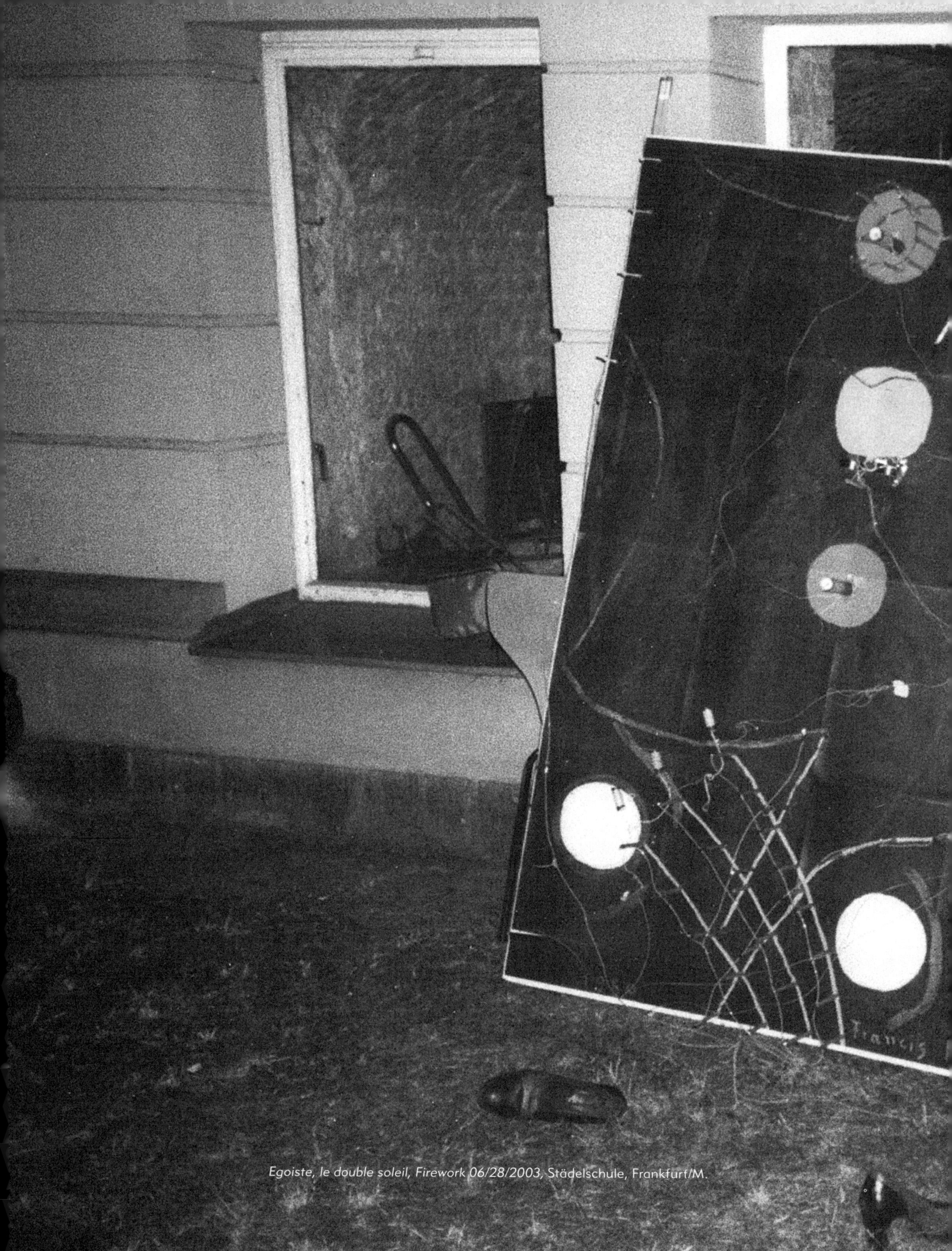

Egoiste, le double soleil, Firework 06/28/2003, Städelschule, Frankfurt/M.

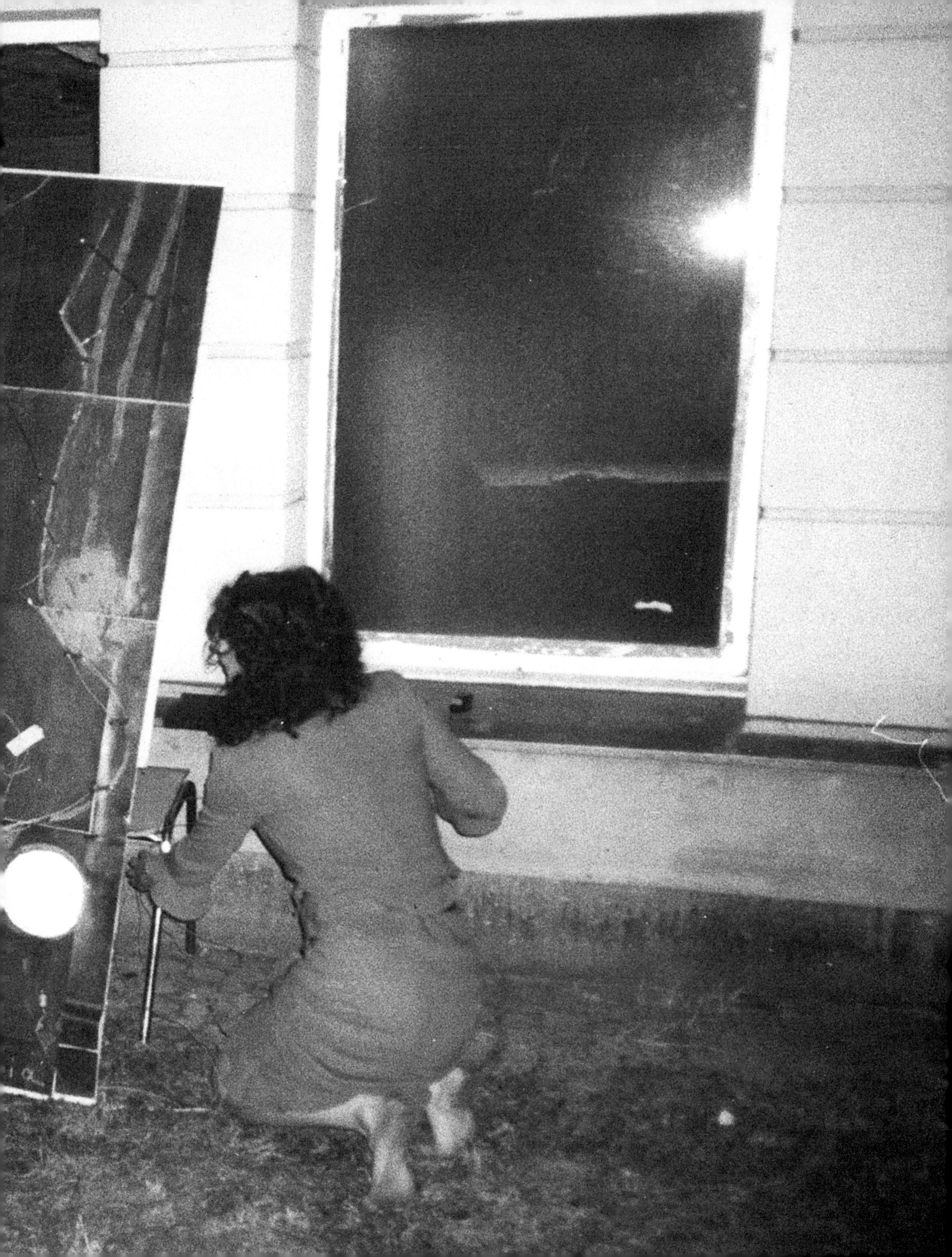

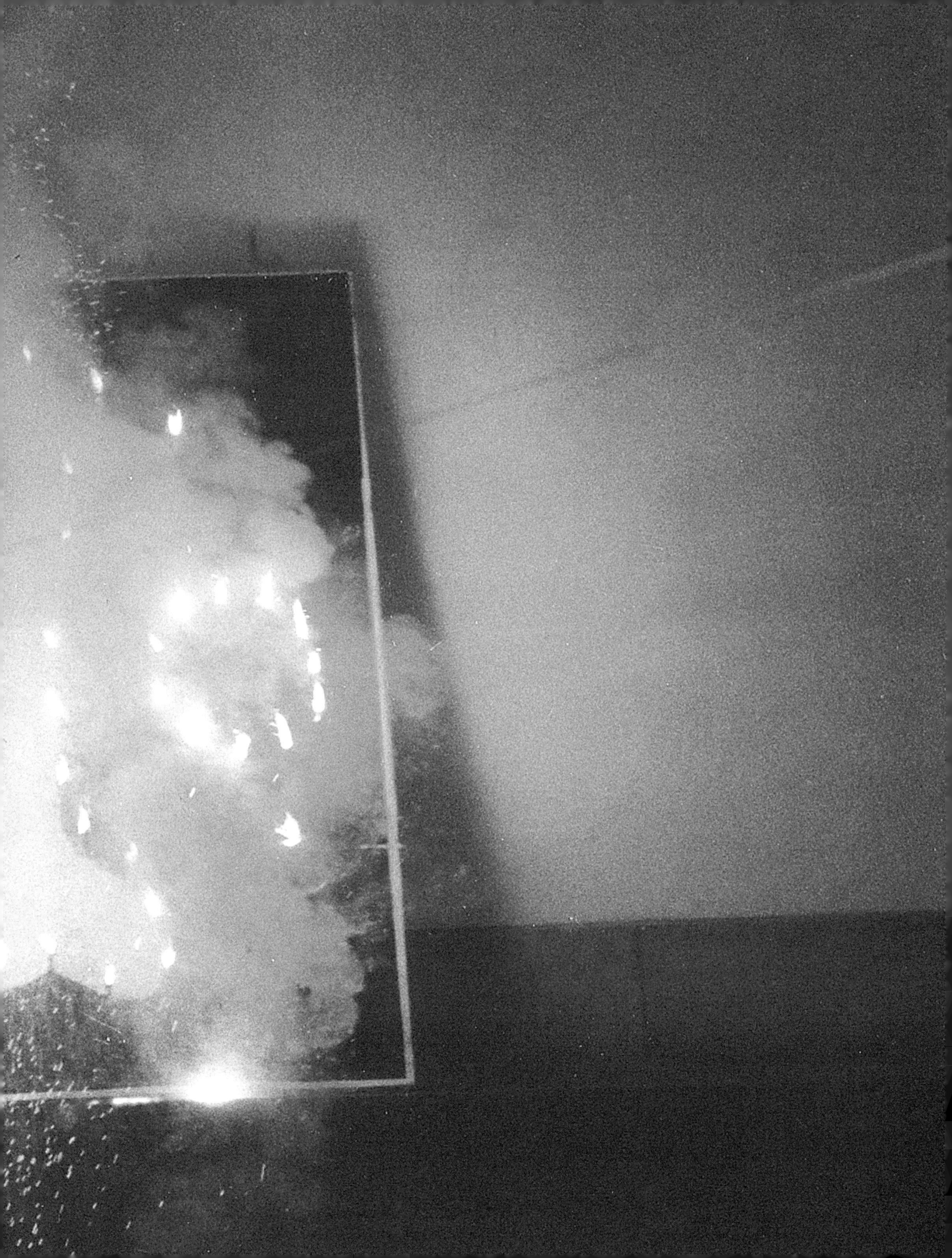

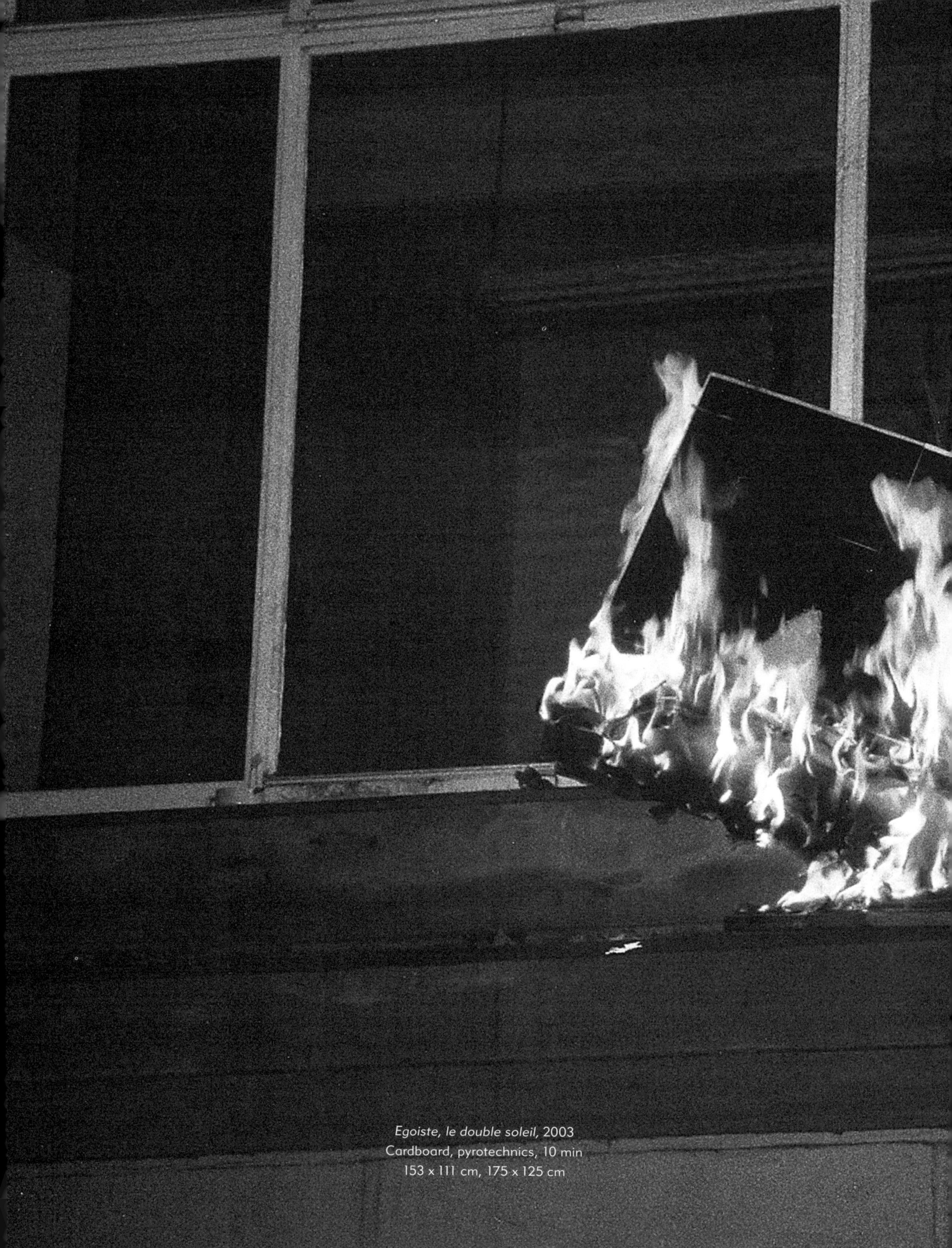

Egoiste, le double soleil, 2003
Cardboard, pyrotechnics, 10 min
153 x 111 cm, 175 x 125 cm

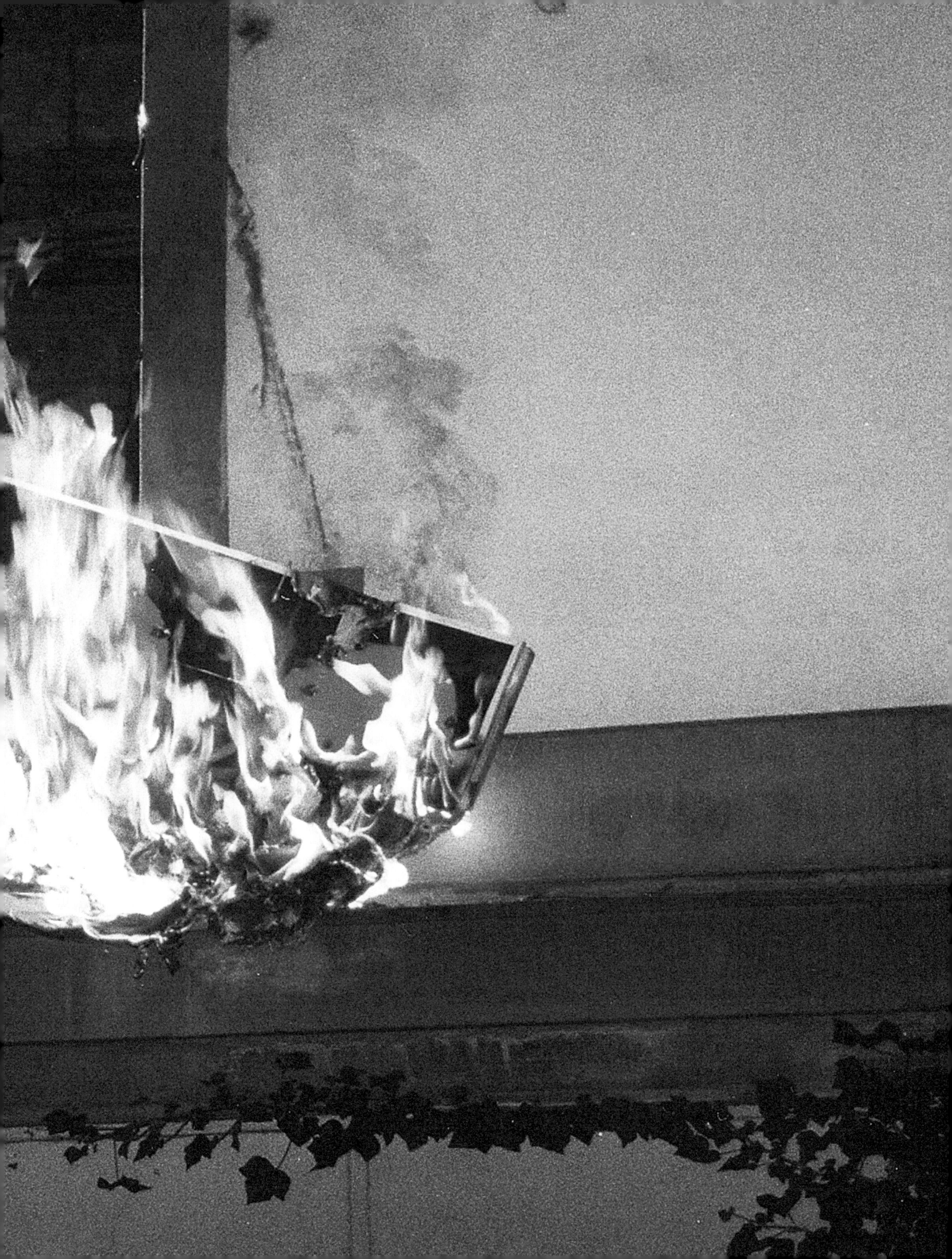

Sandra Kranich –
Mit Licht in den Himmel und in die
Dunkelheit zeichnen

von Astrid Ihle

„A pureza é um mito." (Hélio Oiticica)

Ein skizziertes Quadrat an einer Wand
mit Schmauchspuren, darauf explodierte
Feuerwerkskörper, hie und da baumelt
eine Zündschnur herab – das ist das
Ausgangsbild des Films *Back 3 (Séco 11):*
Stille. Ein unheimliches Zischen, Funken-
sprühen. Wie aus dem Nichts erscheint
plötzlich ein schwarzes trapezartiges
Rechteck, das in Sekundenschnelle
seinen Platz im Bild einnimmt, gefolgt
von weiteren Explosionen sowie von
schwarzen und grauen Vierecken, die
peu à peu, gleich Puzzleteilen, die
Komposition vervollständigen. Ein gleich-
falls dynamisches Szenario entfaltet sich
in *Back 2 (Metaesquema):* Wir sehen eine
geometrische Figur, die sich gleich einem
Feuerrad, immer schneller werdend, dreht
– begleitet von gelbem, rotem und grünem
Funkenregen und einem raketenartigen
Zischen – bis sie sich zur perfekten
Komposition auf weißem Grund einpegelt.
    Die Filme drehte Sandra Kranich
2010 und widmete sie dem Künstler Hélio
Oiticica (1937–1980), dessen Nachlass

im Jahr zuvor bei einem Feuer fast
vollständig vernichtet worden war. Oiticica
ist einer der bedeutendsten brasilianischen
Künstler der Nachkriegszeit, Begründer
und wichtigster Vertreter der Tropicália-
Bewegung, welche die Einheit von Kunst
und Leben zum Ziel hatte. Lange bevor
diese den künstlerischen Diskurs in Europa
und Nordamerika bestimmen sollten, prägte
er Begriffe wie Partizipation, Environment
und Proposition und stellte damit den
traditionellen Kunstbegriff radikal in
Frage. Unter den Werken Oiticicas, die der
Großbrand vernichtete, waren auch eine
Vielzahl früher neo-konkreter Gemälde
und Skulpturen aus den 1950er- und
1960er-Jahren, in denen der Künstler das
abstrakt-geometrische Formenvokabular
der europäischen Vorkriegsmoderne
dynamisierte, ja regelrecht zum Tanzen
brachte. Für ihre Filme rekonstruierte Sandra
Kranich Beispiele dieser frühen Arbeiten
Oiticicas, die sie mit Pyrotechnik versah und
zündete. Den Ablauf der Explosionen ließ
sie filmen, die so entstandenen Kurzfilme
rückwärts ablaufen. Durch diesen kleinen
Kunstgriff verkehrte die Künstlerin das
zerstörerische Potential des Feuers in eine
schöpferische, versöhnliche Geste. Der
Betrachter wird Zeuge eines poetischen,
magisch anmutenden Moments der Genese
aus der Zerstörung.
    Licht und Feuer gehören seit
nunmehr 15 Jahren zu den wichtigsten
Gestaltungsmitteln von Sandra Kranich.
In ihren Skulpturen, Bildern, Installationen
und Filmen veranschaulicht sie einen
Werkbegriff, in dem Konstruktion und
Destruktion, Kontrolle und Zufall aufs Engste
miteinander verbunden sind. Pyrotechnik
spielt dabei von Anfang an eine wichtige
Rolle. Zunächst fertigte Sandra Kranich
Zeichnungen von Weltraumarchitekturen
und Planetensystemen an – zersplitternde,

explodierende oder sich auflösende Formen und Strukturen. Gleichzeitig entstand der Wunsch „mit Licht in den Himmel und in die Dunkelheit (zu) zeichnen"[1]. Die jahrhundertealte Tradition der Feuerwerkskunst bot sich als Möglichkeit an, diese beiden Interessen miteinander zu verbinden, und so die formale Dynamik der an sich statischen Zeichnungen durch die eruptive Sprengkraft der Feuerwerkskörper zum Leben zu erwecken. Ihr erstes Feuerwerk baute Sandra Kranich zum Millenniums-Sylvester: Es bestand aus Hunderten von Streichholzschachteln, die sie zu Türmen und Kugeln zusammensetzte und mit einer Zündschnur untereinander verband *(Firework 12/31/1999)*. Als Ausdehnung ihres Formenrepertoires in Raum und Zeit, verwandelte es die komplexen Geometrien ihrer Zeichnungen in flüchtige Lichtgestalten. Kurz darauf absolvierte sie eine Ausbildung als Pyrotechnikerin, die es ihr alsbald erlaubte, Großfeuerwerke in den Himmel zu schießen sowie in Innenräumen zu intervenieren.

Sandra Kranichs Feuerwerke gleichen komplexen Versuchsanordnungen. Als Basis für ihre Lichtzeichnungen entwickelt sie konstruktivistisch anmutende Skulpturen und Bilder aus Holz, Papier oder Metall, die sie mit pyrotechnischen Vorrichtungen versieht. Im Moment der Zündung entlädt sich die statische Ausgangssituation als funkensprühende Choreografie. Dabei setzt Sandra Kranich gezielt die Farben und Effekte der einzelnen Feuerwerkskörper für die Dramaturgie ihrer Lichtzeichnung ein, die sowohl spielerisch-abstrakt wie auch narrativ angelegt sein kann. Ihre jüngste Werkgruppe, *Echo Return* (2014), stellt unter Verwendung von Feuer, Rauch, Funken- und Konfettiregen einen Raketenstart nach. Trotz der Erarbeitung eines präzisen Zündplans, das heißt der Chronologie, der

Farbnuancen und, bis zu einem gewissen Punkt, der Richtung der Raketenabschüsse, bleibt die endgültige Form der Zeichnung ungewiss. Überzündungen, Kurzschlüsse und andere Unvorhersehbarkeiten zwingen die Künstlerin zur Improvisation: ein Happening-artiger Moment, der den körperlichen Aspekt der Performance betont.

Die Intensität des Feuerwerks steht in Kontrast zum ephemeren Schauspiel der Lichtzeichnung, die nur in der Erinnerung fortbesteht. Feuerwerke sind sekunden-schnelle Spektakel, die Energie entladen. Die Frage nach der Sichtbarmachung, Formfindung und Konservierung dieser Energie rückt wiederum die Skulpturen und Bilder in den Fokus, deren Transformation durch das Feuer von der Künstlerin intendiert ist. Für die Arbeit *Compact Time* (2012) ließ Sandra Kranich die verschossenen Über-reste eines Großfeuerwerks – die Basis-konstruktion aus goldfarbenen Blechdosen sowie die verbrannten Feuerwerksutensilien – zu Blöcken pressen und präsentierte diese als skulpturale Installation. Bei ihren jüngsten Arbeiten handelt es sich um Aluminiumreliefs, deren übereinander montierte geometrische Flächensegmente erst durch das Feuerwerk ihre endgültige Gestalt erhalten. Tatsächlich durchlaufen diese Arbeiten unterschiedliche Metamor-phosen des Bildwerdens – vom dreidimen-sionalen Wandbild über die flüchtige Licht-komposition im Raum zum verschmauchten „informellen" Gemälde. Flammen und Explosionen legen sich in Form von Schmauch- und Brandspuren auf das Metall ab, schreiben sich als komprimierte Erinnerung in die Oberfläche ein. Sandra Kranichs Bilder und Skulpturen funktionieren demnach auch als „Zeitspeicher".

Die Arbeit mit Licht und Feuer eröffnet ein weites Assoziationsfeld, das vom Barockfeuerwerk bis zur zeitgenössischen

Multimediashow reicht. Auch in der
jüngeren Kunstgeschichte finden sich
zahlreiche Anknüpfungspunkte: Man denke
an die Feuerbilder von Otto Piene oder
Yves Kleins Feueranthropometrien, die
explosiven Selbstversuche Roman Signers
oder Cai Guo-Qiangs Zeichnungen mit
Schießpulver; auch die Körperbilder von
Ana Mendieta, die ihre Silhouette mittels
Pyrotechnik in die Erde einbrannte, kommen
in den Sinn.[2] Sandra Kranich gelingt
es, diese unterschiedlichen Einflüsse in
eine zeitgenössische künstlerische Praxis
umzusetzen. Ihr Umgang mit Tradition ist
dabei komplex und spielerisch. Oftmals
verweisen ihre Arbeiten auf bestimmte
Kunstwerke der Moderne und können als
augenzwinkernde Hommage an die von
ihr verehrten Künstler gelesen werden.
So beispielweise die Konstruktion *Firing
Figure* (2008), die einer Skulptur Naum
Gabos (*Model for 'Constructed Torso'*,
1917) nachempfunden ist: Als Zeichen
ihrer Verbundenheit, versah die Künstlerin
ihre pyrotechnische Neuinterpretation
mit einem lächelnden Mund, der beim
Abbrennen des Feuerwerks rot aufleuchtete.
Moment Monument (2011) wiederum lässt
die interaktiv angelegten Konstruktionen
aus bemalten Streichholzschachteln der
brasilianischen Künstlerin Lygia Clark als
großformatige Installation auferstehen,
um sie anschließend in einer fulminanten,
alle Sinne vereinnahmenden Choreografie
komplett abzubrennen. Wie Hélio Oiticica
gehörte Lygia Clark der neo-konstruktiven
Bewegung an. Zu Beginn der 1960er-Jahre
wendete sie sich der Herstellung ephemerer,
manipulierbarer Objekte zu, die erst durch
die körperlich-sinnliche Inbesitznahme des
Betrachters Form und Bedeutung erhielten.
Sandra Kranichs Skulpturen und
Reliefs zitieren das abstrakt-geometrische
Formenvokabular der Moderne und

unterlaufen doch deren Ideale: Rationalität
und Geometrie sind nicht länger Ziele,
sondern manifestieren sich als prekäre
Übergangszustände. Durch die funken-
sprühenden Explosionen wird der „Auf-
bruch in eine unbekannte Dimension der
Reinheit"[3], wie ihn beispielsweise die
Künstler der ZERO-Gruppe im Nachkriegs-
deutschland propagierten, ironisch überhöht
und gleichzeitig ad absurdum geführt.
Tatsächlich kündet die versehrte Oberfläche
der verschmauchten Bilder von Veränderung
und Metamorphose. Anstelle einer Wieder-
geburt im Namen eines utopischen Idealis-
mus steht ihre „Feuertaufe" jedoch für eine
pragmatische, am Alltag orientierte Haltung,
die das Leben mit all seinem Schmutz und
Ballast annimmt und zelebriert.
Bedenkt man zudem, dass Sandra
Kranichs strenge Metallreliefs eine bis heute
männlich konnotierte Praxis der Nachkriegs-
bildhauerei appropriieren, bekommt die
Manipulation der Ausgangsbilder durch
das Feuer eine zusätzliche Bedeutung als
Befreiung von festgefahrenen Traditionen.
Das Element Feuer ist uralt in der
Geschichte der menschlichen Zivilisation.
Es ist eins ihrer konstitutiven Elemente.
In seiner gleichgewichtig kreativen wie
zerstörerischen Funktion wurde es seit jeher
in besonderem Maße als mythische Energie
erlebt.[4] Am effektvollsten und poetischsten
setzte die Künstlerin diese Wesensart
des Feuers vielleicht in ihrem Film *Back 3
(Metaesquema)* um: Dicke Nebelschwaden
legen sich über ein schwarzes Nichts, eine
tachistisch anmutende Leinwand mit weißen
Flecken, einer Urlandschaft gleich oder
Assoziationen an die unendlichen Weiten
des Weltalls weckend ... Langsam lichtet
sich der Nebel, dichte weiße und grüne
Rauchwolken steigen auf, Funkenregen und
ahnungsvolles Zischen begleiten die kurz
aufeinander folgende Serie von Explosionen.

Gleich einem Urknall komponiert sich
die Materie zu drei weißen Quadraten
auf schwarzem Grund: Ein Bild der Ruhe
und Kontemplation, das zugleich auf
die energetischen Urkräfte des Kosmos
verweist.

1)   Sandra Kranich in einem Gespräch mit
Nikola Dietrich und Jochen Volz, in: *Sandra
Kranich. Dark Triangle,* Frankfurt/M., 2009,
o.S.
2)   Vgl. Wagner, Monika, *Das Material der
Kunst. Eine andere Geschichte der Moderne,*
München, 2001, S. 235–249.
3)   Müller, Hans-Joachim, „Die Stunde
der Null", in: http://www.welt.de/kultur/
kunst-und-architektur/article133283884/Die-
Stunde-der-Null.html, Abruf: 24.02.2015.
4)   Kultermann, Udo, „Feuer im Werk von
Otto Piene – das Elementare und die neue
Sensibilität", in: *Otto Piene. Retrospektive
1952–1996,* Ausst.-Kat, Kunstmuseum
Düsseldorf im Ehrenhof; Köln, 1996, S. 25.

Sandra Kranich –
To draw in the sky and in the
darkness with light

by Astrid Ihle

„A pureza é um mito" (Hélio Oiticica)

A square sketched on a wall with traces
of powder, fireworks exploded on it, here
and there a fuse hangs down – this is
the first image we see in the film *Back
3 (Séco 11)*: silence. A spooky hissing,
sparks flying. Suddenly a black rectangle
appears as though out of nowhere, in a
matter of seconds taking its place in the
picture, followed by more explosions, as
well as black and grey quadrilaterals that
gradually, like puzzle pieces, complete the
composition. An equally dynamic scenario
unfolds in *Back 2 (Metaesquema)*: We see
a geometric shape that, like a Catherine
wheel, spins ever faster – accompanied by
a yellow, red and green shower of sparks
and a rocket-like hissing – until it forms the
perfect composition on a white background.
Sandra Kranich shot the films in
2010 and dedicated them to the artist
Hélio Oiticica (1937- 1980), whose estate
had been almost completely destroyed
in a fire the year before. Oiticica is one
of the most significant Brazilian artists of
the post-War era and founder and most
important representative of the Tropicália
movement, which sought to unite art and
life. He coined terms such as participation,
environment and proposition (long before
they were to define artistic discourse in
Europe and the USA) and in so doing
radically questioned the traditional concept
of art. Among Oiticica's works destroyed in
the fire were also a great many early neo-
Concrete paintings and sculptures from
the 1950s and 1960s, in which the artist
lent dynamism to the abstract-geometric
formal vocabulary of the European pre-War
Modern Age, indeed, really got it to dance.
For her films, Sandra Kranich reconstructed
examples of these early works by Oiticica,
to which she attached fireworks and ignited
them. She had the explosions filmed as
they occurred, and the short films played
backwards. By means of this small trick the
artist reversed the destructive potential of
fire, giving rise to a creative, conciliatory
gesture. The observer becomes witness to
a poetic, magical moment of genesis out of
destruction.
For 15 years now, light and fire have
been among the primary media Sandra
Kranich uses in her artistic practice. Her
sculptures, pictures, installations and
films reference a concept of art in which
construction and destruction, control and
coincidence are very closely connected.
Pyrotechnics have played a pivotal role
from the beginning. She initially produced
drawings of outer-space constructions and
planetary systems – fragmenting, exploding
or dissolving forms and structures –
and at the same time wished "to draw in
the sky and in the darkness with light"[1].
The centuries-old tradition of fireworks
presented an opportunity to combine these
two interests. Sandra Kranich made her
first firework on New Year's Eve at the
turn of the Millenium from hundreds of
matchboxes, which she assembled into
towers and orbs and connected together

with a fuse (*Firework 12/31/1999*). It was an extension of her formal repertoire into space and time, transforming the complex shapes of her drawings into ephemeral light figures. Shortly afterward she trained as a pyrotechnician, allowing her to shoot large-scale fireworks displays into the sky, and even to intervene in interior spaces. Sandra Kranich's staged fireworks are like complex experiments. As a basis for her lit drawings she develops constructivist-type sculptures and pictures of wood, paper or metal, which she fits out with pyrotechnic devices. At the moment of ignition the static initial situation is discharged as a spark-emitting choreography. And Sandra Kranich relies on the color and effects of the individual fireworks for the dramaturgy of her fired drawings, which might have a playful, abstract nature or be more narrative in quality. Her most recent work, *Echo Return* (2014), recreates the scene when a rocket is launched using fire, smoke, and raining sparks and confetti. Even though the artist draws up a precise ignition plan, and determines chronology, colour nuances, and up to a certain degree the direction the fired rockets should take, the final shape the drawing will take remains uncertain. Excess explosions, fusing and other unforeseen incidents make the artist improvise: a happening-like aspect, which in turn the physical nature of the performance.

The intensity of the firework forms a contrast to the ephemeral spectacle of the lit drawing, which only continues to exist in the memory. Fireworks are spectacles lasting seconds, which discharge energy. Reflecting on the visualization, emergence and conservation of this energy puts the focus back on the sculptures and images, whose transformation by fire the artist intends. For the work *Compact Time* (2012) Sandra Kranich had remains of a large-scale firework, gold-coloured cans and firework implements, pressed into blocks and then presented these as a sculptural installation. Her most recent works are aluminium reliefs, whose flat geometric segments mounted over one other only receive their final design through the firework. In fact these works undergo different stages before metamorphosing into a final picture – from three-dimensional wall-mounted image via transient lit composition to a powdery "informal" painting. Flames and explosions make their mark on the metal as traces of powder and burned areas, engrave themselves into the surface as a condensed memory. As such, Sandra Kranich's images and sculptures also serve to "store time".

The artist's work with light and fire opens up a wide area of associations that ranges from the Baroque fireworks to contemporary multimedia shows. Numerous connections can also be found in more recent art history: You need only think of the fire pictures by Otto Piene or Yves Klein's fire anthropometries, the explosive experiments Roman Signer conducted on himself, Cai Guo-Qiang's drawings with gunpowder, or the body pictures by Ana Mendieta, who burned her silhouette into the earth using pyrotechnics.[2] Sandra Kranich succeeds in translating these various influences into a contemporary artistic practice, and her handling of tradition is both complex and playful. Often her oeuvre refers to specific Modernist works and can be read as an ironic homage to the artist she reveres, such as the construction *Firing Figure* (2008), which is inspired by a sculpture of Naum Gabo (*Model for 'Constructed Torso'*, 1917): to demonstrate her affinity with the work the artist gave her pyrotechnic re-interpretation a smiling mouth, which lit up in red when the firework burned down.

By contrast, *Moment Monument* (2011) resurrects the interactive constuctions of painted matchboxes by Brazilian artist Lygia Clark as a large-format installation, before burning it down completely in a brilliant choreography that addresses all the senses. Like Hélio Oiticica, Lygia Clark belonged to the neo-constructive movement. At the start of the 1960s she devoted herself to the creation of ephemeral objects that could be manipulated, and which only received their form and meaning by the observer taking possession of them physically and sensually.

Sandra Kranich's sculptures and reliefs cite the abstract, geometric formal vocabulary of Modernism while undermining its idealistic intentions: Rationality and geometry are no longer goals but are manifested as precarious transitional states. Through the spark-emitting explosions the "radical move into an unknown dimension of purity"[3], as advocated say by the artists of the ZERO group in post-War Germany, is ironically exaggerated and simultaneously taken to the absurd. And admittedly the pictures' damaged surfaces with their traces of powder seem to tell of change and metamorphosis, but in place of rebirth in the name of a utopian idealism their "baptism of fire" stands for a pragmatic attitude orientated to the everyday, which accepts and celebrates life with all its filth and burdens.

If you consider as well that Sandra Kranich's austere metal reliefs also appropriate a practice of post-war sculpting that still has a male connotation the manipulation of the initial images using fire also assumes a further meaning as the liberation from set traditions.

In human civilization fire is an ancient element. It is one of its constitutive elements. In its equally creative and destructive function it has been experienced as a mythical energy since time immemorial.[4] The artist can perhaps be said to implement this aspect of fire most effectively and poetically in her film *Back 3 (Metaesquema)*: Swathing mist settles on a black void, a Tachist-looking canvas with white splodges, like a primeval landscape or awakening associations of the infinite expanses of space... Slowly the mist clears and dense white and green clouds of smoke rise up, sparks and sinister hissing accompany the series of explosions following in short succession: Like a Big Bang the material is composed into three white squares on a black background: an image of peace and contemplation, which also refers to the primeval forces of the cosmos.

1)   Sandra Kranich in conversation with Nikola Dietrich and Jochen Volz, in: *Sandra Kranich. Dark Triangle,* (Frankfurt/M., 2009), n.p.
2)   See: Wagner, Monika, *Das Material der Kunst. Eine andere Geschichte der Moderne* (München, 2001), pp. 235-249.
3)   Müller, Hans-Joachim, „Die Stunde der Null", in: http://www.welt.de/kultur/kunst-und-architektur/article133283884/Die-Stunde-der-Null.html; 24.02.2015.
4)   Kultermann, Udo: „Feuer im Werk von Otto Piene – das Elementare und die neue Sensibilität", in: Otto Piene. Retrospektive 1952–1996, exh.cat., Kunstmuseum Düsseldorf im Ehrenhof (Köln, 1996), p. 25.

Sandra Kranich

Geboren / Born in Ludwigsburg

Studium an der / Study at the
Hochschule für Gestaltung / University
of Art & Design, Offenbach/M.
(Prof. Manfred Stumpf und / and
Prof. Heiner Blum)
   Städelschule, Staatliche Hochschule für
Bildende Künste / State University of Fine Arts,
Frankfurt/M. (Prof. Thomas Bayrle)
   Ausbildung als Pyrotechnikerin /
Qualification as pyrotechnician

Einzelausstellungen / Solo Exhibitions

   2015
Opelvillen Rüsselsheim
Rudolf-Scharpf-Galerie des Wilhelm-Hack-
Museums, Ludwigshafen am Rhein
Galerie Sabine Knust, München

   2014
Echo Return, PPC, Philipp Pflug
Contemporary, Frankfurt/M.

   2013
Short Ride in a Fast Machine,
Kunstverein Oldenburg

   2012
Flashforward, Knust und Kunz, München
Knust x Kunz, Galerie Sabine Knust, München

   2010
Firework 8/10/2010, Car Projects, Bologna, I
Shadow, basis, Frankfurt/M.

   2002
Through and Through, rraum 02, Frankfurt/M.

   2000
Silicon Woodcuts, Forum der Frankfurter
Sparkasse 1822, Frankfurt/M.

Gruppenausstellungen / Group Shows

   2014
Installationsansicht, Nassauischer
Kunstverein, Wiesbaden
First Exhibition, PPC, Philipp Pflug
Contemporary, Frankfurt/M.
Im Dschungel, Kunstverein Familie Montez,
Frankfurt/M.

   2013
Hélio Oiticica im Palmengarten, MMK
Museum für Moderne Kunst, Frankfurt/M.
Mothership, Saasfee Pavillon, Frankfurt/M.
Neue Editionen, Galerie Sabine Knust,
München

   2012
about blank, Kunsthalle Darmstadt
Art and the City, Zürich, CH
Against Interpretation, Whatspace, Tilburg, NL

   2011
Moment Monument, Firework 06/27/2011,
Raw, Fundament Foundation, Tilburg, NL
Death and Dada of Everyday Life, Galerie
Suvi Lehtinen, Berlin
Time Tower, Firework 02/10/2011, Schirn
Kunsthalle, Frankfurt/M.

   2010
*Squanto's cold turkey Anti-Massacre
Movement*, Deathanddada, Glasgow, GB
*Twins, Firework 06/11/2010, Der offene
Garten*, Kunsthalle Lingen
Festival des Beaux Arts, Galerie Sabine
Knust, Pinakothek der Moderne, München

prime time, Atelierfrankfurt, Frankfurt/M.
Back 1, Galerie im Regierungsviertel Berlin
Back, The destroyed room, Whatspace
Tilburg, NL
Feuerwerk 06/02/2010, Kunstverein zu
Assenheim, Ursula Blickle Stiftung, Assenheim
Buchpräsentation / Book presentation *Dark
Triangle*, Portikus, Frankfurt/M.

2009
*Lost Star, Firework 06/14/2009, Athens
Biennale*, Athens, GR
Hausfeuerwerk 1, Westfälischer Kunstverein
Münster

2008
Firing Figure, Firework 11/05/2008, T2 Turin
Triennale, Castello di Rivoli, I
Dark Triangle, Firework 30/5/2008,
Neues Museum Nürnberg

2007
*Bag Bang, Firework 04/20/2007, death
of bling*, Frankfurt/M.
*It takes something to make something,
Die Sammmlung Rausch*, Portikus,
Frankfurt/M.

2006
Feuerwerk 06/27/2006, Katholische
Akademie, München
Feuerwerk 03/15/2006, Fine art fair,
Frankfurt/M.

2005
Feuerwerk 07/24/2005, Stadt Crailsheim
Feuerwerk 06/05/2005, Zeichnung, Lübecker
Kunstverein, Overbeckgesellschaft, Lübeck
Jourdan/one, Frankfurt/M.

2004
Feuerwerk 09/10/2004, mit / with Sergej
Jensen, *Arbeiten und ein Feuerwerk*, Galerie
Neu, Berlin

Make it new, Portikus, Frankfurt/M.,
Dresdner Bank Wasserstein

2003
Feuerwerk 11/18/2003, Macht und Tränen,
Arsenal HKM 1, Mainz
*Feuerwerk 10/02/2003, Buon Giorno
Casanova*, Duchcov, CZ
Feuerwerk 09/05/2003, Burgdorf, CH
*Feuerwerk 03/13/2003, Flüchtige
Verfestigung*, Hessischer Rundfunk,
Frankfurt/M.,
Feuerwerk 06/28/2003, Städelschule,
Frankfurt/M.

2000
Through, Proto Academy, Edinburgh, GB
Silicon Woodcuts, Forum der Frankfurter
Sparkasse 1822, Frankfurt/M.
Feuerwerk 05/10/2000, Museum für
Angewandte Kunst, Frankfurt/M.

1999
Feuerwerk 12/31/1999, Historisches
Museum, Frankfurt/M.

Preise und Stipendien / Awards and Grants

2000
Atelierstipendium / Artist Residency,
Burgdorf, CH

2005/06
Reisestipendium / Travel Grant, Hessische
Kulturstiftung / Cultural Foundation of the
State of Hesse

Bibliografie / Bibliography

Solid Signs, New Frankfurt Internationals,
eds. Lilian Engelmann und / and Elke Gruhn,
Kunstverein Frankfurt, Nassauischer
Kunstverein, Wiesbaden, 2015
    Art and the City, a Public Art Project,
Christoph Doswald, JRP|Ringier, Zürich, CH,
2012
    Fundament Foundation, *Raw Stardust,
Excursions in Contemporary Sculpture 2,*
De Oude Warande, Tilburg, NL, 2011
    Der offene Garten, ed. Meike Behm,
Kunsthalle Lingen, Lingen, 2011
Sandra Kranich, *Dark Triangle,* argobooks,
Frankfurt/M., 2009
    Heaven, 2nd Athens Biennale 2009, GR,
2009
    50 Moons of Saturn, Skira, ed. Daniel
Birnbaum, T2 Torino Triennale, I, 2008–
2009
    Kunst macht Schule, An Ort und Ställe,
Saarbrücken, 2007
    Big Bopp, ed. Friedemann Hahn, modo
Verlag, Mainz, 2007
    Macht und Tränen, ed. Friedemann Hahn,
Arsenal HKM1, Mainz, 2003
    Flüchtige Verfestigung, Marielies Hess-
Stiftung e.V., Frankfurt/M., 2003
    Buon Giorno Casanova, ed. Burkhard
Brunn, CZ, 2003
    Silicon Woodcuts, Frankfurter Sparkasse
1822, Frankfurt/M., 2000
    Save the day, Museum für Moderne
Kunst, Frankfurt/M., 1999

Dieser Katalog erscheint anlässlich der
Ausstellung / This catalog is published
on the occasion of the exhibition
Sandra Kranich
Rudolf-Scharpf-Galerie, Wilhelm-Hack-
Museum, Ludwigshafen am Rhein
14. März – 17. Mai 2015

Ausstellung / Exhibition

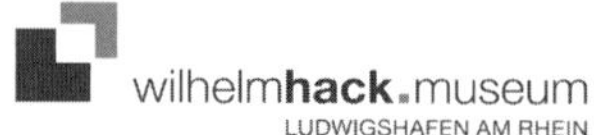 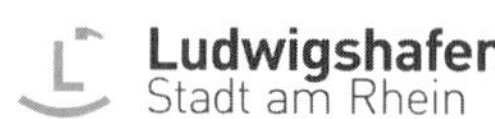

Wilhelm-Hack-Museum
Berliner Straße 23
D-67059 Ludwigshafen am Rhein
Tel + 49 (0)621 504 3045
Fax + 49 (0)621 504 3780
hackmuseum@ludwigshafen.de
http://www.wilhelmhack.museum

Direktor / Director: René Zechlin
Ausstellungskuratoren / Exhibition curators:
Astrid Ihle, Jana Franze
Sammlungskuratorin / Collection curator:
Nina Schallenberg
Presse und Vermittlung / Press and
education: Theresia Kiefer, Regina Pfiester
International Fellow Curator: Öykü Özsoy
Restaurierung / Restauration:
Herbert Nolden
Ausstellungstechnik / Exhibition services:
Udo Baur, Gunter Sachs
Verwaltung und Finanzen / Administration
and finances: Gabriele Herbst
Sekretariat / Secretary: Katja Simeth

Katalog / Catalog

Herausgeber / Editor:
Wilhelm-Hack-Museum
Redaktion / Editing: Astrid Ihle
Lektorat / Proofreading: Nina Schallenberg,
Angelika Pröll
Übersetzung / Translation: Jeremy Gaines
Gestaltung / Design: Harald Pridgar
Fotos / Photographs: Thorsten Arndt, Art
and the City/Zürich, Wonge Bergmann,
Günther Dächert, Diana Djeddi, Petra
Gerster, Wolfgang Günzel, Maren Kindler,
Peter Kranich, Liedeke Kruk, Christian
Lauer, Peter Loewy, Yvonne Pietz, Georg
Pöhlein, Olaf Rahlwes, Siegfried Wameser,
Adrian Williams, Cem Yuecetas
Herstellung / Production: Freiburger
Graphische Betriebe

© 2015 Verlag für moderne Kunst, Sandra
Kranich, Wilhelm-Hack-Museum, Autoren
und Fotografen / Authors and photographers

Alle Rechte vorbehalten / All rights reserved

Printed in Germany

ISBN 978-3-903004-06-1

Bibliografische Information Der Deutschen
Nationalbibliothek
Die Deutsche Nationalbibliothek verzeichnet
diese Publikation in der Deutschen National-
bibliografie; detaillierte bibliografische Daten
sind im Internet über http://dnb.ddb.de
abrufbar.
Bibliographic information published by Die
Deutsche Nationalbibliothek
Die Deutsche Nationalbibliothek lists this
publication in the Deutsche National-
bibliografie; detailed bibliographic data is
available on the Internet
at http://dnb.ddb.de.

Herzlicher Dank geht insbesondere an /
Warm gratitude is extended to Jochem
Hendricks, Nora Hendricks, Monika Kranich,
Andrea Miegl-Kranich, Peter Kranich, Petra
Koller, Eva Mösner, Bernd Münk, HFX
Gunther Haarstark, Sami Akdeniz, Elements
Entertainment Friederike Unverzagt, Hirt
& Co Fireworks Manuel Hirt, Scarpato
Fireworks, Enafsis Fireworks, Wagenvoort
Vuurwerk, Peter Sauer Kunstfeuerwerkfabrik,
Beisel Pyrotechnik Renzo Cargnelutti,
TBC Pyrotec Chris Müller, PPC Philipp
Pflug, Michael Neff, Galerie Sabine Knust
Matthias Kunz, Gertrude Wagenfeld-Pleister,
Jörg Kinner, Christoph Doswald, Dorothea
Strauss, Dr. Beate Kemfert, Charlotte
Birnbaum, Daniel Birnbaum, Dr. Christina
Leber, Dr. Astrid Ihle, René Zechlin, Nadia
Argyropoulou, Jakob Sturm, Felix Ruhöfer,
Dr. Peter Joch, Chris Driessen, Katharina
Dohm, Max Hollein, Car Projects Davide
Rosi Degli Esposti, Meike Behm, Katja
Schröder, Dr. Angelika Nollert, Juliane von
Herz, Jochen Volz, Dr. Eva Linhart, Bernd
Reiss, Elke Gruhn, Harald Pridgar, Dirk
Euler, Anselm Baumann, Bernd Thiele, Mark
Liedtke, Alexandra Papadopoulou, Hanna
Willer, Jacqueline Jurt, Mai Braun, Dirk
Krecker, Koen Delare, Peter Lütje, Hendrik
Zimmer, Sergej Jensen, Oliver Mueller,
Adrian Williams, Kathrin Binner

Der Ausstellungstitel *Short Ride in a Fast
Machine* stammt von einer Komposition
von John Adams / The exhibition title *Short
Ride in a Fast Machine* comes from a John
Adams' composition

Die Publikation wurde grosszügig
unterstützt durch / This publication was
generously supported by

Union Investment Stiftung

Oldenburger Kunstverein